READING C

Stanley Cavell is one of the great minds of our time. To read Cavell as he should be read is to enter into a conversation with him, one in which your entire sensibility and his are involved, and not only your mind and his mind. In this respect, Stanley Cavell is virtually unique.

Hilary Putnam

Stanley Cavell occupies a central and highly distinctive place in twentieth-century philosophy. His influential writings range from painting and music, film studies and literary criticism to Shakespeare, psychoanalysis, Heidegger, Derrida, Wittgenstein and Emerson.

Reading Cavell is a stellar collection of essays by distinguished scholars, covering the full range and implications of Cavell's work. The essays bring to the fore the internal connections in his thought, thus revealing its underlying principles. Cavell's own essay in the volume focuses on his Wittgensteinian vision of language, which informs the other areas of his philosophy. The other contributors extend Cavell's vision of language to investigate his enduring contributions to philosophy: scepticism, exemplification and moral perfectionism.

Together, the essays provide an indispensable resource for understanding Cavell's work, suitable for the seasoned expert as well as those approaching Cavell for the first time.

Contributors: Stanley Cavell, Stephen Mulhall, Alice Crary, Nancy Bauer, Cora Diamond, Hilary Putnam, Sanford Shieh, Paul Franks, Eli Friedlander, Stuart Klawans, and James Conant.

Alice Crary is Assistant Professor of Philosophy at the New School for Social Research in New York. She is co-editor of *The New Wittgenstein* (Routledge, 2000) and editor of *Wittgenstein and the Moral Life* (MIT Press, 2006).

Sanford Shieh is Associate Professor of Philosophy at Wesleyan University, USA. He is co-editor of *Future Pasts: the Analytic Tradition in 20th Century Philosophy*.

READING CAVELL

Edited by
Alice Crary and Sanford Shieh

Routledge
Taylor & Francis Group

LONDON AND NEW YORK

First published 2006
by Routledge
2 Park Square, Milton Park, Abingdon, Oxon, OX14 4RN

Simultaneously published in the USA and Canada
by Routledge
270 Madison Avenue, New York, NY 10016

Routledge is an imprint of the Taylor & Francis Group

Typeset in Goudy by Taylor & Francis Books
Printed and bound in Great Britain by MPG Books Ltd, Bodmin

British Library Cataloguing in Publication Data
A catalogue record for this book is available from the British Library

Library of Congress Cataloging in Publication Data
A catalog record for this book has been requested

ISBN10: 0-415-34640-1   ISBN13: 978-0-415-34640-5 (hbk)
ISBN10: 0-415-34639-8   ISBN13: 978-0-415-34639-9 (pbk)

Taylor & Francis Group is the Academic Division of T&F Informa plc.

CONTENTS

CONTENTS

CONTRIBUTORS

Nancy Bauer is Associate Professor of Philosophy at Tufts University, where she teaches courses in feminism, film, ethics, and nineteenth- and twentieth-century French and German philosophy. She is the author of *Simone de Beauvoir, Philosophy, and Feminism* (Columbia University Press, 2001) and is currently working on a book called *How to Do Things with Pornography*.

Stanley Cavell is Walter M. Cabot Professor Emeritus of Aesthetics and the General Theory of Value at Harvard University. Among his many writings are *Must We Mean What We Say?* (Cambridge University Press, 1976), *The Claim of Reason* (Oxford University Press, 1979), *The Senses of Walden* (North Point Press, 1981), *Pursuits of Happiness* (Harvard University Press, 1981), *Disowning Knowledge* (Cambridge University Press, 1987), and, most recently, *Emerson's Transcendental Etudes* (Stanford University Press, 2003), *Cities of Words* (Harvard University Press, 2004), and *Philosophy the Day after Tomorrow* (Harvard University Press, 2005).

James Conant is Chester D. Tripp Professor of Humanities at the University of Chicago. He received both his B.A. (1982) and Ph.D. (1990) from Harvard University. He taught for nine years at the University of Pittsburgh before moving to Chicago in 1999. He has published articles in philosophy of language, philosophy of mind, and aesthetics, among other areas, and on philosophers such as Wittgenstein, Kant, Nietzsche, Kierkegaard, William James, Frege, Carnap, Putnam, Cavell, Rorty, and McDowell, among others. He is currently working on three projects: a monograph on skepticism, a co-authored work (with Cora Diamond) on Wittgenstein, and a forthcoming collection of essays. He has edited two volumes of Hilary Putnam's papers and co-edited (with John Haugeland) one volume of Thomas Kuhn's papers.

Alice Crary is Assistant Professor in Philosophy at the New School for Social Research in New York. She has written articles on moral philosophy, moral psychology, philosophy and literature, and feminism and philosophy, as well as on figures such as Kant, Wittgenstein, and J.L. Austin. She is co-editor of *The*

New Wittgenstein (Routledge, 2000), editor of *Wittgenstein and the Moral Life: Essays in Honor of Cora Diamond* (MIT Press, 2006), and author of *Beyond Moral Judgment* (2006). She is currently working on a book called *Humans, Animals, Right and Wrong*.

Cora Diamond was Kenan Professor of Philosophy, Professor of Law, and University Professor at the University of Virginia, from which she retired in 2002. She has also taught at Princeton University, Aberdeen University, and the University of Sussex. She is the author of three books *The Realistic Spirit: Wittgenstein, Philosophy, and the Mind* (MIT Press, 1991), *Ethics: Shifting Perspectives* (Harvard University Press), and *Wittgenstein: Finding One's Way* (Oxford University Press). She is also the editor of *Wittgenstein's Lectures on the Foundations of Mathematics, Cambridge 1939* (University of Chicago Press, 1989).

Paul Franks teaches philosophy and Jewish studies at the University of Toronto. He studied at Balliol College, Oxford, and at Harvard University (Ph.D., 1993). He has published on Kantian and post-Kantian themes in philosophy of mind, metaphysics, epistemology, and philosophy of religion, in conversation with the work of Wittgenstein and Cavell, among others. He is Associate Editor of the *International Yearbook of German Idealism*. With Michael L. Morgan, he translated and commented on *Franz Rosenzweig: Philosophical and Theological Writings* (Hackett, 2000). His book *All or Nothing: Systematicity, Transcendental Arguments, and Skepticism in German Idealism* is forthcoming (Harvard University Press, 2005). He is currently working on post-Kantian approaches to metaphysical, epistemological, ethical, and theological problems concerning other minds.

Eli Friedlander is Assistant Professor of Philosophy at Tel Aviv University. He is the author of *Signs of Sense: Reading Wittgenstein's Tractatus* (Harvard University Press) and *J.J. Rousseau: An Afterlife of Words*. He is currently completing a manuscript on Kant's *Critique of Judgment* and is at work on a further book project delineating the philosophical character of Walter Benjamin's writings.

Stuart Klawans has been the film critic of *The Nation* since 1988 and is the author of the books *Film Follies: The Cinema Out of Order* and *Left in the Dark: Film Reviews and Essays, 1988–2001*. He was the recipient of a John Simon Guggenheim Memorial Foundation Fellowship for a projected critical monograph on the films of Preston Sturges.

Stephen Mulhall is Fellow and Tutor in Philosophy at New College, Oxford. He was previously a Fellow of All Souls College, Oxford, and a Reader in Philosophy at the University of Essex. His other publications include *Stanley Cavell: Philosophy's Recounting of the Ordinary* (Oxford University Press, 1994), *Inheritance and Originality: Wittgenstein, Heidegger, Kierkegaard* (Oxford University Press, 2001), and *Philosophical Myths of the Fall* (Princeton, 2005).

Hilary Putnam is Cogan University Professor Emeritus at Harvard University. His books include *Reason, Truth and History, Renewing Philosophy, Pragmatism, The Threefold Cord: Mind, Body and World, The Collapse of the Fact/Value Dichotomy,* and *Ethics without Ontology.*

Sanford Shieh is Associate Professor of Philosophy at Wesleyan University. He has written in philosophy of logic, philosophy of mathematics, and the history of analytic philosophy. He is co-editor of *Future Pasts* (Oxford, 2001) and of *The Limits of Logical Empiricism* (Springer, 2006). He is currently working on a conceptual history of modal logic in the twentieth century.

ACKNOWLEDGEMENTS

We would like to thank the various individuals and institutions who helped us to bring this project to completion. We are indebted in particular to the Wesleyan Center for the Humanities, to its director Henry Abelove, and to the Philosophy Department at the New School. We are grateful for the input and assistance of Jay Bernstein, Richard Bernstein, Mihaela Fistioc, and Nathaniel Hupert, for the generous guidance of Sonja van Leeuwen and Lucie Ewin at Routledge and for Anne van Leeuwen's care in constructing the index. Our deepest debt is to Stanley Cavell without whom this volume would not have happened.

"The Wittgensteinian Event" adapted and reprinted by permission of the publisher from *Philosophy the Day After Tomorrow* by Stanley Cavell, pp. 192–212, Cambridge, MA: The Belknap Press of Harvard University Press, Copyright © 2005 by the President and Fellows of Harvard College.

"Habitual Remarriage: The Ends of Happiness in the Palm Beach Story" by Stuart Klawans was first published in (eds.) Rupert Read and Jerry Goodenough, *Film as Philosophy: Essays on Cinema after Wittgenstein and Cavell*, Palgrave Macmillan 2005.

"The Difficulty of Reality and the Difficulty of Philosophy" by Cora Diamond was fist published in *Partial Answers: Journal of Literature and the History of Ideas* vol. 1, no. 2 (june 2003): 1-26.

Paul Francks, "The Discovery of the Other: Cavell, Fichte, and Skepticism," in *Common Knowledge*, Volume 5, no. 2, pp. 72-105. Copyright, 1996, Oxford University Press. All rights reserved. Used by permission of the publisher.

INTRODUCTION

Alice Crary and Sanford Shieh

This volume assembles a set of papers that, taken together, offer a comprehensive commentary on, and guide to, the philosophy of Stanley Cavell. Its two main aims are (1) to discuss a wide and representative range of the topics explored in Cavell's writings and (2) to display the internal unity of Cavell's thought across his treatments of these topics.

This second aim deserves special emphasis. Over the last two decades, Cavell's work has begun to provoke widespread interest, and to attract critical scrutiny in the many disciplines that it traverses – e.g. philosophy, film studies, literary studies, and cultural studies. But, even though this critical reception reflects the broad range of inquiry that is Cavell's hallmark, it rarely attempts to understand his concerns as contributing to a single, internally coherent, enterprise. The present volume is constructed with an eye to remedying this lack. The papers brought together here focus on disparate areas of Cavell's work; but, considered in each other's company, they illuminate connections among modes of thought distinctive of these areas, thereby shedding light on the broader sweep of Cavell's thought. This collection thus addresses, not only readers familiar with most of Cavell's opus, but also those who are just becoming acquainted with his writings or whose acquaintance extends no farther than one local part of his overall project.

The principle of unity that the volume identifies concerns the role within Cavell's thought of the view or, in Cavell's terms, the "vision" of language that he describes in connection with Wittgenstein's later writings. This view is one that Cavell first presents in his earliest essays on Wittgenstein and in his extended discussion of Wittgenstein's thought in Parts 1 and 2 of *The Claim of Reason*. What distinguishes the view is, very roughly, the idea that the language and concepts we use are invariably "ours" in the sense that they reflect human interests and, further, that this fact about them doesn't undermine their rational authority. On Cavell's reading, Wittgenstein wants us to recognize that our modes of thought and speech express our shared humanity or, to use some of Cavell's terms of art, that they express our "attunement in our criteria." Furthermore, Wittgenstein hopes to combat our tendency to move from this fundamental conception of language to the conclusion that our language is

1

merely natural and as such incapable of supplying the stability constitutive of the exercise of reason. What emerges in Cavell's writings is an image of Wittgenstein as trying to get us in this way to reconcile ourselves, or to make peace, with the observation that our language is "no more than natural" (CR, 178).

The guiding suggestion of this volume is that the vision of language which is Cavell's inheritance from Wittgenstein, and which he also discusses in connection with the work of other philosophers, plays an organizing role within his thought. The individual chapters ask us to understand this image of language as informing both Cavell's selection of many of the major themes of his writings and also his mode of developing them. Among the themes it aims to integrate are those of (1) *J.L. Austin's philosophical procedures*, (2) *the difficulty of philosophy*, (3) *skepticism and the other*, (4) *philosophy and autobiography or voice*, (5) *Emersonian or moral perfectionism*, (6) *philosophy's quarrel with literature*, (7) *the value of film*, (8) *idealism and romanticism*, and (9) *America as a philosophical ideal*.

Each chapter of this volume investigates one or more of these themes in a manner that at least tacitly presupposes Cavell's distinctive view of language. The purpose of this introduction is to give a brief overview of some of the ways in which, as a result, the chapters can be seen as engaging and reinforcing each other.

A helpful place to start is with Cavell's own contribution, which is an extended reflection on his inheritance of Wittgenstein's *Philosophical Investigations*. Cavell draws attention to a web of connections between the view of language that he finds in this book and leading themes of his own writing. He attempts to account for his sense that those passages in the *Investigations* which engage with questions recognized by professional philosophy as its own (e.g. questions about meaning, reference, understanding, consciousness, etc.) cannot, without losing their point, be isolated from remarks in the book that register "literary" responses to these passages. In this connection, he mentions, for instance, Wittgenstein's remarks on how in philosophy we send our words into exile and are called on to lead them back, and on how the exercise of thus leading them back involves a confrontation with ourselves. Cavell tells us that these remarks, far from being mere rhetorical ornamentation on the real business of the *Investigations*, are in fact internal to it. He suggests that the remarks deal directly with the kind of transformed relationship to ourselves that we need to achieve in order to see our language, in the manner prescribed by the philosophically more orthodox passages of the *Investigations*, as simultaneously a matter of individual responsibility and communal attunement. One conclusion Cavell thus invites us to draw is that there is a direct tie between the conception of the difficulty of philosophy that Wittgenstein bequeaths to us and Wittgenstein's view of language. Another conclusion that he invites us to draw is that there are significant links between this view and the view that the style of a work is neither easily nor clearly separable from its content.

In discussing these matters, Cavell revisits things he says throughout his career about fundamental features of the view in question. One topic that he broaches here is that of convergences and divergences between this view and the view of language spelled out in the writings of J.L. Austin. This moment in Cavell's thought is addressed, in different ways, in the chapters by Mulhall, Crary, and Bauer. Mulhall's initial focus is on Cavell's relatively recent criticism of what Austin calls "perlocutionary utterances." Mulhall claims that Cavell's objection is directed to the fact that Austin excludes the perlocutionary from the serious business of language. Austin speaks of the perlocutionary in reference to non-conventional effects that an utterance has on the thoughts and feelings of its audience, and he assumes that it must be possible in principle to grasp the meaning of an utterance without registering any such effects that it has. This is problematic because, Mulhall tells us, Austin thus suggests that "the responsibilities of implication and the rights of desire are two essentially distinct dimensions or aspects of speech." The problem is not only that the suggestion runs counter to the Wittgensteinian view of language that Cavell champions throughout his work, but also that, in some of his recent writings, Cavell introduces a new class of "passionate utterances" that depends for its cogency on rejecting it. The upshot of introducing this new class of utterances, according to Mulhall, is that Cavell reconceives Austin's work so that it is congenial to his own preferred view of language.

This aspect of Cavell's thought is discussed, from a different perspective, in Crary's chapter. Crary offers a close reading of Austin's lectures *How to Do Things with Words* that is compatible with Cavell's attempt to align his own view of language with Austin's. She argues that Austin's treatment of the perlocutionary is flawed by his own lights and that, properly understood, Austin's work accommodates Cavell's notion of the passionate utterance. Crary's larger goal in arguing along these lines is to provide a critique of recent suggestions about the bearing of Austin's work on ethics, and to develop a better account of this bearing. She shows that, when tensions internal to Austin's view of language are resolved, it is possible to attain an Austinian view of language that coheres, not only with Cavell's preferred view of language, but also, at the same time, with Cavell's perfectionist commitments in ethics. A central motif of Cavellian moral perfectionism is the idea that particular modes of affective response are necessary for moral understanding and that it is inevitably possible that new modes of response will bring fresh moral insights within reach – and will in this sense further "perfect" us. Crary's closing claim is that this perfectionist idea becomes available to us when we develop our conception of language to make room for Cavell's passionate utterances.

Where, as we just saw, the emphasis of the chapters by Mulhall and Crary is on investigating Cavell's view of language (and, more specifically, on doing so by following up on his work on Austin), the emphasis of the remaining chapters is on investigating additional areas of Cavell's thought – areas that are, in one way or another, informed by this view. This includes, to proceed in order, the chapter by Bauer. Bauer's contribution both resembles the chapters just discussed in addressing Austin's work and also differs from them in focusing primarily on connections between Austin's work and further problematics and regions of thought of interest to Cavell.

3

Bauer starts from the thought that Austin's project in *How to Do Things with Words* marks a radical departure from the conception of philosophy that informs mainstream analytic philosophy of language. She defends this thought by arguing that the project relinquishes the deeply engrained assumption that it must in principle be possible to pin down the semantics of natural language in advance of "looking and seeing" what we do with our words in particular circumstances, and she brings her argument to bear on a particular example: the appropriation of Austin by analytic philosophers arguing for a feminist position on the regulation of pornography. What specifically interests Bauer is the work of a group of analytic philosophers who maintain that pornography is a kind of illocutionary act whose (alleged) authority over its consumers allows it to systematically introduce – into "the language game of sex" – presuppositions that subordinate and dominate women, for example by eliminating necessary background conditions for their utterances to be understood as rejections of men's sexual advances. Drawing on Cavell's work, Bauer shows that this argument rests on two main philosophical failures. To begin with, it fails to comprehend properly the conventional authority internal to Austin's illocutionary acts, and thus wrongly invokes this conventional authority on pornography's behalf. Bauer traces this first failure to an uncritical inheritance of Austin's official doctrine of the perlocutionary – a misstep that leaves no alternatives beyond the conventional authority of illocutions and the brute force of Austinian perlocutions – and she suggests that one way to avoid it is to appeal to Cavell's notion of the passionate utterance. But Bauer isn't recommending a simple analysis of pornography as passional speech. She also thinks that recent analytic feminist discussions of pornography fail to do justice to the obvious fact that most of pornography is not speech but still or moving images, and so fails to be sensitive to what Cavell, in *The World Viewed* and elsewhere, calls the ontology of photography and film.

The chapter by Cora Diamond represents a break with questions about Austin and about the value of film (the latter question resurfaces in Klawans's chapter; see below) and a turn toward a primary concern with the conception of the difficulty of philosophy that Cavell describes in reference to his preferred view of language. Diamond approaches this topic by first considering moments and aspects of experience that resist our concepts, a resistance that Diamond refers to as "the difficulty of reality." She discusses a number of texts – a poem by Ted Hughes, a story by J.M. Coetzee, a remark of Czesław Miłosz's, and so on – that describe this experience and invite their audiences to confront it as well. Further, she discusses how we are inclined, not to yield to our responses to it, but rather, using one of Cavell's own terms of art, to "deflect" from it and treat it as a merely intellectual problem that can be explained away. Diamond goes on to suggest that deflection occurs in a great deal of traditional philosophy. She claims that it is possible to capture part of what is distinctive about Cavell's work by pointing out that the demand to resist deflection provides a good model for his remarks about the difficulty of philosophy.

4

One case that Diamond considers here is that of Cavell's treatment of skepticism, and her remarks about how for Cavell the challenge of dealing with skepticism is one of resisting the temptation to "deflect" are effectively amplified in the chapters by Putnam and Shieh. Putnam is explicitly interested in the kind of rejoinder to skepticism that Cavell's "projective vision of language" affords. He notes that, for Cavell, our interest in skeptical lines of inquiry is an expression of our tendency to become estranged from our own modes of thought and speech or, in the Cavellian terms that Putnam uses, to lose our "attunement." Further, Putnam also notes that this means that, for Cavell, skepticism, far from being a merely intellectual problem with a solution analogous to solutions of familiar logical paradoxes, is a problem that we only address appropriately in so far as we turn our attention back to ourselves.

At one point in his discussion, Putnam reminds us that Cavell speaks in reference to this basic analysis of skepticism, of "the truth of skepticism." This brings us to the chapter by Shieh, which explores some difficulties of understanding Cavell's teaching on skepticism. Shieh argues that there is something of a convergence of opinion on the overall shape of this teaching, one that stands in some tension with a number of Cavell's characterizations of the philosophical significance of skepticism. In particular, this standard interpretation of Cavell does not account very well for his repeated insistence that his treatment of skepticism and traditional epistemology is not a refutation of these philosophical positions. Shieh argues that, in order to make sense of Cavell's refusal here, one has to recall his account of the procedures of ordinary-language philosophy, procedures that derive from his fundamental Wittgensteinian vision of language. These procedures are aimed, not at establishing empirical generalizations about linguistic behavior, but rather at producing the attunement that is the basis of linguistic community. An insufficiently appreciated aspect of this conception of language is that there is no guarantee for this human attunement. Mutual intelligibility or conviction, in philosophy as in all our other dealings with language, is never a resting place that can be identified and attained antecedently to particular successful attempts to produce it. There is thus no decisive and final refutation of skepticism, and its truth is perhaps just that the very idea of a permanent cure for the plight of the skeptic is itself continuous with the impulse to skepticism. More importantly, this leads to a conception of philosophizing that does not result primarily in the "views" in the traditional sense – i.e. the representation of objective facts – but rather in the activity of bringing a community into being.

The problem of skepticism and this active conception of philosophy are taken up in the essays of Franks and Friedlander, both of which read Cavell by pursuing his remarks on Kant and Kant's inheritors in the German Romantic and Idealist traditions. Franks develops a reading of Cavell as a post-Kantian, a philosopher who accepts that Kant's insight into human finitude marks a fundamental turn in the history of philosophy and yet who remains dissatisfied with Kant's own expression of that insight, especially in the problematic concept of the thing-in-itself. Cavell sees this concept as a critical instance of philosophy's turning the conditions of human knowledge as a disappointing limitation of it, a move rooted in the human drive to deny humanity. Cavell's investigation of skepticism about other minds thus attempts a diagnosis of this drive and a mode of philosophizing that does not recapitulate it. Franks then uses these themes from Cavell to offer a reading of the reaction to Kant of Fichte, one of the key figures of German Idealism. Like Cavell, Fichte was preoccupied with accounting philosophically for the human capacity to deny its humanity. Franks argues that this concern is in fact what led Fichte to realize the need for a rethinking of the Kantian project. This rethinking brought Fichte to the problem of the Other, both as a theoretical problem for a Kantian, and as a skepticism about other minds that played a part in Fichte's own life.

Friedlander's essay highlights the connections between the roots of Cavell's conception of philosophy in the procedures of the ordinary and Kant's notion of aesthetic judgment, through another central idea of Cavell's thought: exemplification. For Friedlander, the ordinary-language philosopher's search for the ground of community, through saying what we say, is a matter of exemplification, using one's inmost convictions to reveal what is common to all. Exemplification is also the showing or enacting of what counts for me that aims at bringing others to speak with me. This notion is used by Friedlander to interpret Kant's judgment of taste as speaking with a universal voice. What makes a judgment aesthetic is not its subject matter but rather a way or manner of judging that exemplifies a possibility. Specifically, it is judging that shows a possibility of making sense of the object of beauty, and thereby gives expression to the presupposition of a common sense of meaningfulness.

The notion of exemplification ramifies in a number of further directions in Cavell's work. The exemplification that allows mutuality becomes mutual exemplification in the idea of conversation that demands an improvisatory interplay in which following and being followed, changing places, taking the lead and being led are essential to the way each reflects for the other further possibilities of the self. This "meet and happy conversation" is central to Cavell's investigation of (re)marriage in a genre of film, and so connects with his transfiguration of the traditional philosophical concept of concept and instance into the notion of genre, discussed at the end of Mulhall's essay. Each member of a genre is an example that further delineates the possibilities of the genre and so further defines what it is for all other members to belong together. Moreover, each member is the possible locus of a conversation over the conditions of membership in the genre. Such a conversation is exemplified in Klawans's essay, an investigation, through the example of a particular film, of the genre of remarriage comedies. Klawans's reading of *The Palm Beach Story* is framed by the question of whether this film belongs to the genre of remarriage comedies. Klawans argues that this film puts great pressure on the notion because, while some of its features – conversation and education – mark it as belonging to the genre, other features undermine the aspirations of those instances of the genre that Cavell has studied. The latter include *The Palm Beach Story*'s pointing up tensions between the attraction to ideals and compromises of real life, a tension embodied in the idea of America as simultaneously making marriage for love possible and yet whose social realities preclude any genuine attempt at living life as adventure. This film thus raises the question of the extent to which one could distinguish a study of the conditions of a genre – which for Cavell is a condition for being a member of the genre – from a deconstruction of that genre.

The themes of moral perfectionism that have been insistently appearing in the essays discussed so far are connected in Conant's essay with the ideas of American philosophy and of America itself as a philosophical concept that has been increasingly important in Cavell's thought since *The Senses of Walden*. Conant develops the main themes of Cavell's discussions of American philosophy by reading them against George Seferis's call for Greek Hellenism in poetry. For both Seferis and Cavell a version of Kierkegaard's "monstrous illusion" stands in the way of being able to perceive the necessity of their projects. For Seferis, the illusion is that a Greek artist can participate in a living Hellenic tradition simply in virtue of speaking Greek, living in Greece, remaining committed to the heritage of Greece, and purifying his or her style of elements deemed not to be Greek. For Cavell, following Thoreau, the illusion is one in which an American citizen can take the existence of America to be unproblematically confirmed by facts such as that he or she lives on a continent called America, in a nation known as the United States of America, in a place where the words used to formulate the promise of America freedom, democracy, equal guarantee of life, liberty and the pursuit of happiness are endlessly repeated in the public discourse. For Seferis the illusion makes invisible the task of a properly Greek Hellenism: a struggle to create a new tradition that can lay rightful claim to having reclaimed some part of the glory that was Greece. For Cavell the illusion obscures the task of taking the discovery and constitution of America to be, not an accomplished fact, but a set of ongoing projects to ensure that America can rightfully claim to live up to its promise. For one who aspires to be an American philosopher, the discovery of America poses particular problems. Conant argues that for Cavell American culture has never really believed in its capacity to produce anything of permanent value, so it consistently undervalues its achievements. The problem for an American philosopher is not why a distinctive American cultural voice has yet to emerge, but why, each time it emerges, for example in the works of Emerson and Thoreau, America fails to acknowledge it as such. Conant shows that Cavell's response to this problem is to work toward dissipating the appearance of America's intellectual barrenness, by bringing the actual contours of the intellectual landscape properly into view. This is the task of Cavell's readings of Emerson and Thoreau, as well as his preoccupation with American films, some of the most passionately consumed but least valued expressions of America.

1

THE WITTGENSTEINIAN EVENT

Stanley Cavell

The text to follow is companion to one that includes a sketch of my indebtedness to Wittgenstein's later work, specifically to his *Philosophical Investigations*, touching on ideas of instruction, hence of the child, and ideas of the ordinary as a field of the incessant risk of pointlessness and of isolation, and perhaps of transfiguration, and follows such possibilities into the novels of two of the greatest observers of the life, or economy, of everyday, recurrent human existence, Jane Austen and George Eliot; it also at least mentions the new difficulty within the strange ease of Wittgenstein's later language, created in part by the pressure on his prose of renouncing reliance on technical philosophical terms.[1] Even terms immediately associated with Wittgenstein's philosophizing, such as "grammar" and "criteria" and "language games," are inventions or extensions that rely on their ordinary senses, as if any and every word in our language might be pressed into, or slip into, theoretical service. The present text is meant to fill in details of the shape that my debt, in particular to the writing of *Philosophical Investigations*, has taken for me, to the extent that I understand the debt and that book.

I leave open how large a change the Wittgensteinian event may represent in our intellectual culture more broadly, I mean beyond professional philosophy; whether it amounts to what Nietzsche calls a great separation (bearing in mind the thought Nietzsche cites at the end of his *Untimely Meditation on Schopenhauer* in words from Emerson's essay "Circles": "A new degree of culture would instantly revolutionize the entire system of human pursuits"); or whether, and how, we should take to heart the epigraph Wittgenstein gives to *Philosophical Investigations*: "It is generally the nature of progress to look greater than it really is." This is almost a dare to look at what one might call the style of the *Investigations*. The text seems to do what it can to make itself at once attractive and uninheritable within professional philosophy – this is perhaps a way to characterize its seductiveness (an admirable, philosophical feature for some, for others deplorable).

It is in this light hardly surprising that *Philosophical Investigations* has no systematic, disciplinary pedagogy unargumentatively associated with it, which is to say that it has no secure place in the current dispensations of academic philosophical instruction. It sometimes seems imaginable to me that the *Investigations* will come to be thought of as belonging to a more or less honorable line of counter-philosophical works whose palpable philosophical eccentricity assures their marginality to a central philosophical curriculum – along perhaps with Montaigne's or Emerson's *Essays*, Pascal's *Pensées*, Rousseau's *Promenades*, Friedrich Schlegel's *Fragments*, Kierkegaard's *Philosophical Fragments*, Nietzsche's *Zarathustra*, works ineradicably tinged with the philosophical whose life, nevertheless, largely depends upon their interesting those beyond the call of professional philosophy. Such a development would, to my mind, lose a singular feature of Wittgenstein's later work (most famous from the *Investigations*), a feature of unfailing fascination for me, which is precisely its demand for an existence at once inside the profession of philosophy and outside of it. The specification "at once" is critical in this formulation; it declares that something essential to the work's fascination is missed if one seeks to keep the palpably philosophical stretches, concerned with problems of meaning, reference, understanding, states of consciousness, language games, grammar, and so on, free from the patently and unembarrassed literary responses to itself, where we are asked to consider such matters as a fly trapped in a bottle, a beetle in a box, talk from a lion, the teeth of a rose.

I have since my first essay on Wittgenstein, "The availability of Wittgenstein's later philosophy," published more than forty years ago, insisted on his remarkable presentation of his philosophizing as internal to his teaching, and it is perhaps primarily because of the persistence of this insistence, in my way of treating it, that I am sometimes called, by the friendly and the not so friendly, an alternative voice in the interpretation of later Wittgenstein, hence perhaps elsewhere in philosophy. For some years I could take a rueful pleasure in such a description of the work I do, but as pleasure in the description faded it was replaced by a certain perplexity: what are the further contours of this sense of an alternative, what difference or set of differences has threatened my welcome within a communal effort? If I am ever to take the measure of this threat, at least to go over in this spirit the range of sketches I have given of stretches of Wittgenstein's work, essentially of the *Investigations*, and see how they add up, there is clearly, at my age, no time like the present.

One way to understand the pedagogical recalcitrance of Wittgenstein's text is to consider that it challenges the fairly fundamental professional assumption that philosophy breaks into separate fields of study. (Heidegger is the only philosopher I think of who has explicitly described himself as shunning the idea of philosophy as a set of fields.) I am responding to this challenge to the separation of philosophical fields when, briefly, I have spoken of the *Investigations'* idea of the solution of a philosophical problem as requiring, or inviting, an aesthetic interpretation; and when, even more briefly, I have suggested that the fervor or urgency of insight that Wittgenstein's writing demands – the air of importance he conveys while at the same time seeming to destroy importance – is to be understood as a form of moral perfectionism. It is as if J.L. Austin's

9

toying with the idea of original sin by putting, in his own voice, a lost garden in conjunction with Berkeley's examples of the apple and the unperceived tree is in *Philosophical Investigations* given a philosophically serious (secular) articulation, human talkers always tormented by possibilities untaken, forever cast down in taking them.

I might summarize the way I see my differences from certain other accounts of Wittgenstein's *Investigations* in the following way: My reading of the text is guided by the idea of taking it not alone as an *object* of interpretation but at the same time as a *means* of interpretation. (Perhaps this is how I view any text I take with full seriousness. It can be seen as characteristic of one way philosophers have from the beginning characteristically confronted or confounded their inheritance. When Aristotle found fault with Plato's account of the Forms underlying or presiding over the metaphysical and epistemological intelligibility of things, he preserved this function of Form as fundamental, but changed its location.) Some members of my generation, struck by the Wittgensteinian event, felt liberated from the sometimes painful draw of philosophy as such, taking its problems as having been finally perceived for what they are worth, and solved. In my case, its changed expectations of philosophy liberated me to think philosophically (according to my lights) about anything, in any medium, in which I found an interest. To my mind Wittgenstein's revision of philosophy is engaged with the revisions introduced by each of the monumental innovators in philosophy, say, just taking obvious modern instances, Descartes, Locke, Hume, Rousseau, Kant, Hegel, Russell, Heidegger, each of whose thinking is involved with a distrust of philosophy, or rather of certain claims to philosophy. The history of philosophy is quite continuously a history of discontinuities.

I should say at once that my interest in Wittgenstein has never been primarily a matter of agreeing or disagreeing with what he says (though I have expressed both reactions about specific matters over the years), but rather, even increasingly, has come from an astonishment that he was able to say the things he says at all, and bring them to philosophical pertinence. I wanted to discover what the conditions are under which that becomes possible. This is more than anything else the desire that has kept me returning to passages of the text of the *Investigations* over what is now more than four decades.

I begin by reassuring myself that the idea of an alternative voice implies some measure of commonality, as of different paths to a similar goal, or of similar vehicles to different goals. For example, I have to assume that claims I have urged about the destruction of what is interesting and important, and about the relation of Wittgensteinian criteria to the idea of the ordinary and to a companion idea of skepticism, however different in conclusion from other views, are recognizable as philosophically companionable work. I know that the emphatic and recurrent attention I give to the idea of the ordinary or everyday in Wittgenstein seems to some excessive, and perhaps that suggests a place to begin a specification of my differences, as I imagine them. One philosophical friend, an influential admirer of Wittgenstein, felt impelled from time to time, over much of a lifetime, to remind me forcibly that Wittgenstein is not an ordinary-language philosopher. For me this essentially means that he is not a philosopher in the mould of J.L. Austin. But differences between these philosophical sensibilities (and of both from that of G.E. Moore) are something I have indeed repeatedly affirmed. Yet I find intersections between passages in texts of Austin's I care about, and passages of *Philosophical Investigations*, that prompt me to want to articulate their differences.

For example, Wittgenstein's saying "What *we* do is to lead words back from their metaphysical to their everyday use" (sec. 116) could almost be said of Austin's practice, except that Austin had no announced conception of, and no patience with, the metaphysical, in this or any other guise, hence no interest in tracing the philosophical, or say the human, craving for the metaphysical (something Wittgenstein once phrases as "a longing for the transcendent"). (This interest has come to seem to me one of the most revelatory of the affinities of *Philosophical Investigations* with the vision of Kant's *The Critique of Pure Reason*, its sense of the essential and implacable restlessness of the human, its distinguished faculty of reason as precisely the faculty that tantalizes itself with the impossible. The associated difference from Kant is Wittgenstein's conviction, as I might put the matter, that no system of concepts – call this a philosophical theory – could as it were establish reliable retreats or reliefs from, or limits which define, this restlessness. I should think Wittgenstein's affinity here is with Schopenhauer's identification of the Will as the thing in itself, to be vanquished only by itself.)

Wittgenstein gives very little direct development of the concept of the ordinary or everyday use of language, but without the concept, his greater development, or portraiture, of the metaphysical in language could not be undertaken. (I have suggested that he is more accurately described as a philosopher of metaphysical than of ordinary language. When he remembers someone striking himself on the breast in the heat of a philosophical discussion, crying out, "No one else can have THIS pain," Wittgenstein's response in effect is that this use of "this" seems to make sense only so long as it remains unspecified, an absolute demonstrative absolutely pointing to an absolute object. A fundamental motive of Wittgenstein's is to understand why we would *seek* such a phenomenon, or non-phenomenon.) The ordinary occurs essentially in *Philosophical Investigations* as what skepticism denies, and what metaphysics would transcend, as it were as a fictional place produced (in retrospect) by philosophy's flight from everyday ungroundedness or prejudices or fixations. (I am alluding here, as I sometimes do, to Plato's Cave as a figure for the ordinary, the place philosophy begins and to which, unlike the aspiration of much of subsequent philosophy, it – so to speak – returns.)

I alluded a few moments ago to Austin's uncharacteristic outburst in his essay "Other minds" at which Austin laments "the original sin . . . by which the philosopher casts himself out from the garden of the world we live in" (*Philosophical Papers*, 3rd edn, p. 90). While this seems to capture something of

Wittgenstein's sense of philosophy's drive to speak outside language games, demanding meaning where none is given or derived (and in effect confesses Austin's – even his – sharing of Romanticism's obsession with the myth of the expulsion from the Garden of Eden), it issues in no serious wish on Austin's part to understand philosophy's perpetual self-defeat (beyond accusing it of such qualities as laziness, drunkenness, wiliness, and morally suspicious claims to profundity). *Philosophical Investigations*, by contrast, at a certain point comes upon what I think of as a counter-myth to that of Eden, a counter-interpretation of our present condition, meant at once to recognize the repetitive force of our temptation to leave it (as if our ordinary lives and language are metaphysical limitations or compromises of the human) and at the same time to indicate how following the temptation will lead to grief. What I am calling the counter-myth runs this way: "We have got onto slippery ice where there is no friction and so in a certain sense the conditions are ideal, but also, just because of that, we are unable to walk" (sec. 107).

An example Wittgenstein gives of this drive to an impossible yet implacable ideal is the thought that if things have the same name they must have something in common, an essence in virtue of which they are said to be the same – a thought as early as Plato's Forms or Ideas, which later philosophy calls universals. Wittgenstein responds: "Don't say: 'There *must* be something common . . . ' but *look and see*" (sec. 66). Can this hopelessly naïve suggestion really dispel a philosophical intuition lasting for millennia, that to know what an object is is to know its essence? Shall we look and see?

What does a tall, small round table at which two bar stools are drawn up have in common with a table of numbers displayed on a page, and both with a water table? (I do not suppose that these further tables are metaphorical.) The common thing cannot be simply that they all have an element that is flat, since the sheet of paper on which the table of numbers is printed is flat, and so is the coaster on the bar table, but we don't call each of these a table (exactly). Then where does the table idea come in these three cases? Well, the instances do all have something in common with a common library table – its horizontal stretch of flatness fits the surface of water; that it is mounted on legs (one or more) fits the round bar table; its rectangularity fits the table of numbers. But is *this* what we thought we meant in insisting that they *must* have something in common? Didn't we mean something more like: they have it in common *in a common or essential way* – a *same* something that calls out for the concept *in each case*?

It seems that Wittgenstein wants to reveal our intellectual disappointment with our philosophical explanations. But when he goes on to suggest that what we see among these instances is no more than what he calls a "family resemblance," this seems, to my mind, even more disappointing, although it has evidently satisfied some who are devoted to Wittgenstein's thought. My sense, rather, is that this is only a preparation for his suggesting that we are right to look for a sense of essence or necessity in our concepts – say a way of understanding our *attachment* to words – but we are looking in the wrong place, in the

12

wrong spirit. This is at stake when he considers that "Concepts ... are the expression of our interest and direct our interest" (sec. 570). So, for example, some tables need legs (when our interest is to sit comfortably at them, namely have them come up roughly to our waists); and our interest in the flatness of others is to allow for a significant measure (the water table); and our interest in the rectangularity of a table of numbers is to achieve the linear clarity necessary to check and to interpret them.

I pause to remark that when I said just now that Wittgenstein's idea of family resemblance does not deny the reality of the philosophical search for necessity, for essence, in our concepts, and characterized this search as a response to our attachment to words, I recognized that characterization as posing a question for my taking, in *The Claim of Reason* (p. 355), Wittgenstein's discussion of seeing an aspect (of seeing-as) to be connected with experiencing the meaning of a word, also as a case of "attachment to our words." These seem opposite criteria for the concept of "attachment to our words." In the aspect case it is the experience of a word, expressed in the idea of its being called forth by an aspect's dawning, that calls forth the concept (the duck aspect in its relation to pictures of ducks); in the case of the draw of essence, it seems to be something like the *absence* of the experience, or distinctiveness, of the *word* that is required, but something like its being called forth by the (experience of the) *reality* of what it conceptualizes, that this thing *is* a table (not an *aspect* of a level of water or of a collection of numbers or of a smallish round flat surface made to sit at – having legs – on a bar stool). Here we come upon the dual service in which criteria are meant to be pressed, to show the necessity in grammatical differences (e.g. between "is a duck" and "is now a duck") and to show the necessity in the relation of the realm of language, of concepts, and the realm of the world (between expecting someone and an environment in which someone is to be expected to appear, or in which there is vanishing hope that he or she will appear).

Why does Wittgenstein express our dissatisfaction with human existence as our getting onto a perfect field of ice where we are unable to walk? How dangerous a consequence is the inability to walk meant to signify? Walking is listed among the handful of capacities that the *Investigations* cites as "part of our natural history" (sec. 25), along with commanding, questioning, recounting, chatting, eating, drinking, playing – so that finding or making ourselves unable to walk (unearthed as it were) would represent a breach in our natural history. This idea of the natural history of the human is not unlike what Heidegger (for example in the essay "The thing") calls the conditionedness of the human, something that presumably may be lost, or denied. (Konrad Lorenz's comparison of animal and human societies, in "Psychology and phylogeny" [*Studies in Animal and Human Behavior*, Vol. 2, Harvard University Press]) where pre-human species, biologically selected for instinctively prepared and released responses to specific environments, are in each case contrasted with human "versatility" (p. 224) and "openness to surroundings" (p. 234) can almost strike one as proposing that the human has no natural history, an idea Lorenz deplored and wished to bring into renewed discussion. I report, without discussion now, that over-conventionalized interpretations of Wittgenstein's notion of life forms seem to me to wish to deny human beings their natural history in its perpetual intersection with human cultivation (a vision linking Wittgenstein with Freud). I would not be surprised to learn that there is some historical connection between "openness to surroundings" (Lorenz attributes the phrase to Arnold Gehlen) and Heidegger's sense of Dasein's openness to Being; I would, I suppose, be surprised to learn that others share my sense that these are related, without historical connection, to Wittgenstein's sense of the essential openness (or exposure) of human concepts (sketched in *The Claim of Reason*, pp. 432–40), and what he calls their criteria, to the world. What a priori limit can we put on the recurrence of what we call, for example, a table, or sociability, or abandonment?

Then how dangerous a loss would a break in our natural history signify? We might try imagining our response to one who begins periodically to move through comfortable rooms and along sunny, unobstructed sidewalks as though they were fields of ice, or paths along a precipice – flailing through an unremarkable apartment, hunching along the sides of buildings – and who professes surprise that we let this interfere with maintaining our end of a conversation with him. The metaphysician conceives of himself as thinking about the essence of human language, while he strikes Wittgenstein as intellectually flailing and hunching. I am, of course, taking the description "unable to walk" not as the description of some specific failure, but as what the *Investigations* elsewhere calls "a symbolical expression [which is] really a mythological description" (sec. 221), presumably in this case signifying something about our inability to move ourselves, physically or intellectually, in accordance with our apparent desires. (We might say of such a one that he or she has gone into his or her "ice walk.") Such symbolical expressions, or uses, are in place where we are trying to make sense of our efforts to make sense of our lives and are led to utterances such as, in wishing to account for the practice of following a rule, "All the steps are really already taken" (sec. 219), which Wittgenstein understands as a gesture in which – while you have said nothing literal – you have expressed "how it strikes you" (cp. ibid.), an expression to which he thereupon pays attention. In mythologizing our requirement for an ideal or pure order of language as a wish to inhabit a medium other than one with human grounding that supports the human gait of walking, the danger of the consequence – as Wittgenstein conceives it – is no less than the danger of our becoming unable to recount or question or play or chat, which is to say, unable to express ourselves or to nourish ourselves by breaking bread with others. Does this suggest that our grounding in the world is weak (because our ground is unsurveyably vulnerable to our capacity for dissatisfaction with ourselves) or that it is strong (because we could not, or would not, actually go so far as to destroy the grounds of our existence, our natural history)?

Wittgenstein ends this counter-myth of escape, as from a false perfection, by exclaiming, "Back to the rough ground!" It is a symbolical expression of what he has described as returning words from their metaphysical to their everyday use. If so, then I might further specify my difference in understanding the importance of the ordinary or everyday in the *Investigations* by noting that the more literal expression about returning words to their everyday use is a gloss on his having just insisted: "When philosophers use a word . . . and try to grasp the *essence* of the thing, one must always ask oneself: is the word ever actually used in this way in the language-game which is its original home?", a remark in which, in turn, I find further clauses in a mythology of human restlessness or strife. This is perhaps harder to see in the published English translation, which I would modify to read more literally: "is the word in fact so used in the language which is its native land?", since "*Heimat*" in the German text is a striking thought and since Wittgenstein here writes "*Sprache*," not "*Sprachspiel*." Then the picture we get is not of the philosopher as not playing the game of the ordinary (to which many have wished to respond: perhaps he has good reason not to), but as casting his words into exile.

That is, casting *our* words. Wittgenstein's "philosopher", in contrast with Austin's (or Moore's), is less some clearly identifiable theorizer, than anyone of us stopped by perplexity, entangled in his or her thoughts. We do not enter adulthood as Socrates, but perhaps as one stunned at the failure of our assertions to convince Socrates. So that we do not know to what extent our ordinary, or say unexamined, lives are spent in exile from our expressions. (Other philosophers, Emerson among them, have spoken of our living as aliens, or rather as in alienation from our thoughts; Kierkegaard says we live as if we are "out," meaning not at home; Wittgenstein will add: not at work. Freud's picture, not altogether unlike Plato's in *The Republic*, is that of our possessing others within ourselves, speaking in our place, as it were out of our mouths. An image, by the way, that Wittgenstein explicitly considers.)

It is an obvious continuation (or inspiration) of this mythological register of exile to speak of leading words *back* (to their homeland), and to urge us to get ourselves *back* (to rough ground). What this specifically expresses as striking us about the act of invoking a language game, or of remembering an ordinary use of a word, is that we have already been at the place we are trying to get to, philosophy has no other. Don't we already know, for example, from our everyday experience, that if I say "I know how he feels about her leaving *only* from what little he tells me, and what less he shows me" my reservation ("only") suggests my sense that he is withholding something from me, and implies that I have in this case little independent means of knowing what it is, for example no other credible informant and no really better opportunity of observing matters for myself. So when Wittgenstein objects to the philosophical or metaphysical assertion that we know others *only* from their behavior (or, rather, attempts to get us to see that this is a philosophically forced assertion) he is asking us to question whether we wish to stand behind the sense that there is something the other is always, necessarily, withholding from us, and affirm the implication that I have in *all* cases *no* independent means of knowing what that is. And if we wish to say that this is undisguised nonsense (all that "necessarily withholding" and "no independent means of knowing" could at most mean here is: he is he and I am I – which, however truly important, conveys no information), then we will want to understand what drives philosophizing into nonsense. And if it is this easy to be exiled, what is, or was, our life in our supposed native land, and what would it mean to "return" to it?

I take the myth of "leading words back" (we haven't interpreted "leading" here, as if words were alive and had to be guided or enticed), to register – since the idea, as I have suggested, should not be that of returning to a *place* – rather the welcome idea of returning words to the circulation of language and its (sometimes unpredictable) projections rather than keeping them fixated in some imaginary service. But this idea does not so far capture the sense of having, in this process, to reverse *ourselves*. This is brought out in the thought not of "return" but of "turn," as when Wittgenstein says "Our investigation must be turned, but pivoted around our real need" (sec. 108). But then the addition of "real need" (*eigentliches Bedürfnis*) has to make its own contribution to mythology, to the characterization of our everyday existence seen from the perspective of philosophy.

The idea of real need adds to the idea of our existence as exile, the suggestion that our lives are characterized, intellectually and otherwise, by *false* needs, or false necessities, as when Wittgenstein cautions, or demands: "Don't say: 'There *must* be something common, or they would not be called "games."'" My taking examples of tables turned out to prompt me to emphasize Wittgenstein's responsiveness to interests in addition to that of needs, and hence to invoke what is for me another of his particularly critical characterizations of his philosophizing, the one in which he turns on himself to ask: "Where does our investigation get its importance from, since it seems only to destroy everything interesting, that is, all that is great and important?", and he replies (I take it to himself): "What we are destroying is nothing but houses of cards." But we have been living in these intellectual edifices since roughly the beginning of systematic philosophy in Plato, not without increasing disturbance since the advent of modern philosophy in the work of, say, Descartes and Hume.

Now a vision of human life as distorted by false necessities links *Philosophical Investigations* with the opening preoccupations of Plato's *Republic*, and Rousseau's *Social Contract*, and Kant's Critiques, and Thoreau's *Walden*, and Marx's *Capital*, and perhaps suggests a way to respond to the feeling – one I have not tried very hard to protect against – that I have already made much too much of Wittgenstein's enticing so-called meta-philosophical remarks about mythological descriptions and symbolical expressions, in emphasizing what are after all only a few patently literary passages out of all proportion to the actual philosophical *work* of the *Investigations*. Evidently my sense, on the contrary, is that what Wittgenstein specifies as the mythological is part of his providing some perspective precisely on what his philosophical work is, what he takes its importance to be, why it is difficult the way it is, why it takes the form it has, and I am taking the obligation to provide that perspective as internal to, called for by, what that work is. (In saying that it is called for I mean to imply that the call may, with reason, be questioned, that one need not take the passages I emphasize to heart as I do. Which is a way of repeating what I urged at the outset, that the work of the *Investigations* is, and should be, professionalizable.)

It is work that can readily seem too trivial to mention (say it is bethinking ourselves of what we say when, and of how that is possible, and sometimes hard to do, and of why it becomes necessary) and then all at once can seem to require a response of particular urgency, as if speaking to a sense of moral or even religious perplexity, as though the philosophical questioning of the use of a word epitomizes, in its apparent triviality and in our resistance to the apparent triviality, a chronic sense that our lives are in mortal question and as such require turning. When Wittgenstein expresses his sense that our investigation seems only to destroy everything interesting and important he adds parenthetically "As it were all the buildings, leaving behind only bits of stone and rubble," thus emphasizing that this impression is our fantasy – no buildings have been destroyed, the things of the world remain as they were. But we, however, in response to trivial requests for saying what we know but do not know how to value, are devastated. This is how a change, urged by philosophy, in our sense of what is interesting, great, important can in the moment make us feel. Shouldn't we ask for something in return? Some liberation, perhaps? But do we trust ourselves to know what liberation looks like?

I might summarize what I have been saying about my interest in the ordinary, I mean about its being that to which we are to turn, or turn again, by saying that the *Investigations* portrays our lives (with their little outbreaks of madness) as something extraordinary, strange, in a sense unnatural. It is to something of this sense that I was responding, in my first book, *Must We Mean What We Say?*, by including in it an essay on Beckett's *Endgame*, which at one point contrasts Beckett's sense of the ordinariness of the extraordinary with Chekhov's portraits of the extraordinariness of the ordinary, in each case marveling at what we, with our cursed and blessed capacity for adaptation or conformity, might judge as either ordinary or out of the ordinary. (And yet this capacity can be nothing other than, must deploy the same powers and constraints as, our capacity for transformation, for, in the Romantic formula, becoming the one you are – so that the path of a human life is the resultant of these contrary forces.) When Wittgenstein remarks, for example, "A philosophical problem has the form: 'I don't know my way about,'" (sec. 123) I understand him – continuing his insistence that philosophy does not seek to teach us anything new – to imply that philosophy does not move us from ignorance to knowledge, but from confusion or chaos to clarity or order, from being lost to finding ourselves, and that the first step of a philosophical answer to a philosophical problem is to demonstrate to us that we are indeed lost, confused, chaotic, even when we think of ourselves as full of conviction. (Thoreau speaks of our enforced certainties or convictions as signifying our being convicted.) Similarly, when in the following

17

section of the *Investigations* (sec. 124) we are told that philosophy "leaves every-thing as it is," I interpret this as speaking to what Heidegger means by openness as "letting-lie-before-us," namely as charging that philosophy is called for by our inability to leave things as they are, namely by the violence of thinking.

In this sequence of thoughts about the ordinary, each way in which, in philosophizing, we come upon ourselves denying our human powers produces a clause in an open-ended mythological description of our everyday lives – as in exile, or making ourselves strange to ourselves, or constructing unsatisfying substitutes for a fantasized lost harmony, or violently asserting a singularity guar-anteed by metaphysics rather than by making our words and deeds our own ("Surely another person cannot have THIS pain!" (striking oneself on the breast) (sec. 253)). For philosophers who, in Nietzsche's words, live in contra-diction to the present (recasting Emerson's description of himself as living in aversion to the present), who link a perception of what they grant to be the actual world with an imagination of an eventual world, there are, we might say, two ordinaries, two polar views of human possibility or adoption – Plato calls them illusion and reality, Kant pictures them as the sensible world and the intelligible world, Emerson speaks of the arenas of conformity and of self-reliance, Nietzsche of philistinism and self-overcoming, Heidegger of the world of the inauthentic transformed by the authentic. Wittgenstein's promise of "peace" or "rest" after restlessness is, in his practice, something lost almost as soon as it is found, not a promise that projects a realm of refuge, so his philo-sophical stance of contradiction and dissatisfaction in effect assumes an independence from whatever world this imperfect one turns out to be.

The specificity of the clauses in Wittgenstein's mythology of the ordinary produces the sense of a continuing effort to recognize the extraordinariness within the ordinariness of our lives, and contrariwise – call it an effort to form a sense or an intuition of "the way we live." This effort is confirmed for me by what I have said in the past in characterizing *Philosophical Investigations* as a kind of philosophy of culture (in "Declining decline") and as containing a portrait of the modern subject (in "The *Investigations*' aesthetics of itself"). I want to say something further about each of these two characterizations.

My idea of Wittgenstein's *Investigations* as a response to, a description and criticism of, its culture (which I am there juxtaposing with Spengler's response in his *Decline of the West*, a text which is well known to have left a marked impression on Europeans of Wittgenstein's and Heidegger's generation) suggests conceiving its sections, in their discontinuities and their continuities, as frag-ments representing details of a complete, sophisticated culture. I was accordingly led to characterize its movement as

> from the scene and consequences of inheritance and instruction and fascination [the child observing his elders], and the request for an apple, and the building of what might seem to be the first building (by builders who seem pre-human hominids), to the possibility of the loss

18

of attachment as such to the inheritance (as in the meditation on "seeing as"); and these moments as tracked by the struggle of philosophy with itself, with the losing and turning of one's way, and chronic outbreaks of madness ("Declining decline", pp. 64–5).

I go on to concede that it is not clear that we can imagine *Philosophical Investigations* as such a portrait, but I add that it should not essentially be harder to imagine than following Wittgenstein's direction, in its section 2, to "Conceive of this [namely, a language consisting of four words] as a complete primitive language," on the assumption I make, that this means conceiving it as the expression of a complete (primitive) culture. (This is part of the significance in my having reported myself imagining the builders as moving and speaking sluggishly, the way I imagine earlier hominids moving and communicating, taking it that what we mean by a culture shapes the self-presentations of its members, from their gaits to their fears and from their temptations to their shows of satisfaction.) I should make explicit as a point of difference in my reading of the *Investigations* that my stress a moment ago on the figure of the child is on a figure who not only appears at the opening of Wittgenstein's text, but also is implied far more often than even the dozen or so citations to the child than an index of Wittgenstein's text will include, namely in its repeated recurrences to ideas of instruction and learning and informing and telling and pointing and ordering and giving directions.

How the child is imagined to be treated is a fateful matter, bearing, for example, on nothing less than Wittgenstein's response to skepticism. I call a frequently cited passage of the *Investigations* its *scene of instruction* – "When I have exhausted the justifications [for following the rule of mathematics, or a criterion of an ordinary concept, in the way I do] I have reached bedrock, and my spade is turned. Then I am inclined to say: 'This is simply what I do.'" I know that Saul Kripke is not alone in taking the passage to be a *strong* gesture. Kripke glosses the scene rather as reading: "Then I am licensed to say: 'This is what I am inclined to do.'" By a strong gesture I mean one in which power in this struggle to reside on just one side, the teacher's, the one undertaking to speak for the culture; and, since it is seen as a power of exclusion, I take it there to be conceived as an expression of political power.

Kripke refers to Wittgenstein's imagining that "If a child does not respond to [a] suggestive gesture [of instruction], it is separated from the others and treated as a lunatic." This idea is broached in Wittgenstein's *Brown Book* (one of two recognizable sets of sketches for *Philosophical Investigations*) but not, I believe, repeated in the *Investigations*. I have called the idea Wittgenstein's Swiftian proposal, implying, fairly obviously I thought, that Wittgenstein's attitude toward the proposal was roughly Jonathan Swift's attitude toward what he names his modest proposal "for preventing the children of poor people in Ireland from being a burden to their parents or country, and for making them beneficial to the public" by establishing a criterion for separating out a portion of them at a certain point of their lives to be prepared as food. I do not mean to say that Wittgenstein's descriptions or discoveries in this area do not raise the issue of a culture's distribution of power (so do Swift's), but only that they do not settle it, do not settle how close our treatment of the helpless can come to Swift's proposals.

Kripke's version of the scene of instruction – concluding "Then I am licensed to say, 'This is what I am inclined to do'" – is, I think importantly, a rendering counter to Wittgenstein's formulation, implying something like, "Do it my way or suffer the consequences." I do not deny the possibility. But I find it at least as plausible to take what Wittgenstein actually writes, namely "Then I am inclined [not: licensed] to say: 'This is simply what I [not: am inclined to] do'" (in which perhaps nothing is imagined to be said) to be a *weak* gesture, even passive, implying something like, "I cannot see here where or how to make myself plainer, but here I am, doing what I do, whenever you find you are interested again." I do not, put otherwise, find that the case generalizes into a surmise, let alone a thesis, of skepticism – that we may at any moment fall into irreconcilable disagreement – since the little myth of instruction strikes me as asking that we take crises or limits of learning case by case, asking ourselves how important it is that we agree, and how thoroughly, in various strains of our form or forms of life, and where we may, or can, or ought to, or must, responsibly tolerate differences, even perhaps be drawn to change *our own* lives – or suffer the consequences.

Illumination by mythological descriptions has its limits. It is, for Wittgenstein (and not, as I have said, for Austin), essential to his philosophizing to account for a certain philosophical vulnerability to, or insistence upon, nonsense, as though the capacity for defeating sense is the same as that for making sense, and serves its own wishes. I shall not try to repeat here my understanding of the role of criteria in the *Investigations*, in connection with grammar, as developed in my *Claim of Reason*, except to say that I take Wittgenstein's idea of a criterion as meant to account both for the depth of our sharing of language and at the same time for our power to refuse this legacy, to account for, as I put it, both the possibility and the recurrent threat or coherence of skepticism. To possess criteria is also to possess the demonic power to strip them from ourselves, to turn language upon itself, to find that its criteria are, in relation to others, merely outer; in relation to certainty, simply blind; in relation to being able to go on with our concepts into new contexts, wholly ungrounded.

Our knack with criteria is shown by Wittgenstein in scores of instances (or reminders), sometimes ones as banal as expecting someone to tea, for which our criteria are such mundane matters as checking the clock, putting on water to boil, setting the table (which imply the less plain matter of the existence, noted earlier, of a context in which someone is *to be expected*), matters which we are given to understand will be connected with criteria for creating an expectation, or with those for an impulsive invitation or a reluctant acceptance, and for awaiting someone impatiently and for being disappointed at a failure of someone to appear, etc. But Wittgenstein reveals at the same time our power to question the power of such criteria in judging the world, for example by finding ourselves pressed to ask whether expecting isn't really a particular feeling (say the one developed in waiting in the dark with others for the birthday person to open the door upon his or her surprise party), and come to the conclusion that either the concept expressed in the ordinary word "expecting" is basically vague or grossly conventional in its reference to a variety of behaviors, or else there really is no such thing as expecting, but at best a collection of unnamed and perhaps unnamable inclinations. If I go on to say to myself "Still, *I* know what expecting is," I am at the verge of an intellectual crisis. It is not *I* who know this. This is what expecting *is*. Everyone knows it. Except, evidently, for some people.

Against this sense of stripping or forgetting ourselves, I sometimes find certain of Wittgenstein's famous terms of criticism insufficiently helpful – such as the idea of running our heads against the limits of language, or being misled by grammar – which may carry the suggestion that such limits, and what he means by grammar, are fixed. I tend rather to emphasize in the *Investigations* other features of what I alluded to as its implied sketch of the modern subject, namely one subject to the philosophical aspirations and perplexities depicted in the fragment-like sections of the *Investigations*. These further features seem to me better to draw out my interest in Wittgenstein's text. I am turning here from the idea of the *Investigations* as a portrait of our culture to the idea of it as a portrait of what I am calling the modern subject.

It was in the course of working on what I say is the *Investigations*' aesthetics of itself, that I tentatively identified eight or nine characteristics that the text may be seen to attribute to this subject. I have earlier here cited specific passages implying lostness, exile, devastation; now I add, fourth, strangeness ("This strange conception [of what a name is] comes from a tendency to sublime the logic of our language – as one might say" (sec. 38)), something I identify with the desire to speak outside language games; fifth, a sense of disappointment with human speech, or with the criteria we share in sharing a world ("A name ought really to signify a simple" (sec. 39)), which pairs, sixth, with perverseness ("Why does it occur to one to want to make precisely this word into a name, when it evidently is *not* a name? – That is just the reason" (ibid.)); which suggests that, seven, sickness ("The philosopher's treatment of a question is like the treatment of an illness" (sec. 255)) is understood both as a sickness of the understanding and a sickness of the will ("[Philosophical problems] are solved . . . through an insight into language *despite* a drive to misunderstand them" (sec. 109)); an eighth characteristic of the subject is a fear of suffocation, of a sort of hysteria ("The ideal, in our thoughts, is unshakable. You can never get outside it. . . . Outside you cannot breathe" (sec. 103)); a ninth is torment ("The real discovery is the one that . . . gives philosophy peace, so that it is no longer tormented by questions which bring *itself* in question" (sec. 133)) – even though, as I have indicated, peace seems to be lost as soon as found.

My way of putting the matter of the restlessness of the finite creature burdened by a longing for the transcendent was, in my first effort to respond to Wittgenstein's later philosophy, to identify (at a minimum) two voices in *Philosophical Investigations*: "The voice of temptation and the voice of correctness are the antagonists in Wittgenstein's dialogues" ("The availability of Wittgenstein's later philosophy," p. 71). It has been suggested to me that " voice of correctness" here should be changed to "voice of correction." That is not a bad idea, but in thus emphasizing society's resemblance to a prison rather than to a school room, it may push too hard to *fix* the power between generations, the power of recruiting resistant new natives of our tongue, since society has also been thought, more or less convincingly, to resemble a hospital, a madhouse, a circus, a herd, a hell, a kaleidoscope, a chorus, a mob, a body, an arcade. In any case, the voices were not meant to exhaust what I am calling the modern subject sketched in, and by, the text, which is capable, in addition, of producing and appreciating the text's humor, its pathos, its parables, its aphorisms, respites from its antagonistic voices.

A more recent instance in my sequence of efforts to register human, or mortal, restlessness (a feature stressed by thinkers as different as Pascal and Hegel) has been to distinguish, in Wittgenstein's often cited invocation of forms of life, between a horizontal or social or conventional direction (where differences between dining and snacking may be significant) and a vertical or biological or natural direction (where differences between eating and feeding, or between tables and troughs, are to the point). An importance of the distinction, beyond cautioning, as said, against what I believe is the more common over-conventionalized reception of Wittgenstein (concentrating more on our capacity to construct language games than on our desire to break free of our disappointment with our constructions), may emerge if we press a step farther Wittgenstein's idea of philosophy as presenting, whatever else, something we can think of as the natural history of the human (notably marked in the *Investigations* by the remarkable number of animals and insects, for a work of philosophy, depicted in its text, from a lion and two flies to one or more beetles and a goose and a dog and a rabbit and two cows) and we take the distinction of directions in life forms to suggest that the human is the animal that is also unnatural (and not only in its epistemology), fated to chronic dissatisfaction with its lot, to torment, disappointment, exile, and the rest – unless you wish to say that the compulsion to escape the human lot, to overcome the human, risking monstrousness, is precisely what *is* natural to the human.

It is, I judge, inevitable that, in periods of distance from the text of *Philosophical Investigations*, one will recur to the sense that the matters I have stressed here, of myth and symbolic expression, are really only matters of style. Then I recall two passages from what appears as Part II of *Philosophical Investigations*: First: "I should like to say that what dawns here lasts only as long as I am occupied with the object in a particular way" (p. 210); and then what is owed is a description of that particular way. (The suggestion is at once, however, that philosophy is not for all moods.) Second: "Is even our style of painting arbitrary? Can we choose one at pleasure?" (p. 230). If one assumes, however, that philosophy serves reason best in thinking of itself solely in connection with science, then perhaps the problem of style will not arise, or will take care of itself.

Only once have I attempted, I think, to start something like an argument to show that for Wittgenstein, as I might put the matter, it is part of philosophy's dedication to reason to account for its literary conditions. (Out of such a dedication one will envy mathematical logic its condition of accounting for every feature of its writing simultaneously with its writing, which means envy the depth of its agreement ahead of time on what its features are, on what counts as a beginning of a stretch of it, on how continuations are validly generated at each point in it, and on when a satisfying end to the stretch has been arrived at.) What I call something like an argument for the presence of the literary, say for the need of the understanding it provides, is a burden of that essay on what I call the aesthetics of and in the *Investigations*, where the idea of a perspicuous presentation, namely what Wittgenstein marks as his form of presentation of his investigations (sec. 122), can be seen to apply not alone to what he calls his signature philosophical procedures of grammatical investigations (as, for example, into the concepts of reading, or of a game, or of being able to do something, or of knowing how to go on, or of something's being simple, or of the difference between saying something and being inclined or tempted to say something), but to apply as well to the extremest and characteristic forms of the literary in the *Investigations*, namely the aphorism and the parable, as when he writes "The human body is our best picture of the human soul" (p. 178), and "A smiling mouth *smiles* only in a human face" (sec. 583). The criteria I emphasize in identifying such instances as perspicuous is that they provide pleasure, that they compose a unity, and that they break off a line of thought. These are, I am supposing, understandable as criteria that also cause Wittgenstein to speak of proofs and of grammatical investigations as perspicuous. In the *Investigations*, accordingly, the literary achievements of aphorism and parable equally represent, together with the methods of language games, instances of the moments of intellectual peace it is for philosophy to achieve, and to relinquish. But in the literary cases, while their words are ordinary, they require something more than an ordinary command of language to produce; they do not continue, but, at least for the moment, stop conversation. This specifies an asymmetry between the roles (not of course always between the persons) in a philosophical exchange, say between those who are in a position to open and to close the exchange and those who are not. (It would follow that the epitomizing of the literary in the *Investigations* is necessary to it, not merely possible for it, only if it were shown that something Wittgenstein wants from philosophizing is given in no other way, in particular not by grammatical investigations. For example, what grammatical investigations achieve through their criteria is, I have claimed, impermanent (not fully resolving restlessness), suggesting an irreducible capacity

23

for disappointment in the human make-up. Further grammatical investigations will not be expected to speak to this capacity.)

But if I say that the distortion in underestimating the writing in *Philosophical Investigations* is as great as my overestimating it here may seem to be, this is perhaps still not to decide whether the writing is to be understood as prior or subsequent to the philosophy it manifests. And here my persistent wish for the work I do to be answerable to professional philosophy means that I take it as correct that pedagogically Wittgenstein belongs, wherever else, in departments of philosophy, and specifically departments of analytical philosophy, that his work cannot fully live intellectually outside their attention. My question is whether his work can fully live intellectually inside their possession.

A word in conclusion about Wittgenstein's encouragement to think of his philosophical methods as like therapies, which some philosophers of my acquaintance have been discouraged by, taking Wittgenstein's proposal as signaling a wish to cure us of the impulse to philosophy. But why take it this way? "Like therapies" suggests that a philosophical question, or a question asked philosophically, is apt to have causes whose origins are not presented, to which a helpful response may be no more like a solution than like a cure, or say no more like finding an answer than like finding a further question. Is it sure that the invocation of therapy is meant to differentiate *Philosophical Investigations* from traditional philosophy, more than it is to assume its place in continuing philosophy, if in its discontinuous way? Has not philosophy itself, at least since Plato, claimed for itself the task of therapy, or say liberation from bonds of illusion, superstition, bewitchment, fanaticism, self-distortion? Wittgenstein's difference lies in his sense that philosophical constructions are as apt to mask as to relieve philosophical perplexity, as if each of us has her or his own countless, diurnal ways of getting lost and of recognizing help. It would follow that philosophy is over only on the assumption that philosophy is exhausted by metaphysics and that metaphysics is exhausted by the attempt to solve problems generated by a skeptical process. But if metaphysics is to tell us how things are, then philosophical procedures otherwise motivated – let's say by wonder – may count as metaphysics, perhaps among them learning to understand what is natural in our history.

Some will feel that philosophy should get out of the liberation business, or perhaps get on with it by joining the more effective liberation represented in the advances of science. I hope I have never denied that the process of acquiring genuine knowledge may itself be therapeutic. But in recent centuries philosophy's allegiance to science, in my part of the philosophical forest, has been in no danger of being lost, unlike philosophy's intimate, if intermittent, argument with, for instance, the great and the small arts. My own sense of liberation in encountering *Philosophical Investigations* (not at first, when I found it arbitrary, unoriginal, and superficial) was that, in freeing me to explore whatever experiences or texts (in whatever medium) genuinely interested me, seemed to call for my attention, it prompted me into regions that my participation in the English-speaking institutionalization of philosophy over the past half-century has seemed sometimes (whatever other causes I have for undying gratitude to it) to wish precisely to forbid me. Put otherwise, I have had occasion to notice that in *Philosophical Investigations* philosophy does not speak first, but rather in response (there, to a moment in Augustine's autobiography), and accordingly taken to heart the idea of philosophy's task as responsiveness, which some will find too passive an ambition for it. I can imagine that it might either lessen or worsen the disapproval of a differently inclined philosopher if I add, in closing, that my claim to an inheritance from the empirical tradition of philosophy lies not in producing, or establishing the justification for, points of empirical evidence for a theory, but in demanding from whatever I am moved to say, its capacity to resist the temptation to become lost to the world of my own experience, to the chance to check and consider it, which would mean to give over my capacity to judge the justice of the world.

Note

1   The article referred to in this sentence is 'Philosophy The Day After Tomorrow' in S. Cavell, *Philosophy The Day After Tomorrow*, Cambridge, MA: Harvard University Press, 2005, pp. 111–131.

2

SUFFERING A SEA-CHANGE

Crisis, catastrophe, and convention in the theory of speech-acts

Stephen Mulhall

In his recent essay, *Passionate and Performative Utterance: Morals of Encounter*,[1] Stanley Cavell investigates and criticizes Austin's treatment of the role of emotion in human speech, as that appears under the heading of the "perlocutionary" aspect or dimension of how we do things with words. In particular, Cavell questions Austin's declaration that "the perlocutionary sense of 'doing an action' must somehow be ruled out as irrelevant to the sense in which an utterance, if the issuing of it is the 'doing of an action,' is a performative" (*HDTW*, 110);[2] for that division between the perlocutionary and the performative is motivated, so Austin declares, by the thought that

> [c]learly any, or almost any, perlocutionary act is liable to be brought off, in sufficiently special circumstances, by the issuing, with or without calculation, of any utterance whatsoever, and in particular by a straightforward constative utterance (if there is such an animal).
>
> (*HDTW*, 110)

In Cavell's view, this justification – with its apparently willful or at least unthinking refusal of the quintessentially Austinian task of actually exploring and classifying the perlocutionary verbs – effectively reiterates Stevenson's notorious claim that "*any* statement about *any* matter of fact which *any* speaker considers likely to alter attitudes may be adduced as a reason for or against an ethical judgement," and thus amounts to a regression on Austin's part to the very patterns of philosophical thinking to which his theory of speech-acts constitutes a radical and devastating rebuttal.

Cavell therefore ends his essay by attempting to avoid that regression. He introduces a category of passionate utterances, understood as a species of perlocutionary acts; and he defines their successful functioning by a list of conditions which aligns them (by pointed contrast) with Austin's six conditions for the category of illocutionary acts:

1   There is no accepted conventional procedure or effect; the speaker is on his or her own to create the desired effect.

2   In the absence of convention there are no antecedently appropriate persons; I must claim the appropriate standing with you, thereby singling you out.

3   In the absence of a conventional procedure, its correct execution is not at issue.

4   In the absence of a conventional procedure, its complete execution is not at issue.

5   In speaking from passion, I must actually be suffering it, in order to demand from you a response in kind, one you are moved to offer.

6   I must make this demand, and you must (if you are so moved) respond to it, *now*.

7   You may contest my invitation to exchange at any of its conditions.

Cavell's essay as a whole is plainly and deliberately open to question and further development at a number of points. In this essay, I find myself moved to respond to it by asking the following question: in exactly what kind of relation does Cavell (in the end, after all) invite us to think that his provocative analysis of passionate utterance actually stands with respect to Austin's theory of speech acts? At first glance, it appears that we should conceive of it as a more or less natural furtherance of the same basic project. In introducing his list of initial examples of passionate utterances, Cavell tells us that "I propose now to *extend* Austin's theory of performative utterances to take account of what I shall call passionate utterances" (*PDAT* 176/*CSC* 178 – my italics), a proposal he describes in the preceding sentence as a means of introducing "some articulation into the region of the perlocutionary act" – thus implying that he is accepting at least the general terms in which Austin characterizes that region. Certainly when he first reaches the point at which he claims that Austin "breaks off his analysis catastrophically early," he criticizes him for "not lifting a finger to count and classify the number of perlocutionary verbs . . . or leaving open the sense that it may be somebody's business to do this" (*CSC* 178); hence he appears to suggest that his main business in the lecture will be precisely this – to set his hand to a quintessentially Austinian task that Austin unaccountably fails to perform.

When, as we have already seen, Cavell goes on to introduce this articulation by specifying the conditions for passionate utterance as a certain kind of negation of those Austin specifies as the conditions for performative utterance, he tells us that they are "essentially working out the consequences of" (*PDAT* 180/*CSC* 192) Austin's own way of differentiating the perlocutionary effect from the illocutionary force of any given speech-act. Hence, passionate utterance appears as a category or mode of speech that Austin's own initial understanding of perlocution can be seen as embodying in embryo, and as sufficiently articulate and robust to constitute a class that can be aligned with that of performative utterance – as sufficiently akin to it, in nature, weight and consequence, to be best explained in contrast with it.

However, when reiterating this fairly straightforward idea of his work as an extension of Austin's later in the same paragraph, Cavell introduces a parenthetical expression of doubt: "My extension (if that is what it is)" (*PDAT* 177/*CSC* 190). And some of what he claims of passionate utterances both earlier and later than this reinforces that doubt. For example, in an early summation of the point of his enterprise, Cavell declares his aim as being "to question a theory of language that pictures speech as at heart a matter of action and only incidentally as a matter of articulating and hence expressing desire" (*PDAT* 159/*CSC* 180). This suggests that even Austin's most general understanding of speech acts as a species of performative action must be fundamentally rethought rather than naturally extended. And much later, when telling us that what he wants from moral theory is "a systematic recognition of speech as confrontation . . . each instance of which directs and risks, if not costs, blood," he concludes: "So, my idea of passionate utterance turns out to be a concern with performance after all" (*PDAT* 187/*CSC* 196).

This last remark does not exactly make it easy to think of passionate utterance as aligned with performative utterance by negation. More importantly, however, it ought to remind anyone familiar with Austin's lectures of the point at which their author found that his own analysis was reaching what Cavell calls a crisis – in which, on Austin's own initial understanding of what a performative utterance is, constative utterances keep on turning out to be a variant or instance of that to which his theory fundamentally opposes it, a revelation from which a deeper understanding of speech is destined to emerge.

I want to follow on this intuition of a certain mirroring or reiteration, a structural analogy between Austin's relation to his own theorizing and Cavell's relation to Austin's. In Britain a few years ago, an insurance company ran a series of commercials whose concluding moral was: "We won't make a drama out of a crisis." My intuition is that Cavell's implicit goal with respect to Austin is to make a catastrophe into a crisis – to transform an overturning of the theory of speech-acts (its undermining by its own assumption that the passional aspects of speech are detachable from it) into a turning-point within its development (a moment when the theory's best possibilities are most vulnerable to disaster, but can nevertheless be turned towards recovery).

In characterizing the moment at which Austin turns from his binary performative/constative distinction to a ternary distinction between locutionary, illocutionary, and perlocutionary aspects of speech-acts as a crisis, to what exactly is Cavell drawing attention? What would be wrong with thinking of this moment as one in which Austin's initial understanding of performative utterance is simply furthered or deepened – say, further articulated? Cavell does not exactly reject such a thought; it is more that he sees that it has a competitor of equal significance. When, for example, he describes Austin's new, ternary distinction as intended "to replace or to articulate further his binary distinction between constative and performative utterances" (*PDAT* 169/*CSC* 186), he implies that Austin's talk of locutionary, illocutionary, and perlocutionary acts could equally be said to dispense with its predecessor – as if this kind of further articulation is also a dismantling. But why is this?

Well, Austin himself talks here of making a fresh start on the problem, and of considering from the ground up how many senses there are in which to say something is to do something; and he is brought to such a new beginning because the old distinction is turning out, under pressure, repeatedly to evaporate, to show itself to be unsustainable in its own terms – in short, to break down. After all, the key terms of the binary distinction simply cannot find equivalent expression in the new, ternary classification; what were previously called constative utterances are reclassified as one sub-type of the fifth general class of utterances that Austin distinguishes according to their illocutionary force (the expositives); and an idea of doing something in saying something that incorporates the speech-act of stating as one of its sub-types is hardly a simple reiteration of one that was characterized by contrast with such utterances. This second typology does not (at all events, not simply) further articulate Austin's initial typology; it utterly transforms it from within. It is not, after all, surprising that Derrida should so admire Austin's staging of such a distinctively deconstructive drama.

Cavell's talk of this transformation as a crisis thus signals his discomfort with those moments in Austin's thinking when he appears to withdraw from his own understanding of the full implications of that crisis – when, for example, Austin claims that

> the doctrine of the performative/constative distinction stands to the doctrine of locutionary and illocutionary acts in the total speech act as the special theory to the general theory. And the need for the general theory arises simply because the traditional "statement" is an abstraction, an ideal.
> (HDTW, 148)

But the traditional conception of constative utterance (understood as opposed to performative utterance) is not an abstract or idealized version of stating (understood as a sub-type of expositive speech acts), and hence not a special version of that general type; it is a radically different way of conceptualizing it.

But Austin has better moments than this – when, for example, he talks of a "sea-change from the performative/constative distinction to the theory of speech-acts" (HDTW, 150). Derrida has helped to focus our attention on the only other passage in these lectures in which Austin resorts to this ostentatiously literary phrase – when, in his opening remarks, he appears deliberately to exclude the literary as such from his understanding of the ordinary.

> A performative utterance will, for example, be in a peculiar way hollow or void if said by an actor on the stage, or if introduced in a poem, or spoken in soliloquy. This applies in a similar manner to any and every utterance – a sea-change in special circumstances.
> (HDTW, 22)

That Austin should use such a literary resource in effecting his exclusion of the literary is worthy of note in itself;[3] but what then are we to make of its reitera-tion in order to characterize the effect of his transition from a binary to a ternary classification of the domain of speech – to characterize what is in effect the central drama of his own theory?

The phrase comes, of course, from act I, scene ii of *The Tempest*, from the song Ariel sings to attract Ferdinand away from his shipwreck and into the field of vision of Prospero and his daughter Miranda:

> Full fathom five thy father lies.
> Of his bones are coral made;
> Those are pearls that were his eyes;
> Nothing of him that doth fade
> But doth suffer a sea-change
> Into something rich and strange.
> Sea-nymphs hourly ring his knell:
> Ding dong
>
> (I. ii. 400–6)

At the very least, then, Austin is acknowledging that this shift in his classifica-tion transforms his theory, and of course the vision of speech that it delivers – that the field of our discussion is rendered as rich and strange as the coral and pearl into which the sea as Ariel envisions it can work human bone and tissue. Might it be further significant that the sea change is effected upon the bones and tissue of a specific individual to whom the one captivated by Ariel's song is related – that the original transformation to which Austin refers is a transfigura-tion of a dead father? Is Austin's new ternary beginning something he thinks of as effecting the death of his own philosophical predecessors – the logical posi-tivists, say – a violence to which he attempts to accommodate himself by picturing it as their transfiguration into philosophical treasure (coral as beauty fabricated from fatality, pearl as wealth fabricated from irritation or anger)? If so, how far has he accommodated, and how far left himself subject to, the further implications of this context of mourning and melancholia – to the fact that the words themselves are speech transfigured in song, and a song sung by an invisible sprite, hence that the vision they embody of the body's vulnera-bility to transformation is given expression by a voice without a body; that they have a seductive or hypnotic effect upon Ferdinand – as if a variant of the beam or ray that Cavell offers as a figure for what Austin sees as the risks in enfolding the perlocutionary into the illocutionary aspects of language – and are them-selves elicited by Prospero's enslavement of Ariel (the result of Ariel's being forced to do Prospero's will in drawing Ferdinand further into the island)? In this, Cavellian, context, it might also be worth pointing out that the purpose of Ariel's vocal seduction of Ferdinand is ultimately Prospero's goal of bringing his daughter together with the dead King of Naples's son; hence this lyric plays a role in an arranged marriage, a romance initiated (rather than opposed or merely acceded to) by the woman's father.

But perhaps we are going altogether too far. For my purposes, I need only the idea that Austin's sense of his theory's rich and strange internal transformation of itself and of its philosophical predecessors gives us an apt figure for understanding Cavell's own attempt to transform what he thinks of as Austin's catastrophe into a crisis. For although Cavell introduces the notion of passionate utterance as a further articulation of Austin's idea of perlocutionary acts, and as a contrastive companion idea to that of a performative utterance – hence apparently as either adding more detail to or adding a further category to Austin's basic theoretical structure – the key aphoristic summation that he provides of the moral of his analysis suggests a rather different kind of operation upon the Austinian notion of a speech-act.

> A performative utterance is an offer of participation in the order of law. And perhaps we can say: a passionate utterance is an invitation to improvisation in the disorders of desire.
>
> From the root of speech, in each utterance of revelation and confrontation, two paths spring: that of the responsibilities of implication, and that of the rights of desire. . . . In an imperfect world the paths will not reliably coincide, but to show them both open is something I want of philosophy. Then we shall not stop at what we should or ought to say, nor at what we may and do say, but take in what we must and dare not say, or have it at heart to say, or are too confused or too tame or wild or terrorized to say or to think to say.
>
> (*PDAT* 185/*CSC* 194)

If this is how a passionate utterance is to be envisioned, then its introduction amounts to a contestation (as well as a further articulation) of Austin's most general sense of how the perlocutionary effect of a speech-act relates to the speech-act itself. For Austin's understanding of that relation is very different from how he envisions the relation between the locutionary and illocutionary aspects of a speech-act and the speech-act itself. Whereas (as Cavell points out) he treats the perlocutionary effect of a given utterance as essentially extrinsic to its sense and force ("Clearly any, or almost any, perlocutionary act is liable to be brought off, in sufficiently special circumstances, by the issuing . . . of any utterance whatsoever" (*HDTW*, 110)), he emphasizes more than once that "the locutionary act as much as the illocutionary is an abstraction; every genuine speech act is both" (*HDTW*, 147). To think, as Cavell encourages us to think in his aphoristic summation, of the path of passion as opening up from each and every utterance, and as being as deeply rooted in speech as is the path of performance, is to think of perlocution as not simply in need of closer and more detailed mapping, but rather as being as internal to any genuine speech-act as are its locutionary and illocutionary dimensions.

But there remains a danger of misunderstanding here; even this way of grasping the sea-change that Cavell wishes to effect upon Austin's theory makes it insufficiently rich and strange. For Cavell's aphoristic talk of two paths springing from speech, and of the contingency of their overlap, appears to imply that the responsibilities of implication and the rights of desire are two essentially distinct dimensions or aspects of speech; hence it implies in turn that Austin's account of speech needs a general supplementation – that the catastrophe it courts is that of failing to see that speech participates not only in an order of law but also in the disorders of desire. My intuition – guided as it is by Cavell's late, apparently passing comment that "my idea of passionate utterance turns out to be a concern with performance after all" – is rather that Cavell wishes his idea of passion internally to modify Austin's idea of the performative, to subject it to internal transformation. His goal is not to counterbalance the idea of order with that of disorder, but to suggest that Austin's idea of the dimension of law in which speech necessarily participates must be one that makes room for – makes possible – the ways in which speech allows us to improvise our way through the disorders of desire. If both paths spring from the root of speech, then the path of desire can no more be entirely without order (improvisation is not anarchy) than the path of implication can be entirely inflexible (to be accountable is not to be enslaved). Rather, the mode of law to which speech is subject must accommodate the disorders of desire, just as the expression of desire's disorders must be a mode of (improvisatory) participation in law.

One way of putting my claim would be to say that Cavell's construction of an idea of passionate utterance by negating the conditions of Austin's idea of performative utterance is also a kind of deconstruction of that idea. Since, as he points out, every condition of passionate utterance he identifies is entailed by his opening negation of Austin's first condition for performative utterance, and since that first condition pivots on Austin's invocation of "a conventional procedure having a certain conventional effect" (HDTW, 14), my intuition is that Cavell's originating negation is in fact an attempt to reconstruct Austin's conception of the order of law in speech as an order of convention. He wants us to rethink Austin's concept of speech as conventional by reconceiving what a convention of speech might be – by distancing ourselves from any idea of the orderliness of speech that is not hospitable to disorder, by rethinking conventions as flexibly inflexible, possessed of a tolerant intolerance.

One advantage of this characterization of Cavell's intentions is that it shows his critique of Austin to mobilize an idea or vision of language that has been central to his work from a very early stage, which sits at the heart of The Claim of Reason[4] in its 'Excursus on Wittgenstein's vision of language," and that is as easy to misapprehend (and in a structurally analogous way) as is the heart of his critique of Austin. Cavell's primary example in that earlier discussion of the ways in which we project our words, hence of the kind of order we can find in their use, is that of the word "feed." We learn to "feed the cat" and to "feed the lions," and then, when someone talks of feeding the meter or feeding our pride, we understand them; we accept this projection of the word. Cavell's view is that tolerating such projections is of the essence of words. We could, of course, have used other words than "feed" for this new context, either by projecting another established word or inventing a new one. If, however, we talked of "putting" money in the meter as we do of putting a dial on the meter, we would lose a way of making certain discriminations (between putting a flow of material into a machine and putting a part made of new material on a machine), we would begin to deprive ourselves of certain of our concepts (could we dispense with talk of feeding our pride and still retain our concept of emotions as capable of growth?), and we would in effect be extending the legitimate range of our alternative word in just the manner we were trying to avoid. If instead we invented a new word, we would lose a way of registering connections between contexts, open up questions about the legitimate projections of this new word, and at the limit deprive all words of meaning (since no word employed in only one context would be a word).

At the same time, however, our projections of our words are also deeply controlled. We can, for example, feed a lion, but not by placing a bushel of carrots in its cage; and its failure to eat them would not count as a refusal to do so. Such projections of "feed" and "refusal" fail because their connection with other words in their normal contexts does not transfer to the new one; one can only refuse something that one might also accept, hence something that one can be offered or invited to accept; and what might count as an offer and an acceptance in the context of a meal is both different from and related to what counts as an offer and acceptance in the context of mating or being guided. These limits are neither arbitrary nor optional; they show how (what Cavell elsewhere calls) a word's grammatical schematism determines the respects in which a new context for a word must invite or allow its projection.

In short:

> [A]ny form of life and every concept integral to it has an indefinite number of instances and directions of projection; and this variation is not arbitrary. Both the "outer" variance and the "inner" constancy are necessary if a concept is to accomplish its tasks – of meaning, understanding, communicating etc., and in general, guiding us through the world, and relating thought and action and feeling to the world.
>
> (CR, 185)

There is a certain tension in this key passage between its surface rhetoric and the underlying tendency of its argument, a tension that is centered on Cavell's talk of "outer" variance and "inner" constancy. For that contrast between outer and inner suggests that the constancy of a concept is more internal or integral to its capacity to accomplish its tasks than its variance. And yet the evident thrust of the passage is to claim that *both* the inner and the outer aspects of the concept are necessary to it. To be sure, Cavell registers a certain sense of discomfort with his own contrast by putting both of its terms within scare quotes; but its apparent implications are not simply in need of softening or qualification to be rendered consistent with his fundamental claim – as if they might mislead but can otherwise make a positive contribution to his argument. In so far as they are taken seriously, they appear to run entirely counter to it.

Suppose, however, we concentrate on the general thrust of the account of concepts that this passage encapsulates, and focus on the claim that a concept needs both outer variance and inner constancy – that, as Cavell puts it, he is "trying to bring out, and keep in balance, two fundamental facts about human forms of life, and about the concepts formed in those forms" (CR, 185). Some good readers of this self-description will naturally find themselves emphasizing the fact of outer variance, and asking whether it is really possible to imagine that any rule-formulation (call it the articulation of a convention) might capture or ground it. Might there be a rule governing the route of projection that our word "feed" displays, not to mention the further steps or leaps we might find ourselves taking with it in the future? But other, equally good readers will find themselves struck by the balancing fact of inner constancy, and ask whether it is really possible to capture it – as it is manifest, say, in our responsibility to show how a concept's new context can tolerate the applications of the concepts to which its criteria relate it – without adverting to some idea of a systematic web of conventions or rules. Surely some such invocation must be made if the fact of outer variance is not to eclipse its inner twin?

Cavell's own talk of attempting to keep two facts in balance suggests that the solution to our problem here is to accept the need for an account of grammar and criteria that accommodates both fundamental facts. Perhaps, then, we should imagine the web of norms, standards, or rules as setting a certain kind of limit on the degree of variance that a concept's projections can be permitted: the rules give constancy, and individual or collective imagination, natural reactions, and so on engender variance, with the life of the concept being formed from the interaction of these two aspects of human forms of life. If we allow one of Cavell's pair of fundamental facts to eclipse the other, our account will be inadequate, unbalanced – in need of extension or supplementation; but the two taken together would provide a complete and balanced picture of the grammatical essence of concepts.

Unfortunately, this picture of compromise and ultimate complementarity would miss the real point of Cavell's vision of Wittgenstein's vision of language as fatefully as its twin would misrepresent the thrust of his passionate critique of Austin. Suppose we return for a moment to his apparently misleading inner/outer contrast, and try regarding the "scare quotes" he assigns to them as quotation marks; for that pair of terms is employed in some of Wittgenstein's most famous remarks about the relationship between the human mind and the human body – as when he declares that "an 'inner process' stands in need of outward criteria" (PI, 580),[5] or that "the human body is the best picture of the human soul" (PI, II. iv). In these contexts, Wittgenstein's point is not to give the inner priority over the outer, or indeed to reverse that order of priority; his concern is to suggest that the inner and the outer are not two independent realms or dimensions at all, but rather internally related to one another – the significance or import of each inseparable from that of the other.

If we transpose that suggestion to the context of Cavell's discussion of the grammatical essence of concepts, it would appear to follow that his characterization of constancy and variance as two fundamental facts is rather more misleading than his characterization of them as inner and outer. For this transposition would allow us to stop thinking of a concept's essence as determined by a conjunction or dovetailing of two separable components or elements (its constancy and its variance); we should rather think of its projectibility as having an indefinitely variable kind of constancy, or an essentially non-arbitrary kind of variation. In other words, Cavell's two fundamental facts are in fact two aspects of a single or singular fact; hence they do not need to be kept in balance, because to downgrade or entirely to overlook one is to distort the other.

What accounts for that single fact, in all its singularity, is identified in a vital early part of Cavell's specification of his (and Wittgenstein's) notion of a criterion.

> [Wittgensteinian] criteria do not relate a name to an object, but, we might say, various concepts to the concept of that object. Here the test of your possession of a concept ... would be your ability to use the concept in conjunction with other concepts, your knowledge of which concepts are relevant to the one in question and which are not; your knowledge of how various relevant concepts, used in conjunction with the concepts of different kinds of objects, require different kinds of contexts for their competent employment.
>
> (CR, 73)

For example, knowing what a toothache is is in part a matter of knowing what counts as having a toothache, what counts as alleviating a toothache, and so on. In other words, what Cavell calls the grammatical schematism of a word is its power to combine with other words –

> the word's potency to assume just those valences, and a sense that in each case there will be a point of application of the word, and that the point will be the same from context to context, or that the point will shift in a recognizable pattern or direction.
>
> (CR, 77–8)

Hence when the acceptability or naturalness of a new projection of a given word is in question, our final judgment will turn upon the speaker's capacity to show that and how the new context into which he or she has projected it either invites or can be seen to allow that projection by inviting or allowing (at least some modified form of) the projection of those other words to which its criteria relate it, and which are accommodated in familiar contexts of the word's use.

Many of Cavell's examples of projections of words in his 'Excursus' are utterly obvious to us; they show the untroubled reach of our mutual attunements. We accept that placing a bushel of carrots in a lion's cage does not count as "feeding" him because (amongst other things) we can see nothing that could count as his accepting or refusing to eat it; but we also accept talk of feeding the meter and feeding our pride despite the fact that much of the word's familiar valences either will not carry over or must be modified in order to do so. We understand someone who says that the meter has refused his or her coins, or that his or her pride refuses to feed on such gross flattery; the valences of "refusal" in these contexts differ not only from one another but also from their more familiar contexts (in the lion's cage or the fast-food restaurant), but the point of their modified retention – the point of the word's application – is clear. In other cases, however, the acceptability or unacceptability of the projection is less clear; it isn't obvious how and why we should accommodate ourselves to it, because it isn't clear how the word's valences might be carried over into its new context. Can we point out Manhattan – could anything count as pointing out Manhattan – to a child who does not yet grasp the concept of maps? Perhaps not, if we're walking with him or her on 58th Street; but what if we are looking out of a window as our plane banks on its approach to LaGuardia Airport? Is a plank stood on end about the height and width of a human being, tipped and braced back slightly from the vertical, into which are fitted at right angles two pegs to go under the armpits and a saddle peg in the middle – is such a thing a chair? Well, would we be inclined to count the tribesman comfortably arranged on its pegs as sitting on it?

Different kinds and instances of questionable projection will elicit different forms of justification and criticism, and reach different kinds of individual and communal resolution. It will not be clear or specifiable in advance exactly what will or might be said to justify or to criticize a disputed projection – that will depend on the disputants' knowledge of the new context for the word, their capacity to give explicit articulation to their implicit grasp of the word's criteria, the depth and range of their imaginations, their willingness to accommodate change in exchange for insight, their sense of a given concept's grammatical center of gravity, and so on. But to know how to speak is to know what kinds of consideration are and are not pertinent to the justification and criticism of a given word's projections; we might see good reason to dispute the suggestion that what the tribesman is doing with his plank is sitting on it, but we thereby acknowledge that determining whether anything might count as sitting on the plank contributes to determining whether that plank counts as a chair. Without that shared grasp of what we might call canons of relevance, there would be nothing of the systematic normativity in language use to which Wittgenstein and Cavell are so sensitive, and without which grammatical investigations could have no claim on our attention.

The phrase "canons of relevance" is one I derive from another stretch of *The Claim of Reason* (its third part), in which Cavell disputes broadly emotivist understandings of moral discourse, and to which Cavell himself makes explicit reference in the lecture on Austin that I have been discussing. There he castigates philosophers such as Stevenson, who claims that any kind of statement that any speaker considers likely to alter attitudes may be adduced for or against an ethical judgment. Cavell, by contrast, argues that morality's claim to rationality (like that of the sciences) depends upon its being constituted by a shared commitment to certain modes of argument – although ones that (unlike those of the sciences) do not necessarily lead to agreement on conclusions. For example, if someone makes a promise, he or she commits himself or herself to performing a certain action; hence, if he or she fails to perform it, he or she must (if he or she is to maintain credibility as a moral agent) explain why the circumstances in which he or she found himself or herself justified this failure to honor his or her commitment, why he or she did not give advance warning of this to the promisee, and so on. His or her interlocutor might dispute the precise weight he or she attached to the factors that led to his or her decision, and offer reasons for that disagreement – reasons that will themselves invoke considerations that must relevantly counter his or her excuse; and the promisor might dispute the weight his or her interlocutor attaches to them, and so on. The rationality of their enterprise is determined by their shared acknowledgement of the canons and procedures that control or limit what might competently be offered as a relevant ground for defense and criticism; but the relevance of these grounds can be acknowledged by both without them both assigning the same weight to any given ground.

> What is enough to counter my claim to be right or justified in taking a certain action is up to me, up to me to determine. I don't care that he is an enemy of the state; it's too bad that he took what I said as a promise.... I can refuse to accept a "ground for doubt" without impugning it as false, and without supplying a new basis, and yet not be dismissed as irrational or morally incompetent. What I cannot do, and yet maintain my position as morally competent, is to deny the relevance of your doubts ("What difference does it make that I promised, that he's an enemy of the state . . . "), fail to see that they require a determination by me.
>
> (CR, 267)

In retrospect we might ask whether Cavell's treatment of the trademark Austinian performative example of promising in this context amounts to an early version of the critique he has only mounted explicitly today. Whatever the truth of this, Cavell's objection to the Rawlsian idea that what counts as an adequate basis for a moral judgment is determined by the practice or institution of morality or justice or promising (an objection that he motivates in part

37

through a long discussion of the role of rules in games) is plainly part of the same argument. The response that a given moral agent makes to a specific moral issue – to accept a ground for doubt another offers him or her, to contest it, or simply to deny its significance – reveals not what the practice impersonally determines the right conclusion to be, but rather what he or she personally regards as justified, what he or she is prepared to be answerable for; it reveals the moral position for which he or she is taking responsibility, and hence it reveals him or her. And it is then open to others to determine their stance towards that position, to determine whether they can agree with it, or disagree with it whilst respecting it (and hence him or her), or discover that he or she and they are not in the same moral universe.

In short, the criteria of relevance shared by those competent in the practice of moral argument open a space in which the right to acknowledge and determine for oneself the relative importance of multiple and competing cares and commitments can coexist with the achievement of a community of mutual understanding and respect. Cavell sees in this human mode of criterially governed interaction a way in which the search for community can be prosecuted without the sacrifice of individuality. And I think we can say that Cavell's objection to Austin's conception of linguistic convention is that it is as overly institutional, as inflexible and resistant to the idea of improvisation, as is that of Rawls.

I hope that the basic pattern of Cavell's thinking, both here and in the apparently more general case of projecting words, is clear. Once seen, its recurrence (with significant variations) throughout his work becomes striking; and it might help to clarify matters further (particularly with the vicissitudes of Ferdinand's and Miranda's romance in play in our present context) if I briefly examine the inflection of it that structures his study of cinematic comedies of remarriage, *Pursuits of Happiness*.[6]

The analytical spine of that book is a highly distinctive notion of genre, which Cavell defines not by a list of essential features that must be manifest in any film that will count as an instance of the genre (as a type of object might be defined by the set of properties that any instance of the type must possess), but rather by the fact that its members share the inheritance of certain conditions, procedures and subjects and goals of composition, and that each member represents a study of those conditions. What distinguishes each member from its fellows is that it bears the common responsibility of its inheritance differently; it may for example introduce new features to the genre, but in so doing it must show how it can be understood either as compensating for any hitherto-standard feature that it lacks, and/or as contributing to a deeper characterization of the genre as a whole. Thus, any genre must be understood as essentially open to change, sometimes very radical change, and no single feature of it can be held to be immune to removal as long as the member in which that removal is effected can be shown to provide a compensation for it. On the other hand, no such alteration in the inheritance can properly be effected without the provision of compensation; and if a film provides no compensation for an absence it effects, if what it provides in its stead cannot be seen as a further interpretation of the genre's inheritance, then it can be said to have negated that feature – and in so doing, it generates or places itself within an adjacent genre, a different inheritance.

Once again, then, we see an inflection of the familiar pattern. Anyone wishing to make a film that is a member of a given genre (call him or her the director) must acknowledge his or her inheritance, which means neither denying its central features nor simply reiterating them, but rather studying them – seeking to deepen his or her own and our understanding of the multiple, inter-related, and multi-dimensional terms of that inheritance by subjecting them to forms of compensatory alteration that can be understood to draw out hitherto-implicit ranges of their significance. We might think of this as the director's capacity to project the genre into a new context, one that we can come to accept as an unpredictable but retrospectively justifiable step in its development. A successful contribution to the genre thus amounts to a non-arbitrary variation in the genre's inheritance, and each such contribution reveals the genre's indefinitely variable constancy.

The relevance of this excursus on film to the matter of Cavell's Wittgensteinian vision of language is, I hope, clear. Since the criteria of any given concept locate it in a system or web of concepts that informs and is informed by human forms of life (call it the word's inheritance), its grammatical schematism possesses a flexible inflexibility, an intolerant tolerance. Its projections into new contexts must show either that its usual valences are carried over into it, or that they can be modified in acceptable ways, or that (and how) the context's inability to tolerate the projection of certain concepts to which the given concept is normally related can itself be tolerated. This is the concept's essential inflexibility, that which allows us to say that what has been projected into the new context is the same old concept. But there are no formulae that determine in advance how broad a field of the concept's related concepts must carry over, or what degree of modification of any given conceptual relation might be acceptable, or whether (and if so when and why) something about a given projection might compensate for the absence of a given conceptual relation. Such judgments will be context-specific, and dependent upon the reach of the speaker's understanding and imagination. This is the concept's essential flexibility, its capacity to elicit new reaches of significance from itself, from those who use it and from the contexts it proves capable of inhabiting.

This means that Wittgensteinian criteria must be so characterized as to bring out the play in their systematicity, the way in which their inter-relatedness establishes structure without occluding individual judgment. This is not a matter of making room in one's account for something other than normativity (say, freedom or individual judgment); it is a matter of showing that and how the kind of normativity they exemplify enables or rather constitutes such freedom of judgment – the openness of our words (and hence ourselves) to an essentially unpredictable (even if retrospectively explicable) future. It is precisely because the grammatical schematism of a word locates it in a horizon of inter-related words embedded in human forms of life that our projections of those words are at once deeply controlled and creative, displaying the kind of imaginative reach that only an acknowledgement of constraint makes possible.

Once we have seen this, however, it seems to me that the question (recently much-discussed by myself and a number of others) of whether this vision of the normativity of language should be given expression in terms of rules becomes essentially otiose. On the one hand, invocations of rule-governed activity – so often exemplified by games such as chess or baseball – might mislead us into thinking that disagreements (particularly deeply charged philosophical disagreements) over the legitimacy of a certain projection of a word can be settled by reference to the impersonal authority of a rulebook containing determinations for every possible eventuality. On the other hand, attempting to motivate or reinforce the rejection of that misconception by rejecting talk of rules altogether might be equally (if oppositely) misleading. For what is needed in place of that misconception is an account of word use that makes room for a speaker's need to take responsibility for determining whether and how they accept a given word's projections, whilst acknowledging that such responsibilities can and can only be exercised within a horizon of linguistic normativity of almost unimaginable range and systematicity.

If that is even roughly correct, then nothing of substance will hang on whether we think of those normative articulations as rules, or talk instead of norms, or standards, or canons. What matters is that we properly acknowledge their distinctive normative character, both in what we say about them and in what we say as philosophers (that is, as recounters of grammar) about anything.

Hence – to return this rather excursive discussion to its source – we can think of Cavell's lecture on Austin as an attempt to clarify further the degree to which what he has previously characterized as the limitations of Austin's conception of language and of philosophy (in comparison to those of Wittgenstein) might be thought of as rooted in Austin's overly conventional or institutional understanding of the order of law in which speech participates. But of course, in reconceiving that understanding, Cavell can and must be thought of as raising the question: to how much variation can a central theoretical concept be subjected before its inner constancy, and hence that of the theory it enables, is subverted? The transmissibility of Austinian philosophy, its continuation into new circumstances by new generations, presupposes its capacity to tolerate some degree of transformation; but there must also be limits to that tolerance. Hence, the deepest question that emerges from Cavell's most recent engagement with Austin is: how far does its originality preclude our seeing it as a projection of a distinctively Austinian inheritance? Has Cavell come to praise his philosophical father or to bury him? Can Ferdinand see his father's eyes in the pearls into which the sea has changed them?

Notes

1 "Passionate and performative utterance". This essay has now been published in two places: in S. Cavell, *Philosophy The Day After Tomorrow*, Cambridge, MA: Harvard University Press, 2005, pp. 155–191 (hereafter *PDAT*), and in R. Goodman, ed., *Contending With Stanley Cavell*, Oxford: Oxford University Press, 2005, pp. 177–198 (hereafter CSC). Since there are small but significant variations between these two published versions of the esssay, all quotations from it will be accompanied by page references to both versions.
2 *How to Do Things with Words* (Oxford: Oxford University Press 1962).
3 As Christopher Ricks has pointed out in "Austin's Swink," in his *Essays in Appreciation* (Oxford: Oxford University Press, 1998), p. 264.
4 Oxford: Oxford University Press, 1979 – new edition 1999.
5 *Philosophical Investigations*, trans. G.E.M. Anscombe (Oxford: Blackwell, 1953).
6 Cambridge, MA: Harvard University Press, 1981.

3

AUSTIN AND THE ETHICS OF DISCOURSE

Alice Crary

One of the most familiar images of J.L. Austin in contemporary philosophy of language is as a source of central pragmatic trends. A prominent theme in recent decades is that a full understanding of a linguistic expression awaits an account of its public use, and this theme is generally developed so that it amounts to a call for a pragmatics of natural language to supplement traditional semantic theory. That is, if we understand "pragmatics" as the study of those features of words that depend on their being used in certain ways, and if we understand "semantics" as the study of those features of the relation between words and world on which truth and falsity depend, then we can say that one of the hallmarks of recent philosophy of language is a tendency to underscore the importance of pragmatics while, at the same time, also depicting its interest as restricted to that of a supplement or auxiliary to semantics. Further, we can also say that this larger pragmatic tendency is often represented as inspired by Austin's work.

In this chapter, I am going to argue that this representation is grounded in a fundamental misunderstanding. One of my goals is to show that, far from wanting to encourage the relevant pragmatic tendency, Austin is in fact centrally concerned to oppose it and, further, that he is therefore properly seen as a much more disruptive figure in the philosophy of language than is generally supposed. My motive for thus reassessing Austin's philosophical legacy is to position myself to say something about the bearing of his thought on ethics. I want to challenge more familiar accounts of Austin's pragmatic concerns in order to suggest that, when these concerns are faithfully rendered, they bring within reach an intuitively appealing account of the nature of moral thought. The model for the things I am going to say about the ethical interest of Austin's philosophy is Stanley Cavell's claim that Austin provides support for a species of "moral perfectionism." I will turn to a discussion of pertinent aspects of Cavell's work in the chapter's last two sections.

1 Introduction: some recent conversations about Austin and ethics

> [T]he question of truth and falsehood does not turn only on what a sentence is, nor yet on what it means, but on, speaking very broadly, the circumstances in which it is uttered.
>
> (Austin)[1]

The interpretation of Austin's view of language to which I want to refer in talking about ethics is unorthodox in the following respect. Austin, as I read him, is centrally concerned to attack a philosophical conception of correspondence between language and the world that continues, more than forty years after his death, to control most philosophical investigations of language. In his 1955 lectures *How to Do Things with Words*,[2] Austin characterizes the conception he repudiates as one on which correspondence to the facts is the exclusive business of propositions that are "bi-polar" in that they describe states of affairs or convey information about the world *either* truly *or* falsely.[3] However, here and elsewhere, Austin makes it clear that his particular target is not the logic of bi-polarity *per se*,[4] but a deeply engrained view of meaning that he thinks feeds philosophical insistence on it – viz., the view that sentences possess what philosophers often call "literal meanings" (i.e. meanings that are given by the meanings of words and the rules of the language, and that accordingly accompany sentences into different contexts of their use).[5] In what follows, I am going to argue that one of Austin's overarching philosophical ambitions is criticizing both this view and also the influential philosophical conception of correspondence between language and the world that it underwrites. My larger aim in doing so is to suggest that Austin's critique has fruitful implications for ethics – implications connected to the fact that the conception of language-world correspondence that it brings into question determines the problem-space within which theories of moral judgment are for the most part developed and debated.

This project has very little in common with ongoing philosophical conversations about the ethical interest of Austin's thought. Most contributions to these conversations presuppose readings on which Austin is taken to be simply helping himself to the idea of literal sentence-meaning. This is most conspicuous in the case of Jürgen Habermas's well-known attempt to show that Austin's work on speech-acts grounds a more or less Kantian account of moral discourse.[6] Habermas's argument draws on an understanding of Austin's theory of speech-acts – one that Habermas inherits relatively directly from John Searle[7] – which enshrines the idea of literal sentence-meaning.[8] Habermas reads Austin as taking an interest in kinds of "communicative failures" that are specifically pragmatic in so far as they result from the employment in inappropriate circumstances of sentences that possess such meaning (and that are therefore presumably kosher from the point of view of syntax and semantics).[9] He claims that Austin's larger aim is to show that even describing is prone to the pertinent kinds of failures, and hence that description, far from monopolizing the serious business of language (as philosophers have often assumed), represents *one* of a variety of ways in which we use – what Habermas conceives as – independently meaningful sentences. The strategy Habermas thinks Austin adopts for attaining this putative goal centers on the development of a theory of speech acts that (as Habermas understands it) functions as a system for classifying different uses of such sentences.[10]

Habermas's account of the ethical significance of this type of (allegedly Austinian) theory proceeds roughly as follows. Habermas assumes that a satisfactory account of moral discourse must not only do justice to our intuitive understanding of such discourse as universally valid but, at the same time, also avoid assimilating it to the descriptive.[11] Further, Habermas is critical of trends in philosophy of language that make it seem as though there is no way of simultaneously meeting both of these demands. He criticizes the tendency of philosophers to focus exclusively on descriptive language and, as a result, to think that the only way in which any stretch of discourse – and *a fortiori* any moral stretch – can be universally valid is by being (descriptively) true.[12] This is the background against which he claims that the type of theory of speech acts he ascribes to Austin is of ethical moment. Habermas argues that such a theory can be used to counter philosophers' descriptive focus and to reveal the possibility of non-descriptive modes of discourse that have legitimate, non-truth-oriented claims to universal validity.[13] What is ethically significant about a theory of the relevant sort, according to Habermas, is that it thus enables us to demonstrate our entitlement to an account of moral discourse as both non-descriptive and universally valid.[14]

There is another set of conversations about Austin and ethical themes that, like Habermas's work and conversations surrounding it, represent Austin as conceiving correspondence between language and the world in terms of the idea of literal sentence-meaning. The inspiration for these further conversations, which take place largely within literary-theoretical circles, is Jacques Derrida's attempt to incorporate Austin's view of language within the "deconstructivist" view he himself favors – specifically, by arguing that Austin is hostile to the notion of fully objective (or universally valid) truth.[15] Derrida's argument comprises two main claims, first, that Austin is concerned to distance himself from the idea of literal sentence-meaning[16] and, second, that Austin is best read as moving from an attack on this idea to the conclusion that there can therefore be no such thing as objective truth.[17]

In so far as Derrida depicts Austin as criticizing the idea of literal sentence-meaning, he differs from philosophers like Habermas who take Austin to retain the idea. But this difference coexists with a philosophically significant similarity in interpretative approach. Derrida depicts Austin as predicating (what Derrida sees as) his rejection of the notion of objective truth on a critique of the idea of literal sentence-meaning. He thus effectively assumes – in accordance with more standard philosophical readings – that Austin takes the idea of literal sentence-meaning to be internal to the notion of objective correspondence. On Derrida's telling, it is only *because* Austin criticizes the idea of literal sentence-meaning that he rejects the notion of such correspondence.

A number of theorists who take their cue from Derrida's interpretative work go on to discuss ethical issues in what they see as an Austinian spirit. Since these theorists agree with Derrida in taking Austin to be denying even descriptive discourse a claim to universal validity, it follows, by their lights, that it would be a sign of confusion to insist (say, with Habermas) that Austin makes room for additional, alternative claims to universal validity in connection with non-descriptive modes of discourse. As these theorists see it, the appropriate way to start a conversation about Austin and ethics is to reflect on consequences, not of the discovery of (what we may be inclined to think of as) *further* universal validity-claims, but rather of the loss of even the kind of universal validity-claim encoded in the notion of objective correspondence between language and world. Thus, e.g., the most outspoken theorists to adopt this allegedly Austinian approach to ethical matters – a group of gender theorists who are primarily concerned with its bearing on identity categories such as "woman" – argue that the categories we employ in moral and political reflection, far from applying to our lives in an objective manner, are non-objective constructs we undertake to "perform."[18]

It is no part of my project here to try to arbitrate the two conflicting suggestions about ethical implications of Austin's view of language I just canvassed. As I see it, both are initially prompted by flawed readings of Austin's work – readings vitiated by a tendency to assume that Austin conceives correspondence between language and the world in terms of the idea of literal sentence-meaning. My aim in what follows is to progress toward a reading that better prepares us to cull a lesson about ethics from Austin's writings by first demonstrating that this assumption is misplaced.

2 The argument of How to Do Things with Words

> Think of how many things are called "description": description of
> a body's position by means of its coordinates; description of a
> facial expression; description of a sensation of touch; of a mood.
> (Wittgenstein)[19]

The best place to turn in this connection is *How to Do Things with Words*. Austin's lectures contain a sustained argument against conceiving correspondence between language and the world as the prerogative of independently meaningful sentences. The argument begins with Austin's efforts, in discussing his distinction between constative and performative utterances, to undermine the view that it is possible to sort sentences as such into different linguistic functions.

i Austin's performance with "performatives"

> If . . . someone says that [a] sentence . . . makes sense to him, then
> he should ask himself in what special circumstances this sentence
> is actually used. There it does make sense.
> (Wittgenstein)[20]

Consider the backdrop against which Austin introduces his distinction. Austin declares that he wants to critically examine the assumption that "the business of a [grammatical] 'statement' can only be to 'describe' some state of affairs, or to 'state some fact', which it must do either truly or falsely" (1). Further, he tells us that philosophers are beginning to depart from this ideal of the 'statement' by insisting that some sentences that have the grammatical form of 'statements' "do not set out to be statements at all" (2) and hence should be regarded (not, as certain logical positivists aver, as nonsensical 'pseudo-statements' but) as linguistic formulas suited for other functions. In this connection he mentions, e.g., the efforts of emotivists to introduce a category of "emotive utterances . . . intended . . . to evince emotion or to prescribe conduct or to influence it in special ways" (2–3).

Notice that the approach to departing from a traditional ideal of the 'statement' that Austin thus describes presupposes that some sentences are perfectly suited for describing the facts and, further, that, in this respect, the approach retains the category of the traditional 'statement'.[21] This is noteworthy because, when Austin turns to his distinction between constatives and performatives, he adopts the same approach. Like the other philosophers he mentions, Austin suggests that while there are some utterances that meet the specifications of a traditional ideal of the 'statement' – he calls them "constatives" – there are also utterances that, although they have the same grammatical form as 'statements', are not suited for describing states of affairs. What distinguishes Austin's particular suggestion is simply his account of the additional utterances that interest him – which he calls "performatives" – as those in which the production of a sentence ("I bet") is the doing of an action (e.g. betting) that "is not normally thought of as just saying something" (7). This means that his work on performatives resembles other strategies for achieving distance from a traditional ideal of the 'statement' in preserving the view, internal to the ideal, that some linguistic formulas are as such in the business of reporting on states of affairs.

This observation should *not* be taken as a sign that Austin thinks we can develop an adequate criticism of the traditional 'statement' without rejecting the view of meaning that informs it. Already at a couple of points in his first two lectures, Austin indicates that he thinks a deeper criticism is required. He tells us that he doubts that isolated linguistic formulas have meanings in virtue of which they can be classified into those suited for stating things and those suited for other purposes, and he says that he is inclined to think that what does the work of constating is "not a . . . sentence" but "an act of speech" (20; see also 1 n. 1). By thus hinting that he disputes the view of meaning that informs the traditional 'statement' (or constative utterance), Austin indicates his willingness to adopt a more radical critical stance. At the same time, he anticipates a conclusion he draws several lectures farther on – viz., that his original classification of utterances into constatives and performatives cannot, in the final analysis, be preserved.[22]

What precipitates the classificatory crisis is Austin's attempt to legitimate the category of the performative by describing dimensions within which performatives (which cannot be said to report on the facts truly or falsely) can be assessed. Austin characterizes the pertinent dimensions – which he refers to as forms of "happiness" and "unhappiness" – as follows. He claims that in order for a performative to be *happy*, the circumstances in which a speaker comes out with a set of words must meet the conditions of a conventional procedure having a certain conventional effect – a procedure that involves the uttering of these words by a person of a certain standing in a certain situation.[23] He mentions two kinds of unhappiness: (1) "misfires" that result in the relevant act – i.e. that for which the verbal form was produced – not coming off at all (e.g. I say "I christen this yacht *Mystic*," but I say it to myself in the bathtub so the act in question, naming, doesn't come off) and (2) "abuses" that result in the act being performed in a less than ideal fashion (e.g. when I say "I guarantee that this food is good" knowing the food is rotten, I do, despite my knowledge, offer a (false) guarantee (18)). These two forms of unhappiness initially appear to hold forth the promise of distinguishing the performative. But after describing the two Austin goes on to claim that constatives, no less than performatives, are subject to them.[24]

What interests him is not only showing that there are statements of fact that might qualify as "abuses" in that they are made in situations in which they are bizarre or inappropriate (e.g. I say "we're almost out of dog food" when a friend and I are in the middle of a serious conversation about our relationship). He also hopes to show that even factual utterances (e.g. "John's children are all bald") can *misfire* or, as he also puts it, turn out to be "null and void" (25; see also 11, 17, 20, and 23) if the circumstances are sufficiently inappropriate (e.g. John has no children) (50–1).[25] Austin is claiming that when the conditions of a certain conventional procedure aren't met it can turn out, not only that a supposed constative utterance is odd or awkward, but also that it's not clear what (if anything) it's in the business of saying. And he is thereby criticizing the assumption – internal to the traditional 'statement' – that we can isolate combinations of words as constative independently of a consideration of how they are used on particular occasions.

Austin's remaining comments about constatives and performatives (Lectures V–VII) further develop this criticism. Austin considers a series of examples of linguistic constructions that, while they may strike us as perfectly suited to express performatives, can nevertheless be used to constate things (e.g. "I censure" when used, not with the performative force of censuring, but to describe the fact that I assign blame (83)). These examples are intended to show that, in different circumstances of its use, a given sentence may have entirely different discursive upshots – and may thus qualify as different kinds of utterance (or, in cases in which it "misfires," no kind of utterance at all). They are supposed to remind us that, in order to figure out what type of utterance (if any) is in question when someone utters a sentence, we need to examine the circumstances in which he or she produces it. It is after considering these examples that Austin declares that he has failed to find a – grammatical – criterion to distinguish constatives and performatives (91).

The tendency of Austin's argument up to this point is toward suggesting that there is something confused about the very idea of such a criterion, and that his

47

failure should not be regarded as a merely accidental shortcoming. Austin presents himself as having shown that the contexts in which we come out with strings of words, far from being external or "merely pragmatic," make an internal contribution to the meaning of our words, and that there can therefore be no such thing as a constative utterance in the (context-independent) sense he originally had in mind. He suggests that it is impossible to classify linguistic constructions into those suited to constate things and those suited to play other linguistic roles, and, further, that any approach to language that presupposes that this is possible – such as, e.g., the approach he himself adopts when he first introduces his distinction between constatives and performatives – must be abandoned.[26]

At this point we have before us Austin's initial argument – presented in the first half of *How to Do Things with Words* – against the view that it is possible to investigate ways in which language functions by looking at isolated sentences.[27] One of his central concerns, later in the lectures, is describing a method for studying linguistic phenomena that incorporates the argument's conclusions. The cornerstone of Austin's method is what he calls a "doctrine of 'illocutionary forces'" (99).[28]

ii Isolating the illocutionary

> The source of the mistake seems to be the notion of thoughts which accompany the sentence.
>
> (Wittgenstein)[29]

Austin defines the illocutionary act as "the performance of an act *in* saying something" (99). He then announces that his "interest in [his] lectures is to fasten on [this] act and contrast it" (103) both with the "locutionary" act, which he defines as the "act *of* saying something . . . with a certain sense and reference" (99–100), and also with the "perlocutionary" act, which he defines as the performance of an act of producing certain consequential effects by saying something (101).

The former of these contrasts has proved to be one of the most controversial points in Austin's lectures.[30] Some of the controversy can be traced to the following subtlety in his account of the locutionary act. Austin initially uses the notion of the locution – in a manner that he himself doesn't ultimately want to endorse – to describe a confusion about the workings of language that he thinks his notion of illocutionary force enables us to avoid. He says he wants to keep us from conceiving questions about such force, as well as questions about other features of language, as questions about how independently meaningful sentences – or, as Austin puts it here, "locutions" – are used. Our willingness to think of linguistic phenomena as matters of "locutionary usage" in this sense will, Austin writes, incline us to slide into what he calls the "descriptive fallacy" – i.e. the fallacy produced by the assumption that some linguistic constructions are as such concerned with describing the facts, or constating things (100; for Austin's initial mention of this "fallacy," see 3).

When Austin speaks of "locutions" in reference to the view of language he himself favors, he stresses that whenever we say something articulate we perform *both* locutionary acts (i.e. acts of saying something with a certain meaning) *and* illocutionary acts (i.e. acts of saying something with a certain force). "To perform a locutionary act is in general . . . also and *eo ipso*," he writes, "to perform an *illocutionary* act" (98; see also 113, 132, and 146). The point Austin is making is that our grasp of the meaning, or locutionary content, of a bit of language depends on our understanding of it as a contextualized act of speech, or illocutionary act. He makes this point by reminding us of the kinds of considerations that originally led him to conclude that "what we [philosophers] have to study is *not* the sentence but the issuing of an utterance in a speech situation" (138). He revisits his discussion of how even apparent constatives can turn out to be "null and void" if the circumstances are sufficiently untoward (136ff.), and, in reference to this discussion, he suggests that we can't be sure we've identified the *locution* expressed by a combination of words until we've figured out what *illocution* is in question.[31]

Austin's aim in thus introducing the notion of the illocutionary act *via* the notion of the locutionary act is to give us an instrument for talking about language that is free from any link to the idea that sentences as such have – "literal" or "conventional" – meanings. To talk about the illocutionary in his sense just is to talk about the meaning or discursive character, not of sentences, but of whole acts of speech.

Would it be premature at this point to represent Austin's remarks on locutions and illocutions as bringing into question the idea of literal sentence-meaning? A fan of the idea might want to protest that nothing in the remarks prevents us from construing the task of identifying the illocutionary force of an utterance as involving the application of a literal sentence-meaning to a speech-situation. But this protest depends for its apparent force on a fundamental misunderstanding. In order to see this, we might examine a further example of the sort that interests Austin. Consider the sentence "This man's children are bald." Here we may seem to be confronted with an exemplary case for the idea of literal sentence-meaning. For it seems plausible to represent this sentence as possessing a stable descriptive meaning which its indexical elements (in concert with contextual features) serve to tie to particular circumstances of its employment. Imagine the following situation:

> G walks into her living room where she finds two of her friends, M and J. As G enters, M says – gesturing at J – "This man's children are bald." G, who has just been outside with J's two ordinarily coifed kids, is perplexed. Nevertheless, since she believes that she grasps (what she thinks of as) the "literal meaning" of M's sentence, and since she believes that she's confronted with circumstances of the most ordinary kind in which (as she sees it) the background conditions for the application of this alleged "literal meaning" are met, she assumes that –

with the guidance of contextual clues etc. – she can determine what M is saying. G accordingly responds: "Of course they're not." M now rejoins: "You misunderstood me entirely. We were getting ready to play a game in which everyone breaks down into two 'gangs', the bald-gang and the hairy-gang. You just heard me assigning J's kids to the former."

The point of this example is not that M's sentence doesn't have the "literal meaning" G takes it to have. The example is neutral on the question of whether the sentence, as M employs it, is properly understood as possessing whatever meaning G originally associated with it. Indeed, it would be in keeping with the spirit of the example to describe a sequel in which G, after appreciating what M is using her sentence to say, asks herself whether the sentence expresses what she initially thought of as its "literal meaning." We need not concern ourselves with how G ultimately answers this question. What's of interest is the fact that it's only once G has appreciated how M's sentence is to be taken that she's in a position intelligibly to ask it. *Now* it seems clear that we're no longer entitled to insist that G's efforts to appreciate what M is saying turn on the application of (what we may have been tempted to think of as) an antecedently available literal sentence-meaning. The example illustrates that if we take for granted Austin's claim about the primacy of the illocutionary there's no room for the idea of "literal sentence-meaning" to play the role philosophers of language traditionally call on it to play.[32]

Austin's discussion of a contrast between *perlocutions* and illocutions is guided by the same concerns that animate his discussion of the contrast between locutions and illocutions. Austin characterizes the perlocutionary in terms of the *consequential* effects that saying something ordinarily has "upon the feelings, thoughts, or actions of the audience, or of the speaker, or of other persons" (101) (e.g. my telling you to look at the sunset may have the effect of your walking into a parking meter). He says that he wants to contrast such consequential effects with the *conventional* effects that flow from the performance of an illocutionary act (e.g. my saying something with the illocutionary force of a bet has the effect of my being committed to a bet) (115 and 119–22). What sparks his interest in this contrast is the reflection that it is possible to isolate the consequential – or perlocutionary – effects of uttering a combination of words without grasping what those words are being used to say. His thought is that, in so far as it's possible to sort utterances according to their perlocutionary forces without understanding them, a system of classifying utterances according to such forces won't threaten the idea that we can grasp the meaning of a sentence without attending to a context of its significant use (esp. 114–15). It is because he realizes that we could accordingly study perlocutions without abandoning the idea of literal sentence-meaning that he insists on distinguishing his interest in illocutions – which is specifically driven by his efforts to rid himself of the idea of such meaning – from an interest in perlocutions.[33]

The aspects of Austin's account of illocutionary force I've been discussing go unrecorded in most philosophical conversations about his work. Austin's talk of illocutionary acts is typically understood, in a manner that simply obscures his efforts to discredit the idea of literal sentence-meaning, as talk of ways in which (what are thought of as) independently meaningful sentences are used. Philosophical commentators tend to characterize Austin's concern with questions of illocutionary force as concern with what he himself disparages as questions of "locutionary usage." And they then often go on to represent themselves as following in his footsteps when they describe schemes for classifying illocutionary forces that are conceived in terms of such questions. This, as we saw in section 1 (above), is the basically Searlian interpretative approach that informs Habermas's attempt to bring Austin's thought to bear on ethics. The larger difficulty with the approach is that, in failing to register Austin's interest in a critique of the idea of literal sentence-meaning, it also fails to register his interest in using such a critique to take a fresh look at what it is for language to correspond to the world.[34]

iii On truth and other dimensions of the assessment of speech-acts

> In real life, as opposed to the simple situations envisioned in logical theory, one cannot always answer in a simple manner whether [a statement] is true or false (142).
>
> (Austin)

When, towards the end of How to Do Things with Words, Austin turns to the question of how we conceive correspondence between language and the world, his accent is on challenging a fixation on truth and falsity – or, in his parlance, a "true/false fetish" (142) – that he thinks is nourished by the idea of literal sentence-meaning. Austin believes that, as long as we remain wedded to a (by his lights, confused) conception of such correspondence as the prerogative of "literally meaningful" sentences, we will be inclined to understand "true" and "false" as philosophically distinct and privileged terms of assessment – i.e. as terms of assessment that, because (as we now see it) they avoid entanglement with our conventions for performing illocutionary acts, are different in kind from terms we employ in assessing speech acts (e.g. "rough," approximate," "fair," "misleading," etc.). A guiding preoccupation of later portions of the lectures is attacking this understanding of "true" and "false," and replacing it with what he sees as a more satisfactory alternative.

What distinguishes the alternative Austin prefers is the thought that relating to the facts is the job of complete speech-acts and hence that "true" and "false" need to be understood as terms for the evaluation of such acts (134 and 138).[35] According to Austin, "truth" and "falsity" are properly understood as standing – not for a relation which is hygienic in that it avoids what we might be inclined to think of as "contamination" by our illocutionary conventions, but rather – for "a general dimension of being a right or proper thing to say as opposed to a wrong thing, in these circumstances, to this audience, for these purposes and with these intentions" (144). It follows, by his lights, that we should see ourselves as appraising descriptive bits of language – not in ways that diverge from our methods of evaluating speech acts, but rather – in "ways involving the employment of a vast array of terms which overlap with those that we use in the appraisal of performatives" (141–2).[36] These are the kinds of considerations that underlie Austin's repudiation of the logic of bi-polarity. Since, within the framework of his preferred conception of correspondence, "truth" and "falsity" resemble other terms of linguistic assessment in being caught up with our illocutionary conventions, it follows by his lights that we need to allow for the possibility that a statement may be – not either true or false but – say, "misleading" or "generally accurate" (141–4).[37]

This concludes my account of the line of reasoning in *How to Do Things with Words* leading up to the claim that primarily interests me here – viz., that corresponding to the world (whether truly, falsely, or in some other manner) is the job, not of independently meaningful sentences, but of illocutions or speech acts. I have entered into a detailed discussion of Austin's defense of this claim in order to provide a counterweight to the tendency of commentators to overlook the claim entirely. Before turning to the claim's ethical significance, I want to say something about how it gets neglected in the work of commentators who aren't guided by any specifically ethical concerns.

iv Is Austin "fair to facts"?

> The truth or falsity of a statement depends not merely on the meanings of words but on what act you were performing in what circumstances (146).
>
> (Austin)

Consider the following structural feature of John Searle's interpretation of Austin. Searle acknowledges that Austin regards corresponding to the world truly (or falsely) as the business of speech acts. But Searle also suggests that this claim is confused and that charity speaks for reading Austin as holding that corresponding is the work of independently meaningful sentences.[38] Searle defends his somewhat revisionist approach to Austin's writings by appealing to an assumption about a necessary link between literal sentence-meaning and objective (or universally valid) truth. Searle maintains – in a manner that relies for its authority on such an assumption – that the *only* way Austin can preserve his entitlement to the notion of objective truth is by retaining the idea of literal sentence-meaning.[39]

Despite the well-known (and notoriously divisive and unproductive) dispute between Searle and Derrida about how to read Austin,[40] there is a basic sense in which their interpretative strategies resemble one another. An assumption about a conceptual tie between literal sentence-meaning and objective truth also informs the exegetical efforts of Derrida and the group of literary-theoretical commentators influenced by him – albeit, as we saw, in a very different manner. Within Derrida's interpretation, the assumption seems to speak for representing Austin – not (as Searle suggests) as hostile to the idea of literal sentence-meaning, but rather – as hostile the notion of objective truth. What accounts for this difference is the fact that Derrida takes Austin to be criticizing the idea that sentences have literal meanings.[41] Derrida acknowledges that Austin represents himself as receptive to the notion of objective truth. But Derrida suggests that such receptivity is in tension with (what he sees as) Austin's appropriate hostility to literal sentence-meaning and that charity speaks for reading Austin as rejecting the notion of objective truth outright.[42] It is in so far as Derrida thus suggests that the *only* way Austin can consistently distance himself from the idea of literal sentence-meaning is by jettisoning the notion of objective truth that he appeals to an assumption – of the same sort that governs Searle's interpretation – about how the notion of objective truth stands or falls with the idea of literal sentence-meaning.[43]

A central contention of this paper is that an assumption about a conceptual tie between literal sentence-meaning and objective truth – an assumption that controls both philosophical and literary-theoretical commentary on Austin's work, and that also governs conversations about its bearing on ethics – is alien to Austin's thought. My contention, is not only that (as I have argued) Austin launches a direct assault on the idea of literal sentence-meaning, but that he does so without suggesting that he has thereby retreated from the notion of objective truth. There is also a more fundamental sense in which it is wrong to approach Austin's work armed with an assumption about a conceptual tie between literal sentence-meaning and objective truth. The more fundamental problem is that the assumption encodes an unstable understanding of the consequences of rejecting the idea of literal sentence-meaning.

Why should we assume that abandonment of literal sentence-meaning is tantamount to the loss of objective truth? Consider what would be involved in abandoning this idea. It would mean giving up an image of ourselves as capable of discoursing about the world from outside our illocutionary conventions, and it would also mean giving up as intrinsically confused the idea of a linguistically formulable conception of the world that doesn't draw on those conventions. *Now* there could no longer be any question of our adducing, as if from an extra-conventional standpoint furnished by such a conception, a priori metaphysical considerations in favor of regarding our current conception of the world as merely relative to whatever illocutionary conventions we draw on in formulating it. For it is an essential feature of the position we are considering that there is no such thing as a non-conventional alternative to our current conception of the world – and hence no such thing as a comparison between our current conception and such an alternative. This means that, in so far as we separate ourselves from the idea of literal sentence-meaning in a rigorously consistent manner, we at the same time deprive ourselves of the sort of metaphysical vantage point from which to discern that our efforts thus to separate ourselves cut us off from objective truth.[44]

The conclusion to draw from this brief argument is that there is good reason to question the assumption – at play in most conversations about Austin's thought – that it is impossible to attack the idea of literal sentence-meaning without risking the loss of objective truth. Since an attack on this idea only appears to sacrifice objective truth when it is contemplated from a metaphysical perspective that at least tacitly retains the idea, it follows that *if* Austin succeeds in discrediting the idea, he by the same token avoids any need for sacrifice. The upshot is that Austin is best understood as endeavoring to put us in a position in which we are obliged, not to deal with the loss of objective truth, but rather to refashion a familiar understanding of what such truth is like.

The kind of refashioning Austin recommends involves a departure from a deeply engrained philosophical conception of objectivity – one often glossed in terms of the idea of a "point-of-viewless" standpoint – which is characterized by the epistemological assumption that we approach an unobstructed view of objective reality by abstracting from all elements of our subjective make-ups (such as, e.g., attitudes, interests, etc.). Austin attempts to show that our efforts to describe the world, no less than our efforts to bring off other linguistic acts, inevitably draw on illocutionary conventions. He thus suggests that our ability to arrive at a genuinely – objectively – accurate understanding of the world, far from calling on us to abstract from all of our attitudes, essentially presupposes modes of appreciation that we possess as participants in practices structured by such conventions. In making this suggestion, Austin invites us to exchange the deeply engrained philosophical conception of objectivity for a conception that, in so far as it no longer requires a blanket abstraction from elements of our subjective make-ups, is characterized by a more permissive, or broader, episte-mological assumption.

The alternative conception of objectivity in question here might be described as, in virtue of its broader epistemology, "wider" than the philosophi-cally more traditional – or "narrower" – conception that Austin criticizes. This terminology enables me succinctly to formulate my main thesis in this paper. My thesis is that Austin favors the wider conception of objectivity and, further, that the move to this conception has far-reaching implications for ethics.

3 Austin, ethics, and objectivity

> [I]n moral or practical affairs, we can know the facts and yet look at them mistakenly or perversely, or not fully realize or appreciate something, or even be under a total misconception . . . even thoughtlessness, inconsiderateness, lack of imagination, are perhaps less matters for failure in intelligence or planning than might be supposed, and more matters of failure to appreciate the situation. A course of E.M. Forster and we see things differently: yet perhaps we know no more and are no cleverer.
>
> (Austin)[45]

One way to approach the question of the ethical interest of the move to the wider conception of objectivity is by considering the significance of the role that the wider conception's narrower counterpart plays in recent work in ethics. It would not be an exaggeration to say that the narrower conception carves out the space of alternatives within which most conversations about the nature of moral judgment take place.

There is a general consensus among philosophers that no plausible ethical theory can accommodate, without some significant correction or qualification, both of two very basic features of our ordinary understanding of moral judgments: viz., (1) the fact that such judgments typically strike us as a matter of sensitivity to features of the world and (2) the fact that they typically seem to us, when they have to do with our immediate practical circumstances, as bearing directly on what we have reason to do. What seems to speak against straightforwardly incorporating both of these two features of ordinary moral experience is, at the most fundamental level, a philosophy of mind that insists on a sharp division between cognitive capacities and their exercise, on the one hand, and affective endowments like attitudes and feelings, on the other. It appears to follow from this philosophy of mind that any judgment that stands in the sort of internal relation to attitudes that permits it to be essentially practical is thereby excluded from counting as fully cognitive or objective. The result is that we seem to be prevented from treating moral judgments as everything they ordinarily strike us as being.

This conclusion is of interest here because the influential philosophy of mind that seems to underwrite it is at bottom nothing more than a variation on the abstract epistemological constraint that distinguishes the narrower conception of objectivity. In advocating a philosophy of mind that calls for a strict separation between cognitive capacities and affective endowments, we are in effect endorsing the idea, constitutive of the relevant constraint, that the world only comes into view, or is only available to thought, from a perspective that abstracts as far as possible from anything affective. We might accordingly say that it is in so far as we endorse the narrower conception of objectivity that we seem to be cut off from taking at face value both of the above two features of our ordinary understanding of moral judgments.

It would be difficult to overstate the influence of the restriction that the narrower conception thus places on an acceptable view of moral judgment. Most ethical theories that straightforwardly incorporate an understanding of moral judgments as a matter of sensitivity to features of the world – i.e. most *realist* or *cognitivist* theories – are presented as earning their entitlement to do so by rejecting an understanding of such judgments as internally related to action and choice.[46] Similarly, most ethical theories that straightforwardly incorporate an understanding of moral judgments as intrinsically practical are presented as earning their entitlement to do so by rejecting an understanding of such judgments as essentially a matter of sensitivity to features of the world.

The latter of these two groups of theories includes, in addition to a variety of familiar ethical *non-cognitivisms* (e.g. prescriptivisms, error-theories, expressivisms, and qualified or quasi-realisms), also the form of non-cognitivism implicit in the deconstructivist outlook that some literary-theoretical commentators, following in Derrida's footsteps, associate with Austin. Moreover, it also includes the kind of *Kantian* approach in ethics that Habermas discusses in connection with Austin's work. Kantian moral philosophers like Habermas resemble non-cognitivists of different stripes not only in insisting that moral judgments are intrinsically practical but also in denying that such judgments are essentially a matter of sensitivity to the layout of the world. What distinguishes their work from different non-cognitivisms is the suggestion that, although (as they see it) moral judgments can't possess the kind of universal validity that is characteristic of descriptive discourse, such judgments nevertheless possess alternative, strictly practical claims to universal validity that are, in Habermas's words, "*analogous to truth-claims.*"[47]

It would not be unreasonable to try to account for the ethical significance of the wider conception of objectivity by first discussing, as I just did, the way in which the narrower conception determines the conceptual space in which most ethical theories (including some that are wrongly associated with Austin's work) are developed and described. We might then go on to observe that introducing the wider conception is tantamount to lifting the restriction that the narrower conception imposes on an adequate view of moral judgment – or, in other words, that it is tantamount to removing narrowly objective obstacles that may once have seemed to keep us from adopting an intuitively appealing view of moral judgments as both essentially concerned with how things are and also intrinsically practical.

These observations put us in a position to credit Austin with bringing the relevant, intuitively appealing view of moral judgment within our reach. They allow us to say that, in so far as Austin defends the wider conception of objectivity, he can be seen as tacitly receptive to such a view. I should emphasize that what is at issue here is nothing more than Austin's *tacit* receptivity to the view of moral judgment that is in question. This deserves emphasis, not only because Austin himself never explicitly considers this view,[48] but also because there is a conspicuous respect in which his system of classifying linguistic phenomena is ill suited to accommodate it.

To the extent that the relevant view of moral judgment is grounded in the wider conception of objectivity, it is capable of accommodating a conception of moral development as essentially a matter of the cultivation of emotional capacities. This means, among other things, that the view makes room for the possibility that bits of language that engage us emotionally can as such play a vital role in the growth of moral understanding. That is, it makes room for the possibility that bits of language that engage us emotionally can as such expand our sensitivity to morally salient features of the world – or, to put it in Austinian terms, that they can as such contribute to our mastery of illocutionary conventions that we draw on in discoursing about the moral life.

In this connection, it is noteworthy that Austin's inventory of linguistic effects doesn't leave room for emotional responses that have the relevant kinds of cognitive powers. Such responses would qualify as what Austin calls *perlocutionary* effects. They would belong to the class of *consequential* effects that saying something may produce on "the feelings, thoughts or actions of the audience" (101). But they would not be consequential in a simple or undifferentiated sense. They would differ from other consequential effects in that a capacity to (at least imaginatively) register them would be internal to a person's ability to grasp what the bit of language that produces them can teach. And they would thus represent a philosophically distinct sub-division within Austin's class of perlocutionary effects.

These reflections underline a respect in which Austin's linguistic apparatus might well be regarded as poorly conceived to incorporate some of its own ethical implications. They suggest the need to criticize Austin for – as Stanley Cavell puts it in a couple of recent discussions of Austin's work – failing adequately "to articulate the perlocutionary"[49] and, more specifically, for failing to isolate a set of perlocutionary effects, of the sort that are of primary interest to naïve ethical realists, that contribute directly to moral understanding.[50]

This criticism depends for its force on an understanding of Austin as an advocate of the wider conception of objectivity. Since commentators of all different persuasions tend to represent him as taking for granted the constraints of this conception's narrower cousin, it should come as no surprise that very few take an interest in the thought, central to the criticism, that some perlocutionary effects are philosophically more interesting than Austin indicates. Where commentators *do* take an interest in perlocutionary effects, their tendency is to suggest – as Habermas, e.g., does – that these effects are without exception merely consequential in a sense that renders them incapable of making anything but an accidental contribution to the growth of understanding.[51]

There is, as we saw, something right about the idea that Austin himself recommends this understanding of the perlocutionary. Nevertheless, to the extent that he refashions familiar philosophical renderings of the notions of truth and objectivity, he effectively recommends a very different understanding - an understanding that makes room for a class of (what Cavell calls) "passionate" perlocutionary effects that are *as such* productive of moral understanding.[52]

4 Conclusion: Austin, Cavell, and moral perfectionism

> I believe that before all else I am a human being, just as much as you are – or, at all events, that I must try to become one. I know quite well . . . that most people would think you right, and that views of that kind [i.e. about how a woman's most sacred duties are to her husband and children] are to be found in books; but I can no longer content myself with what most people say, or with what is found in books. I must think over things for myself and try to get to understand them.
>
> (Nora, in Ibsen's *A Doll's House*)[53]

Acceptance of a conception of moral development that incorporates such effects has significant consequences for how we conceive of challenges of moral reflection, and, before closing, I want to briefly touch on some of these consequences by following up on a line of thought in Cavell's work. The line of thought I have in mind is one that Cavell sometimes develops in reference to an account of Austin's view of language that is congenial to the reading of *How to Do Things with Words* presented above, and that Cavell was already defending as far back as the early 1960s.[54]

It starts with Cavell's description of the dimension of the moral life he calls *moral perfectionism*. Cavell explains that perfectionism, in the sense in which he wants to defend it, "does not imply perfectibility,"[55] and that to talk about a perfectionist dimension of the moral life is to talk about (not perfectibility, but) the possibility of ever further perfection or cultivation of the self. Further, he says that to endorse what he regards as a perfectionist outlook is to leave yourself open to the possibility of new experiences that shape your routes of feeling, give you a more comprehensive understanding of "what you are," and serve as the occasion of a "transformation of the self."[56] A central feature of Cavell's description of perfectionist striving is thus the kind of simultaneously emotional and cognitive growth distinctive of the conception of moral development that, in the last section, I connected with Austin's view of language. In various passages in his work, Cavell suggests a similar connection by declaring that Austin's thought is capable of grounding a perfectionist outlook.[57] Moreover, he also draws attention to a sense in which the conception of moral development that is in play here poses a specifically *moral* challenge to philosophically more familiar, narrowly objective accounts of moral development.

The perfectionist, as Cavell presents her, is an individual who treats her emotional contact with events, people, etc. as capable of making a direct contribution to moral understanding. Since the perfectionist accordingly regards cognitive capacities she draws on in moral reflection as having an ineliminable emotional component, there is for her no question of needing to antecedently regulate her emotional engagements in accordance with the deliverances of (what others may think of as) an independent faculty of reason. However, although an antecedently unconstrained emotional style thus seems appropriate to the perfectionist, it will seem unwarranted to her non-perfectionist critic (i.e. the person who, guided by the logic of the narrower conception of objectivity, excludes the possibility of forms of cognitive growth that have an irreducibly emotional component). To the extent that this critic denies that emotional limitations – even, say, those that result from severe injustices – can as such amount to cognitive ones, she will be inclined to insist that the only morally responsible approach to emotional engagements is one that is directed by the prior dictates of (what he or she understands as) independent cognitive capacities. And, as a result, she will be inclined to regard the perfectionist's resistance to such prior direction as a sign that, in Cavell's words, the perfectionist "lack[s] the concept of morality altogether."[58]

At the same time, although a policy of antecedently regulating emotional engagements appears morally necessary from the standpoint of the critic of perfectionism, from the standpoint of the perfectionist it appears both confused (i.e. in that it seems to presuppose a misguided view of cognition) and also threatening to the growth of moral understanding. The perfectionist will accordingly be inclined to regard the policy as an unnecessary and *moralistic* austerity measure. Speaking for the perfectionist, Cavell puts it this way: "the alternative [to perfectionism] is moralism."[59]

At several points in his work, Cavell mentions the denouement of Ibsen's *A Doll's House* as an illustration of what he sees as dangers of moralism.[60] Cavell argues that the circumstances that lead Nora to leave her husband Torvald and their small children are best understood in perfectionist terms. Cavell is especially interested in the fact that, although Nora isn't convinced by Torvald's claim that morality and religion are on the side of staying, she nevertheless doesn't insist that she is herself in the right. What she does say is that, if she is to figure out "who is right, the world or I,"[61] she needs first to escape from a marriage that (as she now sees it) has infantilized her and kept her from acquiring her own tastes, and to "try to educate [herself]."[62] Cavell hears Nora's demand for an education as a demand for a kind of self-cultivation that is simultaneously emotional and cognitive. It is to the extent that he takes Nora to be claiming the right thus to cultivate herself, even in the face of "all the reasons that can be given her,"[63] that Cavell thinks she embodies the perfectionist spirit. And, by the same token, it is to the extent that he takes Torvald to be disputing this entitlement that Cavell thinks Torvald is the embodiment of perfectionism's moralistic antithesis.[64]

There is an important respect in which the understanding of moralism at play in Cavell's treatment of perfectionism in general – and in his discussion of perfectionist themes in reference to *A Doll's House* in particular – needs to be understood as philosophically distinctive. Although it is possible to find a small cluster of writings within Anglo-American ethics that charge traditional moral philosophy with being moralistic in the same widely objective sense,[65] most conversations about "moralism" equate it, in a manner foreign to these writings, with a moral defect that it is possible to overcome without departing from a narrowly objective account of moral development.[66] One consequence of this is that rejoinders to these writings for the most part fail even to address the specific worry about moralism that Cavell and others hope to air. Since the rejoinders fail to take seriously the (widely objective) possibility that limitations of emotional endowments may directly impair moral judgment, they also fail to take seriously the (similarly widely objective) possibility that insistence on making emotional engagements conform to prior moral judgments may have a tendency to prevent us from overcoming certain impairments (such as, e.g., those that Cavell sees as characteristic of Nora).

Part of what is disappointing about existing discussions of Austin's view of language in relation to ethics is, as I can now put it, that they overlook the

sense in which his view equips us to acknowledge the possibility of simultaneously emotional and cognitive forms of moral growth and, by the same token,
also the sense in which, in making room for this possibility, it comes into
conflict with received views about the challenges of moral reflection. If Austin's
writings are to be brought to bear more faithfully on ethics, they need to be read
as hospitable to the pertinent forms of moral growth, and to the larger picture of
the moral life to which these forms of moral growth belong.[67]

Notes

1   *Sense and Sensibilia* (Oxford: Oxford University Press, 1962), p. 111.
2   Cambridge, MA: Harvard University Press, 1962. All unattributed page references in
    the text and notes of this paper are to this work of Austin's.
3   For talk of "bi-polarity" in connection with propositions that are thus *either* true *or*
    false, see Wittgenstein, "Notes on logic," *Notebooks 1914–1916*, 2nd edn, eds G.H.
    von Wright and G.E.M. Anscombe, trans. G.E.M. Anscombe (Oxford: Basil
    Blackwell), pp. 93–107, pp. 98–9.
4   Austin does not address himself to philosophers (such as Lukasiewicz) whose attacks
    on classical logic lead them to endorse many-valued views of logic. But it is not
    obvious that such views can be excluded from the class that Austin is criticizing
    simply on account of their depiction of assertions as "tri-polar" and not "bi-polar."
    Many-valued theories typically resemble the views that Austin is attacking in repre-
    senting the sense of a sentence as fixed by the conditions under which it is true and
    all other conditions. That these "other" conditions include the conditions in which
    a sentence is false in addition to the ones in which it is neither true nor false does
    not matter to Austin's critique. The heart of the critique, as will emerge, is that
    sentences possess fixed senses prior to and independently of being used on particular
    occasions.
5   What's in question here is, in other words, the simple idea that sentences as such
    have meanings. (In this respect, talk of *literal* sentence-meaning might be thought of
    as pleonastic.) Moreover, the simplicity of the idea is not essentially qualified by
    ways in which it gets further specified. It is characteristic of current accounts of
    literal sentence-meaning to insist that we need to appeal to contextual clues in order
    to arrive at determinations of sentence-meaning and, more specifically, that we need
    to refer to such clues in order to identify the contributions that indexical features of
    a sentence make to its meaning. But current accounts also characteristically insist
    that there must be rules for making such determinations (i.e. rules, for assigning
    values, in particular circumstances, to the parameters that different indexicals pick
    out) and, further, that mastery of those rules must make it possible to give an
    account of what a sentence means independently of an appreciation of the point it is
    being used to make on a particular occasion. For a helpful discussion of these issues,
    see François Recanati, *Literal Meaning* (Cambridge, UK: Cambridge University Press,
    2004), esp. pp. 159ff.
6   Habermas gives his most comprehensive accounts of what he sees as his inheritance
    from Austin in "Universal pragmatics: reflections on a theory of communicative
    competence" (1971), *On the Pragmatics of Social Interaction: Preliminary Studies in the
    Theory of Communicative Action*, trans. Barbara Fultner (Cambridge, MA: MIT Press,
    2001), pp. 67–84, "What is universal pragmatics?" *Communication and the Evolution
    of Society*, trans. Thomas McCarthy (Boston, MA: Beacon Press, 1979), pp. 1–68,
    and *The Theory of Communicative Action*, vol. 1: *Reason and the Rationalization of
    Society*, trans. Thomas McCarthy (Boston, MA: Beacon Press, 1984). For a helpful

overview of the roughly Kantian account of moral discourse Habermas thinks Austin's thought helps to fund, see "Discourse ethics: notes on a program of philosophical justification," *Moral Consciousness and Communicative Action*, trans. Christian Lenhardt and Shierry Weber Nicholsen (Cambridge, MA: MIT Press, 1999), pp. 43–115.

7 Habermas frequently represents Searle as a reliable interpreter of Austin. (See, e.g., "Universal pragmatics," op. cit., pp. 82–3 and "What is universal pragmatics?" op. cit., pp. 25–6, esp. n. 58.) For basic similarities between Habermas's and Searle's approaches to Austin's work on speech acts, see the next three notes. For Habermas's account of certain differences, see note 13, below.

8 See, e.g., "What is universal pragmatics?" op. cit., pp. 27ff. and *The Theory of Communicative Action*, vol. 1, op. cit., p. 297 and pp. 335–7. Searle argues that Austin is best read as endorsing an idea of literal sentence-meaning in "Austin on locutionary and illocutionary acts," *Philosophical Review* 77 (October 1968): 405–24, esp. p. 420. For one of Searle's more general defenses of this idea – i.e. a defense independent of questions of Austin-interpretation – see *Expression and Meaning: Studies in the Theory of Speech Acts* (Cambridge, UK: Cambridge University Press, 1979), ch. 5.

9 See, e.g., "What is universal pragmatics?" op. cit., pp. 27–34. Searle discusses the same sorts of "communicative failures" or (in Searle's jargon) "linguistic improprieties" in both "Assertions and aberrations" (1958), reprinted in T.K. Fann (ed.), *Symposium on J.L. Austin* (London: Routledge & Kegan Paul), pp. 205–18 and also chapter 6 of *Speech Acts: An Essay in the Philosophy of Language* (Cambridge, UK: Cambridge University Press, 1969), pp. 131–56. In these bits of his work, Searle argues that Austin's remarks about "misuses" of language are confusing and, further, that it is only by amending Austin's text that we arrive at (what Searle regards as) a satisfactory picture of linguistic improprieties that involve the inappropriate use of independently meaningful sentences. In this connection, see below note 34.

10 This basic understanding of the nature of Austin's work on speech acts, which guides Habermas's discussions of Austin, is faithful in fundamentals to the understanding Searle describes in *Speech Acts*, op. cit.

11 See, e.g., "Discourse ethics," op. cit., pp. 52–7. I return to philosophical assumptions that inform Habermas's research in ethics below in section 3.

12 See "What is universal pragmatics?" op. cit., pp. 41–4 and 55–7.

13 This is perhaps the right place to note that Habermas takes himself to be departing from both Austin and Searle in arguing that his allegedly Austinian theory of speech acts equips us to talk about non-descriptive modes of discourse with (non-truth-oriented) claims to universal validity. Although he thinks Austin and Searle supply resources for combating philosophers' traditional fixation on the value of truth, he believes both philosophers nevertheless remain fixated themselves (see, e.g., ibid., pp. 55ff). Further, he believes that this alleged fixation is reflected in limitations in the schemes for classifying speech acts both Austin and Searle propose (see, e.g., *Theory of Communicative Action*, vol. 1, op. cit., pp. 309ff. and 319ff.). I am inclined to think that this criticism – although it may have some merit as far as Searle's work on speech-acts is concerned – is driven by a fundamentally flawed interpretation of Austin, and that as far as Austin's work is concerned it fails to even locate its target.

14 See "Discourse ethics," op. cit., pp. 57–62.

15 The relevant paper of Derrida's, which was first delivered in 1971, is reprinted as "Signature event context," *Limited Inc.* (Evanston, IL: Northwestern University Press, 1988), pp. 1–23.

16 See esp. ibid., p. 19.

17 See esp. ibid., pp. 13 and 14 n. 7. I touch on relevant aspects of Derrida's treatment of Austin in section 2 iv, below. One of the most influential theorists to follow in

Derrida's footsteps in making these basic interpretative claims is Stanley Fish. See esp. "How to do things with Austin and Searle: speech-act theory and literary criticism," *Is There a Text in This Class? The Authority of Interpretative Communities* (Cambridge, MA: Harvard University Press, 1980), pp. 197–245 and "With compliments of the author: reflections on Austin and Derrida," *Doing What Comes Naturally: Change, Rhetoric and the Practice of Theory in Literary and Legal Studies* (Durham, NC: Duke University Press, 1989), pp. 37–67.

18 The original impetus for the – now sizeable – body of gender-theoretical work that develops this basic position was provided by Judith Butler's *Gender Trouble: Feminism and the Subversion of Identity* (New York: Routledge, 1990). See also Butler's *Excitable Speech: A Politics of the Performative* (New York: Routledge, 1997).

19 *Philosophical Investigations*, 3rd edn, trans. G.E.M. Anscombe (New York: Macmillan Publishing Co., Inc., 1958), §24.

20 Ibid., §117.

21 I am inheriting Austin's practice of placing "statement" in single quotes ('statement') when referring to the traditional ideal of the 'statement' he wants to criticize. Austin's reasons for employing this notation emerge as his critique proceeds. I return to this topic in note 27, below.

22 It would not be unreasonable, in the light of these considerations, to describe Austin's discussion of constatives and performatives as having the structure of a *reductio*-proof. Austin's larger aim in introducing the distinction is to collapse it and thereby show that the view of meaning that seems to underwrite it (and that seems also to breathe life into the traditional 'statement') is bankrupt. For one suggestion to this effect, see 4 n. 1.

23 Thus – to mention one of Austin's favorite examples – for my uttering of "I pronounce you husband and wife" to be happy, there must be an established procedure for marrying, and I must be an appropriate person in appropriate circumstances.

24 Austin also claims that some utterances that seem to be clear cases of performatives nevertheless resemble constatives in that they are assessed in terms of how accurately they represent the facts (47ff.).

25 See also 136ff. where Austin argues that factual utterances can *misfire* not only when there is some breakdown of reference (as in the example mentioned in parentheses in the text) but also when the circumstances are sufficiently inappropriate in other respects – e.g., when the speaker is "not in a position" to say what he or she utters (138).

26 Austin is not recommending that we banish the *expressions* "constative" and "performative." He thinks that we can go on classifying utterances as constatives and performatives – in a philosophically respectable manner – as long as we bear in mind that what we are doing is drawing a distinction (not between kinds of independently meaningful sentence, but) between kinds of speech-act. So Austin's willingness to continue talking about constatives and performatives later in his lectures should *not* be taken as a sign of any sort of lingering attachment to his original distinction.

27 This puts me in a position to explain the significance of Austin's practice of using single quotes when referring to a traditional ideal of the 'statement'. (See note 21, above.) Because he rejects the view that linguistic constructions have meanings independently of circumstances of their use, he insists on drawing a sharp distinction between merely grammatical entities, on the one hand, and our use of such entities to say things on particular occasions, on the other. He speaks of *sentences* in reference to a class of the latter, and he speaks of *statements* in reference to the use of sentences on particular occasions. And he uses single quotes when discussing a traditional ideal of the 'statement' to indicate that he thinks that this ideal, although it gets touted as an ideal of the *statement*, is better understood as an ideal of the *sentence* (i.e. since it presupposes that meanings attach themselves to isolated

sentences). Here I should add that ultimately Austin will speak of statements, not in connection with all meaningful uses of sentences, but only in connection with those that report on the facts. (See, e.g., 146–8 and also "Truth," *Philosophical Papers*, 3rd edn, eds J.O. Urmson and G.J. Warnock (Oxford: Oxford University Press, 1961), pp. 117–33, p. 131.)

28 Notice that it would be wrong to object to Austin's discussion of constatives and performatives on the ground that, if, in accordance with it, we give up the idea of literal sentence-meaning, we thereby commit ourselves to the ridiculous view that the words that get used in a particular context contribute nothing to the meaning of the utterance in which they figure. The person who, following up on Austin's treatment of constatives and performatives, distances himself or herself from the idea of literal sentence-meaning is making, not this ridiculous proposal, but rather the quite reasonable proposal that what the words used in a given context contribute to the meaning of the utterance in which they figure is a set of past uses in terms of which similarities can be established between the relevant past contexts and the context currently at hand.

29 Ms. 110, stress in the original, cited and translated by David Stern, *Wittgenstein on Mind and Language* (Oxford: Oxford University Press, 1995), p. 105.

30 For a central excerpt from the controversy, see, e.g., Searle, "Austin on locutionary and illocutionary acts," op. cit.

31 Let me add a note here about a couple of passages in which Austin comments on his treatment of the locutionary act in relation to the illocutionary act. Austin tells us that he devotes almost no attention to the locutionary *alone* (95), and at one point he admits that in the final analysis he "is not sure whether [the distinction between the locutionary and the illocutionary] is sound" (148). These passages need to be situated within the context of the larger argument of Austin's lectures. It would be wrong to read them – as some commentators have proposed – as indicating that Austin lacks confidence in his account of both the locutionary act and the illocutionary act. In these passages, Austin is admitting that it isn't clear to him whether or not the notion of the locutionary act has significant philosophical interest *by itself*. But he is not questioning its usefulness as a (at least transitional) tool for isolating the illocutionary act.

32 It would be wrong to represent this attack on the idea of literal sentence-meaning, as Peter Geach once famously did, as undermined by the Fregean observation that a thought that occurs unasserted in discourse (say, because it is the antecedent in a condition or a disjunct in a disjunction) may nonetheless have a determinate content. (See *Logic Matters*, (Oxford: Blackwell, 1972), pp. 254–8.) This observation only appears to amount to a telling objection if we assume that the attack has to do with whether thoughts are asserted in the sense that Geach has in mind. But this assumption is clearly false. Austin is claiming that sentences depend for their content, not on being asserted in Geach's sense, but rather on being used to say something to someone in a particular context. And this claim applies to complex sentences involving clauses that express unasserted thoughts just as it applies to simpler sentences. (For a helpful discussion of limitations of Geach's objection, see Recanati, *Literal Meaning*, op. cit., pp. 154–5.)

33 Although Austin's distinction between illocutions and perlocutions hasn't proved as controversial as his distinction between illocutions and locutions, this area of his work has inspired a lively debate about the philosophical interest of the category of the perlocutionary. I turn to relevant issues in section 3.

34 Another problem with this approach to inheriting from Austin is that it obscures connections between the theoretical concerns that guide Austin's analysis of the workings of language and the *linguistic method* he employs throughout his work. It is characteristic of Austin to proceed philosophically by investigating how particular

expressions are ordinarily used and arguing that philosophers misuse those expressions – thereby lapsing into "nonsense" or "meaninglessness" (e.g. *Sense and Sensibilia*, op. cit., pp. 10, 15, and 19). Moreover, when Austin explicitly discusses his characteristic method (see esp. "A plea for excuses," *Philosophical Papers*, op. cit., pp. 175–204, esp. pp. 181–9), he makes it clear that he takes this charge of nonsense to represent, not a *merely pragmatic* objection (i.e. one that is consistent with our having a grasp on what it is philosophers are saying), but rather a *logical* objection (i.e. one whose upshot is that, even though philosophers are employing sentences that we know perfectly well how to use in other contexts, it's not clear what, if anything, they are saying). This logical criticism depends for its cogency on Austin's rejection of the idea of literal sentence-meaning. It takes for granted his thought that it is impossible to grasp the locutionary act someone is performing in uttering a set of words apart from a grasp of the illocutionary force with which he or she utters them and hence that *all* illocutionary performances – even, say, those philosophical ones that strike us as having the form of descriptive statements or constatives – are subject to circumstantial infelicities that render them "null and void." Stanley Cavell discusses Austin's interest in this logical form of criticism in "Must we mean what we say?" and "Austin at criticism" (reprinted in *Must We Mean What We Say?: A Book of Essays* (Cambridge, MA: Harvard University Press, 1969), pp. 1–43 and pp. 97–114). But Cavell's contribution to Austin scholarship is in this respect exceptional. The general tendency of philosophical commentators is either to overlook indications that Austin is interested in this sort of logical criticism (see, e.g., Paul Grice, "Prolegomena," *Studies in the Ways of Words* (Cambridge, MA: Harvard University Press, 1989), pp. 1–22) or to treat such indications as signs that he is confused about methodological ramifications of his own view of language (see, e.g., Searle, "Assertions and aberrations," op. cit.).

35 See also the epigraph to section 1.

36 Austin draws a similar conclusion elsewhere in his work. In "Unfair to facts" (*Philosophical Papers*, op. cit., pp. 154–74), he presents a list of adjectives, apart from "true" and "false," that we use in assessing statements ("precise," "exact," "rough," and "accurate") and then declares that he is happy to claim "that these are the important terms to elucidate when we address ourselves to the problem of 'truth'" (161).

37 The point here is not *simply* that Austin claims that sometimes statements are neither true nor false – and that sometimes they are, say, "roughly true" or "largely false." This claim might well be advanced by a thinker who endorsed the very view of sentence-meaning from which Austin is here trying to distance himself. Such a thinker might try to defend the claim by arguing that there are situations in which we grasp (what he or she sees as) the literal meaning of a sentence that is being used to make a statement – and in which, moreover, we see how the sentence's indexical elements pin it to the particular circumstances – but are unable to determine whether the sentence is true or false. Although a thesis about the indeterminacy of literal meaning might thus lead a thinker to be critical of bi-polarity, his or her criticism would nevertheless not be Austin's.

38 In "Austin on locutionary and illocutionary acts" (op. cit.), Searle argues that Austin's claim that some speech acts have truth-values is the product of an error in his analysis of statements and, further, that what Austin should have said is that independently meaningful sentences are the sole bearers of such values (see esp. pp. 421–3).

39 Searle defends the pertinent assumption in "Rationality and reason, what is at stake?" *Daedelus* 122 (1992): 55–84.

40 The dispute includes Derrida's "Signature event context," op. cit., first published in *Glyph* 1(2) in 1977; Searle's response in "Reiterating the differences: a reply to

Derrida," in H. Sussman and S. Webster (eds), *Glyph* 1(2) (Baltimore, MD: Johns Hopkins University Press, 1977); and Derrida's counter in "Limited inc. a b c . . . ," *Limited Inc.*, op. cit., pp. 29–110.

41 Derrida describes what he sees as Austin's rejection of the idea of literal sentence-meaning in these terms. He says that Austin moves from a classical view of meaning to a view on which the distinguishing mark of linguistic signs is their "iterability" or "citability" – i.e. their capacity for projection into multiple contexts. (See, e.g., "Signature event context," op. cit., p. 7.) Here Derrida refers specifically to the moment at which Austin declares that he cannot find a grammatical criterion to sort linguistic formulas as such into constatives and performatives. Derrida writes that "[iterability] is what creates this embarrassment and makes it impossible . . . 'to lay down even a list of all possible criteria'" (ibid., p. 23, n. 10). Now, to the extent that Derrida thus represents Austin as rejecting the idea of literal sentence-meaning, his interpretation resembles the interpretation defended in the pages above. But this initial similarity co-resides with a philosophically fundamental difference. (See the following three notes.)

42 Derrida offers the following diagnosis of Austin's alleged misstep. He argues that there is a moment at which Austin betrays (what Derrida sees as) his repudiation of the idea of literal sentence-meaning. He suggests that Austin holds that the *intentions* with which a speaker produces a set of words secure those words against mishaps that would deprive them of meaning (ibid., pp. 14–15). This suggestion – which unfortunately has been repeated by many theorists influenced by Derrida – is clearly unfounded. For although Austin does mention intentions in connection with the "infelicities" to which he thinks all speech acts are subject, he clearly denies that the presence of appropriate intentions constitutes any sort of semantic guarantee. But, however misguided, the suggestion is the centerpiece of Derrida's explanation of how Austin is led – wrongly, as Derrida sees it – to "reintroduce the criterion of truth in his description of performatives" (ibid., p. 22, n. 7). Moreover, since Derrida thinks that Austin's interest in objective truth reflects philosophical confusion, it appears to him that Austin is best read as rejecting such truth – and, more specifically, that he is best read as wanting "to free the analysis of the performative from the authority of the truth *value* . . . and to substitute for it at times the value of [illocutionary or perlocutionary] force" (ibid., p. 13, stress in the original).

43 In his paper on Austin, Derrida offers a brief argument for this assumption. He argues that there is an important sense in which a view of language that rejects the idea of literal sentence-meaning or, in his terms, an "iterable" view (see note 41, above) is paradoxical. Derrida writes that, within the context of iterability, "the condition of the possibility of [linguistic] effects is, simultaneously, once again, the condition of their impossibility" (ibid., p. 10). His thought is that here the very thing that – allegedly – enables signs to convey meaning (viz., their iterability) at the same time prevents them from serving as metaphysical guarantees of the delivery of meaning (i.e. since their iterability is what exposes them to mishaps that render them "null and void"). This strikes him as paradoxical because he thinks that, if signs lack meaning in isolation, the validity of whatever meanings they have in particular contexts must be relative to the illocutionary conventions governing their use in those contexts. So the putative paradox is that the very iterability that enables signs to convey meaning at the same time prevents them from doing so except in a qualified (non-objective or relativistic) manner.

44 The line of thought traced out in this paragraph implies a criticism of Derrida's claim that there is something paradoxical about a view of language free from the idea of literal sentence meaning. (See the previous note.) The point of this paragraph is, as I can now put it, that the appearance of a paradoxical threat to objective truth is only sustained by the tacit retention of a bankrupt metaphysical perspective. Stanley

Cavell concisely formulates this point in a relatively recent discussion of Derrida on Austin. Cavell writes: "Derrida's sense of . . . 'paradoxicality' . . . seems to insist on the pathos of the philosophical view of language he combats" ("Counter-philosophy and the pawn of voice," *A Pitch of Philosophy: Autobiographical Exercises* (Cambridge, MA: Harvard University Press, 1994), pp. 53–128, p. 72).

45 "A plea for excuses," op. cit., p. 194.

46 One of the most influential and interesting realist theories that is *externalist* in this sense (i.e. in the sense that it represents moral judgments as only externally related to action and choice) is laid out by Philippa Foot in *Virtues and Vices* (Berkeley, CA: University of California Press, 1978). (However, in more recent work Foot champions a non-externalist realism more congenial to the larger concerns of this paper. See *Natural Goodness* (Oxford: Clarendon Press, 2001).) There is also a rough family of externalist realisms put form by a group of philosophers – including Richard Boyd, David Brink, and Nicholas Sturgeon – who share affiliations to the Cornell Philosophy Department and might thus naturally be thought of as forming a "Cornell School."

47 "Discourse Ethics," op. cit., p. 56, stress in the original. The classic model for these alternative, practical claims to universal validity is, of course, Kant's categorical imperative.

48 To be sure, Austin *does* clearly indicate that he thinks his critique of the traditional 'statement' undermines a familiar philosophical distinction between factual 'statements' and emotive utterances. He opens his lectures by adducing such a distinction as an example of a linguistic classification that presupposes that some linguistic constructions are as such in the business of constating things (see section 2 i), and he then goes on to attack the pertinent presupposition in a manner that implies a deep criticism of the familiar distinction. Moreover, in his closing lecture, he explicitly follows up on this suggestion when he declares that his main line of argument enables him to "play Old Harry . . . with the value/fact fetish" (150) and that it shows that "the familiar contrast of 'normative or evaluative' as opposed to the factual is in need, like so many dichotomies, of elimination" (148).

49 "Counter-philosophy and the pawn of voice," op. cit., p. 82. See also Cavell's more involved critique of Austin's treatment of the perlocutionary in "Passionate and performative utterances," *Philosophy The Day After Tomorrow*, Cambridge, MA: Harvard University Press, 2005, pp. 155–191.

50 Since one of my aims in this paper is hinting that there are more significant parallels between Austin's and Wittgenstein's views of language than is generally assumed (see, e.g., the epigraphs to sections 2 and 2 ii), I want to acknowledge that this paragraph identifies an important *discontinuity* between Austin and Wittgenstein. Wittgenstein is properly credited with taking an interest in the kind of perlocutionary effects, neglected by Austin, that are at issue here. In this connection, see, e.g., Wittgenstein's remarks in *On Certainty*, eds G.E.M. Anscombe and G.H. von Wright, trans. Denis Paul and G.E.M. Anscombe (London: Basil Blackwell, 1969) on what he sees as the intrinsically cognitive character of certain *persuasive* modes of discourse.

51 Although he has on several occasions revised details of his view of perlocutionary effects, Habermas endorses this basic understanding of them (viz., an understanding on which all such effects stand in a merely external relationship to cognitive development) throughout his work. His revisions target, not this basic understanding, but rather, more locally, his early – and surely mistaken – suggestion that all intended or foreseeable perlocutionary effects are deceptive or, in his parlance, "strategic" (*The Theory of Communicative Action*, vol. 1, op. cit., pp. 288f). For a relatively recent account of the revisions he thinks are called for, see "A reply" in *Communicative Action: Essays on Jürgen Habermas's Theory of Communicative Action*, eds A. Honneth and H. Joas (Cambridge, MA: MIT Press, 1991).

52 Cavell introduces the moniker "passionate" in "Passionate and performative utterances," op. cit.

53 *A Doll's House, The Wild Duck, Lady from the Sea*, trans. R. Farquharson Sharp and Eleanor Marx-Aveling (London: J.M. Dent & Sons Ltd, 1958), p. 68. (I have amended the translation, at the suggestion of Robert Haraldsson.)

54 For remarks on convergences between Cavell's approach to Austin and the approach defended in this paper, see above notes 34 and 44, and also the last three paragraphs of the previous section.

55 *Conditions Handsome and Unhandsome: The Constitution of Emersonian Perfectionism* (Chicago, IL: Chicago University Press, 1990), p. 3. The introduction to this book contains Cavell's most detailed discussion of what moral perfectionism amounts to.

56 Ibid., p. 7; see also pp. 2 and 46.

57 See, e.g., ibid., p. 35 and *A Pitch of Philosophy*, op. cit., p. 118. It is worth observing that Cavell originally speaks of moral perfectionism in reference to an ethical outlook he finds expressed in Emerson's work and, further, that although he doesn't yet use the label 'perfectionism' in some of his early discussions of Emerson, he nevertheless already connects what he sees as Emerson's ethical outlook with Austin's and Wittgenstein's views of language. See, e.g., *The Senses of Walden*, expanded edn (San Francisco, CA: North Point Press, 1981), pp. 143–4.

58 *Conditions Handsome and Unhandsome*, op. cit., p. 2.

59 Ibid., p. 7; see also pp. 13 and 46.

60 See ibid., pp. 108–15 and *Pursuits of Happiness: The Hollywood Comedy of Remarriage* (Cambridge, MA: Harvard University Press, 1981), pp. 20–4.

61 *A Doll's House*, op. cit., p. 69.

62 Ibid., p. 67.

63 Cavell, *Conditions Handsome and Unhandsome*, op. cit., p. 109.

64 Cavell claims that there is an important sense in which Torvald's embodiment of moralism is imperfect. Cavell's thought is that, at the play's close, Torvald moves quickly from moralistic impatience with Nora to a more promising effort to comprehend her. See ibid., p. 113 and also *Pursuits of Happiness*, op. cit., p. 23.

65 See, e.g., Cora Diamond, "Moral differences and distances: some questions," Lilli Alanen, Sara Heinämaa, and Thomas Wallgren, *Commonality and Particularity in Ethics* (New York, NY: St Martin's Press, 1997), pp. 197–234 and Annette Baier, "Moralism and cruelty: reflections on Hume and Kant," *Moral Prejudices: Essays on Ethics* (Cambridge, MA: Harvard University Press, 1994), pp. 268–93.

66 The class of such rejoinders includes, conspicuously, the efforts of a broad range of contemporary Kantian moral philosophers – such as, e.g., Marcia Baron, Barbara Herman, Thomas Hill Jnr, Christine Korsgaard, and Onora O'Neill – to discredit the suggestion that Kant's ethical theory is moralistic.

67 This paper began its life as an attempt to follow up on Stanley Cavell's claim that Austin's thought underwrites a species of moral perfectionism. My debt to Cavell here is pervasive. I am also indebted to Jay Bernstein and Pablo Gilabert for many helpful suggestions about Habermas's work on Austin, and to Nancy Bauer, Jay Bernstein, Robert Haraldsson, Nathaniel Hupert, and Mark Richard for many useful comments and criticisms.

4

HOW TO DO THINGS WITH PORNOGRAPHY

Nancy Bauer

My title is of course a twist on the one J.L. Austin gave to the series of twelve William James lectures he delivered at Harvard fifty years ago. And since my understanding of what is going on in Austin's lectures both deeply informs what I am doing in this paper and at the same time is pointedly at odds with the standard way of taking them, I think it best for me to start with some general remarks about how I read *How to Do Things With Words*.[1]

One way to gesture at my beef with the standard interpretation of Austin's lectures is to say that it fails to take seriously his entitling them according to the conventions of an instruction manual. Ironically, one won't even be able to make out the title unless one already knows how to do things with words. Perhaps you are inclined to take this irony merely as an instance of Austin's legendary cleverness. (Let us not forget *Sense and Sensibilia*, which involves a play both on Jane Austen's title and on their homonymous names.)[2] But you won't take it so lightly if, like me, you are convinced that Austin's central concern was precisely to show that his contemporaries in professional philosophy *didn't* in fact know, or perhaps had ironically managed to repress, what they couldn't fail to know: namely, that we don't just *say* things with our words but also *do* things with them. Austin suggested in his lectures that philosophers had led themselves to focus exclusively on a single aspect of our use of words, namely, the meaning of sentences, which is to say, given the conception of meaning bequeathed to us by Frege, their "sense," understood as the determinant of their truth value. What philosophers had failed to notice, Austin claimed in his lectures, is the extent – extremely great indeed, he argued – to which our use of words consists in more than claim-making: it gets things done. We use language not just to convey sense and reference, but also to apologize and to promise and to bet and to accuse and to forgive. To read the philosophy of his day, Austin implied, was to get the impression that philosophers had lost sight of this basic function of words and thus literally stood in need of an instruction manual, of being taught, or, better, re-taught, how to do things with them.

The rebuke that Austin issued to his peers is ordinarily construed quite narrowly, as though his aspiration were merely to found a new cottage industry in what was just coming to be called the philosophy of language, the business of which would be to construct theories of how people *use* words – to do "prag-matics," as we now call it. On my reading, however, this understanding of Austin's legacy turns on an impoverished grasp of his ambitions and achieve-ments.[3] There is no sign in *How to Do Things with Words* that Austin sees himself as modestly gesturing toward a smallish expanse of unexplored philo-sophical territory adjacent to the vast swath that was being colonized by philosophers of language. To the contrary, there is every indication that he wishes to challenge the foundational premises of this incipient movement, most notably the assumption that well-formed sentences (or their parts) invariably and inherently possess, in some absolute sense, "literal" meanings on which their linguistic powers stand and fall. This challenge runs very deep – even deeper, I think, than many of Austin's admirers and fellow skeptics about the importance of "literal meaning" are wont to go.[4] For Austin's goal is not to argue that there is no such thing as literal meaning or to claim that it plays a more modest role in the workings of language than others had assumed. He does not, that is, wish to propound some counter-*theory*. Rather, he is worried about the very idea that there must be some one thing or other at the heart of language use, some overarching theory that philosophers can and ought to endorse about how utterances say and do what they do. In effect, then, Austin is challenging the coherence and importance of the central project that philosophers of language understand themselves to be undertaking. He is suggesting that doing philosophy – getting a productive philosophical grip on *how things are with the world* – does not require that we be able to pin down the semantics of natural language in advance of what Wittgenstein, at least here on the same page as Austin, calls "looking and seeing."

On my reading, then, *How to Do Things with Words*, addressed quite explic-itly to Austin's colleagues in professional philosophy during the heyday in Anglophone circles of the idea that philosophy was all about analyzing language, audaciously accuses philosophers not just of failing at the enterprise of understanding how language works but in fact of not knowing the first thing about it. The philosopher Austin has in mind lacks a sense not just of what words in general can do, though that is true enough; more specifically, he is deeply misguided about what he himself is (and perhaps more importantly, is not) doing with his words. In so far as he sees himself as in the business of constructing an a priori semantic theory, he reveals himself not to know how to do things with his own words. The way back to philosophical sense-making will have to rest on what he already knows, but to his peril has ignored or repressed, about what words – and, in particular, *his* words – do.

How to Do Things with Words is not the only expression of Austin's convic-tion that much of what passed for philosophy in his day was in fact a kind of wheel-spinning. Elsewhere, for example, Austin takes aim at the ideas – ideas that were absolutely central to the philosophy of his day – that (1) our percep-tions of the world are mediated by mental representations (in *Sense and Sensibilia*); (2) ethical theory could not proceed other than by attempting to pin down the meanings of terms like "good" and "right" (in "A plea for excuses," "Ifs and cans," and "Three ways of spilling ink"); and (3) knowledge is to be understood as incorruptibly true belief and therefore, since it is never the case that our certainty with respect to the truth of a proposition is absolute, cannot be secured (in "Other minds"). In all of these writings, it is generally agreed, Austin is commending to our attention not an *addition* to an established research program but, at best, a *replacement* for it – or sometimes, as in the case of his discussion of "the problem of other minds," a call to abandon it altogether. Though many people of course find these writings quite uncongenial, no one misses the radical aspirations that are driving them. And yet, curiously, *Words* is routinely taken "straight," as though here – and only here – Austin was perfectly content to till the same old philosophical soil and wished merely to draw attention to some adjacent virgin land.[5]

The repression that Austin points up in calling his book *How to Do Things with Words* thus finds its ironic twin in his inheritors' collective failure to grasp the nature of his (and, it follows, their own) enterprise – to discern the serious note in his clever title. And I am now in a position to say that my twist on that title is meant to mark what I see as a further repression in this inheritance, one that concerns the way Austin has been taken up by certain contemporary feminist philosophers who are motivated by sympathy for the idea that the proliferation of pornography, at least under the current circumstances, constitutes a violation of women's civil rights. I confess to being dubious about this understanding of pornography's powers, but my primary goal here is not to contest it. Rather, what concerns me is the *method* these particular inheritors of Austin are employing. Specifically, I am worried about "using" or "applying" what are taken to be Austin's ideas, or slight modifications thereof, in service of having a philosophical say about pornography. What worries me about this method is twofold. First, I am convinced that it constitutes a very bad way to do feminist philosophy – very bad from the point of view of philosophy and, at least as importantly to me, of feminism. Second, this appropriation of Austin, in so far as it unquestioningly takes up the standard attenuated reading of *How to Do Things with Words*, obscures the various ways in which the book might genuinely help feminists think about how to combine philosophy with the furthering of our political aims. The present paper aims to make these two worries vivid or at least to provoke feminist philosophers to think carefully about what our words actually say and do.

To grasp why feminist philosophers of a certain stripe have been attracted to his views, we will of course need to get clear on what specifically Austin, in remarking on philosophers' failure to attend to the way words do things, is accusing his colleagues of overlooking; for he acknowledges early on in *Words* that he has a very specific phenomenon in mind. He concedes that some of his contemporaries had evinced interest, albeit "somewhat indirectly," in certain ways we do things with words, namely the way we use them to *express* our attitudes or to *sway* other people to adopt those attitudes.[6] These philosophers had argued that "'ethical propositions' are perhaps intended, solely or partly, to evince emotion or to prescribe conduct or to influence it in special ways."[7] Here, Austin is alluding to the central tenets of the forms of ethical non-cognitivism most prominent in his day, namely *emotivism*, which holds that our moral utterances, while apparently statements with sense and reference, are in fact devoid of propositional content and instead merely express a speaker's approval or disapproval of one or another view; and *prescriptivism*, which adds to emotivism's main thesis the idea that such utterances also function to exhort the speaker's auditors to follow suit. According to prescriptivism, when I say that euthanasia is wrong, I am not putting forth a proposition about how things are with the world – as I would be if I were to say, e.g., that whether or not euthanasia is morally permissible is a controversial issue. I am merely giving the (emotivist) thumbs-down to euthanasia with the (prescriptivist) intention of getting my audience to follow suit. In *How to Do Things with Words* Austin evinces virtually no explicit interest in the expressive powers of speech – that is to say, the dimension that engages the emotivist. On the other hand, he is directly concerned with the power of speech to sway an audience, the power that engages the prescriptivist, which Austin calls its "perlocutionary" force. And yet Austin's interest in the perlocutionary powers of language is limited For perlocutionary effects – those consequences that I bring about *by* ("per") my locutions – are, he thought, essentially a chance *by-product* of our utterances: depending on the audience and perhaps the time or place or other circumstances, the same utterance might generate very different perlocutions. (I *enrage* you when I say that euthanasia is wrong; but I *inspire* Fred.) Austin was interested not in the way that, at least on his understanding, words *happen* to do things – not, that is, in their perlocutionary force – but in the way they *inherently* do them.[8]

What the philosophers of Austin's day had not noticed, what Austin was trying to highlight, was the extent to which an utterance, delivered under the right circumstances, *in and of itself* constitutes a doing of something with words – regardless of the reactions it produces in its audience. When, for example, I say, "I forgive you," I'm not merely *putting forth a proposition* about the condition of my soul, nor am I merely *expressing* my feelings about what you've done or *trying to get you* to do or think or feel something. I am performing the act of forgiving you. When I promise you I'll meet you at five, I'm not just stating my intentions or expressing my commitment to you or trying to get you to the church on time; I am, literally, giving you my word. When I say, "I christen this ship the *Queen Elizabeth*," I'm not just announcing the name of the ship or expressing my pride in it or trying to impress you; I'm christening the ship. Of course, not just any old utterance of the sentence "I christen this ship the *Queen Elizabeth*" will actually count as the act of christening the ship. Certain conditions need to be in place: I need, for instance, to be the person officially designated to christen the ship, and my utterance must occur at the right time and in the right place, and I need to have a champagne bottle in my hand. Admittedly, some of these conditions are more vital to the success of my act of christening than others. If I am the captain of the ship and smash a bottle of sparkling grape juice against its hull, all may be well; but it certainly won't be if I simply get it into my head to go down to the harbor and undertake to name some random ship. Similarly, if I swear I'll be there at five and yet lack any intention of meeting you, then my act of promising, like my ill-conceived christening venture, will be "infelicitous" or "unhappy," to invoke Austin's terms of art.[9]

A central goal of Austin's in drawing attention to what he calls the "perfor-mative" or, later in his lectures, the "illocutionary" power of speech, its inherent power not just to say but also to do things, is to disrupt philosophers' fixation on the idea that the only philosophically pertinent measure of our utterances is their truth value. Once we evaluate what Austin calls "the total speech act in the total situation" (148), we see that the truth or falsity of an utterance (or, more precisely, the truth or falsity of the facts presupposed, implied, entailed by, or otherwise associated with that utterance) is only one dimension of the utter-ance's success or failure. In addition to involving, first, the issuing of a "locution" with sense and reference, which implies a "truth/falsehood dimen-sion," virtually all utterances will at least aim at the execution of a performative act ("illocution"), which is to be judged according to what Austin calls a "happiness/unhappiness dimension" (148). (An utterance often will also involve, third, the evincing and effecting of states of mind and behavior in ourselves and others; that is, it may have certain "perlocutionary" effects.) Because our utterances constitute speech *acts*, the things we say are not only "heir to [the] kinds of ill which infect all *utterances*" but also "subject to [the] unsatisfactoriness to which all *actions* are subject" (21, my emphases).[10]

Austin's intention in making such observations, as he says quite explicitly at the end of his last lecture, is to produce a "programme" (164) for philosophers, one that must begin with their abandoning certain fixations and tendencies toward oversimplification – "which," he observes, "one might be tempted to call the occupational disease of philosophers if it were not their occupation" (38). At the end of *Words*, in his only example of how this new program might go, he discusses his contemporaries' tendency – quite dominant in the philosophy of the mid-twentieth century – to imagine that moral philosophy must start with a pinning down of the meaning of the word "good." Certain influential philoso-phers had suggested, Austin notes,

> that we use it for expressing approval, for commending, or for grading. But we shall not get really clear about this word "good" and what we use it to do until, ideally, we have a complete list of those illocutionary acts of which commending, grading, &c., are isolated specimens – until we know how many such acts there are and what are their relation-ships and inter-connections.
>
> (163–4)

Here, clearly, Austin is accusing his colleagues of severely undercounting the number of acts that involve the use of the word "good," of succumbing to the occupational temptation to oversimplify things. But how to generate a "complete list"? I suggested above that here is a place that Austin and Wittgenstein are in agreement: both think that finding one's way out of a philosophical dead end requires what Wittgenstein calls "looking and seeing." (A crucial difference here is that Wittgenstein never seems to suggest – at least on my reading of him – that a philosopher can avoid any given dead end once and for all.)

But what does "looking and seeing" involve? Is it empirical work? Well, do I have to *investigate* how we use a word such as "good"? Do I have to leave the proverbial study and concretely observe the way that other people talk? Or am I to stay in my study and proceed abstractly, by way of the logical analysis of concepts? Tellingly, Austin rejected both of these paths. His favorite method for generating his lists of things that words do was to sit around a table with students and colleagues, and float proposals. The authority of the lists generated during these sessions – of, for example, the various categories of illocutions he details at the end of *Words* – was therefore to rest neither on observations of other people talking nor on the inexorability of abstract logical thinking but on Austin's own experience as a user of English words – his own ear – as tested against other people's experience (and ears). In rebuking his fellow philosophers for not knowing how to do things with words, then, Austin was in effect accusing them of avoiding their own experience. This avoidance for Austin amounted to a failure on the part of his colleagues to recognize the locus of their authority as philosophers – that is to say, the authority required to speak in the voice of the universal, to make claims about how things, in general, are. Their commitment to the *idées fixes* that were preventing them from noticing how words do things was also, therefore, blinding philosophers to the ways in which their own words were idling. *How to Do Things with Words* is therefore to be read as a plea for philosophers to pay heed not only to what people in general do with words but also to what they themselves are – or are not – doing with them.

As it turns out, Austin would live to see very little of the response to this plea. He died in 1960, just a few years after he delivered the lectures that constitute *How to Do Things with Words* and before the lectures were published as a book. Given the unlikely places in which appeals to this work have surfaced in the mean time, I suspect that Austin long ago stopped turning over in his grave. Surely he did not anticipate that his lectures would come to preoccupy the likes of Jacques Derrida and the legions of deconstructionist literary theorists captivated by Derrida's views or to provide a centerpiece notion (that of "performativity") for the Foucaultian thinking that has led to the development of university departments of Queer Studies. More controversially, I would like to imagine that Austin might have been, if not surprised, then troubled by the interpretation and appropriation of his work that has gained ascendancy among his fellow analytic philosophers, an inheritance epitomized in the work of John Searle and others who understand themselves to be working on "pragmatics" in the philosophy of language.[11] By now, in any event, one can hardly imagine a use of *How to Do Things with Words* that would be shocking enough to disturb Austin in his eternal slumber. (As he himself says at the end of his BBC lecture on performative utterances, "life and truth and things do tend to be complicated.")[12]

Given the colorful history of the reception of *How to Do Things with Words*, we perhaps ought not be surprised to learn of a movement within analytic feminist philosophy of the last decade whose aim is to show how Austin's work might be deployed to bring pornography out from under the protective wing of free-speech law. The argument is advanced most powerfully and carefully in a number of papers authored by the philosophers Rae Langton and Jennifer Hornsby, who have achieved the (alas) still unusual feat of garnering respect for both their "mainstream" philosophical writing as well as their explicitly feminist work on pornography.[13] Langton and Hornsby start with the fact that in many progressive societies – most notably the United States – the production and use of pornography is protected on the grounds that curtailing its traffic would constitute a violation of a right to free speech.[14] The rationale for this protection turns on the assumption that pornography, like all speech in the legal sense of the term, is (mere) expression: it advances a certain opinion or point of view. But – and here's where Austin comes in – it's a mistake, Langton and Hornsby warn, to assume that a piece of speech is invariably just an expression. What *How to Do Things with Words* shows us is that speech is often *performative* (or "illocutionary"), that it often accomplishes certain things in and of itself, that ordinarily to speak is to *act*. Admittedly, certain conditions must be in place for any speech-act to come off – to be "felicitous" or "happy," in Austin's argot; and the case of pornography is no exception. But if we can specify these conditions and establish the plausibility of the claim that they're in place in contemporary culture, then we can show that pornography does not merely express a certain set of opinions but in fact acts both to *subordinate* women and to *silence* them. And in so far as it inherently and differentially harms women, pornography constitutes a kind of sex discrimination and thus ought at least in principle to be actionable.

My discussion of this argument will focus on two of its features. First, there is a question about whether pornography has the *authority* that Langton and Hornsby claim it must have in order to do what they say it does – for example to subordinate women by ranking them as sex objects.[15] Of course, as Langton and Hornsby readily concede, individuals rank people all the time without materially *subordinating* anyone. For subordination to occur, the issuers of what Austin at the end of his lectures (153–5) calls "verdictive" speech must have the right sort of authority in, of course, the right sort of circumstances. (Indeed, though Austin doesn't quite say so, the power of a verdict will *often* depend heavily on the authority of an utterer.) But it's very difficult to say what sort of "authority" pornography could possess apart from an account of what authority, and especially the kind of authority that's not ceremonially invested in a person or group, is or could be. It's clear enough that the United States Supreme Court has the authority to strike down a law that a majority of its members deem unconstitutional. But it's certainly not obvious what it would mean for pornography or its producers or purveyors or consumers to enjoy authority in a culture at large. We cannot even count on agreement about what pornography *is*, although of course that might just indicate where we need to start in thinking through any question about its authority.

My second concern in this paper will be with an assumption that runs throughout the literature on this subject, namely, the assumption that pornography is speech. To get my worry on the table, let me quote the first paragraph of "Speech acts and unspeakable acts," Langton's most influential article on pornography and Austin:

> Pornography is speech. So the courts declared in judging it protected by the First Amendment. Pornography is a kind of act. So [the well-known feminist legal scholar and anti-porn crusader] Catharine MacKinnon declared in arguing for laws against it. Put these together and we have: pornography is a kind of speech act.
>
> ("Speech Acts," p. 293)

But why *should* we put these two things together? A great deal of pornography is not speech, *except* in the legal sense of the word. Much pornography consists in photographs, still or pixelated, of actual human beings on display before a camera. If we are going to talk about the performative effects of pornography, then, we will need to know something about what Stanley Cavell, following André Bazin, has called the ontology of photography and film.[16] It's of course quite central to what Austin is doing in his lectures that, as the title indicates, he's talking about how to do things with *words*. And this is true even though, as Austin explicitly observes (119), we can achieve both illocutionary and perlocutionary acts non-verbally, as when we throw a tomato in protest (that would be the illocutionary act) and humiliate our speaker (the perlocutionary act). So in drawing attention to the fact that Austin is talking about the phenomenon of human speech, I am not denying that pornography might have both illocutionary and perlocutionary force. Rather, I am wondering *how* photography and film do the things they do. To elide the legal and ordinary senses of "speech" seems to me to occlude this issue from the start.[17] Austin stresses in his lectures that "there cannot be an illocutionary act unless the means employed are conventional" (119). If he is right, then in order to determine what illocutionary act a photograph or film might perform, we need to think about whether these media really are governed by conventions and, if so, what they are. And even if "convention" need not play a role in the performance of every successful illocutionary act, as Hornsby, for one, thinks it need not, we still have an open question about how the media of photography and film play on our sensibilities – how they achieve the effects they achieve, and how we understand the role of the picture taker or director (or purveyor of pornography or consumer of it) in the achievement of these effects.[18] This is to say that the question of authority, or authorship, will be pertinent here as well. I will not make much headway on these issues in this paper. My goal is simply to get them on the table.

Why are Langton, Hornsby, and others as invested as they are in the specific project of using Austin to try to argue that pornography constitutes a form of sex discrimination? An understanding of their motivations will begin to emerge from a brief look at a signal instance in the history of the feminist anti-pornography movement.

In 1984, the city of Indianapolis attempted to enact an ordinance making the traffic in pornography civilly actionable. At the heart of the ordinance, authored for Indianapolis by Catharine MacKinnon and fellow anti-porn activist Andrea Dworkin, was the claim that "pornography is a systematic practice of exploitation and subordination based on sex which differentially harms women."[19] Without much ado, the ordinance was struck down by a district court on the grounds that, in the words in which Circuit Court Judge Easterbrook affirmed the lower court's ruling, "the ordinance regulates speech rather than the conduct involved in making pornography."[20] And of course the regulation of "speech" – or more specifically, of human beings' attempts to express their opinions – is prohibited by the First Amendment to the United States Constitution. But, oddly, Judge Easterbrook at the same time explicitly agreed in this landmark decision, *American Booksellers Association, Inc. et al. vs. Hudnut*, that pornography is in fact a *practice* of exploitation and subordination. How, then, could he justify the idea that it is protected *speech* as opposed to harmful, and therefore actionable, *conduct*?

Perhaps Judge Easterbrook did not fully realize what he was doing in endorsing MacKinnon's understanding of pornography as a kind of practice. Indeed, a lower-court judge accused MacKinnon of lodging her claim that pornography might not just *cause* subordination but actually *be* a kind of subordination via "a certain sleight of hand."[21] The trickery would consist in MacKinnon's failure to flag an equivocation in her implicit characterization of, if you will, the ontological status of pornography. This characterization is expressed in three claims at the beginning of the ordinance, all of which Easterbrook seconds in *Hudnut*:

1 Pornography is a discriminatory practice based on sex which denies women equal opportunities in society.
2 Pornography is central in creating and maintaining sex as a basis for discrimination.
3 Pornography is a systematic practice of exploitation and subordination based on sex which differentially harms women (*In Harm's Way*, p. 439).

Claims one and three both say that pornography is a practice – of discrimination, of exploitation, and of subordination. If these claims are correct, then as a practice pornography is a form of sexism, just as discrimination, exploitation, or subordination on the basis of someone's skin color constitutes a form of racism. Claim two, on the other hand, is a claim not about what pornography is but about what it *causes*: namely, the use of sex "as a basis for discrimination." And, from a legal point of view at least, this looks to be a very different sort of claim, a claim about what a reader of Austin might be tempted to call pornography's perlocutionary effects. For if pornography (merely) causes sex discrimination, then, plausibly, it's (merely) a form of (legal) speech, albeit, perhaps, an extremely powerful one, as Judge Easterbrook – who fails to see any difference in status between claim two and claims one and three – opines:

> We accept the premises of this legislation. Depictions of subordination tend to perpetuate subordination. The subordinate status of women in turn leads to affront and lower pay at work, insult and injury at home, battery and rape on the streets. In the language of the legislature, "pornography is central in creating and maintaining sex as a basis of discrimination. Pornography is a systematic practice of exploitation and subordination based on sex which differentially harms women. The bigotry and contempt it produces, with the acts of aggression it fosters, harm women's opportunities for equality and rights [of all kinds]." (Indianapolis Code §16–1(a)(2).) Yet this simply demonstrates the power of pornography as speech. All of these unhappy effects depend on mental intermediation.
>
> (*Hudnut*, section III)

Though Easterbrook explicitly identifies pornography as a "systematic practice of exploitation and subordination based on sex which differentially harms women," he in the same breath insists that pornography is ultimately to be characterized as "speech," that is, as a phenomenon whose "unhappy effects depend on mental intermediation." In Easterbrook's opinion, pornography, no matter how systematic its discriminatory effects, cannot be said to discriminate against women *in and of itself* and therefore must count, legally at least, as a protected form of expression.

Call this the "liberal" view of pornography. Not only is this liberal view encoded in American law, but it also has been vigorously defended by famous liberal philosophers, including, perhaps most influentially, Thomas Nagel and Ronald Dworkin.[22] The view is sometimes seen as having its roots in the second chapter of John Stuart Mill's *On Liberty*, "Of the liberty of thought and discussion," in which Mill is taken to have argued that what tends in the liberal literature to get called the "free marketplace of ideas" is essential to the flourishing of humanity. Mill's arguments in this chapter are pretty much unabashedly utilitarian: he champions free speech – and thought – on the grounds that encouraging people to think and say what's on their minds is the only way that the ideas most beneficial to humankind – that is to say, the truthful ones – will come to the fore.[23] But in their discussions of pornography, both Nagel and Dworkin are careful not to endorse any utilitarian rationale, since they are of the same mind in judging that the proliferation of pornography is highly unlikely to bring about a better world. Indeed, for the sake of argument, Dworkin assumes that it will bring about a *worse* world. Nonetheless, he, like Nagel, argues that curtailing pornography would violate our *human* (and not just legal) rights.

Dworkin claims that human beings have what he calls a "right to moral independence," the right

> not to suffer disadvantage in the distribution of social goods and opportunities, including disadvantage in the liberties permitted to them by the criminal law, just on the ground that their officials or fellow-citizens think that their opinions about the right way for them to lead their own lives are ignoble or wrong ("Pornography," p. 353).

The legal right to free speech is a guarantor, then, of a *moral* right, if I can put the idea that way, to a certain lack of interference in one's private life. And Nagel argues that anti-pornography activists dangerously conflate the sphere of privacy with the sphere of what he calls "public space" and do so, he speculates (and so does Dworkin ("Pornography," p. 356)), because they find other people's sexual fantasies abhorrent (see Nagel's "Personal rights," pp. 104ff.). Both Nagel and Dworkin suspect that those who would exempt pornography from protection by free-speech laws are motivated by a revulsion for sexual fantasy – their own and others' – which interferes with their ability to acknowledge the line that any decent theory of human rights draws between the private and public spheres.

The liberal stance epitomized in the writings of Nagel and Dworkin is tailor-made to contest the view that the problem with pornography is that it's *indecent* speech, a view that has in fact been codified in US laws allowing communities to restrict public displays of what they deem "obscene."[24] To label pornography "obscene" is to suggest that it offends decent sensibilities to such a degree that curtailing its expression at least on the local level is legally tolerable. Now, according to the liberal view, any right you have not to be offended by what turns me on is going to be dwarfed by my right to privacy (figured, if you like, as what Dworkin calls "moral independence"). But the liberal argument doesn't touch the likes of MacKinnon, at least not on this particular ground. For MacKinnon deplores the idea that what's wrong with pornography is that it's obscene; indeed, she finds this idea as odious as the phenomenon of pornography itself. The "obscenity" claim, according to MacKinnon, both reinforces the view that pornography is a kind of expression, so that its only badness could be its giving of a kind of offense (that is to say, to invoke the Austinian terminology, its having a certain perlocutionary effect), and diverts us from noticing that pornography is a *discriminatory practice that differentially harms women.*[25] It follows from MacKinnon's position that fighting pornography on obscenity grounds is a self-defeating way for feminists to proceed, since the very idea that pornography is obscene reinforces precisely the fundamental liberal claim that feminists ought to contest, namely, that it is at heart merely expressive speech. Even if the obscenity objection were to result in a reduction in the traffic in pornography, its grounds, MacKinnon insists, are intolerable from a feminist point of view.

Like many anti-pornography feminists of a certain stripe, MacKinnon is inclined to endorse instead a strategy that fits with her second claim in the Indianapolis ordinance about pornography's harms, the claim that "pornography is central in creating and maintaining sex as a basis for discrimination." This strategy is to adduce scientific evidence that men's use of pornography *causes* them to harm women in various ways, from viewing them with contempt and disrespect (and thereby, perhaps, not taking them seriously as workers or thinkers or human beings) to, some argue, raping or otherwise physically harming them. The most famous experiments designed to support this point were conducted some years ago by Edward Donnerstein, a psychologist whose work is invoked frequently in the feminist anti-pornography literature. Donnerstein and his colleagues conducted a series of experiments in which they measured men's reactions – both verbal and, as it were, penile – to violent pornographic images. They found an association between men's pornography-related arousal levels and their sensitivity, or lack thereof, to violence against women; and they concluded from this data that some men who consume pornography may be more likely than other men to hurt women.[26] Notoriously, this rather weak conclusion entails a number of controversial assumptions, for example that men's use of pornography must be a *cause* of their desires and attitudes, rather than a symptom of them. Still, a very charitable reading of Donnerstein's conclusions *might* support the view that pornography causes *some* men to harm some women.

But that conclusion is not strong enough to undergird MacKinnon's understanding of pornography as a discriminatory practice that harms women. It is not enough, in particular, to defeat the liberal view of pornography as protected speech. In other words, MacKinnon's second claim, about the harms pornography *causes*, is bound to be trumped by the liberal argument against controlling the traffic in pornography. What needs to be shown, in order for MacKinnon to prevail, is how to make sense of the central idea in claims one and three of the Indianapolis ordinance: the idea that a bunch of magazines, films, books and webpages could constitute, in and of themselves and regardless of what effects they happen to produce, a subordinating and exploitative practice of discrimination against women. This is where Langton and Hornsby enter the picture.

Let us now examine more carefully Langton's argument in support of what I will henceforth call *the subordination claim*, the claim that pornography can be seen as having "the illocutionary form of subordination" ("Speech acts," p. 313). Langton's proposal is that we recognize pornography, in Austinian terms, as (1) *verdictive* speech that "*ranks* women as sex objects" and (2) *exercitive* speech that "legitimates sexual violence" against them ("Speech acts," pp. 307–8).[27]

Verdictives, Austin says, are "judicial acts" as opposed to "executive acts"; they are judgments about how things *are* that are based on *evidence*, rather than opinions about how things *should be* that are based on *preferences*.[28] Two of Austin's examples of verdictives are an umpire's ruling whether a ball is out of bounds and a jury's finding an accused party guilty or innocent – though, as Austin notes, a successful verdictive can be issued in an unofficial context, too; he lists "reckon" and "calculate" as examples. In addition to their force as judgments, Austin observes, "verdictives have obvious connexions with truth and falsity, soundness and unsoundness and fairness and unfairness." For of course "the content of a verdict is true or false": there is a fact of the matter about whether the ball was fair or foul or whether the defendant committed the crime or not. And yet, as Austin explicitly recognizes, verdictives, "as official acts," have the power to "make law" regardless of whether their content is true; hence, their "connexions" with fairness and soundness. "A jury's finding makes a convicted felon" even if the judgment that the accused is guilty is wrong, unfair, and unsound.

In her argument that pornography performs the verdictive act of ranking women as inferior to men, Langton is particularly interested in the implications of Austin's observation that an "official" verdictive can, if I can put the matter this way, substitute a faulty judgment for a fact of the matter – can make it the case that the batter is "out" even if she in fact beat the ball to the bag.[29] Though she does not quite say so explicitly, Langton wants to focus our attention on cases in which the authority of a verdictive-issuing judge is not patent. When it comes to ball games and murder trials, and other such public events, the fact of a verdict's having been issued is obvious and the truth of the verdict's content is therefore subject to debate, at least in principle. But when the power invested in the judge is not ceremonial, the possibility of mistake, unfairness, injustice, or other forms of unhappiness may not be salient. The judgment and the fact of the matter may become hopelessly conflated, in which case the verdictive will have *created* the reality that the judge purports merely to describe. The teacher tells Johnny that he is a failure and so, in his own mind, he becomes one (and, of course, the teacher's judgment may then become a self-fulfilling prophecy). The evangelist declares that homosexuality is an abomination, and so, in the minds of his parishioners, it is. And, under the right circumstances, Langton argues, pornography's ranking of women as inferior to men, as mere sex objects as opposed to genuine human subjects, might be precisely what makes it the case that women are subordinate to men. By "the right circumstances," Langton seems to imply, she means simply that the recipients of the verdictive take the judgment of its issuer to be (1) authoritative, which means, more specifically, that (2) he is regarded as a reliable judge who (3) thereby induces the relevant people to conform to the picture of the world of which the verdict, if I may put it this way, is a snapshot. So in so far as pornography's picture of the way things are is authoritative in this sense, it might actually *construct* women as the second sex.

Langton offers us a very similar story about the second way in which she thinks pornography plausibly subordinates women, namely, by functioning as "exercitive speech that *legitimates* sexual violence."[30] Here is what Austin has to say in *How to Do Things with Words* about exercitives, which, he notes, constitute "a very wide class":

> An exercitive is the giving of a decision in favour of or against a certain course of action, or advocacy of it. It is a decision that something is to be so, as distinct from a judgement that it is so: it is advocacy that it should be so, as opposed to an estimate that it is so; it is an award as opposed to an assessment; it is a sentence as opposed to a verdict.
>
> (p. 155)

In this passage Austin implies, congenially enough for Langton, that an exercitive, when used by an authoritative person under the right circumstances, has the power to make the content of the utterer's judgment a reality. "Annul" is an exercitive verb, as are "veto" and "repeal." Notice that all of these examples (unlike, say, the examples "entreat" or "recommend") are typically associated with formal procedures, and all can be felicitously used only in conjunction with the right kind of authority, ordinarily that of the state. Although Austin does not include Langton's "legitimate" in his examples, it seems to fit the bill: to legitimate some practice, say, does indeed seem to constitute "a decision that something should be so." To my ears, "legitimate," while perhaps not as solidly associated with formal procedures and civil authority as an exercitive like "veto," nonetheless seems to require that the party doing the legitimating cannot just be any old person: she or he must command a certain authority. To legitimate a practice, one must have the power to make that practice come to be, or rather come to be taken as, legitimate. I draw attention to the distinction here only to make explicit the obvious fact that an authority's declaring something to be legitimate does not automatically make it legitimate, in the sense that it would be if it were just or reasonable. Langton of course concurs: indeed, her argument implicitly rests on the claim that the pornographer's legitimation of violence against women is unjust and unreasonable, to say the least. What Langton needs in appealing to the idea that pornography is exercitive speech that legitimates violence against women is only the idea that an authority's legitimating of a practice provides its practitioners with an official, conventionally recognized justification for their action, should they find themselves in need of one.

So much, at least for now, for the two faces of the subordination claim. Let us turn to the second claim advanced by MacKinnon and analyzed separately and in slightly different ways by both Langton and Hornsby: that pornography has the illocutionary force of *silencing* women. The idea is that in addition to legitimating violence against women pornography performs a second exercitive function, that of *depriving* women of the background conditions that must be in place in order for their voices to be heard. Langton calls this silencing "illocutionary disablement."[31] It occurs when someone can utter the words she wishes to utter but is doomed to fail to do what she wishes to do in uttering them. A man says "I do" during a marriage ceremony; but his partner is also a man and so he fails to marry.[32] An actor trying to alert another character on stage to a pretend fire suddenly spots an actual fire in the back of the theater; he yells "fire!" but the audience takes this as more dialogue and so he fails to warn. Linda Lovelace, the star of the notorious *Deep Throat*, writes a book, called *Ordeal*, about her horrendous experiences making the film; but the book is routinely marketed as pornography, and so she fails to protest. A woman wishing to repel the sexual advances of a man says "No!" but, because pornography has made it the case that men hear this "no" as a "yes," she fails to refuse.[33]

Before I discuss this last and, for Langton and Hornsby, most pertinent example in depth, let me draw attention to an important feature of the silencing claim, which is that it does not say that pornography has the *perlocutionary* effect of causing women not to speak – though of course one could argue that, in addition to silencing women in the way Langton and Hornsby think it might, pornography causes women to feel intimidated about uttering the words they are inclined to say. The claim at stake here, though, is that pornography silences women at the level not of their locutions but of their illocutions: it makes it the case that some of the *illocutionary* acts that women attempt to perform are overwhelmingly likely to misfire. Pornography, according to the silencing claim, denies women a reasonable chance of being able to make their auditors understand the force of certain of their utterances and thus to achieve certain acts – notably, the act of refusing sex. It makes it impossible, to put the point in the Austinian terms that Langton finds congenial, for certain of women's utterances to obtain "uptake."[34] Take the case, now, of a woman who wishes to refuse sex with a man. Except under unusual circumstances, she will of course be able to *say* "no" or its equivalent – to *attempt* to refuse the man. However, the argument goes, if the man is conditioned not to recognize the woman's words as an attempt at refusal, then she will be unable to refuse. And it's plausibly the case, according to supporters of the silencing claim, that pornography teaches men that, for example, to cite Hornsby's words, "women who do not behave with especial modesty or dress with especial circumspection are ready and willing to gratify men's sexual urges, but will feign unwillingness, whether through a pretended decency, or through a desire to excite."[35]

More specifically, according to Hornsby, pornography might "create a *presumption* of [a] woman's being insincere."[36] In a discussion of how pornography could be seen to produce women's illocutionary disablement by conditioning men in a certain way, Langton and a co-author, Caroline West, try to understand exactly how the creation of such a presumption might come about. For, certainly, pornography does not proffer a verbal *argument* that when a woman says "no" she is in fact not refusing sex. Indeed, if it were to offer such an argument, we would have more reason to construe it as what the law calls "speech" than we have if it determines men's attitudes by a process of psychological conditioning.[37] To see how this conditioning happens, how certain presumptions get into men's heads, Langton and West ask us to consider a pictorial spread from *Hustler* magazine, the first photograph of which depicts a waitress being pinched by a male pool player "while his companions look on with approval."[38] The captions accompanying the spread reportedly read as follows:

> Though she pretends to ignore them, these men know when they see an easy lay. She is thrown on the felt table, and one manly hand after another probes her private areas. Completely vulnerable, she feels one after another enter her fiercely. As the three violators explode in a shower of climaxes, she comes to a shuddering orgasm.

Here, Langton and West observe, we have a case (a typical case, we might note) in which a woman is not represented as explicitly refusing sex – as saying "no." And yet, they argue, the most natural and obvious way of making sense of what is going on in the pictorial requires that one *presuppose* that

> the female waitress says "no" when she really means "yes"; that, despite her protestations to the contrary, she wanted to be raped and dominated all along; that she was there as an object for the men's sexual gratification; that raping a woman is sexy and erotic for men and women alike.
>
> ("Scorekeeping," p. 311)

Langton and West want the concept *presupposition* here because it allows them to understand the pictorial in terms proposed by David Lewis in his influential paper "Scorekeeping in a language game" (1979).[39] Lewis is interested in the way that certain things we *don't* say routinely come to play an important role in conversation. For example, suppose we are talking about the difficulty of an exam and I remark that "even Jane could pass." Even though I don't *say* that Jane is incompetent, my remark introduces into the conversation the presupposition that Jane is incompetent. According to Lewis conversation tends to be governed by a "rule of accommodation" that allows a presupposition like "Jane is incompetent" to be tacitly introduced and then, as long as no one explicitly challenges it, to exercise an influence over what can and cannot properly be said thereafter. Lewis urges us to think of the tacit introduction of presuppositions into a conversation as a kind of "move" in a rule-governed "language game," a move that changes the "score" of the game. If none of my interlocutors challenges my remark about Jane, then the presupposition that Jane is incompetent is, to quote Langton and West's way of putting the matter, "immediately established as part of the score" of the language game and thereby makes it the case that saying "even Jane could pass" counts as a correct move in that game.[40] Moreover, this change of score may license, for example, the making of jokes at Jane's expense, further disparaging of her talents, and so on (see "Scorekeeping," p. 310). Even more insidiously, Langton and West argue, because presuppositions are often implicit, they are less salient than explicit claims, hence more difficult to challenge, hence more *unlikely* to be challenged than overt attempts to change the conversational score.

With this picture in place, one can understand pornography as implicitly establishing rules in the various "language games of sex" by introducing presuppositions into these games – presuppositions that, because they are tacit, are more likely to go unchallenged than if they were explicit. Because the introduction of these presuppositions by and large in fact goes unchallenged, certain utterances in the language games of sex have come to be seen as counting as correct moves in those games. This is how a pornographic photo spread like the one from *Hustler* has come to change the score of the language games of sex, despite its not making an explicit claim that a woman's "no" should not count as an act of refusal. For by successfully introducing into the conversation, as it were, the tacit presupposition that a woman's "no" does not constitute an act of refusal, *Hustler*, along with other such pornographic speech, has made it the case that the rule "do not take her 'no' as an attempt at the illocutionary act of refusal" comes to govern what does and does not count as a correct response to a woman's "no" – has made it the case that men are, according to the rules of this particular language game, *right* not to take a woman's "no" as an act of refusal.[41] In so far as pornographic speech sets up the rules in the language games of sex in this sort of way, Langton observes, it constitutes a particularly powerful kind of speech, namely, "speech that determines the kind of speech there can be" ("Speech acts," p. 326). And in so far as pornographic speech has this determining power, it will be able to disable women's attempts at refusal, to silence them at the level of their attempted illocutions.

What Langton and West are arguing, then, is that the presuppositions that pornography introduces into our cultural conversation about sex go unchallenged not just because they are insidiously tacit but because pornography has the *authority* to determine, via its own illocutionary acts, what sex is in the culture. Langton is fully aware of the pivotal role that this claim about pornography's authority plays in her arguments. In "Speech acts and unspeakable acts," for example, she writes as follows:

> If pornography sets up the rules in the language games of sex – if pornography is speech that determines the kind of speech there can be – then it is exercitive speech in Austin's sense, for it is in the class of speech that confers and removes rights and powers. We saw that the claim that pornography subordinates requires the premise that pornography is authoritative speech, otherwise it could not rank and legitimate. We can now see that the claim that pornography silences requires the same premise: pornographic speech must be authoritative if it is to engender the silence of illocutionary disablement.
>
> ("Speech acts," p. 326)

The question now becomes: what is the nature of the authority that pornographic speech must enjoy in order to subordinate and silence women?

The answer to this question is not at all obvious. Even if we feel morally certain that pornography is a thoroughly pernicious influence in the culture, we may well have difficulty cashing out this influence in terms of the notion of authority. For since pornography is not *formally* invested with whatever illocutionary power it has, we need to think about exactly how it might possess the authority to subordinate or silence women. This, it is important to me to note, is something that Austin's anti-pornography appropriators do not do. They simply claim that "it may be that pornography has all the authority of a monopoly" for "hearers who ... do seem to learn that violence is sexy and coercion legitimate."[42] My impatience with this claim stems not from a sense of its implausibility or any dearth of evidence – I have no problem with the strategy of putting empirical questions on the back burner – but from its resolute avoidance of the question of what authority might come to in this instance. Ironically, at this crucial juncture in the appropriation of Austin we find a profoundly un-Austinian moment. Austin's procedures are everywhere and always characterized by dogged attention to the terms in which we are inclined to express ourselves, by a sense of the fatefulness of how we count things and how they count for us. If pornography's illocutionary powers rest on its authority, then we cannot hope to understand these powers absent reflection on what we have in mind in recurring to the word "authority."

What form might pornography's authority take? Langton's claim that pornography (plausibly) has the power to legitimate violence against women suggests that perhaps what is at stake is a kind of authorization, a granting of permission to men to hurt women who appear to be refusing sex. (Notice that "authorizing" is a kind of illocutionary act.) Consider a certain type of adolescent boy cruising the Internet who comes upon some explicit photographs of naked men, presented in an explicitly affirmative context. It does seem to me that this boy's sense of relief – or of belonging, or of finding a concept for his longing, or of increased longing – might be construed as something that the site he is gazing at is authorizing. Note that "authorize" in this context would mean that the boy would understand himself to have reason to think that his feelings, of whatever kind, are shared by others and, hence, not inhuman. To put the point in a slightly different way, the boy would perhaps experience the fact of the exis- tence of others like himself as permission to see himself as something other than completely – and disturbingly – sui generis. This feeling of authorization is likely to be even more intense for Internet surfers who have extremely unusual sexual desires. Indeed, there are countless websites devoted to people who are sexually aroused by blowing up balloons (for some, to the point of popping; for others, just before the popping point); by pretending that they have an ampu- tated digit or limb; by expressing physical love for dolphins; by watching people in high heels step on bugs; and by having other people feed them to the point of gross obesity.[43]

But of course it is a very different question whether a website could possibly *justify* our dolphin-lover in his practices. True, a website might provide informa- tion about the formal permissibility in a given domain of sexual encounters with dolphins and so in that way reveal that certain types of human activities with dolphins are or are not (legally) authorized. But could a website give the dolphin-lover reason to construe his behavior and attitudes as authorized in some absolute, context-less sense? "Authorized" here would have to mean some- thing like: absolving the dolphin-lover of responsibility for his fetish. But what or who in a culture has such powers of absolution *überhaupt*, that is to say, apart from the faith that individuals place in it or him or her?

Perhaps, though, these fetish cases are misleading. Perhaps we should be considering pornography that purveys and reinforces conventional discrimina- tory constructions of what it is to be a woman, pornography that portrays women as essentially sex-hungry beings who love penetration in all forms and who live to provoke men to orgasm. The authoritative force of such pornog- raphy, one might argue, comes from the sheer ubiquity of it: when men (and women) live in a conventionally pornographic world, when they are told over and over again that this is what women are like, then they will participate in the subordinating and silencing of women almost involuntarily. Consider the boy who searches the Internet for heterosexual porn and then (I mean subse- quently, not, or not necessarily, consequently) presses sex on his girlfriend. Suppose that the boy has discovered and pored over lots of photographs of men forcing sex on resistant women. In this case, unlike that of the latently gay

young man, we are not inclined to imagine the boy as experiencing an authorization of what he took to be his idiosyncratic desire to deny the humanity of
his girlfriend. But this is because it is hard to imagine that the boy ever felt
alone in conceptualizing women as mere sexual commodities, as bodies that are
there for the taking. Unless one never sees magazine covers or billboards or
watches TV or goes shopping for clothes, one cannot help but learn that huge
numbers of people conceptualize women that way. So the boy who claims to feel
authorized by pornography to conceptualize his girlfriend as a sexual object is
being grossly disingenuous. There is nothing in the case to *be* authorized: the
idea that women are essentially sexual objects for men, along with the idea that
the happiest and most womanly women embrace this status, is ubiquitously
accepted in our culture.

Still, imagine that the boy who assaults his girlfriend attempts to excuse
himself by claiming that he did so because a pornographic website authorized
the act. What are we to say? That, given our society's essentially pornographic
outlook on women, the boy was in fact authorized by the website to assault her?
But then we would have to accept his excuse. What we want to say is that
nothing could authorize what he has done. This is not just because what he has
done is horrific. It's not even just because, at the end of the day, we are loath to
absolve rapists of their crimes on the grounds that our society is insidiously or
even explicitly rape-friendly. It's because no person or institution that is not
formally invested with the authority has such authority apart from individuals'
granting it to them – because we understand human beings of a certain age as
bearing responsibility for the way they see the world. We understand them this
way because we wish to attribute to them the power to think for themselves –
the power, that is, to be philosophical in the best sense of the word. (Not coin-
cidentally, this understanding of what it is to be philosophical is, I take it,
Austin's understanding; to do philosophy, for Austin, was to investigate what it
is to be a human being not by conducting empirical research but by reflecting
on what one's experience reveals as, for example, the difference between a
mistake and an accident.)[44]

But perhaps I am exploring the wrong sense of authority. There is also the
sense to which we appeal when we speak of authoritative editions of texts. But
to call a text authoritative is simply to make a claim that this particular edition
is more tightly connected with its *author* than any other. If one were to challenge the text's authority, a defender of it would tell a story that would end at
the author's doorstep. The story might be fallacious or mendacious, needless to
say; but the basis of the claim to authority would be clear. Consider now our use
of the term "authority" to refer to an expert in a certain field. To call someone
an authority in this sense is to claim that the person's views are, or ought to be,
influential. And it's at least plausible that pornography might be authoritative
in this sense: it might have a very strong, even exclusive power to shape certain
of people's beliefs and attitudes about the world and particularly about how we
should construe sex difference.

But I doubt that this sense of "authority" can at the end of the day do the work that Langton *et al.* need it to do. What they need is a conception of authority on which pornographers can be seen to enjoy exclusive power to *fix* the conventional signification of pornographic images and words – or, if you like, the rules in the language games of sex. But the power to fix conventions is a far stronger sort of power than the power, however great, to influence people's beliefs and attitudes. And it's not at all clear that any authority could possess the stronger sort of power, at least when we're talking about an entire culture's ways of understanding the conventional signification of some phenomenon. For the fixing of conventional signification rests, as David Lewis in his work on convention suggests, not (or not simply) on what some authority *ordains* it to be but on what those who abide by the convention *recognize and accept* it to be.[45] This means that the conventional signification of a piece of pornography – if indeed pornography has conventional signification – will be a matter not of the pornographer's authority to fix it but of consumers' acquiescence to the pornographer's point of view. In so far as pornography's authority consists in its power to get us to acquiesce to the way it sees the world, its effects are not conventional, not what Austin might call illocutionary, but rather, if anything, perlocutionary. One might be tempted to think that pornography virtually inevitably *makes* people see the world in a certain way. But even that is simply to say that it has a certain very strong perlocutionary force. The question then becomes: why?

The answer to this question surely has something to do with our culture's persistent misogyny, not to mention racism, homophobia, and other sorts of entrenched prejudices, hates, and fears. But it also seems to me that Langton *et al.* have grossly under-described the way that pornography plays on human sensibilities. That pornography can be and no doubt frequently is influential in a pernicious, sexist way seems to be obviously true. But it is equally obvious that pornography meets the needs and desires of a huge number of people, both men and women; and the idea that it alone has manufactured these needs and desires is as implausible as the idea that the invention of the telephone has manufactured our needs and desires to talk to people who are not within shouting distance. This is not to suggest that the invention of the telephone has manufactured *no* new needs, nor is it to contradict the obvious fact that it has transformed certain old ones. Marx famously says that there is no such thing as a raw human need, that all needs take a culturally specific form.[46] And in *Civilization and Its Discontents*, Freud observes that apparent advances in civilization – and he singles out various technological developments, including the invention of the telephone – seem actually to have deepened human misery. But Marx does not suggest that we have no inherent human needs, and it is one of Freud's goals in *Civilization and Its Discontents* to show that the new needs are permutations of the old. If the invention and proliferation of the telephone (and perhaps even more dramatically the cellular phone and the Internet) means that some of us can now bear to live farther away from our loved ones than we once might have, it does not mean that we never before longed to hear the voices of or see those loved ones when they or we did have to leave home. And if the invention and proliferation of video technology means that some of us can now meet our sexual needs and desires more conveniently and more privately than we once might have, it does not mean that we never before longed for the various satisfactions that are peculiarly sexual (which is to leave open the question of the dimensions and terrain of the field of such satisfactions).

As the feminist film theorist Linda Williams notes in *Hard Core*, the pornographic use of film has been with us since the invention of the moving picture. The first man to achieve the taking of photographs in fast enough succession to produce a primitive film, Eadweard Muybridge, produced hundreds upon thousands of sequences of naked men and women engaging in various activities. And the so-called "stag film," the crude, ordinarily black-and-white, ordinarily narratively sloppy films made for viewing in a booth in a sex shop or at a bachelor party, can trace its origins to the earliest period of film history. These facts alone cannot of course prove the claim that pornographic film meets certain human needs. But we get closer to a proof if we consider what Stanley Cavell says, in *The World Viewed*, about the power of the medium of film to present us the human body as something that is "*dressed* . . . hence potentially undressed."[47] It follows that when we see a desirable human being in a film – potentially *any* human being in *any* film, Cavell implies – we are "looking for a reason" for this human being's clothes to come off.[48] Cavell continues,

> When to this we join our ontological status – invisibility – it is inevitable that we should expect to find a reason, to be around when a reason and occasion present themselves, no matter how consistently our expectancy is frustrated. The ontological conditions of the motion picture reveal it as inherently pornographic (though not inveterately so).
>
> (p. 45)

The implication here is that the desire to see another human being naked is something that film is prone to *adduce*, not to create. Again, this is to leave open the possibility that in its adducing of desire, a particular film may reveal it for the first time or transform it or make it stronger or show it to be in competition with a set of moral rules to which I thought I was eternally committed. Indeed, it seems to me that unless you are open to the idea that pornography has these particular powers, you will misunderstand whatever illocutionary force it has.

Even if I'm wrong about pornography's powers, I still want to claim that Langton *et al.* are pressing what I was calling the liberal argument in favor of not curtailing the traffic in pornography in the wrong place. The reason these thinkers are so invested in the idea that pornography's force is *illocutionary* is that if pornography is *merely* a kind of expression, then by definition it's protected speech. But I want to insist – and here I once again follow Stanley Cavell, this time in a recent paper of his called "Passionate and performative utterances"[49] – upon the obvious fact, one that even Austin underplays, that expression has the power to wound, a power that is certainly much stronger, precisely *because* it's less conventional, than the analogous power to do things manifested by the illocution.

Take the expression "I'm bored," Cavell suggests. If it needs saying, "it may also be obvious, perhaps should be obvious, without saying; then saying it would place a demand that I may be unwilling or unable to face, a demand that you acknowledge the obvious." And now take the case of a woman's "No!" to a man's sexual advances. It seems to me that the same analysis applies. What forces the woman's silence is not the authority of pornography, but the man's failure (which can take more than one form) to acknowledge the obvious. Can we imagine an instance in which the *only* way a woman is attempting to refuse a predatory man is by saying "no" (simply, flatly, with no note of desperation in her voice, with no accompanying body language)? The scandal is not, or not merely, that the man has heard her "no" as a "yes," if indeed he has; it's that he no longer reads anything she does in anything resembling conventional human terms. He no longer treats her as a human being. The woman's "no" strikes me as a desperate, and, in Cavell's sense, desperately passionate, utterance. Her failure to stop the man is a product not of the fact that the felicity conditions for the success of her illocution are not in place, but the fact that there is not a human exchange going on here: the perlocutionary failure of the woman's utterance is, given this man's intentions, foreordained. Is it plausible to suggest that what has gone wrong is *only* that the man has been taught by pornography to ignore the woman's humanity, that pornography is the necessary and sufficient goad to his brutishness and brutality? The answer to that question must depend in part on what pornography is.

But we will not arrive at a meaningful understanding of pornography if we ignore the passionate *power* of expression, which means in this context its ability to take us into a no man's land of hurt and pain. The courts are wrong to conceptualize expression as inherently *neutral*, to take its lack of conventionality to mean that its utterers are not responsible for its perlocutionary effects. When an utterance has caused pain, it will be absolutely necessary for us – I mean, for anyone interested in what has happened, including the people directly involved – to make judgments about who is responsible for which effects. When we are in the domain of the perlocutionary we cannot rely on convention to sort out the question of responsibility. (I leave it to others to judge whether and how this observation might bear on any attempt to ask the courts to regulate pornography.)

All of this leaves unaddressed the question of whether pornography *is* a kind of expressive speech. This question might be unproblematic when it comes to pornographic *words*. But even if we can decide such a question fairly straightfor-wardly, we're left with the question of the nature of pornographic photographs and films. Here, I think, what is required is an understanding of the mysterious erotic power of photographs of human beings. Developing such an under-standing is a project for another paper, one that, I think, might start by juxtaposing Cavell's writings on photography with those of Linda Williams on pornographic film. In *The World Viewed*, Cavell suggests that photography, as a medium, in so far as it has satisfied a human wish, has satisfied a wish peculiar to the modern world, a wish vividly expressed in Descartes' *Meditations*, for an escape from what he calls "metaphysical isolation" (p. 21). It satisfies this wish, he says, "by *automatism*, by removing the human agent from the task of repro-duction" and thus by maintaining "the presentness of the world by accepting our absence from it" (p. 23). In *Hard Core*, Linda Williams suggests that what is sought in pornographic film is a confirmation of the existence of the woman's orgasm, which would mean of her sexuality, which in turn, I take it, would mean of the legitimacy of the man's sexual desire for her.[50] Cavell writes, "A photograph does not present us with 'likenesses' of things; it presents us, we want to say, with the things themselves" (*World Viewed*, p. 17). Whether we can or will say this – that is to say, will rest content with this way of expressing our intuitions – is another matter. And Williams claims that the pornographic film "obsessively seeks knowledge through a voyeuristic record of confessional, involuntary paroxysm, of the 'thing' itself" (*Hard Core*, p. 49).

What is the relationship between the quest for knowledge of the thing itself, or things in themselves, and human sexual desire? What sort of epistemological wish, if any, is involved in the desire to gaze at pornographic photographs and films? Whatever answer one might be inclined to propose, it is clear that this wish cannot be identified or accounted for simply by the idea that pornography is a kind of speech. One wants to ask: who is doing the speaking? The subjects of the photographs? (And are they subjects or objects, or both?) The pornogra-phers? And what exactly is being said? And to whom? And why are people so aroused by looking at *photographs* and *films* of other people's naked bodies and their sexually explicit activity?

There is work to be done here. What surprises me is that none of the people on either side of the pornography debates appears to be interested in doing it. (Linda Williams's work, and the work that has followed in the wake of it, constitutes something of an exception, although without asking important ques-tions about what photography is and what film is, and so without aspiring to get to the heart of the matter.) Perhaps this is because what is required would be an honest accounting of our investments, both positive and negative, in the phenomenon of pornography, which might entail looking at a lot of pornog-raphy, if one hasn't already, and looking differently at a lot of pornography, if one has. Austin's work reminds us philosophers that it is possible to look at something very familiar – ordinary words, in his case – in a new way, one that shows the perversity of our history of imagining that words bespeak themselves

91

and stolidly wear their truth conditions (and nothing else) on their proverbial sleeves. The example Austin sets gives us reason to imagine that we will feel at least as much exhilaration as despair or shame when we recognize the depth of our own implication in what our words – and, I am suggesting, our pictures – say and do.[51]

Notes

1   For me, a second reason for beginning this paper, for this Festschrift, with a discussion of *How to Do Things with Words* is equally important: the fatefulness of Austin's lectures for Stanley Cavell. A 1985 interview of Cavell by James Conant begins with Cavell's articulation of this fatefulness:

> In 1948, I found myself in Los Angeles and enrolled as a special student at UCLA. Its philosophy department was very fine, had lots of different kinds of people in it, very sympathetic people. But I couldn't for a long time tell whether I thought this was the beginning of something which down the road would become what I wanted to spend my life at. This doubt moved with me when I moved to Harvard three years later to continue graduate studies, and indeed though I was rewarded at the subject of philosophy, and there were moments in which I was exhilarated, what I was doing was still not the thing that somehow in my mind I thought there must be for me. What that might be did not get answered distinctly until J.L. Austin appeared at Harvard to give the William James Lectures in 1955 and to offer seminars in other of his interests. Then I had the experience of knowing what I was put on earth to do. I felt that anything I did from then on, call it anything you want to, call it philosophy, will be affected by my experience of dealing with this material. It is not necessarily that in Austin I found a better philosopher than my other teachers had been, but that in responding to him I found the beginning of my own intellectual voice. (James Conant, "An interview with Stanley Cavell," *The Senses of Stanley Cavell*, eds Richard Fleming and Michael Payne (Lewisburg, PA: Bucknell University Press, 1989), pp. 35–6)

Were I confident that I had found the beginning of my own intellectual voice, I would be inclined to characterize my first encounter with Stanley Cavell – which also dates to 1985 – in the terms in which he describes his indebtedness to Austin. A difference might be this: among the splendid teachers I have had, none has been a better philosopher than Cavell. One way to put the aim of the present paper – indeed, of all of my philosophical writing – is this: I'm trying to transplant what I've learned, and continue to learn, from Cavell into my own philosophical garden. (The metaphor is appropriated from Simone de Beauvoir, who herself is appropriating the image from Voltaire, when she suggests at the beginning of *Pyrrhus et Cinéas* (Paris: Gallimard, 1944) that overcoming skepticism about philosophy's powers to transform a life requires not only a willingness to find one's own garden but also, first, imagining that there's one out there to be found.)

2   See Stanley Cavell's account of Austin's delight in this particular instance of wordplay in "Austin at criticism," *Must We Mean What We Say?* 2nd edn (New York: Cambridge University Press, 2002), pp. 97–114.

3   In a monograph-length version of the present paper, which is also called *How to Do Things With Pornography* and which I am presently completing, I defend this reading of Austin in much more detail.

4   Here I have in mind work in pragmatics by some of its most influential practitioners: John Searle, Kent Bach, François Recanati, and Charles Travis.

5   I borrow the metaphor from Austin's discussion of his philosophical method in "A plea for excuses," in which he notes that

> we should prefer a field which is not too much trodden into bogs or tracks by traditional philosophy, for in that case even "ordinary" language will often have become infected with the jargon of extinct theories, and our own prejudices too, as the upholders or imbibers of theoretical views, will be too readily, and often insensibly, engaged.... Granted that our subject is ... neighbouring, analogous or germane in some way to some notorious centre of philosophical trouble, then ... we should be certain of what we are after: a good site for *field work* in philosophy. Here at last we should be able to unfreeze, to loosen up and get going on agreeing about discoveries, however small, and on agreeing about how to reach agreement. (*Philosophical Papers*, 3rd edn (Oxford: Clarendon Press, 1979), pp. 182–3)

6   *How to Do Things with Words*, eds J.O. Urmson and Marina Sbisá, 2nd edn (Cambridge, MA: Harvard University Press, 1975), p. 2.

7   *Words*, pp. 2–3. Let me note that it is not at all clear that Austin is here *endorsing* a form of ethical non-cognitivism. Indeed, it seems clear that he is dubious about the doctrine. Two pieces of indirect evidence here. First, the paragraph in which the sentence I've just quoted is embedded takes digs at various fashions in the philosophy of Austin's day no fewer than five times. The context of the remark about "ethical propositions" is this: Austin first notes the development of the view that certain statements – those that are not "verifiable" (his scare quotes) – are in fact pseudo-statements and then notes a "second stage" in this development, in which pseudo-statements are reconceived as utterances that were never intended to be stating things in the first place. "Ethical propositions" exemplify – "perhaps" – such (non-) pseudo-statements. Second, on pp. 19–20, when Austin is in the middle of his discussion of the "infelicities" to which all attempts to act, via words or otherwise, are subject, he says this:

> A great many of the acts which fall within the province of Ethics are *not*, as philosophers are too prone to assume, simply in the last resort *physical movements*: very many of them have the general character, in whole or part, of conventional or ritual acts, and are therefore, among other things, exposed to infelicity.

If you put this together with what Austin says in the sentence to which this note is attached, you see how much of a stretch it is to imagine that he is agreeing with non-cognitivists that "ethical propositions" are intended as prescriptivists say they are. His view, rather, seems to be that ethics is about acts, verbal or otherwise; and therefore the question of whether "ethical propositions" are genuine propositions does not arise. (See also this passage, in the paragraph after the "province of Ethics" sentence: "The more we consider a statement not as a sentence (or proposition) but as an act of speech (out of which the others are logical constructions) the more we are studying the whole thing as an act" (20).)

8   In a recent, essay on *How to Do Things with Words* ("Performative and Passionate Utterance"), Cavell has forcefully suggested that Austin's characterization of the perlocutionary powers of speech leaves much to be desired. Cavell puts pressure both on Austin's lack of interest in the expressive powers of speech and on his insinuation that the relationship between a given stretch of speech and the perlocution it achieves is essentially arbitrary. This essay is published in Cavell, *Philosophy the Day After Tomorrow*, Cambridge, MA: Harvard University Press, 2005.

9 For the record: there are important distinctions between the sorts of infelicity that we find in these two cases. In the christening case, Austin observes, we will say that the ship was not christened – that, because I am not authorized to christen your ship, the procedure does not come off, that it "misfires." But my insincerity in swearing that I'll be there at five does not nullify my promise, though what I've done constitutes an "abuse" of the procedure and renders my act of promising "hollow" or "void."

10 Jennifer Hornsby, in a series of papers on the role of illocution in a theory of language (cited in note 13 below), especially one sensitive to the moral and political dimensions of linguistic communication, argues that Austin's characterization of illocution suffers from his failure to distinguish carefully between the concept of an "action" and that of an "act." In particular, she thinks, Austin's sloppiness here made it impossible for him to draw a principled line between illocution and perlocution. Later in the present paper, my disagreement with Hornsby's reading of Austin will occasionally become explicit. In *How to Do Things with Pornography*, I go into much greater detail about my concerns with the way that Hornsby and other philosophers of language have understood the ramifications of Austin's views.

11 This claim of course needs fleshing out. What I have in mind is the way that Searle and certain other "speech-act theorists" (e.g. Kent Bach and François Recanati) embrace the standard division of labor in contemporary philosophy of language according to the categories of syntax, semantics, and pragmatics. On my view, Austin's work constitutes a radical challenge to the enterprise of making sweeping claims about how our use of words works and thus to the very idea of "philosophy of language," at least as it is currently construed. For a start on a defense of this claim, see my *How to Do Things with Pornography*.

12 *Philosophical Papers*, 3rd edn (Oxford: Oxford University Press, 1990), p. 239.

13 Langton has written a book on Kant and has published numerous papers in moral and political philosophy and metaphysics. Hornsby is a well-known philosopher of mind and language. Langton and Hornsby have developed very similar, though not completely identical, appropriations of Austin in service of arguing for the coherence of the idea that pornography doesn't just *say* things but also inherently *harms* women. Their many papers on this topic include the following: Rae Langton, "Speech acts and unspeakable acts," *Philosophy and Public Affairs* 22(4) (autumn 1993): 293–330; Langton, "Sexual solipsism," *Philosophical Topics* 23(2) (fall 1995): 149–87; Langton and Hornsby, "Free speech and illocution," *Legal Theory* 4 (1998): 21–37; Langton, "Subordination, silence, and pornography's authority," *Censorship and Silencing: Practices of Cultural Regulation*, ed. Robert Post (Los Angeles: Getty Museum Publishing, 1998); Langton and Caroline West, "Scorekeeping in a pornographic language game," *Australasian Journal of Philosophy* 77(3) (September 1999): 303–19; Hornsby, "Things done with words," in *Human Agency: Language, Duty, and Value*, eds Jonathan Dancy, J.M.E. Moravcski, and C. Taylor (Stanford: Stanford University Press, 1988); Hornsby, "Speech acts and pornography," *Women's Philosophical Review*, November 1993, reprinted in an amended version in *The Problem of Pornography*, ed. Susan Dwyer (Florence, KY: Wadsworth, 1995); Hornsby, "Illocution and its significance," *Foundations of Speech Act Theory*, ed. Savas L. Tsohatzidis (New York: Routledge, 1994); Hornsby, "Disempowered speech," *Philosophical Topics* 23(2) (fall 1995): 127–47; and Hornsby, "Free and equal speech," *Imprints* 1(2) (1996): 59–76.

14 As Hornsby notes, the right to "free speech" is notably more sacrosanct in the United States – where it is constitutionally protected – than it is in other democracies (where it is not). See e.g. Hornsby's "Free and equal speech," pp. 59–60.

15 See "Speech acts," pp. 307–8.

16 See Cavell's *The World Viewed* (Cambridge, MA: Harvard University Press, 1979), chapter 2, and Bazin's "The ontology of the photographic image" in his *What Is Cinema?*, vol. 1 (Berkeley: University of California Press, 1967), pp. 9–16.

17 In the context of arguing that we need the techniques of analytic philosophy or language if we are to understand properly what the word "speech" means in the concept "free speech," Hornsby acknowledges that "most pornographic material is not linguistic" and that some people "move, without any argument, between 'speech' in a narrow sense (confined to the linguistic) and 'speech' in the broadest sense (including all 'expression')." But, as an analytic philosopher of language, she is not interested in thinking about how non-linguistic pornography does whatever it does. See "Free and equal speech," p. 62.

18 On Hornsby's view, Austin's claim about the importance of convention to illocution was rash; it stemmed, she thinks, from his paying too much attention to highly ritualized illocutions, such as marrying, christening ships, baptizing, and so on. Hornsby argues that in many cases a sufficient condition for the success of a person's illocution is simply that her utterer grasps that she is attempting to perform it. For example, if you understand me to be trying to tell you something, then I will have successfully performed the illocution of *telling*. See Hornsby, "Illocution and its significance."

19 Catharine A. MacKinnon and Andrea Dworkin, *In Harm's Way: The Pornography Civil Rights Hearings* (Cambridge, MA: Harvard University Press, 1998), p. 439.

20 United States Court of Appeals, Seventh Circuit, *American Booksellers v. Hudnut*, 771 F.2d 323 (1985), section I.

21 This accusation, from *American Booksellers v. Hudnut*, 598 F. Supp. 1316, 1334 (S.D. Ind. 1984), is quoted in Langton, "Speech acts," p. 294.

22 See, e.g., Nagel, "Personal rights and public space," *Philosophy and Public Affairs* 24(2) (spring 1995): 83–107; Dworkin, "Do we have a right to pornography?" *A Matter of Principle* (Cambridge, MA: Harvard University Press, 1985), pp. 335–72; Dworkin, "Liberty and pornography," *The New York Review of Books* 38(14) (15 August 1991); Dworkin, "Women and pornography" (a review of Catharine MacKinnon's *Only Words*), *The New York Review of Books* 40(17) (21 October 1993); and Dworkin (in an exchange with Catharine MacKinnon in the wake of his review of her book), "Women and pornography," *The New York Review of Books* 41(5) (3 March 1994).

23 Hornsby and Langton see a certain irony in liberals' understanding their view as grounded in Mill's, for they read Mill in his famous chapter on the liberty of thought and expression to be championing not just the freedom to think and say what one wishes but, more essentially, the freedom to *do* things with one's words – what they call "freedom of illocution." For reasons that will, I hope, become clearer as this paper progresses, I have doubts about whether this notion is coherent. I discuss these doubts at some length in *How to Do Things with Pornography*.

24 A landmark obscenity case, which defines "obscenity" in terms of what would offend "the average person" with respect to "community standards," is *Miller v. California*, 413 U.S. 15, 24 (1973).

25 See, e.g., MacKinnon, "Equality and speech," *Only Words* (Cambridge, MA: Harvard University Press, 1993). See also her essay "Not a moral issue," *Feminism Unmodified* (Cambridge, MA: Harvard University Press, 1988), pp. 162–4, and her letter to the editor of *The New York Review of Books* in response to Ronald Dworkin's review of *Only Words*, in "Pornography: an exchange," *NYRB* 41(5) (3 March 1994).

26 See, e.g., Edward I. Donnerstein, Daniel Linz, and Steven Penrod, *The Question of Pornography: Research Findings and Policy* (New York: Free Press, 1987).

27 Austin introduces the category of "verdictives" on pp. 153–5 of *Words*. Until further notice, all of the quotations from Austin are from this section of the book.

28 The latter type of illocutions are "exercitives," which I discuss directly later.

29 See pp. 267–70 of Langton's "Subordination, silence, and pornography's authority," referenced in note 13 above.

30 Langton, "Speech acts and unspeakable acts," referenced in note 13 above, pp. 307–8; my emphasis.

31 See "Speech acts," pp. 315ff.

32 Happily, given recent judicial rulings in, e.g., my home state of Massachusetts, there is reason to hope that this example will become archaic in the foreseeable future.

33 Langton considers all of these examples in some depth in "Speech acts." See pp. 316–17 for her discussion of the first two examples and pp. 320–2 for her treatment of the second two.

34 For various reasons that are not relevant here, Hornsby, in her somewhat different treatment of illocutionary silencing, prefers to think of illocutionary silencing as involving not a failure of "uptake," *per se*, but of what she calls "receptivity." Hornsby discusses the reasons for her way of understanding what's at the crux of illocutionary success in all of her writings on this subject (see note 13 above for a list). See especially "Illocution and its significance."

35 "Illocution and its significance," p. 206, n. 28.

36 "Illocution and its significance," p. 199.

37 For the idea that pornography "works by a process of psychological conditioning," see Langton and West's "Scorekeeping in a pornographic language game," cited in note 13 above, p. 303.

38 The *Hustler* spread is discussed in "Scorekeeping in a pornographic language game," p. 311. Langton and West thank Catherine Itzin for drawing their attention to this example, which appears on p. 30 of *Pornography: Women, Violence, and Civil Liberties*, edited by Itzin (Oxford: Oxford University Press, 1993). The *Hustler* spread apparently is from the January 1983 issue; I have been unable to obtain a copy of it.

39 David Lewis, "Scorekeeping in a language game," *Journal of Philosophical Logic* 8 (1979): 339–59, reprinted in Lewis's *Philosophical Papers*, vol. I (Oxford: Oxford University Press, 1983), pp. 233–49.

40 The Jane example is from Langton and West's "Scorekeeping," pp. 309–10. I can only briefly note here what I regard as the irony of Langton's decision to help herself to *Lewis's* notion of a language game, rather than that of Wittgenstein, from whom Lewis appropriates the term. Lewis's goal is to unearth a certain deep structure he presumes governs human conversation, one, specifically, that allows the presuppositions with which interlocutors are operating to be introduced in a tacit but conventional way. The idea that in our talk we rely on a species of attunement with one another is important to Wittgenstein. But his work contests the notion that this attunement is a kind of *convention*. Unlike Wittgenstein, Lewis is not inclined to wonder whether our linguistic attunement with one another is deeper or more complicated than the notion of "convention" implies. I have come to appreciate the idea that we ought to wonder about this, and that developing the notion of attunement requires a kind of Gestalt shift for those who describe human conversation as resting on "agreement" or convention, from Stanley Cavell. See Cavell's sustained discussion of Kripke's (mis)characterization of Wittgenstein's views on conversational attunement in "The argument of the ordinary," *Conditions Handsome and Unhandsome* (Chicago: University of Chicago Press, 1990), pp. 64–100.

41 Langton and West do not have much to say about exactly what constitutes a "language game of sex." One gets the sense that by this concept they intend to include all attempts at illocutionary acts that have to do with sexual matters. This would mean that a woman's unspoken attempt at a refusal of sex – her look of horror or revulsion, say – would count as part of such a language game, albeit one in which the woman's attempt to pull off the illocutionary act of refusal does not count as a

correct move in the game, given the presuppositions that pornographic materials have introduced into it without challenge. In my book *How to Do Things with Pornography*, I worry more about whether thinking about the way that pornography has an influence on the culture is helped along by the notion of "language games of sex." See note 40 above for an indication of the direction in which my worries run.

42 Langton, "Speech acts and unspeakable acts," p. 312.
43 For examples, see: www.deviantdesires.com, www.overground.be, www.dophinsex.org, www.theagitator.com/archives/004764.php,and also www.dimensionsmagazine.com /Weight_Room/anonymous.html.
44 See Austin's "A plea for excuses," *Proceedings of the Aristotelian Society* 57 (1957), p. 11. The paper is reprinted in Austin's *Philosophical Papers*, 3rd edn (New York: Oxford University Press, 1980), pp. 175–204.
45 The Lewisian *locus classicus* here is *Convention: A Philosophical Study* (Cambridge, MA: Harvard University Press, 1969). I could take a different tack in worrying about the relationship between authority and convention. But I am here referring to Lewis's views since Langton apparently takes Lewis to be authoritative himself with respect to the issue of authority.
46 See, e.g., Marx's *Economic and Philosophical Manuscripts of 1844–1845*, *The Marx–Engels Reader*, ed. Robert C. Tucker, 2nd edn (New York: Norton, 1978), pp. 66–125.
47 Cavell, *The World Viewed*, enlarged edn (Cambridge, MA: Harvard University Press, 1979), p. 44.
48 Unlike certain film theorists, Cavell is not suggesting that film-watchers (contemporary human beings, that is) are inherently voyeuristic, though that may be so. Rather, he is fleshing out a set of claims about film's power as a medium to transfigure the human body.
49 See note 8.
50 Linda Williams, *Hard Core: Power, Pleasure and the "Frenzy of the Visible"* (Berkeley: University of California Press, 1999).
51 I owe my interest in this subject to Sally Haslanger, who invited me to participate in a panel discussion of Langton and Hornsby's work at MIT in January 2000. I have presented the views in this paper at a conference on Austin in Amiens, France, in March 2001; at Harvard University in April 2001; at the Pacific Division meetings of the American Philosophical Association in Seattle in March 2002; and the conference honoring Stanley Cavell organized by Sanford Shieh at Wesleyan in May 2002. I thank the audiences at these events for helpful questions and suggestions. I have also benefited from discussions of this material with Stanley Cavell, Alice Crary, Michael Glanzberg, Kathrin Koslicki, Mark Richard, participants in a seminar on pornography and hate speech I gave at Tufts in the spring of 2001, and members of the Boston-area Workshop on Gender and Philosophy, especially Ishani Maitra and Mary Kate McGowan.

5

THE DIFFICULTY OF REALITY AND THE DIFFICULTY OF PHILOSOPHY

Cora Diamond

I am concerned in this paper with a range of phenomena, which, in the first four sections of the paper, I shall suggest by some examples. In the last three sections, I try to connect the topic thus indicated with the thought of Stanley Cavell.

1 A single exposure

First example: a poem of Ted Hughes's, from the mid-1950s, called "Six young men." The speaker in the poem looks at a photo of six smiling young men, seated in a familiar spot. He knows the bank covered with bilberries, the tree and the old wall in the photo; the six men in the picture would have heard the valley below them sounding with rushing water, just as it still does. Four decades have faded the photo; it came from 1914. The men are profoundly, fully alive, one bashfully lowering his eyes, one chewing a piece of grass, one "is ridiculous with cocky pride." Within six months of the picture having been taken, all six were dead. In the photograph, then, there can also be thought the death of these men: the worst "flash and rending" of war falling onto these smiles now forty years rotted and gone.

Here is the last stanza:

That man's not more alive whom you confront
And shake by the hand, see hale, hear speak loud,
Than any of these six celluloid smiles are,
Nor prehistoric or fabulous beast more dead;
No thought so vivid as their smoking blood:
To regard this photograph might well dement,
Such contradictory permanent horrors here
Smile from the single exposure and shoulder out
One's own body from its instant and heat.

What interests me there is the experience of the mind's not being able to encompass something that it encounters. It is capable of making one go mad to

98

try, to bring together in thought what cannot be thought: the impossibility of anyone being more alive than these smiling men, nothing being more dead. (No one is more alive than is the person looking at the photo; no one is more alive than you are, reading the poem. In section 6, I turn back to the 'contradictory permanent horrors' of the imagination of death.)

Now it's plainly possible to describe the photo so it does not seem boggling at all. It is a photo of men who died young, not long after the picture was taken. Where is the contradiction? – Taking the picture that way, there is no problem about our concepts being adequate to describe it. Again, one might think of how one would teach a child who had been shown a photo and told it was a photo of her grandfather, whom she knows to be dead. If she asks "Why is he smiling if he's dead?" she might be told that he was smiling when the picture was taken, because he was not dead then, and that he died later. The child is being taught the language-game, being shown how her problem disappears as she comes to see how things are spoken of in the game. The point of view from which she sees a problem is not yet in the game; while that from which the horrible contradiction impresses itself on the poet-speaker is that of someone who can no longer speak within the game. Language is shouldered out from the game, as the body from its instant and heat.

What Hughes gives us is a case of what I want to call the difficulty of reality. That is a phrase of John Updike's,[1] which I want to pick up for the phenomena with which I am concerned, experiences in which we take something in reality to be resistant to our thinking it, or possibly to be painful in its inexplicability, difficult in that way, or perhaps awesome and astonishing in its inexplicability. *We take things so.* And the things we take so may simply not, to others, present the kind of difficulty, of being hard or impossible or agonizing to get one's mind round.

2 A wounded animal

Few of us are not in some way infirm, or even diseased; and our very infirmities help us unexpectedly.
(William James, The Varieties of Religious Experience)

Second example: the example is complex – part of it is the set of lectures delivered by the South African novelist J.M. Coetzee as his Tanner Lectures. These lectures were published under the title *The Lives of Animals*, together with an introduction by Amy Gutmann and comments by several other people; the introduction and comments also form part of the example as I want to understand it.[2] Coetzee's lectures themselves take the form of a story. In the story, an elderly woman novelist, Elizabeth Costello, has been invited to give an endowed lecture at Appleton College. She is a woman haunted by the horror of what we do to animals. We see her as wounded by this knowledge, this horror, and by the knowledge of how unhaunted others are. The wound marks her and isolates her. The imagery of the Holocaust figures centrally in the way she is haunted, and in her isolation. For thinking this horror with the imagery of the Holocaust is or can be felt to be profoundly offensive.[3]

I want to describe Coetzee's lectures, then, as presenting a kind of woundedness or hauntedness, a terrible rawness of nerves. What wounds this woman, what haunts her mind,[4] is what we do to animals. This, in all its horror, is there, in our world. How is it possible to live in the face of it? And in the face of the fact that, for nearly everyone, it is as nothing, as the mere accepted background of life? Elizabeth Costello gives a lecture, but it is a lecture that distances itself in various ways from the expectations of a lecture audience. She describes herself as an animal exhibiting but not exhibiting, to a gathering of scholars, a wound that her clothes cover up, but which is touched on in every word she speaks. So the life of this speaking and wounded and clothed animal is one of the "lives of animals" that the story is about; if it is true that we generally remain unaware of the lives of other animals, it is also true that, as readers of this story, we may remain unaware, as her audience does, of the life of the speaking animal at its center.

I say that that is how I want to describe Coetzee's lectures; but it is not how the commentators on the lectures describe them. Amy Gutmann, in her introductory essay, sees Coetzee as confronting the ethical issue of how human beings should treat animals, and as presenting, within a fictional frame, arguments that are meant to support one way of resolving that issue. Peter Singer also reads Coetzee as having been engaged in the presenting of arguments within the frame of a fiction, arguments for a kind of "radical egalitarianism" (p. 91) as the appropriate way to organize our relations to animals. He thinks the arguments in Coetzee's lectures are not really very good ones, since they fail to make clear the source of the moral significance of the lives of animals.[5] The fact that the arguments are those of a character in a story he sees as simply making it possible for Coetzee to distance himself to some degree from them and to avoid taking full intellectual responsibility for them. Another one of the commentators, Wendy Doniger, takes the lectures to be deeply moving, but begins her response by attempting to identify the ideas implicit in the lectures. She reads the implicit idea as an argument from the appropriate emotions toward animals and emotional bonds with them to conclusions about appropriate actions toward them. And Barbara Smuts, a primatologist, describes the Coetzee lectures as a text containing a "discourse on animal rights."

For this kind of reading, the wounded woman, the woman with the haunted mind and the raw nerves, has no significance except as a device for putting forward (in an imaginatively stirring way) ideas about the resolution of a range of ethical issues, ideas that can then be abstracted and examined. For none of the commentators does the title of the story have any particular significance in relation to the wounded animal that the story has as its central character. For none of the commentators does the title of the story have any significance in how we might understand the story in relation to our own lives, the lives of the animals we are.

So we have then two quite different ways of seeing the lectures: as centrally concerned with the presenting of a wounded woman, and as centrally concerned with the presenting of a position on the issue how we should treat animals. The difference between the two readings comes out especially sharply if we consider the references to the Holocaust, references that are of immense significance in Coetzee's lectures. Gutmann treats them as a use by Coetzee of an argument from analogy.[6] Singer also treats the Holocaust imagery as playing a role in the argumentative structure that he reads in the lectures. He sees the references to the Holocaust as part of the argument by Elizabeth Costello for her brand of radical egalitarianism. There would, he believes, be nothing illegitimate in arguing that both the behavior of the Nazis toward the Jews and the world's response, or failure of response, to it have some points of resemblance to our treatment of animals and our failures to attend to what we do to animals. But the problem he sees with Elizabeth Costello's argument is that she equates the cases, which ignores the differences in moral significance between killing human beings and killing animals.[7]

Gutmann and Singer, then, take the Holocaust imagery in the lectures as constituting part of an argument. That there is a woman haunted by the Holocaust as it seems to be replaying itself in our lives with animals, that there is a wounded woman exhibiting herself as wounded through talk of the Holocaust that she knows will offend and not be understood – this drops totally away in Singer's reading and almost totally in Gutmann's. Gutmann does consider the presence in the text of a character, Abraham Stern, who takes Elizabeth Costello's use of the Holocaust to verge on blasphemy; Gutmann sees the presence of Stern as enabling Coetzee to represent the difficulties we may have in understanding each other's perspectives. But "perspective" is too general and bland a term for the rawness of nerves we have in both Stern and Costello, in contrast with the unjangled, unraw nerves of the other characters. The contrast is made sharply present through Costello's own allusion to one of the most searing poems about the Holocaust, with its image of the human being in the ash in the air, as part of her portrayal of how we protect ourselves with a dullness or deadness of soul.[8] (Gutmann describes Stern as Costello's "academic equal," but they are better seen as equals rather in the way their rawnervedness propels them toward or beyond the borders of academic decorum.)

The difference between the two contrasting types of readings concerns also the question whether Coetzee's lectures can simply be taken to be concerned with a moral or ethical issue. Or, rather, this isn't a question at all for one of the two kinds of readings: neither Gutmann nor Singer considers whether there is any problem in taking the lectures that way, which is the way they themselves understand discourse about "animal rights."[9] Of course, Coetzee's lectures might indeed be intended to grapple with that ethical issue; but since he has a character in the story he tells, for whom it is as problematic to treat this supposed "issue" as an "ethical issue" for serious discussion as it is problematic to treat Holocaust denial as an issue for serious discussion, one can hardly, I think, take for granted that the lectures can be read as concerned with that "issue," and as providing arguments bearing on it. If we see in the lectures a wounded woman, one thing that wounds her is precisely the common and taken-for-granted mode of thought that "how we should treat animals" is an "ethical issue," and the knowledge that she will be taken to be contributing, or intending to contribute, to discussion of it. But what kind of beings are we for whom this is an "issue"? (It is important here that the lectures bring us to the writings of Jonathan Swift and to questions about reading Swift, while none of the commentators except Garber even mentions Swift, or takes the pages devoted to Swift to be significant in their reconstruction of what Coetzee is concerned to do.)[10]

Elizabeth Costello says that she doesn't want to be taken to be joining in the tradition of argumentation. She is letting us see her as what she is. She is someone immensely conscious of the limits of thinking, the limits of understanding, in the face of all that she is painfully aware of (p. 45). So what then is the role of the argument-fragments that are contained in the Coetzee lectures? My comments on this are inconclusive, but are meant to reflect the idea that we cannot understand their role in Coetzee's lectures without first taking seriously how argument is treated within the story, by Elizabeth Costello. She does not engage with others in argument, in the sense in which philosophers do. Her responses to arguments from others move out from the kind of engagement in argument that might have been expected. She comments on the arguments put to her, but goes on from them in directions that suggest her own very different mode of approach. She does not take seriously the conventions of argumentation of a philosophy text, as comes out in her image of the dead hen speaking in the writings of Camus on the guillotine. (This is clearly, from the point of view of the conventions of argumentation, no way to respond to the argumentative point that animals cannot speak for themselves and claim rights for themselves as we can. The image itself is reminiscent of Wittgenstein's image of the rose having teeth in the mouth of the cow that chews up its food and dungs the rose.) Elizabeth Costello's responses to arguments can be read as "replies" in the philosophical sense only by ignoring important features of the story, in particular the kind of weight that such responses have in Costello's thought. In the life of the animal she is, argument does not have the weight we may take it to have in the life of the kind of animal we think of ourselves as being. She sees our reliance on argumentation as a way we may make unavailable to ourselves our own sense of what it is to be a living animal.[11] And she sees poetry, rather than philosophy, as having the capacity to return us to such a sense of what animal life is.[12] (Another way of trying to confront the issues here: to think of Coetzee's lectures as contributing to the "debate" on how to treat animals is to fail to see how "debate" as we understand it may have built into it a distancing of ourselves from our sense of our own bodily life and our capacity to respond to and to imagine the bodily life of others.)

I am not sure how helpful it is to say "Coetzee's lectures have to be read first of all as literature," because it is not clear what is meant by reading them as literature. But what is meant not to be done is at least somewhat clear: not pulling out ideas and arguments as if they had been simply clothed in fictional form as a way of putting them before us. (This is perhaps particularly clear in connection with the use of Holocaust imagery, where the desire to see the point being made by Coetzee by using the imagery leads to various formulations of the point in general terms: Coetzee is making clear the question whether there is any way of resolving ethical conflicts in cases in which people's sensibilities are far apart (Gutmann); or he is engaged in putting forward an argument, which he himself may or may not accept, for radical egalitarianism (Singer). – Elizabeth Costello asks herself, at the end of the story, whether she is making a mountain out of a molehill. The mind does, though, have mountains; has frightful no-man-fathomed cliffs: "Hold them cheap may who ne'er hung there." What is it like to hang there? What comfort is offered by her son? "There, there, it will soon be over"? "Here! creep, wretch, under a comfort serves in a whirlwind: all life death does end and each day dies with sleep." If we do not see how the Holocaust imagery gives a sense of what it is to hang on these cliffs, what it is to have nothing but the comfort of sleep and death in the face of what it is to hang on those cliffs, it seems to me we have not begun really to read the lectures. But it equally seems we may be driven, or take ourselves to be driven, to such a reading by philosophy, as we hear it pressing on us the insistent point that that portrayal is simply the portrayal, however moving it may be, of a subjective response, the significance of which needs to be examined.)

If we take as central in our reading the view Coetzee gives us of a profound disturbance of the soul, it may seem natural to go on to suggest something like this:

We can learn from the "sick soul" how to see reality, as William James said in his Gifford Lectures. The "sick soul" in the Coetzee lectures lets us see one of the difficulties of reality, the difficulty of human life in its relation to that of animals, of the horror of what we do, and the horror of our blotting it out of consciousness.

The trouble with that view of what we may learn from the lectures is that it is fixed entirely on Elizabeth Costello's view, and implicitly identifies it as Coetzee's. But he shows us also that her understanding of our relation to animals seems to throw into shadow the full horror of what we do to each other, as if we could not keep in focus the Holocaust as an image for what we do to animals without losing our ability to see *it*, and to see fully what it shows us of ourselves. So there is a part of the difficulty of reality here that is not seen by Costello: so far as we keep one sort of difficulty in view we seem blocked from seeing another. And there is also a further important theme of the lectures that we cannot get into view so long as we stay entirely with her understanding, the difficulty of attempting to bring a difficulty of reality into focus, in that any such attempt is inextricably intertwined with relations of power between people. Elizabeth Costello responds to the allegations that dietary restrictions, and arguments in favor of them, are a way of allowing some group of people to claim superiority over others; but the lectures themselves leave us with a picture of complex dynamics within her family, in which her grandchildren's responsiveness to animals and to eating baby animals cannot be pulled apart from the mutual resentment between her and her daughter-in-law.

Elizabeth Costello, talking about Ted Hughes, says that writers teach us more than they are aware of; writing about Wolfgang Koehler, she says that the book we read is not the book he thought he was writing. Garber says that we can take both remarks to be about Coetzee, but she then more or less drops the point. I would pick it up and use it this way: Coetzee gives us a view of a profound disturbance of soul, and puts that view into a complex context. What is done by doing so he cannot tell us; he does not know. What response we may have to the difficulties of the lectures, the difficulties of reality, is not something the lectures themselves are meant to settle. This itself expresses a mode of understanding of the kind of animal we are, and indeed of the moral life of this kind of animal.

3 Deflection

I have suggested that Coetzee's lectures present a mode of understanding of the kind of animal we are, where that understanding can be present in poetry, in a broad sense of the term. There is also the idea that an understanding of the kind of animal we are is present only in a diminished and distorted way in philosophical argumentation. Philosophy characteristically misrepresents both our own reality and that of others, in particular those "others" who are animals. What we then see in the response to Coetzee's lectures by Gutmann and Singer (and to a lesser degree by Doniger and Smuts) is that the lectures are put into the context of argumentative discourse on moral issues. I want a term for what is going on here, which I shall take from Cavell, from "Knowing and acknowledging." Cavell writes about the philosopher who begins (we imagine) from an appreciation of something appalling: that I may be suffering, and my suffering be utterly unknown or uncared about; "and that others may be suffering and I not know" (1969b: 247). But the philosopher's understanding is *deflected*; the issue becomes deflected, as the philosopher thinks it or rethinks it in the language of philosophical skepticism. And philosophical responses to that skepticism, e.g. demonstrations that it is confused, further deflect from the truth here (p. 260). I shall return to Cavell's ideas; here I simply want the notion of deflection, for describing what happens when we are moved from the appreciation, or attempt at appreciation, of a difficulty of reality to a philosophical or moral problem apparently in the vicinity.

Let me go back briefly to my first example, the poem from Ted Hughes. What is expressed there is the sense of a difficulty that pushes us beyond what we can think. To attempt to think it is to feel one's thinking come unhinged. Our concepts, our ordinary life with our concepts, pass by this difficulty as if it were not there; the difficulty, if we try to see it, shoulders us out of life, is deadly chilling. How then can we describe the philosophical deflection from a difficulty of reality, as we see it in Gutmann and Singer? I have in mind centrally their taking Coetzee as contributing to the discussion of a moral issue: how we should treat animals. Should we eat them, should we grant them rights? And so on. Philosophy knows how to do this. It is hard, all right, but that is what university philosophy departments are for, to enable us to learn how to discuss hard problems, what constitutes a good argument, what is distorted by emotion, when we are making assertions without backing them up. What I have meant to suggest by picking up Cavell's use of the term "deflection" is that the hardness there, in philosophical argumentation, is not the hardness of appreciating or trying to appreciate a difficulty of reality. In the latter case, the difficulty lies in the apparent resistance by reality to one's ordinary mode of life, including one's ordinary modes of thinking: to appreciate the difficulty is to feel oneself being shouldered out of how one thinks, how one is apparently supposed to think, or to have a sense of the inability of thought to encompass what it is attempting to reach. Such appreciation may involve the profound isolation felt by someone like Elizabeth Costello. Recall here her reference to her body as wounded: her isolation is felt in the body, as the speaker in Hughes's poem feels a bodily thrownness from the photograph. Coetzee's lectures ask us to inhabit a body.[13] But, just as, in considering what death is to an animal, we may reject our own capacity to inhabit its body in imagination,[14] so we may, in reading the lectures, reject our own capacity to inhabit in imagination the body of the woman confronting, trying to confront, the difficulty of what we do to animals. The deflection into discussion of a moral issue is a deflection that makes our own bodies mere facts – facts that may or may not be thought of as morally relevant in this or that respect, depending on the particular moral issue being addressed (as our sentience, for example, might be taken to be relevant to our having "moral status"). So here I am inviting you to think of what it would be not to be "deflected" as an inhabiting of a body (one's own, or an imagined other's) in the appreciating of a difficulty of reality. This may make it sound as if philosophy is inevitably deflected from appreciation of the kind of difficulty I mean, if (that is) philosophy does not know how to inhabit a body (does not know how to treat a wounded body as anything but a fact). I shall return to that question later, and also to Coetzee on imagining one's own death, on having a genuinely embodied knowledge of being extinguished. For that is another important point in the lectures, not mentioned by any of the commentators.

4 Beauty and goodness, and spikiness

I said at the beginning that I was concerned with a range of phenomena; and so far I have had only two examples, which cannot by themselves adequately suggest the range. I want briefly to mention some other examples to go a part of the way to remedying that.

My first example involved a poem about life and death; the second example involved the horror of what we do to animals. But I would include in what I call the difficulty of reality some things that are entirely different. Instances of goodness or of beauty can throw us. I mean that they can give us the sense that *this* should not be, that we cannot fit it into the understanding we have of what the world is like. It is wholly inexplicable that it should be; and yet it is. That is what Czesław Miłosz writes about beauty: "It should not exist. There is not only no reason for it, but an argument against. Yet undoubtedly it is." And he writes of the mystery that may seem to be present in the architecture of a tree, the slimness of a column crowned with green, or in the voices of birds outside the window greeting the morning. How can this be? – In the case of our relationship with animals, a sense of the difficulty of reality may involve not only the kind of horror felt by Elizabeth Costello in Coetzee's lectures, but also and equally a sense of astonishment and incomprehension that there should be beings so like us, so unlike us, so astonishingly capable of being companions of ours and so unfathomably distant. A sense of its being impossible that we should go and *eat* them may go with feeling how powerfully strange it is that they and we should share as much as we do, and yet also not share; that they should be capable of incomparable beauty and delicacy and terrible ferocity; that some among them should be so mind-bogglingly weird or repulsive in their forms or in their lives. Later I will come to Cavell's remarks about human separateness as turned equally toward splendor and toward horror, mixing beauty and ugliness, but those words, which he calls on to help give the felt character of human separateness, are very like words we might call on to express the extraordinary felt character of animal life in relation to our own.

Ruth Klüger, in her memoir *Still Alive: A Holocaust Girlhood Remembered*, describes her own astonishment and awe at the act of the young woman at Auschwitz who first encouraged a terrified child, Ruth at twelve, to tell a lie that might help save her life, and who then stood up for her, got her through a selection. Klüger says that she tells the story in wonder, that she has never ceased to wonder at that girl's doing, the "incomparable and inexplicable" goodness that touched her that day (pp. 103–9). In discussing Hughes's poem, I mentioned that the photograph and what it shows would not be taken to boggle the mind by everyone. The men were alive, and now are dead; what's the problem? Klüger says that when she tells her story in wonder, "people wonder at my wonder. They say, okay, some persons are altruistic. We understand that; it doesn't surprise us. The girl who helped you was one of those who liked to help." Here, as in the case of the Hughes poem, what is capable of astonishing one in its incomprehensibility, its not being fittable in with the world as one understands it, may be seen by others as unsurprising. Klüger asks her readers not just to look at the scene but to listen to her and not take apart what happened, to "absorb it" as she tells it (pp. 108–9). She asks for a kind of imagination that can inhabit her own continued astonishment. The "taking apart" that she asks us to eschew would be a distancing from the story, a fitting of what went on into this or that way of handling things, a deflecting from the truth.

(In a discussion of concepts of the miraculous, R.F. Holland sets out one such concept as that of the occurrence of something that is at one and the same time empirically certain and conceptually impossible. The story in the New Testament of water having been turned into wine is "the story of something that could have been known empirically to have occurred, and it is also the story of the occurrence of something which is conceptually impossible." To be the miracle story it is, Holland says, it has to be both; the sort of occurrence he means is one that, for us, is impossible to think, and yet it is there. Klüger, in introducing the story of what happened to her, describes it as an act of grace, and I do not want to suggest that that is the same as seeing it as a miracle, in Holland's sense. But I do want to connect the astonishment and awe that Klüger expresses as related to the astonishment and awe that one would feel at a miracle in Holland's sense, and indeed to the astonishment Miłosz expresses at the existence of beauty.)

Mary Mann's story, "Little brother," is described by A.S. Byatt (in her intro-ductory essay for *The Oxford Book of English Short Stories*) as "plain, and brief, and clear and terrible." Mann's telling of the story is "spiky with morals and the inadequacy of morals." Byatt says no more than that; and it is therefore not entirely obvious what she means by the telling's being spiky with the inade-quacy of morals, and how that is related to the terribleness of what is related. (What is related is the playing of two poor children, who have no toys, with the corpse of their newborn, stillborn brother. His stiff little body is the only doll they have had. The narrator had told the mother what she thought of the dese-cration; the last word is given to the mother.) The telling, fully felt, shoulders us from a familiar sense of moral life, from a sense of being able to take in and think a moral world. Moral thought gets no grip here. The terribleness of what is going on and the terribleness of the felt resistance of the narrated reality to moral thought are inseparable. (A story that seems to me comparable in its "spikiness" with morals and the inadequacy of morals is Leonard Woolf's "Pearls and swine." On one level, the story is a criticism of racism and colonialism; but it is also a telling of the kind of terribleness that, fully felt, shoulders one from one's familiar sense of moral life.) Again here I should want to note that the sense of this or another narrated reality as resisting our modes of moral thought is not something everyone would recognize.

5 Turned to stone

Hughes's poem again: The contradictory permanent horrors shoulder out one's body from its instant and heat. To look is to experience death, to be turned to stone. Losing one's instant and heat, being turned to something permanent and hard and cold, is a central image in Cavell's discussion of skepticism and knowl-edge in *The Winter's Tale* and *Othello* (CR: 481–96). He says of *The Winter's Tale* that Hermione's fate of being turned to stone can be understood as her under-going what is in a sense the fate of Leontes. Leontes's failure or inability to recognize her makes her as stone; "hence," Cavell says, that is what it does to him. "One can see this as the projection of his own sense of numbness, of living death"; and Cavell then asks why that was Leontes's fate (p. 481). Cavell links the two plays with a play on words: in both plays, "the consequence for the man's refusal of knowledge of his other is an imagination of stone" – stone as what is imagined and stoniness as what has befallen the imagination. Othello imagines Desdemona's skin as having the smoothness of alabaster (pp. 481–2). He imagines her as stone, says that she stones her heart. It is Othello, though, who "will give her a stone heart for her stone body"; his "words of stone" transfer to her what he himself has undergone, a heart turned to stone (p. 492). What does this to Othello is the intolerableness to him of Desdemona's existence, her separateness. About the possibility of that separateness Cavell says that it is precisely what tortures Othello: "The content of his torture is the premonition of the existence of another, hence of his own, his own as dependent, as partial" (p. 493). Separateness can be felt as horror;[15] such a response is what puts Othello "beyond aid."

Cavell has in many of his writings traced connections and relations between, on the one hand, the multifarious forms in which we take in or try to take in or resist taking in that difficulty of reality that he refers to most often as separateness and, on the other hand, skepticism: skepticism as itself both a presence in our lives and as, intellectualized, a central part of our philosophical tradition. The early direction his thoughts took on these issues can be seen in his statement of one form of the "conclusion" toward which he took those thoughts to be heading, that "skepticism concerning other minds is not skepticism but is tragedy."[16] Earlier still, he had been particularly concerned, in "Knowing and acknowledging" (1969b), with what he took to be inadequate in the Wittgensteinian response to skepticism: I mean the response of such Wittgensteinians as Norman Malcolm and John Cook, not that of Wittgenstein. Malcolm and Cook had taken the skeptic about other minds to be confused about what can be said in the language-game in which we speak about our own sensations and those of others, in which we express our own feelings and in which we may speak of what we know of the feelings of others, what we doubt or are certain of. Thus Cook (1965) had criticized the idea that it is some sort of limitation on us that we cannot actually feel what another person feels, cannot have that very feeling; such an idea reflects (he thinks) one's taking the inaccessibility of the feeling as like the inaccessibility of a flower in a garden on the far side of a wall over which one cannot see. What Cook was criticizing was the idea I may have of the position that I cannot be in in respect to the pain of the other person, the position that that person himself is in, the decisive position. His argument was an attempt to show that the skeptic takes to be a kind of inability what is really a matter of the difference between two language-games: in the language-game with pain, there is no such thing as the position in which one has *that which* the other person has. We are not "unable" to be *there* if there is no there where we are unable to be. Cook's account was thus meant to enable us to see the confusion in the skeptic's view. Cavell's response was astonishing. He places Cook's argument in the situation from which the skeptic speaks; leads us to imagine that situation and to recognize the pressures on words; shows us what may happen with our experience of distance from what others undergo. When we put, or try to put, that experience in words, the words fail us, the words don't do what we are trying to get them to do. The words make it look as if I am simply unable to see over a wall that happens to separate me from something I want very much to see. But the fact that the words are apparently too weak to do what I am demanding from them does not mean that the experience here of *powerlessness* has been shown to involve a kind of grammatical error. But why, then, since words seem not to be able to do what I want, did I call on them? Why, in particular, does the experience appear to be an experience of not being able to know what is there in the other because I cannot have what he has? Cavell says "I am filled with this feeling – of our separateness, let us say – and I want you to have it too. So I give voice to it. And then my powerlessness presents itself as ignorance – a metaphysical finitude as an intellectual lack" (1969b: 263). His criticism of Cook, then, takes the form of allowing us to hear Cook's own voice differently. When Cook, in repudiating the skeptic's idea, speaks of it as "inherently confused," Cavell lets us hear his voice as responding with "correctness" to the voice of philosophical skepticism.[17] When I spoke of Cavell's response as astonishing, I meant his teaching us a way of hearing both Cook and the skeptic whom he is criticizing, a way of hearing these voices that puts them back into the situation within which the humanness of the other seems out of reach, and thereby shows us where and how philosophy has to start. – This takes us back to the subject of deflection.

In section 3, I quoted Cavell's description of how we may be filled with a sense of the facts, the ineluctable facts of our capacity to miss the suffering of others and of the possibility of our own suffering being unknown and uncared about; we may be filled with a sense of these facts, of our distance from each other, and our appreciation be deflected, the problem itself be deflected, into one or another of the forms it is given in philosophical skepticism. I quoted also Cavell's remark about the anti-skeptical response as a further deflection, a deflection that ignores the fundamental insight of the skeptic (1969b: 258–60), the sense the skeptic has of the other's position with respect to his own pain, and the light in which it casts his position in relation to that other. The image of deflection is implicit also later on in Cavell's writings, when he describes the difficulty of philosophy as that of not being able to find and stay on a path (*This New Yet Unapproachable America*, 1989: 37); for we can here see deflection as deflection from a path we need to find and stay on; but it is also deflection from seeing, deflection from taking in, the tormenting possibility central to the experience of the skeptic. What he sees of the human condition, what unseats his reason, is converted into and treated as an intellectual difficulty (CR: p. 493). I shall come back to this, but first I want to make further connections with Coetzee's lectures and Hughes's poem.

6 Correctness and exposure

There is in Coetzee's second lecture a response by a fictional philosopher, Thomas O'Hearne, to Elizabeth Costello's ideas (1999: 59–65). It is implicitly a response also to some of the arguments in favor of animal rights put forward by philosophers like Singer and Tom Regan. But here I want to consider a response by a real philosopher, Michael Leahy, a response that has some resemblances to O'Hearne's but which will more easily enable us to see the connections with Cavell's thought. Leahy's argument has two parts. He first tries to establish what the language-game is within which we speak of animals and their pains and desires and so on.[18] His argument is that animal liberationists characteristically fail to recognize that the language-game in which we speak of the mental life of animals, of a dog fearing this or a chimpanzee believing that, is "vitally different" from the language-game in which we use such terms of human beings (pp. 138–9). Leahy relies on that point when he goes on to argue that the practices within which we use animals in various ways (as pets, food, experimental subjects, sources of fur and so on) "dictate the criteria for our judging what constitutes needless suffering" (p. 198), and that is the second part of the overall argument. The two parts of his argument together are thus meant to undercut the case made for animal rights. Leahy's response to the liberationists is not unlike Cook's response to skepticism about other minds: like Cook, he takes the failure to recognize the difference between distinct language-games to be the ultimate source of the confusion he wants to diagnose. There are various questions that might be raised about how the two parts of his argument are connected, about whether the recognition of the differences between the language-games has the practical implications that Leahy thinks it has.[19] But that is not my concern here. I am interested rather in Leahy's voice, and its relation to the anti-skeptical voice exemplified for Cavell in "Knowing and acknowledging" by the voices of Malcolm and Cook. The Coetzee case is not an exact parallel to Cavell's; and the philosophical debates about animals cannot be treated as more than partially parallel to the debate about skepticism.[20] But we are concerned in both cases with a repudiation of the everyday; with a sense of being shouldered out from our ways of thinking and speaking by a torment of reality. In both cases, the repudiation may be heard as expressing such-and-such position in an intellectual-ized debate; in both cases, the opposite sides in the debate may have more in common than they realize. In the voices we hear in the debate about animal rights, those of people like Singer on the one hand and those of Leahy and the fictional O'Hearne on the other, there is shared a desire for a "because": because animals are this kind of being, or because they are that kind of being, thus-and-such is their standing for our moral thought. If we listen to these voices in the way Cavell has taught us to, can we hear in them a form of skepticism? That is, a form of skepticism in the desire for something better than what we are condemned to (as the kind of animal we are)? But what might we be thought to be "condemned to"? Cavell, in *The Claim of Reason*, uses the word "exposure" in discussing our situation: Being exposed, as I am in the case of "my concept of the other," means that my assurance in applying the concept isn't provided for me. "The other can present me with no mark or feature on the basis of which I can *settle* my attitude" (p. 433). He says that to accept my exposure, in the case of my knowledge of others, "seems to imply an acceptance of the possibility that my knowledge of others may be overthrown, even that it ought to be"; it implies acceptance of not being in what I may take to be the ideal position, what I want or take myself to want (p. 439; see also p. 454). Our "exposure" in the case of animals lies in there being nothing but our own responsibility, our own making the best of it. We are not, here too, in what we might take to be the "ideal" position. We want to be able to see that, given what animals are, and given also our properties, what we are like (given our "marks and features" and theirs), there are general principles that establish the moral significance of their suffering compared to ours, of their needs compared to ours, and we could then see what treatment of them was and what was not morally justified. We would be *given* the presence or absence of moral community (or thus-and-such degree or kind of moral community) with animals. But we are exposed – that is, we are thrown into finding something we can live with, and it may at best be a kind of bitter-tasting compromise. There is here only what we make of our exposure, and it leaves us endless room for double-dealing and deceit. The exposure is most plain in the Coetzee lectures at the point at which Elizabeth Costello is asked whether her vegetarianism comes out of moral conviction, and replies that it doesn't; "It comes out of a desire to save my soul," and she adds that she is wearing leather shoes, and carrying a leather purse.[21]

The title of this essay is "The difficulty of reality and the difficulty of philosophy," but a word I'd want to add to the title is: *exposure*. Ted Hughes's poem is about *a single exposure*, but the single exposure is *our* exposure, as we find for ourselves, or are meant to find, in a shuddering awareness of death and life together. In the background is perhaps a reference to Wilfrid Owen's "Exposure," in which the sense of war as not making sense, the sense of loss of sense, is tied to death literally by exposure, exposure to cold that transforms the men to iced solidity. – I have not more than scratched the surface of Cavell's use of the idea of exposure; but there is also more to the idea in Coetzee's lectures. Elizabeth Costello, in Coetzee's first lecture, speaks of her own knowledge of death, in a passage that (in the present context) takes us to the "contradictory permanent horrors" spoken of in Hughes's poem. "For an instant at a time," she says, "I know what it is like to be a corpse. The knowledge repels me. It fills me with terror; I shy away from it, refuse to entertain it." She goes on to say that we all have such moments, and that the knowledge we then have is not abstract but embodied. "For a moment we *are* that knowledge. We live the impossible: we live beyond our death, look back on it, yet look back as only a dead self can." She goes on, making the contradiction explicit:

> What I know is what a corpse cannot know: that it is extinct, that it knows nothing and will never know anything anymore. For an instant, before my whole structure of knowledge collapses in panic, I am alive inside that contradiction, dead and alive at the same time (p. 32).

The awareness we each have of being a living body, being "alive to the world," carries with it exposure to the bodily sense of vulnerability to death, sheer animal vulnerability, the vulnerability we share with them. This vulnerability is capable of panicking us. To be able to acknowledge it at all, let alone as shared, is wounding; but acknowledging it as shared with other animals, in the presence of what we do to them, is capable not only of panicking one but also of isolating one, as Elizabeth Costello is isolated. Is there any difficulty in seeing why we should not prefer to return to moral debate, in which the livingness and death of animals enter as facts that we treat as relevant in this or that way, not as presences that may unseat our reason?

7 The difficulty of philosophy

Can there be such a thing as philosophy that is not deflected from such realities?[22] This is a great question for Simone Weil. She wrote in 'Human Personality':

> Human thought is unable to acknowledge the reality of affliction. To acknowledge the reality of affliction means saying to oneself: "I may lose at any moment, through the play of circumstances over which I have no control, anything whatsoever that I possess, including those things which are so intimately mine that I consider them as being myself. There is nothing that I might not lose. It could happen at any moment that what I am might be abolished and replaced by anything whatsoever of the filthiest and most contemptible sort."
>
> To be aware of this in the depth of one's soul is to experience non-being.
>
> (Weil 1986: 70)

Weil's writings show that she saw the difficulty of what she was doing as the difficulty of keeping to such awareness, of not being deflected from it. I give her as an example of a philosopher concerned with deflection from the difficulty of reality, but a philosopher very different from Cavell.

In the concluding two paragraphs of *The Claim of Reason*, Cavell speaks of Othello and Desdemona, lying dead.

> A statue, a stone, is something whose existence is fundamentally open to the ocular proof. A human being is not. The two bodies lying together form an emblem of this fact, the truth of skepticism. What this man lacked was not certainty. He knew everything, but he could not yield to what he knew, be commanded by it. He found out too much for his mind, not too little. Their differences from one another – the one everything the other is not – form an emblem of human separation, which can be accepted, and granted, or not.
>
> (CR: 496)

Cavell returns to the audience: "we are here, knowing they are 'gone burning to hell.'" He asks: "can philosophy accept them back at the hands of poetry?" and answers, "Certainly not so long as philosophy continues, as it has from the first, to demand the banishment of poetry from its republic. Perhaps it could if it could itself become literature. But can philosophy become literature and still know itself?" (p. 496).

What follows is not meant to answer that last question, but to bear on it.

It may seem as if Cavell is here taking for granted that literature can accept – no problem! – such realities as throw philosophy. I do not think that that is an implication, but I won't discuss it.[23] I want to look instead at Cavell's question whether philosophy can accept Othello and Desdemona back, at the hands of poetry. For philosophy to do so would be for philosophy to accept human separateness as "turned equally toward splendor and toward horror, mixing beauty and ugliness; turned toward before and after; toward flesh and blood" (p. 492); for philosophy not to accept them back is for philosophy not to get near, but to get deflected from, the forms that our exposure to that separateness takes. But if that suggests a conception of the difficulty of philosophy, the difficulty of staying turned toward before and after, toward flesh and blood, toward the life of the animals we are, how is it related to what Cavell says elsewhere about the difficulty of philosophy?

In "Notes and afterthoughts on the opening of Wittgenstein's *Investigations*," Cavell says that the medium of philosophy, as Wittgenstein understands it, "lies in demonstrating, or say showing, the obvious"; he then asks how the obvious can fail to be obvious. What is the hardness of seeing the obvious? – And he then says that this must bear on what the hardness of philosophizing is (1996: 271–2). This question is present also in his reflections on Wittgenstein's aim of bringing words back from their metaphysical to their everyday use. What can the difficulty be, then, of bringing or leading words back? What is the everyday, if it is so hard to achieve? It is within the everyday that there lie the forms and varieties of repudiation of our language-games and distance from them, the possibility of being tormented by the hiddenness, the separateness, the otherness of others (1989: *passim*). As a form of repudiation of the language-game in which there is no contradiction between the young men being profoundly alive and then totally dead may be in the life of the Hughes poem; which is itself not to be thought of as outside life with the words we use for thinking of life and death.

In section 1, when I introduced the phrase "a difficulty of reality," I said that, in the cases I had in mind, the reality to which we were attending seemed to resist our thinking it. That our thought and reality might fail to meet is itself the content of a family of forms of skepticism, to which one response is that the very idea of such a failure is confused, that what I have spoken of as the content of such forms of skepticism is not a content at all. A language, a form of thought, cannot (we may be told) get things right or wrong, fit or fail to fit reality; it can only be more or less useful. What I want to end with is not exactly a response to that: it is to note how much that coming apart of thought and reality belongs to flesh and blood. I take that, then, to be itself a thought joining Hughes, Coetzee, and Cavell.

Notes

This paper was presented at a symposium, "Accounting for Literary Language," at the University of East Anglia in September 2002, and at the Hannah Arendt/Reiner Schürmann Memorial Symposium, on Stanley Cavell, held at the New School in New York, in October 2002. I am very grateful for the comments of the audience on both occasions. I was helped to think about the issues by Anat Matar's reply to my paper at the conference in East Anglia. I am also very glad to have had comments and suggestions from Alice Crary and Talbot Brewer. The paper was originally published in *Partial Answers* 1 (2003), and I am grateful for many suggestions and careful editorial attention from Leona Toker and her assistants.

1   I believe I read it in a *New Yorker* essay of his in the 1980s, but cannot trace it.
2   The two Coetzee Lectures have been reprinted as Lessons 3 and 4 in Coetzee 2003.
3   The description of her as "haunted" has, for me in this context, two particular sources. One is Ruth Klüger's discussion of Sylvia Plath and of Plath's use of Holocaust imagery in her poetry, her defense of Plath against those who object to her taking over what has happened to us, to the Jews, in expressing a private despair. (She was writing about Alvin Rosenfeld in particular, but had in mind others who shared his view, and who felt as he did that there was an "unforgivable disproportion" in Plath's expression of her own anguish in language drawing on the Holocaust. See Klüger 1985, especially pp. 184–5.) Klüger speaks of how "others" (other than we who ask the world to remember what happened to us) may be "haunted by what has happened to the Jews and claim it as their own out of human kinship, as part of their private terrors and visions of death." The second source is Coetzee's story, in which Elizabeth Costello mentions Camus and the haunting imprint on his memory made by the death-cry of a hen, which, as a little boy, he had fetched for his grandmother, who then beheaded it (p. 63).
4   I use the word "mind" here with some hesitation, since (within the context of discussion of animals and ourselves) it may be taken to suggest a contrast with bodily life. Conceptions of mind are at stake within the lectures. In particular, there is involved a critical stance towards the idea that, if one were to imagine what it is like to be a bat or other animal, or to be another human being, one would need to imagine what is going on "in its mind," rather than to imagine its fullness of being (see, e.g., pp. 33, 51, 65). So, to speak of Elizabeth Costello as having a haunted mind in a sense of "mind" which takes that understanding of embodiment seriously is to speak of how her life is felt.
5   "Fail to make clear" is my way of putting the criticism; see Singer, pp. 87–90. Singer's response doesn't take on Elizabeth Costello's rejection of the form of argument that Singer thinks is appropriate, an argument that responds to the *therefore*-arguments of those who justify treating animals as we do by their own different *therefore*-arguments. She comments on such arguments after one of the other characters in the fiction speaks of the "vacuum of consciousness" within which animals live (p. 44). We say such things as that they have no consciousness, but what she minds is, she says, what comes next: "They have no consciousness *therefore*. Therefore what?" Against those who say that therefore we may treat them as we like, she does not reply that animals are conscious, *therefore* we may not eat them, or that they have other relevant properties, *therefore* we should recognize their rights, etc. See also below, note 12.
6   See "Introduction," p. 8. When she describes Coetzee as arguing by analogy, Gutmann is actually speaking about Marjorie Garber's discussion of Coetzee's use of

the Holocaust, but interestingly Garber herself, although she has quite a long discussion of the use of analogies by Coetzee and others, never refers to the cases in question as the presentation of a kind of argument. While I would disagree with Garber's reading, she does at any rate, unlike all the other commentators, begin by taking for granted that we have in front of us something to be thought about in literary terms, and that this matters.

7 I do not in this essay try to judge, or even to examine what would be involved in trying to judge, Elizabeth Costello's use of the imagery of the Holocaust. Later in the present section I do, though, discuss how the effort to take in one difficulty of reality may block us from seeing another.

8 I had meant Paul Celan's "Todesfuge"; I am indebted to Ruth Klüger for pointing out to me that Nelly Sachs makes use of that image too ("Dein Leib im Rauch durch die Luft").

9 See especially the opening paragraph of Gutmann's introduction, intended to help fix the terms of our reading of the rest of the book: the lectures, she says, focus on an important ethical issue – the way human beings treat animals; cf. also the following page, where that description is repeated.

10 I cannot here go into the discussion of Swift in Coetzee's lectures. It is important for various reasons, among which is that it takes up the question where we might get if we push Swift's tales further than we usually do, and suggests an "ex-colonial" perspective on what, thus pushed, the tales might say about the kind of being we are.

11 There is an issue here that I can merely indicate. I have found, in teaching undergraduates how utilitarians discuss the killing of babies, that my students react very strongly indeed to claims that killing a baby does not wrong the baby, that it does not interfere with what the baby might be taken to want for itself, since the baby is not as yet capable of grasping such a choice. Killing an older child might (on this view) go against what it wants, but that is possible only because the older child can understand what it is to go on living, and can therefore want to do so. – In response to that sort of argument, the students say that you are wronging the baby; that the baby is attached to life: In the struggle of a baby or animal whom someone is trying to kill, you can see that it is clinging to life. They reject the idea that there is no interference with what a baby or animal might be said to want. Their rejection of the utilitarian argument is connected with their rejection of the kind of argumentative discourse in which the utilitarian wants the issue cast, a form of discourse in which one's imaginative sense of what might be one's own bodily struggle for life, one's imaginative sense of an animal's struggle for life, cannot be given the role they want it to have. It is as if they felt a kind of evisceration of the meaning of "wanting to go on living."

12 Gutmann in fact does recognize some of the features of the lectures that I have just described, but takes Costello's responses to argument as showing that she is after all willing to engage in argument to at least a limited degree. She speaks of Costello as employing philosophy in demonstrating the weakness of arguments opposed to her own view, but Gutmann's treatment of the argument-fragments that the story contains is shaped by her basic reading of the story as a way of presenting a stance on an ethical issue. My reading of the arguments in the Coetzee lectures would go in a different direction, and would focus on some of the specific cases, in particular Elizabeth Costello's rejection of the *therefore*-arguments that go from characteristics of animals to it therefore being permissible to treat them this or that way, as we do. Earlier I mentioned Singer's response to such arguments with contrasting *therefore*-arguments; a very different response that in some ways resembles Elizabeth Costello's is that of Rush Rhees, in "Humans and animals: a confused Christian conception," which is not an essay but two sets of exploratory notes and a letter to a friend. A theme in the notes and in the letter is the unexamined use of *therefore*-arguments, the conclusion of which is the supposed greater importance of human life; in fact a criticism of the "*therefore*" is the starting point of the first set of those notes, which

characterize such arguments as reflecting "the illusion of a *reason* which justifies one in treating animals with less respect or less consideration than human beings." So a question for Rhees in these informal notes is how to think his own response to what he takes to be illusion.

13 See p. 51; here I am taking a remark of Elizabeth Costello's as deeply Coetzee's.

14 Central to the lectures: see p. 65; also p. 32. I return to this region of Coetzee's thought in section 6.

15 Cavell says that human separateness is "turned equally toward splendor and toward horror, mixing beauty and ugliness; turned toward before and after; toward flesh and blood" (p. 492). My discussion is partial at this point, emphasizing as it does horror over splendor. But see also pp. 494–6.

16 Foreword to *The Claim of Reason* (1979: xix). What Cavell says is more complex than my quotation: He says that he knew (in 1973 and 1974) the direction that the conclusion of his work in progress was "hauling itself toward," and that that conclusion had to do with the connection of "Knowing and acknowledging" and "The avoidance of love," "the reciprocation between the ideas of acknowledgment and of avoidance, for example as the thought that skepticism concerning other minds is not skepticism but is tragedy" (pp. xviii–xix).

17 "Knowing and acknowledging" (1969b: 259–60); the term "voice of correctness" comes from Cavell's "The availability of Wittgenstein's later philosophy" (1969a: 71).

18 All of Chapter 5 of *Against Liberation* (1991) is relevant, but p. 126 is particularly helpful in making clear Leahy's method and aims.

19 There are also questions about the first part of the argument, the attempt to establish the differences between the language-game in which we speak about the thoughts, feelings and intentions of animals, and that in which we speak about our own. One question would concern the idea of there being just the two language-games he describes. The question is particularly acute in connection with the writings of Vicki Hearne, which Leahy discusses and criticizes at various points in the book. One way of putting her understanding of what is involved in talking about animals is that talking about animals in connection with their "work" (in her sense of that term) is itself a distinctive language-game. This language-game she takes to be inseparable from the trainer's activity; the activity itself is carried on through such talk, and the talk gets its sense through what it achieves in the shared "work." See, in addition to *Adam's Task* (Hearne 1986, the target of Leahy's criticism), her essay "A taxonomy of knowing: animals captive, free-ranging, and at liberty" (1995).

20 For one thing, I don't want to suggest that Leahy's use of the concept of criteria in his argument is an appeal to criteria in Cavell's sense. But more important than that, there is a significant difference between the two cases in the conceptions of knowledge in play. The sort of knowledge to which Elizabeth Costello appeals when she discusses the attachment of animals to life can be contrasted with that which Othello takes himself to want. See, on knowledge and forms of perception in *Othello*, and on Othello's desire for proof, Naomi Scheman's "Othello's doubt/Desdemona's death: the engendering of skepticism," in *Pursuits of Reason*. Scheman's essay itself helps to bring out also a connection between the issues I have been discussing and issues concerning gender, both within Coetzee's lectures and more generally.

21 To forestall misunderstanding here, I want to note that I am not (in this section or anywhere else) denying a role, indeed a large and deeply significant role, to "because" in moral thinking, and indeed to argument. I am suggesting we look with some serious puzzlement at attempts to establish moral community, or to show it to be absent, through attention to "marks and features."

22 Alice Crary has pointed out to me that my descriptions, earlier in this essay, of how philosophical argument can deflect us from attention to the difficulty of reality may

seem to have implied the answer "No" to my question whether there can be a non-deflecting practice of philosophy. That there can be such a practice, and that argument may have an essential role in it, is not something I would wish to deny. There are here two distinct points: philosophical argument is not in and of itself any indication that attention has been or is being deflected from the difficulty of reality, and (more positively) philosophical argument has an important role to play in bringing to attention such difficulty and in exploring its character, as well as in making clear what the limits or limitations are of philosophical argument, and indeed of other argument. See, for example, Cavell's arguments about the argument that the human embryo is a human being (1979: 372–8).

23 The kinds of difficulty that literature may have in the face of a "difficulty of reality" are emphasized by Simone Weil in remarks about the representation of affliction. See "Human personality" (1986: 72).

Bibliography

Byatt, A.S. (1998) "Introduction," in A.S. Byatt (ed.), *The Oxford Book of English Short Stories*, Oxford: Oxford University Press, pp. xv–xxx.

Cavell, Stanley (1969a) "The availability of Wittgenstein's later philosophy," in *Must We Mean What We Say?* New York: Scribner's, pp. 44–72.

——(1969b) "Knowing and acknowledging," in *Must We Mean What We Say?* New York: Scribner's, pp. 238–66.

——(1979) *The Claim of Reason: Wittgenstein, Skepticism, Morality, and Tragedy*, Oxford: Clarendon Press.

——(1989) "Declining decline," in *This New Yet Unapproachable America: Lectures after Emerson after Wittgenstein*, Albuquerque: Living Batch Press, pp. 29–75.

——(1996) "Notes and afterthoughts on the opening of Wittgenstein's *Investigations*," in Hans Sluga and David G. Stern (eds), *The Cambridge Companion to Wittgenstein*, Cambridge: Cambridge University Press, pp. 261–95.

Coetzee, J.M. (1999) *The Lives of Animals*, ed. Amy Gutmann, Princeton: Princeton University Press.

—— (2003) *Elizabeth Costello*, New York: Vicking

Cook, John (1965) "Wittgenstein on privacy," *The Philosophical Review* 74: 281–314.

Doniger, Wendy (1999) "Reflections," in Coetzee 1999, pp. 93–106.

Garber, Marjorie (1999) "Reflections," in Coetzee 1999, pp. 73–84.

Gutmann, Amy (1999) "Introduction," in Coetzee 1999, pp. 3–11.

Hearne, Vicki (1986) *Adam's Task: Calling Animals by Name*, New York: Knopf.

——(1995) "A taxonomy of knowing: animals captive, free-ranging, and at liberty," *Social Research* 62: 441–56.

Holland, R.F. (1965) "The miraculous," *American Philosophical Quarterly* 2: 43–51.

Hughes, Ted (1957) "Six young men," in *The Hawk in the Rain*, London: Faber & Faber, pp. 54–5.

James, William (1960) *The Varieties of Religious Experience*, London: Collins.

Klüger, Ruth (Angress, Ruth K.) (1985) "Discussing Holocaust literature," *Simon Wiesenthal Center Annual* 2: 179–92.

——(2001) *Still Alive: A Holocaust Girlhood Remembered*, New York: The Feminist Press at the City University of New York.

Leahy, Michael P.T. (1991) *Against Liberation: Putting Animals in Perspective*, London and New York: Routledge.

Mann, Mary (1998) "Little brother," in A.S. Byatt (ed.), *The Oxford Book of English Short Stories*, Oxford: Oxford University Press, pp. 93–6.

Miłosz, Czesław (1988) "One more day," in *The Collected Poems*, New York: Ecco, pp. 108–9.

Rhees, Rush (1999) "Humans and animals: a confused Christian conception," in *Moral Questions*, Basingstoke: Macmillan, pp. 189–96.

Scheman, Naomi (1993) "Othello's doubt/Desdemona's death: the engendering of scepticism," in Ted Cohen, Paul Guyer, and Hilary Putnam (eds), *Pursuits of Reason: Essays in Honor of Stanley Cavell*, Lubbock: Texas Tech University Press, pp. 161–76.

Singer, Peter (1999) "Reflections," in Coetzee 1999, pp. 85–91.

Smuts, Barbara (1999) "Reflections," in Coetzee 1999, pp. 107–20.

Weil, Simone (1986) "Human personality," in Siân Miles (ed.), *Simone Weil: An Anthology*, New York: Weidenfeld & Nicolson, pp. 50–78.

Woolf, Leonard (1921) "Pearls and swine," in *Stories of the East*, Richmond: Hogarth Press, pp. 21–44.

6

PHILOSOPHY AS THE EDUCATION OF GROWNUPS

Stanley Cavell and skepticism

Hilary Putnam

At the close of the section titled "Natural and conventional" in *The Claim of Reason*, Stanley Cavell wrote the following remarkable words:

> In philosophizing, I have to bring my own language and life into imagination. What I require is a convening of my culture's criteria, in order to confront them with my words and life as I pursue them and as I may imagine them; and at the same time to confront my words and my life as I pursue them with the life my culture's words may imagine for me: to confront the culture with itself along the lines in which it meets in me.
>
> This seems to me a task that warrants the name of philosophy. It is also the description of something we might call education. In the face of the questions posed in Augustine, Luther, Rousseau, Thoreau . . . we are children; we do not know how to go on with them, what ground we may occupy. In this light, philosophy becomes the education of grownups.

When I was invited to write a "*Nachwort*" to a collection of Stanley Cavell's writings that was recently published in Germany,[1] I opened my essay by saying that Stanley Cavell is one of the great minds of our time, but he is not a founder of movements or a coiner of slogans or a trader in "isms". I described him as "a writer who always speaks to *individuals* – and that means, one at a time". To read Cavell as he should be read is to enter into a conversation with him, one in which your entire sensibility and his are involved, and not only your mind and his mind.

In this respect, Stanley Cavell is virtually *unique*. And this uniqueness extends not just to the *way* he speaks, but to *what* he has to say to us – indeed, the idea that one can "factor" what Cavell says into a *way* of speaking, a "style", and a substance independent of the way it is said and the way it is listened to is as wrong as the idea (that Cavell has brilliantly criticized)[2] that we can do this with Wittgenstein's writing. The purpose of this essay will be to bring out the way in which Stanley Cavell's reflections on *skepticism* are unique, and the way in which they exemplify the idea of philosophy as the education of grownups. But this will require a good deal of stage setting.

1 Skepticism

If Cavell's interest in skepticism is well known, it is also frequently misunderstood, which is unfortunate because properly understood it is the key to understanding his Wittgenstein interpretation – or, rather, a proper understanding of each of these is essential to a proper understanding of the other.

Here is an example of what I have in mind. Although leading Wittgenstein interpreters on both sides of the divide that separates Stanley Cavell and Peter Hacker[3] have long pointed out that Wittgenstein is not a behaviorist, the idea that he must be remains widespread. Yet the textual evidence for the behaviorist reading is, to put it mildly, extremely slim. Why then does it continue to appeal?

The answer, I think, has to do with the following question, which I often hear from students: "If Wittgenstein wasn't a behaviorist, what *was* his answer to skepticism about other minds?"

Although most "orthodox" (non-Cavellian) interpreters no longer read Wittgenstein as a behaviorist, they do read him as having *shown* that skepticism about other minds cannot even be coherently expressed, and, in that sense, as a philosopher – indeed, as *the* philosopher – who has refuted skepticism (and not only about other minds). But to understand either *The Claim of Reason* or Cavell's other writings on the topic of skepticism, the first thing one needs to be clear about is that Cavell's Wittgenstein is not out to "refute skepticism". Accept this, and what Cavell has to say about "criteria", about the philosopher's context being a "non-claim context", and other subtle issues connected with his reading of *Philosophical Investigations* will fall into place. Miss it, and all this will be inscrutable.

Yet, the idea that Wittgenstein is *not* "refuting" skepticism can also be misunderstood. When Cavell denies that Wittgenstein is out to "refute" skepticism by showing that the skeptic has committed a conceptual blunder – when Cavell even speaks of "the truth in skepticism"[4] – he is not *agreeing* with those philosophers who would say that the skeptic (who, after all, speaks outside the normal language games in which the word *know* figures) makes perfect sense.[5] Cavell is not saying that skepticism is intelligible and (wholly or partly) right. Rather he is making two points: first, the *concern* of *Philosophical Investigations* – and, importantly for what I am going to say in this essay, Cavell's own purpose in *The Claim of Reason* is not to do anything that could be called "refuting skepticism". To read either *Philosophical Investigations* or *The Claim of Reason* as if it were a longer and more careful attempt to say what John Austin said in "Other minds" is to look at Wittgenstein's work and Cavell's work in the wrong way.

Second, if the skeptic's utterances don't clearly fail to make sense, neither do they clearly make sense. In the end (but *The Claim of Reason* thinks this is something still to be shown in detail)[6] there *is* something we ought to find nonsensical about the skeptic's claim that we "don't know", something we are not in attunement with. (Still, Cavell wants us to ask, "Who is the 'we' here?") But, the question this raises for Cavell (and, he argues, for Wittgenstein) is:

what is the *source* of the skeptic's being out of attunement? And why are we all moved, at certain moments, to be "the skeptic" ourselves?

That his failure to make what *we* call "sense" is, at bottom, a failure of *attunement*, is something the skeptic will regard as a *confirmation* of skepticism. If Cavell, and Wittgenstein read through Cavell's eyes, increase our understanding of skepticism, they may well increase our unease, our "conflicts", in the face of its presence, inside ourselves as well as outside. This is all that I mean by speaking of the "uniqueness" of these philosophers; whereas English-speaking philosophers who write about skepticism generally think of themselves as "epistemologists", and are concerned to "answer" the skeptic's arguments (or to defend them, or to find new arguments for skepticism if they think the skeptic is right),[7] Cavell (and Wittgenstein as Cavell reads him) are concerned to make us see something that troubles the skeptic, something that can and should give us a sense of "vertigo" at certain times, without causing us either to become skeptics or to find illusory comfort in over-intellectualized response. If I find this even more in Cavell than I do in Wittgenstein, it is because it is, after all, Cavell who uses the disturbing expression "the truth in skepticism".

But it is not just a turn of phrase that is new. To see a "truth in skepticism" without seeing some "truths of skepticism" marks, I believe, a decisive shift in the treatment of epistemological questions, and it was the great achievement of *The Claim of Reason* to highlight that shift.

Is it helpful to think of skepticism as an "antinomy"?

Thinking about the uniqueness of Stanley Cavell's approach to skepticism had an effect on me that I did not anticipate: it caused me to recall with a certain chagrin something I wrote about skepticism a few years ago. I want to share with you what I wrote then and why, when I think about what I wrote in the light of Cavell's insights, I find it – not exactly wrong – but something perhaps worse than wrong, namely superficial.

Here is the passage I suddenly recalled:

> The reason skepticism is of genuine intellectual interest – interest to the *nonskeptic* – is not unlike the reason that the logical paradoxes are of genuine intellectual interest: paradoxes force us to rethink and reformulate our commitments. But if the reason I undertake to show that the skeptical arguments need not be accepted is, at least in part, like the reason I undertake to avoid logical contradictions in pure mathematics (e.g., the Russell Paradox), or to find a way to talk about truth without such logical contradictions as the Liar Paradox; if my purpose is to put my own intellectual home in order, then what I need is a perspicuous representation of our talk of "knowing" that shows how it avoids the skeptical conclusion, and that my *nonskeptical* self can find satisfactory and convincing. (Just as a solution to the logical paradoxes does not have to convince the skeptic, or even convince all philosophers – there can be alternative ways to avoid the paradoxes – so a

solution to what we may call "the skeptical paradoxes" does not have to convince the skeptic, or even convince all philosophers – perhaps here too there may be alternative solutions.) It is not a good objection to a resolution to an antinomy that the argument to the antinomy seems "perfectly intelligible", and, indeed, proceeds from what seem to be "intuitively correct" premises, while the resolution draws on ideas (the Theory of Types, in the case of the Russell Paradox; the theory of Levels of Language in the case of the Liar Paradox – and on much more complicated ideas than these as well, in the case of the follow-up discussions since Russell's and Tarski's) that are abstruse and to some extent controversial. That is the very nature of the resolution of antinomies. What I have tried to provide in this essay is an argument *that convinces me* that *the skeptic cannot provide a valid argument from premises I must accept to the conclusion that knowledge is impossible.* In the same way, Russell showed that (after we have carefully reconstructed our way of talking about sets) a skeptic – or whoever – cannot provide a valid argument from premises we must accept to the conclusion that mathematics is contradictory, and Tarski showed that (after we have carefully reconstructed our talk about truth) a skeptic – or whoever – cannot provide a valid argument from premises we must accept to the conclusion that talk about truth is contradictory.[8]

Here I compared skepticism to an "antinomy" in the sense that word has acquired since Russell and Tarski. And I now think that this was "not exactly wrong", but superficial. So let me explain "not exactly wrong" and "superficial" in turn.

2 "Not exactly wrong"

It is no accident that I chose the Rusell Paradox and Tarski's formalization and treatment of the ancient Liar Paradox.[9] These are the two great examples that gave the notion of an "antinomy" (or "logical paradox") the sense it has in modern logic. I don't know if anyone ever did, but it would have been perfectly possible for someone in the Victorian era with a penchant for logical paradoxes (Lewis Carroll, for example) to write the following sentence on a piece of paper:

(1) The sentence (1) is not true.

Lewis Carroll would then (let us imagine) have gone on to point out that if (1) is true, then it is not true. So, by *reductio ad absurdum*, (1) is not true. But we have just proved (1)! So (1) must be true after all! So (1) is both true and not true, which is an absurdity.

Prior to having any special reason to spend time worrying about this curiosity, a plausible response would be to be amused, and then forget all about it. After all, one might think, when in our ordinary use of the word "true" do we ever encounter puzzles like this? We don't need to be able to say "what is wrong" with the Liar sentence to go on using the word perfectly successfully. (And the Russell Paradox cannot even be explained without first explaining the Cantorian notion of a "set", as something that can itself have "sets" as elements). But once reasons arise for worrying about the Liar – and there *are* good reasons for worrying about it *in certain mathematical and formal-logical contexts* – what one naturally does is to write down the assumptions that generate the contradiction. There are a number of ways of doing this – for example one may highlight the role of what we now know as Tarski's T-schema:

"*P*" is true iff *P*

and, in the present case, the particular instance ("T-sentence") –

"The sentence (1) is not true" is true iff the sentence (1) is not true"

– by taking it as the relevant assumption.[10] In more sophisticated treatments, one may make explicit the role of the assumption that "true" can be thought of as a single predicate, rather than a hierarchy of predicates (as in Tarski's solution to the Liar Paradox),[11] or the assumption that sentences are true, and not "statements" or "propositions", or the role of the assumption that there is just *one* relevant interpretation of the sentence (1),[12] or the assumption that there as *at most one* relevant interpretation of the sentence (1). In still more complicated treatments, one may challenge the idea that there is even such a thing is a *totality* of all relevant interpretations.[13] And one may show how giving up one or more of these assumptions enables one to use the word "true" in metalogical contexts without risk of formal contradiction.

Obviously, what I was thinking of when I wrote the passage I am now dissatisfied with was that one can similarly turn a standard skeptical argument – say, Descartes's in the First Meditation – into a formal proof, not, to be sure, of a contradiction, but of "I do not know that *p*", where *p* can be *any* proposition "about the external world". In a sense, this is what Thompson Clark's famous essay "The legacy of skepticism" did.[14] In *The Significance of Philosophical Skepticism*, a book strongly influenced by Clarke's essay, Barry Stroud offers the following example of a skeptical argument (which I state in my own words):[15] suppose I am at a party, and someone asks whether John is coming. I reply that he is. Asked by my skeptical host, "How do you know?", I reply "I just spoke to him on the phone, and he told me he is on the way." My host points out (or, better, claims) that "it is possible that John will be struck by a meteorite on the way." Although Stanley Cavell's and my beloved friend Rogers Albritton always regarded this as a highly suspicious use of the word "possible", Stroud accepts that

It is possible that John will be struck by a meteorite and prevented from coming to the party; and hence

I don't know that John won't be struck by a meteorite and prevented from coming to the party. But

If John is struck by a meteorite and prevented from coming to the party, then John won't come to the party.

So, IF (and, surprisingly, this is the only premise that Stroud thinks is problematic in this reasoning!)

X knows that p, and X knows that p implies q, together imply that X knows that q –

It obviously follows that if I know that John is coming to the party, then I know that he won't be struck by a meteorite and prevented from coming, and since we have agreed that I don't know any such thing, it follows I *don't* know that John is coming to the party. My knowledge claim is defeated![16]

Stroud's analysis of Descartes's dream argument is very similar. Stroud thinks it is undeniable that it is possible that D is somewhere else and only dreaming that D is sitting in front of the fire, and clearly that statement implies that D is not sitting in front of the fire. And D knows the implication. So, if (4) ["closure of knowledge under known implication"] holds, then Descartes is correct in his most skeptical moment. He doesn't *know* that he is sitting in front of the fire.

Interestingly, Stroud doesn't conclude that (4) must be given up; he thinks it is a mysterious and deep problem whether it can be.[17]

Here we have skepticism about "knowledge of future events" and skepticism about "the external world" nicely laid out as an antinomy. (Although Stroud isn't sure that it is an antinomy, and not a sound argument to the truth of skepticism.) And I do indeed think that it is important to see at what point in these proceedings we have departed from the concept of knowledge we actually have – the concept we are normally "attuned" in employing – although I would start at a very different place than Stroud does start, in fact, by questioning Stroud's Gricean assumption that "know" and "possible" have context-independent truth-conditions. But even this – seeking for what Wittgenstein would have called a "perspicuous" overview of our uses of "know" and "possible" – is very different from the kind of thing Russell and Tarski were concerned to do.

Russell and Tarksi were involved in constructive mathematical enterprises (as well as philosophical ones, to be sure), constructive enterprises I find of great value. But the "Theory of Knowledge" is hardly a formal, mathematizable affair. The problem here is not "consistent axiomatization", and is not likely ever to be that. And to treat the skeptic's argument as a purely intellectual puzzle, an "antinomy" to be removed, as I suggested we do, is to *trivialize* skepticism. "Look," I was in effect saying in the passage I quoted earlier, "here are some premises from which I can deduce 'I don't know that p', for any p about 'the external world'. Let's try to find a 'neat' way of giving up one of the premises, so we don't 'get' that conclusion." Surely this was a shallow response to a deep issue, for skepticism *is* a deep issue.

3 The depth of skepticism

What I want to bring out now is the way in which Stanley Cavell has taught me to *see* skepticism as a deep issue, thus illustrating the education of at least one "grownup". In a sense, this means that I want to explore the internal relation between Part Four of *The Claim of Reason* and parts One, Two, and Three. In those parts, Cavell was concerned to do justice to the very complex ways we speak of "knowing", and to understand how it can be that "masters of the language"(like Barry Stroud?) find skeptical arguments (all but) irresistible. It cannot be the case that Austin was right to adopt the school-masterly tone he did, to treat the skeptic as someone who is just being childishly unreasonable.[18] The long and subtle discussion in the first three parts of *The Claim of Reason* includes, among many other things, the presentation of what Cavell calls "the projective vision of language", the vision of language as everywhere dependent on human attunements, attunements in projecting words into novel contexts. This is something I have written about elsewhere, and I shall not repeat that discussion here.[19] But one feature I do have to mention is that there are also attunements in what we don't say, don't ask, don't question. That we don't so much as raise the question "Do I know I am sitting here by the fire?" when we are comfortably sitting by a fire – or that only philosophers raise it (or pretend to raise it) is no trivial fact, on the one hand, nor is it just evidence of the lack of philosophical insight on the part of the mass of mankind, on the other. That there is no clear *job* for that question to do in those circumstances is a fact that, if we reflect on it, can guide us in perceiving at least some of the jobs that talk of "knowing" does do. That epistemologists continue to take it completely for granted that "I know" I am sitting in a chair, when I am, that "I know" I am eating a sandwich, when I am, etc., and do not so much as consider the Cavellian claim that my relation to the chair, the sandwich, etc. isn't one of *knowing* is something I find extremely disappointing.

But as long as we stick to examples involving chairs and fireplaces and sandwiches, it might still seem that skepticism is a purely "intellectual" affair, even if it is one that raises significant questions concerning the most perspicuous way to view human life with and within language. It is when Cavell shows us that skepticism about *other minds* is not a purely intellectual matter, in the way that skepticism about tables and chairs seems to be, that the true depth of the problem of skepticism really comes into view.

The stage is set for this by early examples in *The Claim of Reason*. For example, the following passage (from pp. 69–70):

And then perhaps the still, small voice: Is it one? [is the man having a toothache?] Is he having one? Naturally I do not say that doubt cannot insinuate itself here. In particular I do not say that if it does I can turn it aside by saying "But that is what is *called* having a toothache." That abjectly begs the question – if there is a question. But what is the doubt now? That he is actually suffering. But in the face of that doubt, *in the presence of full criteria*, it is desperate to continue: "I'm justified in saying, I'm almost certain." My feeling is: There is nothing any longer to be almost certain about. I've gone the route of certainty. Certainty itself hasn't taken me far enough. And to say now, "But that is what we call having a toothache" would be mere babbling in the grip of my condition. The only thing that could conceivably have been called "his having a toothache" – his actual horror itself – has dropped out, been withdrawn beyond my reach. – Was it always beyond me? Or is my condition to be understood in some other way? (What is my condition? Is it doubt? It is in any case expressed here by speechlessness.)

When we reflect on this passage we of course see how strange it would be to ask, "Do I know so-and-so is in agony?" when he obviously is. But it is also strange to ask "Do I know I am standing on a floor?" when I obviously am. A difference between the two cases – a big one – is that the latter question doesn't *hurt* the floor. It isn't a mark of a "lack of respect for floors" or "an inhuman attitude to floors". But to really stop and ask the skeptical question when someone is in agony (in what Cavell called "the horror" of toothache), to ask it *about* the agony, would manifest a failure of humanity. It would be a refusal to acknowledge the other as a person, indeed, as Cavell describes the phenomenology, the other doesn't so much as exist for me as a person if I am in that state of non-acknowledgement. His agony has "been withdrawn beyond my reach". And what is not yet said, at this stage in *The Claim of Reason*, but what we already begin to perceive, is that even if we do not go to the extreme of mediating about "the problem of other minds" in the presence of someone in agony, we do all, at moments, fail to acknowledge the suffering of others. Non-acknowledgement is a real human possibility – an ever-present one, in fact.

In the closing pages of Part Four of *The Claim of Reason* this is illustrated, not by the example of a moral monster, a Himmler, say, a figure of "radical evil", but by "a study of Othello" (pp. 483–96). Othello is, in a sense, a genuine skeptic about one other mind – Desdemona's. His problem – and this is the horror of his situation – isn't that he lacks "evidence" of Desdemona's faithfulness. It is that *no* evidence is good enough. And even to imagine one of the minor ordinary-language philosophers of the 1950s and 1960s saying to Othello "This is what we *call* conclusive evidence of Desdemona's faithfulness" (or: "This is what we *call* having an unreasonable doubt") makes one want to vomit. That is why *The Claim of Reason* may be described as a defense of Wittgenstein *against* "ordinary-language philosophy", not a defense of Wittgenstein *as* an ordinary-language philosopher.

My imaginary ordinary-language philosopher might have put the emphasis in a different place, and thereby said something more interesting, by saying "This is *we* call conclusive evidence" – but then it would be evident that Othello is no part of that "we". Yet it isn't that Othello is part of a different "we" either. Othello resembles the philosophical skeptic in that he simultaneously treats "Do I know that *p*" (that Desdemona is faithful) as a serious question, an all-important question, *and* makes it impossible for it to receive an affirmative answer; makes it so that nothing could count as showing to *his* satisfaction that *p*. And what good could it do to "show" Othello that this is "logically absurd"?

Our fundamental relation to the world, Cavell teaches us, isn't one of knowledge but of acknowledgment. But for Othello there is no acknowledgment – and the cry, "I don't know if she is faithful", however "inappropriate" when all the criteria for knowing have been suspended, is the natural, the inevitable, expression of despair in such a situation. It isn't just an intellectual error.

One might grant all this, however, and see Othello as a tragic example of a pathology, a sort of spiritual cancer, from which (one might comfort oneself by supposing) most of us fortunately do not suffer. But this sort of comfort is something that Cavell wants us to repudiate. What is important – and this connects with many of Cavell's other interests – in Emersonian perfectionism, for example, and likewise with the ways in which Cavell takes films and operas as subjects of philosophical reflection – is that if Othello's is a pathology, it is an exaggerated form of, so to speak, a *normal* pathology. The point of saying this is not simply to awaken us to the suffering of others, as Levinas does (although I have heard Cavell speak about Levinas with deep respect); it is also to get us to see that an idea of being totally free of skepticism, in this deep sense, is itself a *form* of skepticism.[20]

To explain this last remark I have to touch on – I don't have space to do more than touch on it – some of the most profound and difficult parts of Cavell's philosophy. But touching on them seems to me a fitting way to conclude a chapter in a volume honoring Stanley Cavell.

4 Conclusion

One of the pitfalls into which many Wittgenstein interpreters have fallen is the pitfall of reading the Private Language Argument as some sort of "transcendental argument", say, a transcendental argument to the effect that a private language is impossible. James Conant, himself a student of Stanley Cavell, has beautifully explained why and how this is a misreading.[21] Cavell, needless to say, avoids this pitfall. But what is "shown", not by some controversial set of paragraphs in *Philosophical Investigations*, but by the whole "projective vision of language" that Cavell finds in that work, is that language speaking in a normative sense, fully *human* use of language, necessarily involves both individual responsibility and community. Speaking without rising to the level of full responsibility for one's projections of words into situations – the sort of speaking that Emerson's great essay on self-reliance taught us to call "conformist" – is parroting; but "speaking" by means of projections that do not and cannot make sense to a human community is "acting out"; an imitation of human language just as much as parroting is. And one of the deepest suggestions that I find in Part Four of *The Claim of Reason* is that skepticism universalized, skepticism that refuses to acknowledge any human community, is, to the extent that it is possible, a posture that negates not only its own intelligibility, but also the very existence of a speaking and thinking subject, negates the skeptic's own existence and the world's.

The refusal to acknowledge a human community need not take a form that is "skeptical" on the surface, however. Every ideological posture that purports to free us from our human limitations, whether by means of political "revolution" or magical "therapy" or absolute religious "enlightenment", in the end replaces the real imperfect and limited acknowledgment of the other of which we are capable by a fantasy. That is why I said that the idea of being totally free of skepticism is, in the end, a form of skepticism in Cavell's sense, is something that "repudiates or undercuts the validity of our criteria, our attunement with one another".[22]

Notes

1 Stanley Cavell, *Die Unheimlichkeit des Gewöhnlichen und andere philosophische Essays*, eds Davide Sparti and Espen Hammer (Frankfurt a. M.: Fischer Taschenbuch Verlag, 2002).

2 Stanley Cavell, "Epilogue: the *Investigation's* everyday aesthetics of itself", in Stephen Mulhall, *The Cavell Reader* (Oxford: Blackwell, 1996), pp. 369–89.

3 I discuss the "divide" in "Rules, attunement, and 'applying words to the world'; the struggle to understand Wittgenstein's vision of language", in Chantal Mouffe and Ludwig Nagl (eds), *Deconstruction and Pragmatism* (Bern and New York: Peter Lang Press, 2001).

4 E.g.

> The bond [between the teachings of Wittgenstein and that of Heidegger] is one, in particular, that implies a shared view of what I have called the truth of skepicism, or what I might call the moral of skepicism, namely, that the human creature's basis in the word as a whole, its relation to the world as such, is not that of knowing, anyway not what we think of as knowing (*The Claim of Reason: Wittgenstein, Skepticism, Morality, and Tragedy* (Oxford, Oxford University Press, 1979), p. 241).

5 Barry Stroud, in *The Significance of Philosophical Scepticism* (Oxford: Oxford University Press, 1984), is such a philosopher.

6 Cf. *The Claim of Reason*, p. 220, "This is no more than a schema for a potential overthrowing or undercutting of skepticism."

7 As Peter Unger did in *Ignorance: A Defense of Philosophical Skepticism* (Oxford: Oxford University Press, 1975). (But he takes a different position in *Philosophical Relativity* (Oxford: Oxford University Press, 1984).)

8 Hilary Putnam, "Skepticism," in Marcelo Stamm (ed.), *Philosophie in synthetischer Absicht* (Stuttgart: Klett-Cotta, 1998), pp. 239–68. The passage about skepticism as an "antinomy" is on 255–6.

9 For a detailed examination of the latter, see my Tarski Lectures, "Paradox revisited", in *Between Logic and Intuition; Essays in Honor of Charles Parsons*, eds Gila Sher and Richard Tieszen (Cambridge: Cambridge University Press, 2000), pp. 3–26.

10 Since the sentence (1) = "The sentence (1) is not true", this implies

> "The sentence (1) is not true" is true iff "The sentence (1) is not true" is not true – which is a contradiction.

11 Alfred Tarski, "Der Wahrheitsbegriff in den formalisierten Sprachen", *Studia Philosophica*, vol. I (1935); translated as "The concept of truth in formalized languages" in Tarski, *Logic, Semantics, Metamathematics; Papers from 1923 to 1938*, trans. J.H. Woodger (Oxford: Clarendon Press, 1956).

12 As proposed by Charles Parsons, "The Liar Paradox" in his *Mathematics in Philosophy* (Ithaca: Cornell University Press, 1983).

13 See my "Paradox revisited".

14 Thompson Clark, "The legacy of skepticism", *The Journal of Philosophy*, 69(20) (9 November 1972): 754–69.

15 Stroud states it thus:

> Suppose that as soon as I had hung up the telephone from talking with John and had said that I knew he would be at the party, the boorish host had said, "But do you really know he'll be here? After all, how do you know he won't be struck down by a meteorite on the way over? You don't know he won't be." ... Not only is this "challenge" ... unfair and inappropriate ... it is difficult to understand why he even brings up such a consideration at this point and thinks it is a relevant criticism. His doing so would normally suggest that there have been a lot of meteorites hitting the earth lately in this general area, some of them rather big and capable of causing harm. If that were so, perhaps I should have thought of it and considered it – or at least if I didn't know about it my ignorance might threaten my claim to know John would be there. But in the absence of any such special reason, the "challenge" seems ... outrageous.

However, Stroud does *not* think that the fact that the "boorish host" is speaking "outrageously" means that the "challenge" is unintelligible; Stroud thinks that what the "boorish host" says may well be *true*. For he immediately goes on to write:

> My act of asserting that John would be at the party was made on just about the most favorable grounds that one can have for saying such things. It is no reflection on me or on my saying what I did that I had not ruled out or even thought of the meteorite possibility. But once the question is raised, however inappropriately, can it be said that I do know that that possibility will not obtain? It seems to me that it cannot. ... I do not think it was true when I hung up the telephone that I knew that John would not be hit by a meteorite. So, again, part of what the host says is true. I did not know any such thing. But still I said I knew John would be at the party (*The Significance of Philosophical Scepticism*, p. 61).

16 I critically examine Stroud's argument in "Skepticism, Stroud and the contextuality of knowledge", in *Philosophical Explorations* 4(1) (2001): 2–16.

17 Actually, given all the premises that Stroud grants the skeptic, (4) is not needed for the skeptical conclusion.

18 This is what Cavell sees Austin as doing in "Other minds". See Chapter III of *The Claim of Reason*.

19 See "Rules, attunement, and 'applying words to the world'."

20 I elaborate on this idea in my preface to *Pursuits of Reason: Essays Presented to Stanley Cavell* (Lubbock: Texas Tech University Press, 1992), edited with T. Cohen and P. Guyer.

21 James Conant, "The earlier, the later, and the latest Wittgenstein"; published as "Le premier, le second et le dernier Wittgenstein" in *Wittgenstein, dernières pensées*, eds Jacques Bouveresse, Sandra Laugier, and Jean-Jacques Rosat (Marseilles: Agone, 2002), pp. 49–88.

22 *The Claim of Reason*, p. 46. A topic I want to suggest we might want to reflect on in the future is that – if these last remarks are at all on the right track – there is a way of seeing "skepticism about tables and chairs" as also a "deep" matter. It cannot, after all, be an accident that the Idealist tradition in philosophy has always, in one way or another, passed through a skeptical moment, and that "external-world skepticism" has regularly been linked to something called "solipsism." (Neurath once remarked that "it is hard to say what the difference between 'methodological solipsism' and real solipsism is.") But "solipsism" is just the attempt – or the feigned attempt – to universalize the non-acknowledgment of the other that Cavell speaks of.

7

THE TRUTH OF SKEPTICISM

Sanford Shieh

One of the most distinctive and fundamental aspects of Stanley Cavell's work is his reading of Wittgenstein's relation to philosophical skepticism. The basic contours of this reading, known to all those familiar with Cavell's work, may be captured in this passage:

> [The work of Austin and the later Wittgenstein] is commonly thought to represent an effort to refute philosophical skepticism, as expressed most famously in Descartes and in Hume, and an essential drive of my book *The Claim of Reason* . . . is to show that, at least in the case of Wittgenstein, this is a fateful distortion, that Wittgenstein's teaching is on the contrary that skepticism is (not exactly true, but not exactly false either; it is) a standing threat to, or temptation of, the human mind – that our ordinary language and its representation of the world *can* be philosophically repudiated and that it is essential to our inheritance and mutual possession of language, as well as to what inspires philosophy, that this should be so.[1]

That skepticism is "not exactly false" points to what Cavell calls "the truth of skepticism, or . . . the moral of skepticism, namely, that the human creature's basis in the world as a whole, its relation to the world as such, is not that of knowing, anyway not what we think of as knowing."[2]

These characterizations of the philosophical significance of skepticism call forth a number of questions, the most basic of which are:

1   What, for Cavell, is Wittgenstein's response to skepticism, if it's not a matter of refuting it?
2   What exactly is the "truth of skepticism"; in particular, is it a skeptical thesis that Cavell accepts?

In addition, one might ask:

3   Why is skepticism a *standing* threat to or temptation of the human mind?

4   Why is the possibility of the repudiation of ordinary language that underlies
    skepticism essential to our inheritance and possession of language?
5   Why is this possibility essential to what inspires philosophy?

These questions are naturally not new; in the critical literature surrounding
Cavell's work one can find most of them, implicitly or explicitly, stated and
answered. Although some of this discussion is useful and illuminating, the questions have remained, for me, not satisfactorily resolved. A substantial part of this
essay elaborates the reasons for my dissatisfaction. The main excuse for thus
publicly indulging in my continuing preoccupation with these questions is that,
by reflecting on their difficulties, I hope to sketch a way of looking at Cavell's
philosophical project that makes more explicit its originality and its divergences
from the philosophical traditions with which it is in continuing conversation. As
will become clear, I have rather more to say about the first two questions than
the last three. This is not, of course, to claim that what I do have to say goes any
further than the beginnings of a way of taking up Cavell's philosophical work.

1 A refutation of skepticism?

I begin with Cavell's repudiation of the idea that Wittgenstein aims at refuting
skepticism. What this means, of course, depends on what counts as refuting a
philosophical position. In *The Claim of Reason* Cavell explicitly contrasts his
account of Wittgenstein's notion of criterion against that of those early readers of
Philosophical Investigations, Norman Malcolm and Rogers Albritton, who take
"Wittgenstein's motivation with respect to skepticism as that of showing it to be
false" (CR, 7, my emphasis). To these sympathetic readers of Wittgenstein we
might also add critical ones, such as Jerry Fodor and Charles Chihara;[3] all of them
took Wittgensteinian criteria to constitute conditions in some way sufficient to
guarantee, albeit not by deductive entailment, the existence of that for which the
criteria are criteria. Thus, in particular, Wittgensteinian criteria of mental
concepts consist of (types of) behaviors that guarantee the existence of mental
states instantiating these concepts. As Malcolm puts it in the case of criteria for
pain: "The satisfaction of the criterion of y establishes the existence of y beyond
question. . . . [I]t will not make sense for one to suppose that another person is not
in pain if one's criterion of his being in pain is satisfied."[4] Hence on the basis of
knowing that the criteria for pain are satisfied we can know that someone is in
pain; this shows the falsity of the skeptical thesis that we cannot have knowledge
of other minds. On this interpretation Wittgenstein naturally appears, as he did to
Chihara and Fodor, as advocating a variety of behaviorism.

More recently this way of reading Wittgenstein's account of skepticism and of
mental concepts has lost its vogue, and Wittgenstein scholarship has come to
emphasize a different set of terms of criticism. These other terms are already
suggested by the words I quoted from Malcolm, which might be read with the
emphasis on the claim that "it will *not make sense* . . . to suppose that another

person is not in pain" in face of satisfaction of criteria, and therefore that for Wittgenstein the skeptic's doubts are senseless rather than false. To take a central example, the most prolific exegetes of the later philosophy of Wittgenstein, Peter Hacker and Gordon Baker, hold that in the sense in which Kant sought a Refutation of Idealism, by proving that the conclusions and theses of Idealism are false, Wittgenstein would not seek a refutation of skepticism. Hacker writes, "Skepticism is not to be answered by proving that we do know what the skeptic doubts, but rather by showing that the skeptical doubts make no sense."[5] The underlying basis of this newer style of interpretation is Hacker's and Baker's account of the foundation of Wittgenstein's later philosophy. On their view Wittgenstein departed decisively from a long-standing conception of philosophy as aimed at discovering facts about reality; instead, Wittgenstein envisioned the task of philosophy as setting out grammatical rules that demarcate what makes sense from what does not, and that thereby delimit the ways in which it is possible to depict reality. In addition, on this interpretation, much of Wittgenstein's later work consisted of criticisms of traditional philosophy on the ground that its supposed theses and arguments turned on confusions over or violations of the rules of grammar, and thus are in fact nonsense.[6] Here is a characteristic application of this way of reading Wittgenstein to skepticism about other minds, taken from a collection of critical essays selected more or less at random from recent books on Wittgenstein: "Whereas the skeptic takes the meaningfulness of certain questions for granted and then sets directly about answering them, Wittgenstein points out that meaningful doubts can be raised, questions asked and answers given only within particular language games"; for example, the skeptic's claim that "one can regard all behavioral evidence . . . as evidence of deceit is . . . senseless."[7]

Given Cavell's explicit rejection of the Malcolm–Albritton account of the relation between criteria and skepticism, this newer emphasis in reading Wittgenstein leads to a rephrasing of my first question: is Cavell's account of Wittgenstein's relation to skepticism in broad agreement with it? That is, does Cavell take Wittgenstein to be arguing that skeptical theses are nonsensical rather than false? On this question there is, it seems to me, something of a consensus among much of the significant critical discussions of Cavell's writings on skepticism and traditional epistemology.[8] As we shall see in more detail, Cavell is generally read as arguing, along with and on behalf of Wittgenstein, that there is some sort of failure of intelligibility in skepticism, even if he does not claim that skepticism consists of nonsense.

The fundamental source of my dissatisfaction with this reading is that it seems to fit poorly with Cavell's overall characterization of skepticism. To begin with, one may well think that if Wittgenstein sought to show that skepticism is in some way unintelligible, akin to nonsense, then it matters little whether we call his argument a refutation or not. If the premises or assumptions or conclusions of the skeptic are not intelligible, then that is surely no less forceful a ground for rejecting skepticism than proving that its conclusions are false. Indeed, this perhaps explains why some readers of Cavell seem unable to take seriously his explicit disclaimers; because they read *The Claim of Reason* as aiming to show the senselessness of skepticism, they find it hard to see Cavell as aiming to offer anything other than what Michael Williams calls a "definitive refutation" of skepticism.[9] Furthermore, if for Cavell skepticism is unintelligible, then it is *prima facie* unclear why he insists on a truth in skepticism, or why he claims that skepticism is a standing threat to the human mind, or, indeed, connected in some way to the very possibility of language and of philosophy. How could there be any truth in something unintelligible? And if it has been *demonstrated* that skeptical "theses" are somehow lacking in sense, why does skepticism remain a standing threat to the mind? Why shouldn't we, in view of this demonstration, take skepticism to be, in Richard Rorty's words, "as obsolete as . . . controversies about the nature and elements of the Eucharist"?[10]

2 Reading Cavell on skepticism

I turn now to the details of some representative interpretations of one set of Cavell's arguments concerning skepticism and traditional epistemology, occurring near the end of Part Two of *The Claim of Reason*, in the sections titled "The philosopher's basis," "The philosopher's context is non-claim," and "The philosopher's conclusion is not a discovery" (CR, 204–25); this stretch of text is generally taken to constitute Cavell's central argument concerning the nature of skepticism. Specifically, I will draw on Marie McGinn's *Sense and Certainty*,[11] Michael Williams's *Unnatural Doubts*,[12] and Stephen Mulhall's book-length study, *Stanley Cavell*.[13] Before beginning, I would like to note some limitations and conventions of the ensuing discussion. First, for my purposes, I will simply accept the assumption, made in these accounts of Cavell, that traditional epistemology, at least to the extent that it takes skepticism seriously as a position worth refuting, is continuous in philosophical motivation and method with skepticism. Second, an important caveat is that I will not, *in propria persona* as it were, discuss Cavell's text in much detail, even though I do think that a close reading of it would be welcome; my aim is to discuss the reception of this text. Third, this means, in particular, that in this and the next four sections I will not sort out those representations of Cavell's views with which I agree from those with which I do not; hence I do not claim in any of these five sections to be voicing my own conception of Cavell's treatment of skepticism. That comes only in the last three sections. Thus, finally, I would like the reader to assume that, before section 7, when I ascribe views to Cavell I am presenting these representative interpretations.

The overall context of the arguments under discussion is Cavell's interpretation of traditional epistemology, represented in Descartes's *First Meditation*, as the examination of a "best case" of knowing. For present purposes it will be enough to note the following points about this interpretation of traditional epistemology:

1   The traditional epistemologist's investigation of knowledge of the external world focuses on purported cases of knowledge of objects considered generi-

cally, "generic objects" for short. This means that no one (among the epistemologist and his audience) is in a better position than anyone else to identify these objects of knowledge, to say *what* they are. No one has any special training, any opportunities for observation not available to others, etc. This also means that these objects do not naturally raise, in the context of epistemic assessment, any question of identification. The only epistemically relevant question that might arise for such objects is whether they exist.

2   The consideration of a particular case of purported knowledge of a generic object is the basis for a conclusion about knowledge as a whole. This generalization is reasonable because no one is in any better position than anyone else to claim to know what such objects are, hence whatever epistemic position anyone is in with respect to them is the best that anyone could be in.

3   Much of the skeptic's progress does not depart from ordinary, "fully natural," procedures of questioning and assessing claims to knowledge. But two aspects of the starting point of the skeptical recital are not fully natural: the apparent entering of a claim to knowledge about a generic object that is the focus of investigation, and the skeptic's ground for doubting those apparent claims.

The relevant sections at the end of Part Two focus on the first of these aspects of the skeptical starting point. They evidently advance arguments for at least two major conclusions. The first is that "no concrete claim is ever entered as part of the traditional investigation" of knowledge (CR, 217). Instead, the epistemologist only imagines that a claim has been made. The second conclusion is that the traditional epistemologist faces a "dilemma": "the traditional investigation of knowledge ... must be the investigation of a concrete claim if its procedure is to be coherent, it cannot be the investigation of a concrete claim if its conclusion is to be general. Without that coherence it would not have the obviousness it has seemed to have; without that generality its conclusion would not be skeptical" (CR, 220).

The critical notion for understanding the first conclusion is that of a "concrete claim." This notion is based on "the grammar (conditions) of saying (claiming) something" (CR, 217), namely, "there must ... be reasons for what you say, if what you say is to be comprehensible" (CR, 206). This is taken to mean that certain conditions have to be fulfilled in order for it to be possible to understand someone as making a claim or an assertion at all. That is, there are rules or norms governing what has to be the case in order for someone to qualify as making a claim or an assertion, norms constitutive of claiming and assertion. Thus, for Mulhall, making a "concrete" claim is saying something intelligible, which "is a species of assertion, and so a speech-act; and like any other particular type of human action not just anything people do will be (will count as) asserting something" (SC, 99). Specifically, as McGinn puts it, "[i]n order for an utterance to be an intelligible act of assertion it is, as a matter of 'logic' or 'grammar', essential that the act have some recognizable point; a pointless utterance ... cannot be an intelligible act of assertion" (*SAC*, 89). In order for a speech act to have a "recognizable" (*SAC*, 89) or "definite" (*UD*, 152) point, the speaker has to be in a "special context" (*SC*, 98), one in which he or she has "specific grounds or reasons for making the claim"[14] apparently expressed by his or her utterance. In sum, the conditions for claiming are that a speaker has to produce his or her utterances in contexts in which it is possible for him or her to have a recognizable or definite point or reason for those utterances.

What if an utterance fails to satisfy the conditions for being a concrete claim? What is Cavell's assessment of the starting point of the traditional epistemologist? According to Mulhall, "[w]hat the skeptic is doing is *violating* the conditions under which something can intelligibly be said" (*SC*, 99). For Williams, the skeptic enters "his claims in a way that *violates* the conditions for fully meaningful speech" (*UD*, 151). Similarly, McGinn explains "Cavell's argument" as

> an attempt ... to show that the universal constraint of intelligibility limits us to operating within the normal forms of human action; the philosopher's attempt to perform an act of assertion without meeting the demands on normal human action results in something that is, as it were, *beyond* the bounds of sense. The argument is intended to ... expose ... the skeptic's words as entirely empty or idle (*SAC*, 92).

All these readers are careful to point out that the term of criticism that Cavell applies to skepticism is not straightforwardly the category of meaninglessness or nonsense. Cavell writes that when he claims that the skeptic "imagines himself to be saying something when he is not" (*CR*, 221), and does not "know what [he] means, nor even that [he] means nothing" (*CR*, 225),

> this is not the same as saying that the expressions [he] is then using in themselves, as it were, 'mean nothing' i.e., are nonsense; 'nonsense', used as a term of criticism in recent philosophizing, registers that concentration on 'expressions themselves', i.e., apart from their human use, which I have found a pervasive temptation of the tradition generally (*CR*, 225).

In particular, "[w]e can understand what the *words* mean apart from understanding why [someone says] them; but apart from understanding the point of [her] saying them we cannot understand what [*she*] means" (*CR*, 206).

This distinction is understood as a contrast between the meaningfulness of the sentences uttered by a speaker and the intelligibility of what the speaker is doing in making those utterances. For example, according to Williams,

> whereas verificationists focus on the skeptic's words, asking what they might mean, Cavell thinks we should turn our attention to the skeptic

himself, asking what he might mean by them. On this approach, the meaning of sentences is not primary but rather derived from what sentences are used to mean on particular occasions. The meaning of words, as a function of their role in sentences, is therefore an abstraction from an abstraction. The critical potential in this thought lies in its opening up the possibility that uttering a meaningful sentence – i.e. a grammatically correct sentence composed of meaningful words – does not guarantee fully meaningful speech (*UD*, 151).

The result of unleashing this potential, as McGinn formulates it, is the conclusion that "[t]he . . . epistemologist . . . can[not] be construed as a rational human agent engaged in an intelligible form of human action" (*SAC*, 89–90). As Mulhall puts it, "[The skeptic] is not . . . depriving his words of meaning (they may mean what they always did, what dictionaries say they mean) but rather depriving his utterance (his saying of them) of any meaning" (*SC*, 99).

Before going on to the second main conclusion, the dilemma of traditional epistemology, I would like to note two points. First, the interpretations of Cavell's treatment of skepticism that we have seen so far make it seem a combination of the concerns of contemporary epistemic contextualism with those of H.P. Grice.[15] With the former, there is the idea of the dependence of meaning on context; with the latter, there is the idea that there are dimensions of sense distinct from and not founded on "literal" meaning. Second, I would like to say something about how this account of skepticism might be connected to Cavell's reading of Wittgenstein. As we saw above, Cavell more or less explicitly equates the conditions for claiming with (part of) the grammar of claiming. Now, Cavell points out that for Wittgenstein "what we discover in the course of [a grammatical] investigation, when we ask, 'Under what circumstances, or in what particular cases, do we say . . . ?', are our criteria" (*CR*, 30). Thus, it seems that the conditions of claiming something must either be or be based on our criteria for claiming. From this perspective, the essence of Cavell's argument is that at the starting point of his argument, the skeptic violates our criteria for the concept of an intelligible claim.

Now, what about the dilemma of traditional epistemology? This is, of course, in part an explanation or diagnosis of how the traditional epistemologist ends up in this position of failing to meet the conditions of intelligibility. But this argument could also be taken to be a separate criticism that "reinforces" (*SAC*, 90) the basic charge of violating the conditions of intelligibility. The dilemma is the result of the tension between two aspects of the skeptic's position. On the one hand, the essence of traditional epistemology is to discover the fate of human knowledge of the world in general by examining a particular, representative, "best" instance of (purported) knowledge. This project requires that no features of the instance of claim to knowledge under investigation restrict the conclusions of the investigation to just this particular case. So the claim in question must be made in contexts in which there are no special reasons,

reasons tied to those contexts, for making that claim. On the other hand, the conditions governing assertion require that a human being have specific grounds, grounds special to the context in which he or she makes an utterance, in order for him or her to count as having made an intelligible claim. The conflict between the skeptic's project and the requirements for concrete claims is evident: the contexts of utterance demanded by the former are precisely those ruled out by the latter as ones in which any genuine claim, and so *a fortiori* any claim to knowledge, can be made. This argument clearly aims to show more than that the starting point of traditional epistemology in fact, perhaps inveterately, violates the conditions of intelligibility; it aims to show that the very nature of traditional epistemology insures that it cannot but begin from such a violation. As McGinn puts it: "meaninglessness is, as it were, endemic to the philosopher's extraordinary investigation" (SAC, 91). Note that this account of the dilemma of traditional epistemology displays the way in which the skeptic does not merely "fall" or "stray" into unintelligibility, but chooses the path of unintelligibility. It is open to the skeptic to speak intelligibly, by placing her words in certain contexts, but in order to carry out her project, she has to *choose* different contexts for her words. In making this choice the skeptic, as Mulhall puts it, deprives her utterances of meaning.

3 Reading the truth of skepticism

Among discussions of Cavell, Mulhall's and Malcolm Turvey's[16] are two of the few that explicitly attempt to explain what the truth in skepticism consists in. I will focus on Mulhall.

The background of Mulhall's account, I take it, is Cavell's claim that the focus of the traditional epistemologist's investigation is an object considered generically. Thus no one, in the context of epistemic assessment, is in any better position than anyone else to say what the object is, i.e. to identify it. It is for this reason, I believe, that Mulhall claims that propositions concerning it

> are not specific beliefs at all: they are not arrived at or brought under suspicion by the gathering of specific evidence; they do not express 'facts' that some are in a better position than others to have learnt, or 'claims' that some are in a better position than others to make (SC, 105).

Now Mulhall nevertheless claims that these propositions "do seem to be true"; indeed "there may be nothing of which we are more convinced than" these propositions. But, since we are all in equally good position to say what the object or phenomenon is, none of us could have a "special reason" to *claim to know* what it is. This means that "these [propositions] are not things which it makes sense for us to claim to know"; they do "not function in our lives in the way that pieces of knowledge characteristically do" (SC, 105). This account of the object of the skeptic's investigation yields an elaboration or explanation of why the skeptic's contexts are "non-claim." The point here is not just that in order to make any claim at all one must have particular reasons, but also that the choice of object of investigation precludes the skeptic from having reasons for making a *knowledge* claim. Now, the "realization" that the skeptic's contexts are ones in which no claims to knowledge can intelligibly be made

> is the truth or moral that can be derived from skepticism. For the skeptic is right in so far as he thinks that such propositions do not encapsulate something we can be said to know. . . .
>
> None the less in so far as the skeptic's final position amounts to substituting the concept of doubt for that of certainty, he participates in the misapprehension evinced by his opponents; in this sense, as Cavell puts it, the truth in skepticism is not exactly a truth (SC, 105–6).

This account of the truth of skepticism makes it into a meta-linguistic truth whose least misleading formulation would use some sort of semantic ascent. What I have in mind is this. Recall the old dispute between Russell and P.F. Strawson on the references of definite descriptions.[17] Strawson's view, roughly, is that in certain contexts an utterance of 'The present King of France is bald' fails to make a statement and so is neither true nor false, even though the sentence (type) has a determinate meaning. By parity of reasoning, in these same contexts an utterance of 'The present King of France is not bald' also fails to make a statement, and so is also neither true nor false. Nevertheless, we might say that if we characterize the first of these utterances in its context by uttering 'It is not the case that the present King of France is bald,' we come close to stating a truth, for what we have uttered can be interpreted as an attempt to say that it is not the case that the utterance (in the context in question) of 'The present King of France is bald' makes a true statement. But by the very reason for which we come close to stating a truth in this case, we would also come close to stating a truth by uttering 'It is not the case that the present King of France is not bald.'

We can understand Mulhall's account of the truth of skepticism analogously. In the contexts of the traditional investigation of knowledge, e.g. when I'm wide awake, sitting by the fire in my dressing gown, free of cares, etc., an utterance of 'I know that I'm sitting in front of a fire' fails to make any intelligible claim at all, even though the sentence is perfectly meaningful. But, equally, in such a context an utterance of 'I don't know that I'm sitting in front of a fire' fails to make an intelligible claim. Nevertheless, we might say that if someone characterizes these utterances in these contexts by uttering 'It is not the case that I know I'm sitting in front of a fire,' she would come close to stating a truth, for what he has uttered can be interpreted as an attempt to say that it is not the case that the utterance (in the context in question) of 'I know that I'm sitting in front of a fire' is an intelligible claim. In this way the skeptic may be taken to have come close to stating a truth. But now also, by the very reason for which the skeptic comes close to stating a truth in this case, the anti-skeptic would also come close to stating a truth by uttering what seems to be the denial of what the skeptic says, namely, 'It is not the case that I don't know I'm sitting in front of a fire.'

It is not essential to this account of the truth of skepticism that the utterances of the traditional epistemologist be characterized in Mulhall's way, as simultaneously expressing propositions and failing to constitute intelligible claims. One might object to such a characterization, on the ground that since propositions are precisely those entities that are either true or false, if such utterances expressed propositions, then they do have truth-values. Thus, the skeptic can escape criticism by focusing on the question of whether her utterances expressed true propositions about knowledge, conceding that they do not make any claims to knowledge.[18] But a slight revision of Mulhall's account in the direction of contemporary contextualist epistemology can overcome this worry. The familiar idea underlying contextualist epistemology is that the meaning of 'know' shares a number of features with the meanings of words such as 'here' and 'I'. In the case of the latter, facts about the contexts in which they are uttered have a significant effect on how statements made with these utterances are evaluated as true or false. So, in the case of the word "know" and related epistemic terms, facts about the context in which they are used affect the requirements that have to be satisfied in order for knowledge to be correctly ascribed by or to the person who uses them. Now, the standard schema for contextualism specifies that the fulfillment or otherwise of these requirements are the bases for assessing the relevant statement's having one of two truth-values. But there is *prima facie* no incoherence in extending this schema to encompass the position that the context of utterance may prevent the utterance from expressing a proposition with any truth-value at all, or even from expressing any proposition at all. Indeed, this is one natural way of interpreting Strawson's view. If to express a proposition is to state something true or false, then since according to Strawson in certain contexts utterances of 'The present king of France is bald' fail to make any statements with truth-values, these utterances also fail to express any propositions.[19]

Thus, one might revise Mulhall's account by adding two theses: (1) in "non-claim" contexts, utterers of (some) sentences involving 'know' (and related epistemic terms) fail to perform any intelligible speech-act at all, and so, *a fortiori*, fail to express any truth-valued propositions, or any propositions at all, and (2) these failures do not generalize beyond "non-claim" contexts. The truth of skepticism is then the meta-linguistic theory consisting of these two theses, together with Mulhall's account of what makes a context "non-claim." Now we can make coherent sense of how Cavell's argument about skepticism extracts a truth from it without agreeing with any apparent claim of the skeptic, or her anti-skeptical adversary. The skeptic's project requires her to begin her investigation of knowledge in contexts in which her utterances render her unintelligible. But those utterances can be understood as attempts to express a particular instance of the truth that is thesis (1), and so skepticism is not exactly false. Moreover, the anti-skeptical traditional epistemologist is forced, by his project, to utter strings of words that seem syntactically the negations of sentences apparently uttered by the skeptic, in contexts in which *he* is unintelligible. But his utterances can also be understood as attempts to express another instance of the truth that is thesis (1), and so skepticism is not exactly true either.

Call the interpretation outlined in this and the last sections the standard interpretation of Cavell on skepticism. This interpretation in essence takes Cavell's project to rest on certain claimed facts about conditions of intelligibility, and about traditional epistemology's position with respect to those conditions. And so it is not surprising that some proponents of this interpretation criticize Cavell by questioning whether he has successfully established that these conditions hold, or whether he is right in his depiction of the traditional epistemologist's position with respect to those conditions. An example of the first type of criticism is Stroud's claim that Cavell fails to give "a description, or even a sketch, of the conditions that must be present in order for a claim to have been made."[20] A criticism of the second type is given by Williams, who argues that even if "normally" a skeptic's "exemplary proposition" fails to "featur[e] in a concrete claim," "this does not mean that no claim is entered when such an example is introduced into a philosophical inquiry as a best case of knowing" (*UD*, 155); that is, for all that Cavell has argued, the requirements for making a claim "in the context of philosophical reflection" (*UD*, 155) are satisfied by the skeptic. This type of point is also made by McGinn. Like Williams, she agrees that in order for the traditional epistemologist's words to be intelligible they must have a point, but she argues that Cavell does not succeed in showing that they lack a point. She takes Cavell to argue that the words of the skeptic lack a point because they seem to constitute an obviously true statement, and so are not worth saying. But on McGinn's account, the skeptic precedes his introduction of the obviously true purported claim by "general reflections" which he or she takes to establish that his or her knowledge in general rests on propositions he or she has taken for granted and never justified. These are the apparently obvious truths with which he or she begins his or her inquiry, and so the skeptic's general epistemological reflections give a point to making and assessing a claim that seems obviously true.

4 The standard of interpretation and orthodox Wittgensteinianism

Prima facie, Cavell's treatment of skepticism, according to the standard interpretation, *is* in broad agreement with the newer style of interpretation of Wittgenstein's view of skepticism. Cavell's discussion appears, in these lights, to accuse skepticism, or the skeptic, of a form of failure of intelligibility. There are three salient differences between Cavell and the more orthodox Wittgensteinian account. First, the orthodox account focuses on the words of the skeptic, claiming that they are nonsensical, while Cavell focuses on the skeptic's act of uttering her words apart from conditions in which she can be intelligible as making a claim. Second, on the orthodox account, the rules of grammar determine what makes sense and what doesn't, and this suggests that whether the skeptic's attempts at performing speech-acts succeed in being intelligible is not up to the skeptic. In contrast, on these readings of Cavell, the skeptic has a choice to be intelligible, but is driven by her project to "deprive" her speech-act of intelligibility. The final difference is Cavell's insistence on a truth in skepticism. But we saw in the last section how this truth may be understood as nothing other than the meta-linguistic characterization of the unintelligibility of the skeptic when she utters what she does in those contexts required by her project. So these differences seem to be in detail rather than general approach: both Cavell and the orthodox Wittgensteinian are concerned with questions of "sense and meaning," but while for the latter these questions apply to words, for the former they apply to, say, linguistic actions and their agents.

As I mentioned at the outset, the standard interpretation raises a number of puzzles about Cavell's overall characterization of skepticism. On this interpretation, Cavell's main argument is that the skeptic's project insures that at the very starting point of any attempt to advance skeptical arguments the skeptic is not intelligible, and so the skeptical argument has no consequences for (attempted) knowledge claims in general. But doesn't this argument then furnish a decisive reason to close off skepticism as viable philosophical option? Surely this is why McGinn characterizes "Cavell's argument" as "intended to show us why we do not need to hearken to the skeptic's argument, why the argument does not constitute a genuine criticism of ordinary practice," to "reveal . . . the skeptic's criticisms as worthless and earn . . . our commitment to unqualified common sense" (SAC, 91). And surely this is why, as noted above, Williams sees Cavell as attempting a "definitive refutation" of skepticism. And since the traditional anti-skeptic starts from the same point as the skeptic, anti-skeptical arguments are equally, necessarily, unintelligible. So, doesn't Cavell's argument, if sound, yield a *definitive* reason for rejecting the viability of traditional epistemology? If so, then, as I noted above, one need not insist on calling this argument a "refutation" in order to take it to be a reason to close off traditional epistemology as a philosophical option. Moreover, if this is so, it is puzzling why Cavell would maintain that skepticism remains a *standing* threat to the human mind. When we become convinced of the truth of Cavell's premises and the validity of the inferences he makes, we should, shouldn't we, have good reason to abandon traditional epistemology once and for all.

It is also unclear how one would answer the fourth and fifth questions posed at the opening of this essay, if the standard interpretation is right. Since the skeptical enterprise, on this reading, necessarily transgresses the conditions of intelligibility, it is natural to assume that this violation is what Cavell means by the repudiation of ordinary language that he appears to identify with skepticism.

So, one might surmise that the possibility of this repudiation underlies what inspires philosophy because, if such a repudiation were not possible, then there wouldn't be such a thing as traditional epistemology. But what about Cavell's own philosophical work? On the standard reading it must consist fundamentally of the identification of conditions of intelligibility and their violation by the skeptic. But then why is an essential part of the inspiration of this work that these conditions can be violated? Why would the depiction of the conditions of intelligibility have to be motivated by their violations? Furthermore, on the standard reading the skeptical repudiation leads to an unavoidable loss of intelligibility. So, it would seem that we have to refrain from such a repudiation in order to achieve mutual intelligibility, and doesn't that mean that we have to refrain from this repudiation in order to achieve our possession of language? If this is so, how could the possibility of this repudiation underlie our possession of language?

5 Violation and refusal

The standard interpretation, as I have formulated it in sections 3 and 4, seems committed to attributing to Cavell the claim that skepticism is generated by a "violation" or "transgression" of the conditions of intelligibility. This attribution has been criticized by Steven Affeldt, who argues that for Cavell the skeptic "does not *violate* the conditions of intelligible speech by trying to say something in a context in which it cannot be said."[21] In this section I will show that there is a way of understanding this criticism that allows it to be assimilated to the standard interpretation. I don't take this to be the only, or the best, or the intended, way of understanding Affeldt's criticism. But I hope through this interpretation to bring out more fully the bases of the standard interpretation.[22]

Mulhall's account of the skeptic's dilemma seems to presuppose that the context of the skeptic's initial example is given, or settled, independently of the utterance and interpretation of his or her words. Properties of the context, together with the grammatical rules for determining the intelligibility of utterances, then justify the assessment of the skeptic's utterance as unintelligible. On Affeldt's view, a central point in Cavell's account of skepticism is a rejection of this independence of context from the interpretation of speech. How we understand, or try to understand, an utterance is at least part of what determines its context. Thus,

> there is, for Cavell, nothing about, for example, looking at an envelope under ideal observational circumstances which precludes one from having reason for claiming that one knows that one sees it. . . . And, perhaps with some, but not much, effort, we can imagine reasons for someone, staring at an envelope in his hand, claiming to know that he sees it. . . . And the reasons that we imagine need not be especially exotic or the non-reason 'because it is true' (GM, 19).

In other words, it is open to the traditional epistemologist to make sense of his starting point, by supplying a context for it, or accepting one, that would make the words he imagines being uttered intelligible, or make him, in producing those words, intelligible as a (normal) human being. However, as is by now familiar, the skeptic's project requires her to investigate a particular claim to knowledge that has implications for knowledge as such, and so she must take herself not to have any reason for making that claim which is special to it, which would then block the desired generalization. Now, as Affeldt reads Cavell, this requirement

> means that [the skeptic] must *refuse* all particular reasons and so concrete claims. Schematically, the skeptic's problem is not that his *context* or *setting* militates against his entering any intelligible claim to know, it is that his *project* prohibits him from accepting as what he means any of the various perfectly intelligible claims that he might be (understood as) making. It is in this sense that *he* can enter no concrete claim. The skeptic does not *violate* the conditions of intelligible speech by trying to say something in a context in which it cannot be said. His project prohibits him from *satisfying* the conditions of intelligible speech by saying anything in particular. He is not driven into necessarily unintelligible assertion, but into (for him) *necessary muteness*, into a refusal of expression, meaning, and intelligibility (GM, 19–20; last emphases mine).

But what exactly is the difference between "violating" the conditions of intelligible speech and "refusing to satisfy" such conditions? One way to understand it is this. On the "violation" reading, there is something, whose identity is known, or at least unproblematic, that the skeptic is trying to do, which turns out not to be doable. The skeptic is trying to perform a specific speech-act whose identity is given and unproblematic, in a fixed context; but, it turns out, the conditions governing intelligibility prevent this attempt from succeeding in the given context. On the "refusal" reading, there is no specific act that the skeptic is trying to perform, *because* she has to reject all of the ways in which he or she could *make* the context in which she imagines herself speaking into one in which she would be intelligible as performing some specific linguistic action. The skeptic refuses to do any of the things that would put her in a position to make a concrete claim. So there is nothing, as Cavell puts it, "that [we] cannot say" (CR, 215); we could say it if only we would allow ourselves to undertake the work of saying it, a work that goes beyond making noises or abiding by the requirements of (logical) syntax and semantics.

Perhaps another way of pinpointing the differences between these two readings is in terms of the notions of activity and passivity with respect to conditions of intelligibility. On the "refusal" view, "the context" of speech is *not already fixed* and so *not beyond the control* of the skeptic; it is always open to her to make the context into one that makes her words intelligible. In contrast, on the "violation" view, the boundary between sense and nonsense in the performance of speech-acts is fixed by the rules of grammar together with properties of the context in which the words are placed; this boundary is out of the control of the speaker, it constitutes a standard of assessment independent of what we might do to make sense in what we say. Once we know where the boundary lies, we can simply place ourselves on the right side of it, and thereby guarantee that our speech is intelligible. But the other side of the coin is that if we don't know where the boundary is, and happen to be on the wrong side, then there is no escaping the fate of unintelligibility. Affeldt suggests that this conception of the passivity of speakers with respect to intelligibility in fact also partly underlies skepticism. Since the skeptic conceives (tacitly) of her words' possession of meaning as independent of what she does with them, she fails to see that she needs to make them make sense. Thus, she sees no reason why she can't fulfill the requirements of her project by refusing all the ways of giving a particular point to her utterances, which is what leads to the skeptic's dilemma.

The distinction between these two readings of skepticism is, however, rather difficult to keep in sharp focus. Once again, what does it mean to claim, on the "refusal" account, that there are all sorts of reasons for the skeptic's utterance that we can offer her or that she could imagine, but for her project she *has to* attempt to make a claim without these reasons? Isn't this, after all, to claim that there is *something* that the skeptic *cannot* do? Isn't a crucial presupposition of the "refusal" reading of Cavell's argument that it is *impossible* for the skeptic to be making a (concrete) claim without accepting any of the particular reason that could be made available to her? Otherwise how could she be driven into "*necessary* muteness"? Now, on Affeldt's account of Cavell's Wittgensteinian notion of criteria, they "elaborate or articulate the structure or logic of our talk and conduct" (GM, 15), where this structure or logic is *not* something independent of our language that underlies its possibility, but something *in* our language as it stands. So, to paraphrase Affeldt, to elaborate criteria for making a knowledge claim is to "call attention to the fact that" if you are a normal speaker of the language, and if, e.g., you are looking at an envelope under ideal observational circumstances, and you claim that you see it, then there is a certain open-ended range of reasons that you *must* be prepared to supply or accept (cf. GM, 15). What is this necessity, this "must"? Doesn't it precisely derive from the "logic of our talk and conduct"? And what is that except a set of conditions governing when we can be mutually intelligible as normal speakers of a language?

What I am suggesting is that a natural reading of the modal vocabulary used in stating the "refusal" interpretation is that it is normative vocabulary. Read in this way, this interpretation appeals tacitly to certain standards, standards in, as opposed to underlying, language. These standards govern what a person has to do in order for him to be in a position to be intelligible as a normal speaker making an assertion. This is exactly how Mulhall reads the "refusal" interpretation:

[Are] the conditions that govern our speech . . . fixed or given? Well –
not just anything we do will count as making a knowledge-claim; the skeptic
*cannot simply ignore the fact that claims to know something are a species of
assertion, and that not just anything (even anything true) can (intelligibly)
be asserted to anyone at any time.* And how do we *know* this? *Because, as
the skeptic's confusion invites us to remind ourselves, we grasp the criteria for
knowledge-claims, the shared grammatical framework of assertion.* On the
other hand, there is no fixed catalogue of grammatical rules that will
tell us just what can (intelligibly) be asserted at any particular time by
any particular person – there are no rules to tell us exactly what is
worth saying when and to whom

(GG, 43–4; emphases mine)

What is fixed or given is not, as it were, a determinate function taking contexts
and utterances as inputs and yielding judgments of sense or nonsense as outputs.
Rather, what is given is a connection between the intelligibility of any (normal)
speech-act and the speaker's undertaking to make himself intelligible in certain
non-arbitrary but not antecedently determined ways. Note, moreover, that this
passage suggests that for Mulhall we *know* certain facts about these norms of
normal intelligibility, and that these facts bind the skeptic. "Cannot simply
ignore" seems to mean something like: ignoring this fact, failing to abide by it,
has costs. For instance, not just any driving behavior will constitute obeying
traffic regulations, and one cannot simply ignore, e.g., the fact that a red light
requires one to stop, without (potentially) incurring certain costs. The cost to
the skeptic, one surmises, is "necessary muteness." That is to say, perhaps the
skeptic does not violate *particular* rules fixing the intelligible application of
specific words in *particular* contexts. But does his project not require him to
(attempt to) violate the general or underlying norm that sense or intelligibility
requires *some* act or the other of assuming a position in speaking, of investing
one's utterances with a point?

Perhaps we can get at this worry from another angle by considering what the
traditional epistemologist might say in response to the "refusal" characterization
of his dilemma. Isn't he being told something about his (attempted) use of
language that he did not know? That, contrary to what he had always been
tacitly assuming – indeed, what, until now, he or she had not even been aware
he had been assuming – there are more conditions to the making of any claim
or remark or assumption than just uttering meaningful words, even in combinations in which there is no equivocation over the logical roles played by those
words. So, moreover, by failing to use words in accordance with these conditions, he is not making sense, i.e. normal speakers don't understand him. But
then isn't it urgent to figure out whether there really are such conditions on the
use of language or on the intelligibility of performers of linguistic actions? (And
how can we figure such things out?) Alternatively, might the traditional epistemologist not agree that his critic has correctly identified the general constraint

on intelligibility, but respond: "Is it really the case that I have failed to satisfy them?" Why is "because it is true" a "non-reason"? Why couldn't it be a perfectly good reason "in the context of philosophical reflection," as, at the end of section 3, we saw Williams suggest? Alternatively, why hasn't the skeptic already made, through "general epistemic reflection," the occasion of his words one in which there is a point to questioning even the most apparently obviously true claims, as, at the end of section 3, we saw McGinn suggest?

We seem now to have come back to the point we reached in section 3. According to the "refusal" interpretation, the skeptic's project prohibits her from doing what is necessary to meet the conditions for saying anything at all. So, skepticism consists, necessarily, of the skeptic's uttering words in such a way that she (tacitly) refuses to render herself intelligible, to normal speakers of the language, as saying anything at all. But isn't this to say that skepticism results in necessary emptiness, unintelligibility, or abnormality? And are these results not excellent reasons for rejecting altogether any philosophical position that leads to them? Moreover, the refusal interpretation seems clearly compatible with the meta-linguistic account of the truth of skepticism. That the skeptic has to refuse to say anything particular at all implies that she necessarily keeps her words from accomplishing that which the saying of something particular normally accomplishes. And isn't one of those normal accomplishments the expression of a proposition? In that case, the violation and the refusal readings would agree in a meta-linguistic conclusion about the skeptic: necessarily, her words express nothing true or false. And this conclusion could be taken to be the truth of skepticism.

6 Reading Cavell's refusal of refutation

Mulhall is also one of the few readers of Cavell who explicitly attempts to account for Cavell's insistence that he does not offer a refutation of skepticism. I will discuss three of the reasons Mulhall presents.

First, Mulhall points out that "Cavell wishes to dissociate himself from any version of a claim often made by Wittgensteinian philosophers, namely, that criteria confer certainty" (SC, 103). That is to say, skeptical doubts are not simply falsified by criteria and do not arise from "a simple failure to apprehend the true nature of ordinary language"; indeed, "there is no crucial piece of knowledge about language that skeptics lack or have forgotten, and that the rest of us possess" (SC, 103). This reason seems perfectly in line with the standard interpretation: Cavell disavows refutation because the trouble he discerns in skepticism is not falsity but unintelligibility. This appears to be confirmed by the fact that Mulhall goes on to say that "the inevitable consequence of succumbing to the skeptical impulse [is] that that impulse cannot be given intelligible expression" (SC, 104). But if this is indeed Mulhall's interpretation, then it fails to answer our earlier puzzle: does inevitable unintelligibility not furnish a conclusive reason for rejecting any philosophical position, and is not the refusal to title such conclusive reasons a "refutation" a quibble?

Mulhall, it seems to me, does have a more persuasive account to offer, in the second and third reasons he gives on behalf of Cavell. The second reason begins by ascribing to Cavell a characterization of skepticism that, on the face of it, differs from the standard interpretation just discussed. Skepticism is now said to result from "the termination or withdrawal of . . . agreement or consent" to "employing and deploying" our criteria (SC, 103). According to Mulhall, one of Cavell's reasons for "rejecting the idea of refuting skepticism" is that

> we cannot 'refute' the possibility that someone will decide (or find, or be driven to the conclusion) that he no longer agrees with others, that his attunement with them has limits; we cannot 'refute,' the possibility of repudiating an agreement, however fundamental that agreement may be (SC, 103).

It is hard to make sense of this reason, because it is unclear what would count as refuting a possibility, and so it is hard to see how anyone would even be tempted by the idea of refuting skepticism, if it involves the dubiously coherent idea of refuting possibilities. However, by looking at the third reason Mulhall offers, we can see better that what he has in mind is in fact an inflection of the standard interpretation. Here is Mulhall's third reason for why Cavell does not advance a refutation of skepticism:

> [G]iven that Cavell . . . regards agreement in criteria as the presupposition of mutual intelligibility, he is committed to thinking that the consequence of repudiating them will be a failure of intelligibility – an inability to mean what we think we mean, or to mean anything, by what we say; so a mismatch between what the skeptic says and what he wishes to mean remains the *inevitable consequence* of succumbing to the skeptical impulse, such that that impulse *cannot* be given intelligible expression. But this merely provides a third reason for rejecting the idea of refuting skepticism: for on this account of its *necessary* fate, the skeptical impulse is not best characterized as a commitment to a body of beliefs or hypotheses which might be based upon inadequate evidence or invalid arguments and so might be open to refutation; it is rather an impulse to repudiate or deny the framework within which alone human speech is possible, and so exemplifies one way in which human beings attempt to deny their conditionedness (their condition) (SC, 103–4; emphases mine).

The key to understanding Mulhall's view, I hold, is that he attributes to Cavell a distinction between criteria, which constitute "the framework within which alone human speech is possible," and the claims and arguments that are made possible only on the basis of accepting these criteria. This distinction is a version of the distinction made by Hacker and Baker between the grammatical rules that demarcate what make sense from what do not, and moves in the language for which these rules are normative – stating facts, gathering evidence, supporting claims – which are possible only on the basis of the grammatical rules. Given this distinction, one could argue that the very concept of refutation is coherently applicable only to claims or arguments made within the language, not to the rules that constitute the language. The idea of refutation is the idea of showing that certain claims or arguments are *incorrect* and so should be rejected, and this makes no sense except on the basis of standards demarcating correctness from incorrectness. The rules of grammar are, of course, these standards of correctness; hence there is no such thing as a refutation unless the rules of grammar are accepted. It follows that this acceptance cannot itself be refuted. By the same token, the concept of justification, of showing that certain claims or arguments are *correct* and so should be accepted, is equally inapplicable to the rules of grammar. It follows that whatever "repudiating" criteria might be, it cannot be based on an argument showing that one should not accept criteria, nor can there be an argument against this repudiation, showing that one should accept criteria.[23] On Mulhall's reading of Cavell, it is for this reason that there is no refutation of skepticism.

Unfortunately, this principled account against refuting skepticism is still not altogether satisfactory. The problem arises from the conjunction of two claims that we have already seen Mulhall ascribing to Cavell. First, skepticism is based not on factual mistakes but on a decision or action, so that "there is no crucial piece of knowledge about language that skeptics lack or have forgotten, and that the rest of us possess" (SC, 103). Yet, second, "the inevitable consequence" of making the skeptical decision is "a failure of intelligibility." Now, if unintelligibility is skepticism's "necessary fate," how could there be "no crucial piece of knowledge about language that skeptics lack or have forgotten, and that the rest of us possess"? Isn't it a crucial piece of knowledge about language use that it is not possible to make an intelligible claim without any particular reason? If the skeptic knows this fully well, i.e. knows that if she attempts to make a claim without any particular reason, then she will inevitably, necessarily, be unintelligible, then how can she arrive at the point of deciding, or finding, or concluding, that she can, after all, make an intelligible claim without any particular reason? If "the skeptic cannot simply ignore the fact that . . . not just anything . . . can (intelligibly) be asserted to anyone at any time," how could she still try to do so if she is fully apprised of the costs of such an attempt? Wouldn't the skeptic then be like someone who knows very well that it is impossible to trisect an angle with ruler and compass, but yet decides, or finds, or concludes, that it is possible after all?

149

In the last section I sketched a response, on behalf of the traditional epistemologist, to the "dilemma" in which he is said to be caught. The response comes
down to questioning whether the conditions of intelligibility he is accused of
having to refuse to fulfill really do hold, or whether he really has to refuse them. I
offered this response *not* primarily because it is *in fact* a characteristic response of
readers of Cavell such as Stroud, McGinn, and Williams. Rather, I offer it chiefly
because it strikes me as a natural, i.e. a reasonable, response to the sort of criticism ascribed to Cavell by the standard interpretation. Perhaps we can bring out
further why it seems natural by contrasting it to a response that seems unreasonable. Suppose that the traditional epistemologist replied: "Of course I know that
my philosophical project requires me to be unintelligible; but that's alright, I
have decided to be unintelligible, because my project is more important than
mere intelligibility." If I am right that this strikes us as an unreasonable, indeed,
irrational, thing to say, then we can explain why Mulhall's account is unsatisfying. Irrationality is surely a strong, even decisive, ground for rejecting a
philosophical position. On Mulhall's account, we cannot refute a position based
not on ignorance of facts but on making a choice. But what we have seen is that
in order to make the choice that the skeptic, according to Mulhall, makes *in full
knowledge of the (normative) facts*, one has to be irrational, and that becomes, after
all, grounds for a final rejection of skepticism. Indeed, one might wonder
whether this ground is really any different from the earlier ones considered; can
we really understand someone who is irrational in the sense described as a
normal human being?

Of course, it might be insisted that the type of ignorance internal to the concept
of refutation must be ignorance of those facts whose depiction presupposes, and so
are conceptually posterior to, the rules of grammar, rather than ignorance of the
rules themselves. But now again it is hard to see this as more than a quibble.

It might be argued that while the skeptic neither "lacks" nor "has forgotten"
the crucial normative facts about language, he or she nevertheless does not have
full knowledge of these facts. Perhaps he or she knows, but has repressed this
knowledge; perhaps his or her knowledge is not explicit or theoretical but practical or implicit. *Something* prevents the skeptic from acknowledging or accepting
Cavell's account of the normative facts, and thereby seeing that in philosophizing he or she has become unintelligible. Perhaps, as the last long quotation
from Mulhall suggests, this something is endemic to the human condition. Now
this reply, it seems to me, does not clear the skeptic from the charge of irrationality; at most it offers an explanation or motivation for that irrationality.
Moreover, how does the claim that the skeptic does not have full knowledge of
her unintelligibility yield a reason for not offering this "inevitable" unintelligibility as a refutation of skepticism? Surely skepticism is not any more viable as a
philosophical position simply because philosophers who hold it resist their
(implicit? repressed?) knowledge of its or their incoherence.

This discussion perhaps suggests another way of understanding Mulhall's
claim that one cannot refute the possibility of withdrawing consent to an agree-

ment. Perhaps the point is that showing the unintelligibility of skepticism is not sufficient for overcoming the skeptic's resistance to accepting her knowledge of her unintelligibility. If so, this suggests that, on Mulhall's reading, Cavell's concern is with the skeptic rather than with skepticism. On this view the epistemologist's dilemma might show that as a philosophical position traditional epistemology is either unintelligible or irrational; but it will not be enough to overcome the repression necessary to being an actual skeptic or an actual traditional epistemologist. This raises (at least) the following question. Do we have any reason to think that overcoming the resistance of the skeptic is a *philosophical* task? That is, nothing in this view seems to rule out that the skeptic's resistance has nothing to do with the philosophical conclusion that skepticism is untenable. A consequence of the interpretation of Cavell's project I will propose next is an account of how and in what sense a concern with the skeptic, as opposed to her doctrine, can be philosophically central.

7 Beyond the standard interpretation: proceeding from the ordinary

In this section I offer a way of thinking of Cavell's project that partially resolves some of the questions I have raised about the standard interpretation.

These questions are hard to answer, I hold, because on this interpretation Cavell's project is an instance of a traditional and widely accepted conception of philosophical criticism. The fundamental model underlying this conception is that philosophical criticism begins from what Frege would term a "conflict of opinions,"[24] in which the critic disagrees with the claims that constitute a philosophical position. As Frege saw it, to the extent that such a disagreement is genuine and rational, it is inextricably linked to the possibility of asking "Who is right?" and of determining an answer to this question on the basis of standards of correctness that are impersonal and objective in the sense of being independent of what any of the parties to the conflict takes to be correct.[25] The philosophical critic proceeds by attempting to ascertain, on the basis of these impersonal standards, the incorrectness of the claims he or she criticizes. The fact that the standards are impersonal implies that this incorrectness provides a ground for rejecting these claims that is rationally compelling on those who hold the position constituted by the claims.

At first glance, Cavell's opposition to traditional epistemology, understood according to the standard interpretation, does not quite fit this basic model. Since Cavell's criticism is supposed to be that the skeptic is not intelligible as making any claims, his conflict with skepticism seems to have to be something other than disagreement. However, a moment's reflection shows that this criticism is merely a variation on the basic model. Recall that Cavell's argument is supposed to rest on a set of conditions – based on or articulated by criteria – for a human being to be intelligible as making a claim. What this means is that the norms to which Cavell appeals for his assessment of skepticism are of the intelligibility rather than the correctness of (utterances intended to express) claims.

151

In addition, recall that we could find no clear argument against taking the unintelligibility of the skeptic's utterances to provide rationally compelling grounds for abandoning the attempt to maintain skepticism as a philosophical position. Finally, in our discussion of the traditional epistemologist's response to this critique, we see that a disagreement simply shows up in a different way or a different place, as a disagreement over whether Cavell has correctly represented the norms of intelligibility.

This leads to a characterization of the traditional conception of philosophical criticism as involving five principal elements. First, philosophical criticism originates from the critic's opposition to a set of purported claims that constitute the philosophical position under assessment. Second, the adjudication of this conflict must appeal to impersonal and objective norms that determine facts about properties of the philosophical position relevant to its critical appraisal. Third, when these facts are conjoined with the values we attach to those properties, we attain a rationally compelling basis for critical appraisal. For example, since incorrectness and unintelligibility are surely universally acknowledged (maximally) undesirable properties of philosophical positions, any positions with these properties are, as McGinn puts it, "worthless." Fourth, the impersonality and objectivity of the norms mean that appeal to them amounts to an identification of facts about the object of criticism that hold independently of the conflict or its resolution. One might say that, on this view, philosophical criticism has an essentially theoretical component, the discovery of objective features of the object of criticism. Finally, it is because the facts and values that are the bases of appraisal are independent of the act of criticism or of its reception that the critical judgment can be rationally compelling on those who hold the position under criticism.

It should be fairly clear why, if Cavell's treatment of skepticism is taken to be an instance of traditional philosophical critique, it would be difficult to understand why Cavell explicitly refuses to treat his argument as a definitive rejection of skepticism. Suppose a critic takes himself to have correctly identified the properties of the philosophical position he is investigating, and suppose some of these properties are generally taken to be completely undesirable, thereby qualifying that position as having no value. From the vantage point of such a critic, it is surely hard to see how anyone could have good reason to take up such a position; this is what it means for the critique to be rationally compelling. But then what reason could this critic have to refuse to claim that the position in question should be rejected altogether? A keen sense of human fallibility would not be enough, since it would only furnish a reason, in the first instance, to question whether one has made the correct identification of the properties in question (and perhaps also of the extent to which the relevant properties are taken to be undesirable). To put it in another way, if one thinks one has discovered that a philosophy is worthless, what would stand in the way of pronouncing it obsolete? Moreover, why would such a critic think that this philosophical position, which from his or her perspective no one has good reason to adopt, nevertheless remains a standing threat to the human mind? From his perspective, anyone who understands and accepts his arguments but yet takes up this position would be doing so knowing fully that it is intellectually worthless. Such a person is surely irrational, and so her adoption of the position is hardly a threat to the human mind. Of course it is compatible with this picture to think that we might come to change our minds about the value of the properties in question; we might, for instance, come to think that unintelligibility is not so undesirable after all. But in such a situation a reappraisal of the position is required, the outcome of which would clearly not be that the position is worthless, and so its adoption no longer ground for censure.

This discussion suggests that in order to provide a satisfactory answer to my first opening question, one can try to show how Cavell's project is something other than traditional philosophical criticism. I begin this task by looking at one of the most fundamental aspects of Cavell's work, his account of the nature of Wittgenstein's and Austin's appeal to ordinary language in their philosophical practices. I take it to be central to this account that "when Wittgenstein, or . . . any philosopher proceeding from ordinary language 'says what we say', what he is doing is not producing a generalization" (CR, 19), and I understand this claim to mean that such an appeal is not an attempt to *capture the facts* of our linguistic behavior. Rather, what a philosopher appealing to ordinary language produces is

> a (supposed) instance of what we say. We may think of it as a sample. The introduction of the sample by the words 'we say . . .' is an invitation for you to see whether you have such a sample, or can accept mine as a sound one. One sample does not refute or disconfirm another; if two are in disagreement they vie with one another for the same confirmation. The only source of confirmation here is ourselves (CR, 19).

The relationship between the philosopher's sample and its confirmation Cavell describes as follows. If I disagree with the philosopher's sample,

> he is not obliged to correct his statement in order to account for my difference; rather he retracts it in the face of my rebuke. He hasn't said something false about 'us'; he has learned that there is no us (yet, maybe never) to say anything about (CR, 19–20).

Thus, when there is a failure in philosophizing, by the lights of the appeal to ordinary language, it is not because there is a mistake about the facts, but because a sample is not acknowledged; one might say that a fact of agreement has not come into being. And this is to say, I would claim, that when there is philosophical success by proceeding from the ordinary, i.e. when I acknowledge a sample, the agreement need not reflect a fact about us that exists antecedently to my being presented with the sample. Rather, the agreement may be brought about through the sample's effect on me, through its getting me to acknowledge it. Thus, "[t]he philosophical appeal to what we say . . . [is] a [claim] to community. And the claim to community is always a search for the basis upon which it can or has been established" (CR, 20). The notion of a "search" here I would understand, not as the attempt to discover an independent fact, but as an attempt to bring the basis of a community into being. Understood in this way, it should be unclear how the attempt can so much as proceed, much less succeed, independently of the one(s) to whom it is addressed.

The consequences of this account of the philosophical appeal to ordinary language to our discussion of traditional epistemology can be seen as follows. Recall that on Cavell's reading of Wittgenstein, "what we discover in the course of [a grammatical] investigation, when we ask, 'Under what circumstances, or in what particular cases, do we say . . . ?', are our criteria" (CR, 30). Thus, saying what we say, the core practice of the philosophical appeal to ordinary language, is how we conduct a (Wittgensteinian) grammatical investigation, and thereby elicit our criteria. So the search for the basis of community is "the search for our criteria on the basis of which we say what we say" (CR, 20). Given Cavell's conception of proceeding from the ordinary, it follows that eliciting our criteria, just like saying what we say, is not the identification of a set of facts concerning either what we actually go on, or to what we hold ourselves accountable, when applying the concepts for which the criteria are criteria. Rather, it is a search, an attempt to bring about the possibility of a community whose use of concepts is bound by those criteria. As we saw above, the criteria for saying, claiming, and asserting are centrally at stake in Cavell's treatment of skepticism. But now that we have a different conception of what it is to elicit criteria, we should have a correspondingly different conception of what this treatment amounts to. Specifically, since Cavell's treatment of skepticism goes through the eliciting of criteria, it is, or at least requires, an attempt to make possible a community bound by norms whose authority to settle the bounds of intelligibility goes no further or deeper than this attempt and its acknowledgement, and so is essentially dependent on the act of philosophical criticism and its reception.

If this is roughly on the right track, then the difference between Cavell's account of skepticism and the orthodox Wittgensteinian's may be seen as a version of the opposition between philosophy proceeding from ordinary language and traditional philosophy. One partial way of characterizing this opposition is as a difference in conception of how the conditions for making sense are related to philosophizing. Here are some questions that divide them. For example, is philosophy the identification of those facts that, *by themselves*, guarantee, underlie, and limit what it is to make sense? Or is it the attempt to bring about those conditions under which the philosophical critic and his audience can be mutually intelligible? Are there conditions of making sense available to us, identifiable by us, antecedently or independently of what we do philosophically – of our attempts to make ourselves intelligible to one another, and of our acknowledgements of these attempts? If a contrast to the idea of the theoretical in philosophy is the practical, then this conception of philosophy, one might say, is ineliminably practical all the way through.[26]

The kind of philosophical criticism I have sketched makes the idea of a definitive refutation of a philosophical position problematic. If there can be a norm that mutually binds the traditional epistemologist and his critic only to the extent that he acknowledges the criteria articulated by the latter as his, then there is no such as thing as identifying, once and for all, the bounds of sense on whose wrong side traditional epistemology is located. There remain only specific philosophical encounters, particular occasions in which a philosophical critic seeks to bring forth a community of intelligibility with her interlocutor(s) (who, we of course all know, may well not be anyone other than the critic herself). There is no conception, antecedent to such an occasion, of what the outcome of any such exchange should be, no guarantee of the objective correctness of any side.[27]

8 Attunement and its fragility

We have now, I think, the beginnings of an answer to the first of my opening questions. We reached this point primarily by focusing on just one way in which Cavell's account of skepticism departs from the model of traditional philosophical criticism, namely, for Cavell the path to a resolution of philosophical conflict does not go through the identification of properties of the opinions underlying the conflict on the basis of objective standards of correctness holding independently of the attempt to resolve the conflict. This is merely the beginnings of an answer; it calls forth and leaves unaddressed many questions, the most pressing of which are perhaps the following two. Why should one proceed in philosophy by searching for the criteria that would bring the possibility of a community into being? How does the production of a sample accomplish this? By developing some answers to these questions, I hope to make more explicit the nature of the philosophical conflicts in which Cavell is interested. As I hope we will see, Cavell's view of what constitutes such conflicts indicates further the distance between his conception of philosophical criticism and the traditional one.

I will get to my answers by first considering a way in which the conception of philosophizing from the ordinary might seem disquieting. The idea that when proceeding from the ordinary a philosopher attempts to bring about with his audience the criteria by which they are mutually bound may well suggest that the normativity of our speech and thought is just, as it were, made up on the spot, at will, *ad hoc*. But then it is not clear that it is genuine normativity. Here again Mulhall's reaction is instructive. Commenting on an idea he takes to be suggested by Affeldt, that Wittgensteinian grammatical investigations are undertaken "only when . . . we encounter specific confusions or crises in going on with our words" (GG, 40), Mulhall writes that this idea makes it seem as if criteria are absent in the absence of such problems, as if our uncontested or unconfused everyday linguistic judgments are not always already shaped or informed by criteria, as if in such circumstances we have judgments without criteria. This would not only make it hard to comprehend Cavell's and Wittgenstein's frequent talk of being recalled to or reminded of our criteria by philosophical and non-philosophical confusions – talk which seems to imply that whilst criteria may be discovered through such confusion, they are not created thereby. It would also leave little room for talk of our everyday judgments as normative, as open to evaluation as correct or incorrect. For such talk presupposes the existence of standards of correctness, of norms; it must be possible for us to justify how we go on, and as Wittgenstein tells us, "justification consists in appealing to something independent of that which is being justified" (*PI*, 265). It is that justification that, on my account, criteria provide (GG, 40).

Mulhall's worry is based on two claims about criteria: first, they are discovered, not created, in grammatical investigations, and second, unless criteria are discovered, they cannot play the role of that by which justification proceeds. But why does it follow from the claim that criteria are constituted through grammatical investigations that they cannot be standards of correctness in justification?

A first possible answer is that Mulhall conceives of a grammatical investigation as something a philosopher can pursue independently of an audience, in which she simply claims to make explicit the rules that we acknowledge as norms. If her articulation of these rules is not constrained to be faithful to the actual norms that govern our language independent of this articulation, then an appeal to the criteria she makes explicit cannot constitute for her a genuine justification. Without an independent check, there's no distinction between what he or she takes to be the norms and what the norms really are; but then there is no reason to believe that whatever she has done yields a rule that is objectively binding in justification. If this is the right account of Mulhall's worry, then there seems to be a fairly simple reply. Philosophizing from the ordinary, as we have seen, is essentially addressed to an audience, and aimed at bringing about the possibility of a community bound by criteria. Only if the samples introduced are acknowledged can there be a common possession of criteria to which the philosopher and her audience can hold themselves accountable. Since acknowledgement functions as a constraint on the articulation of criteria, what any participant in such a philosophical exchange says cannot be simply identified with the criteria that would emerge from a successful appeal to ordinary language.

This reply is not likely to seem fully satisfactory. There is another way of understanding what Mulhall is getting at. On his version of the standard interpretation, criteria are norms of justification not only for "everyday linguistic judgments" but also for assessments of the intelligibility of philosophical claims and the adjudication of philosophical conflicts. Now consider what the conception of philosophizing I have been sketching looks like from the perspective of traditional philosophical criticism. It must seem to allow that the standards for adjudicating philosophical conflicts are not given independently of these conflicts, but may themselves be instituted or altered for any particular conflict. It is as if, in order to determine the outcome of any particular game of chess, the players may together make up or change what counts as checkmate or draw. Our intuition in the latter case is that the players are changing the game rather than determining the outcome; so, in the former case, our intuition is that the disputants are changing the topic rather than determining which side is favored by the balance of reasons.[28]

It is tempting to respond to this worry by suggesting a slight change in the idea of instituting or changing norms: perhaps we can take eliciting criteria to be proposing their adoption. This suggestion amounts to a (re)interpretation of Cavell's philosophical practice as sharing its aims with some varieties of pragmatism. On such an interpretation, this philosophical practice is apt to seem insufficient for achieving its goal: for surely a proposal for adopting certain criteria would be more compelling if accompanied by some reasons in favor of the adoption? There are many possibilities for supplementing proposals for adopting criteria. For example, a proponent of the standard interpretation might say: are not intelligibility and rationality sufficiently compelling incentives? Pragmatists, who tend to be more tolerant, might suspend judgment on the intelligibility of the skeptic and her use of words, but urge that standards for epistemic assessment which lead to doubts about every empirical belief are surely less useful for science and everyday life than ones which do not.[29]

To my mind, this response remains at odds with what is central to Cavell's conception of his conflict with skepticism and the possibilities of its resolution. An indication of this is that pragmatism is still an instance of traditional philosophical criticism. Systems of thought or of claims here replace (attempted) claims as what philosophical positions comprise. Philosophical conflict becomes the determination of which system to adopt, and its resolution still appeals to objective standards that determine properties of the systems relevant to their evaluation, for example their overall utility. And criticism is still aimed at offering rationally compelling grounds in favor of one system.

The depth of Cavell's difference with the tradition cannot be fully measured until we grasp that for him philosophical conflict is not a disagreement, however disguised, over claims, not an opposition of theses. In order to see how this is so, let's begin by reading a well-known and much-quoted passage from one of the earliest of Cavell's discussions of Wittgenstein, "The availability of Wittgenstein's later philosophy":

> We learn and teach words in certain contexts, and then we are
> expected, and expect others, to be able to project them into further

contexts. *Nothing* insures that this projection will take place (in particular, not the grasping of universals nor the grasping of books of rules),
just as *nothing* insures that we will make, and understand, the same
projections. That on the whole we do is a matter of our sharing routes
of interest and feeling, modes of response, senses of humor and of
significance and of fulfillment, of what is outrageous, of what is similar
to what else, what a rebuke, what forgiveness, of when an utterance is
an assertion, when an appeal, when an explanation – all the whirl of
organism Wittgenstein calls 'forms of life'. Human speech and activity,
sanity and community, rest upon nothing more, but nothing less, than
this. It is a vision as simple as it is difficult, and as difficult as it is (and
because it is) terrifying.[30, 31]

I would like to emphasize two ideas that can be discerned in this passage. The
first is the fundamental status of human agreement. That human beings "agree
in the *language* they use,"[32] converge in judgments and reactions, is a fact, for
which no "philosophical explanation," "say, in terms of meanings or conventions or basic terms or propositions," "is needed, or wanted" (CR, 32). It is this
agreement that is foundational; on *it* rests "[h]uman speech and activity, sanity
and community."

Cavell emphasizes that this agreement is *not* like "coming to or arriving at an
agreement on a given occasion" (CR, 32). Seeing why this is so is critical for my
purposes, so I will sketch what I take to be a clear case of coming to an agreement on an occasion, in order to contrast it with the foundational agreement
among human beings. At a department meeting I may propose to my colleagues
that a course in elementary logic should not be required for completing our
undergraduate major in philosophy, because our students tend to be bored by
such a course and learn too little to help their participation in other philosophy
courses. After some discussion, my colleagues and I conclude that these disadvantages do indeed outweigh the advantages and so decide to adopt my
proposal. In such a case it is clear that we first understand what is being
proposed, then consider its merits, then conclude that it should be adopted.
About such a situation we would surely say that my colleagues and I have come
to an agreement about major requirements. Moreover, on the pragmatist interpretation and supplementation, the project of eliciting criteria is essentially like
this: a proposed criterion is presented, understood, reasons for and against it are
weighed, and then it is adopted or rejected on the basis of these reasons.

As I understand it, for Cavell's Wittgenstein, what we share are fundamental
ways of responding to one another and to the world, and *ways* of acting toward one
another and in the world. Among other things, we share ways of saying, expecting,
naming, understanding, describing, thinking, making sense, taking something to be
useful, concluding, agreeing, adopting. . . . It is on the basis of sharing these ways
that there exist, for *us who share* them, such things as saying, concluding, agreeing,
etc. It follows that we don't first understand a description of how to do such things,

and then think about whether it makes sense, or is useful, for us to do them in these ways, and then, if we conclude in favor, agree to adopt these ways. I take it that something like this line of thinking forms, at least in part, Cavell's reason for marking the singularity of the fact of human agreement by calling it "attunement." If agreement in criteria is part of this attunement, then it is more natural to say that we agree *in our criteria*, as we agree in our language, than to say that we *agree to use* (to "employing and deploying") *criteria*, for such-and-such reasons.

The second idea, which is perhaps somewhat under-appreciated, might be termed the fragility of our attunement and so our mutual possession of language. This is the idea that our attunement is, as it were, *merely* a fact. There is no guarantee that human beings are, or will remain, or will achieve attunement. That human being sometimes fall out of attunement is evidenced, in particular, by philosophy; the disagreements that arise in philosophizing "are typically not those of philosophers with one another but of philosophers with the words of ordinary human beings" (CR, 32). The nature of our attunement gives the sense in which and the reason for which nothing insures that we remain in it. As I read Cavell, a guarantee of attunement would be a set of rationally compelling grounds for us to remain in or return to attunement. But, as we have just seen, a convergence in judgment and reaction is what makes possible our practice of giving one another reasons; hence ultimately we cannot give someone reasons why he or she should judge or react in the ways in question.

Against the background of these two ideas, we are in better position to grasp what for Cavell constitutes Wittgenstein's philosophical criticism. In contrast to the traditional conception, the philosophical conflict at its origin is not one of opinions, not of (systems of attempted) claims. From Wittgenstein's perspective, the plight of the traditional philosopher is to have fallen, somehow, out of attunement with other human beings and with himself when not philosophizing. So Wittgenstein would take his conflict with traditional philosophy to be a loss of attunement with the ways of traditional philosophizing; the conflict is not, as traditional philosophy would take it to be, that he rejects certain attempted claims on the grounds that they are objectively incorrect or unintelligible.[33] It follows that Wittgenstein's differences with traditional philosophy include a difference over how they differ; this provides a sense in which Wittgenstein's philosophical ambition includes altering the self-understanding of traditional philosophy.

The task of philosophical criticism is to restore the traditional philosopher to attunement with the ways of ordinary human beings. But since nothing rationally compels one to share one's judgments and reactions, this task cannot be accomplished by identifying reasons, which apply to the traditional philosopher no matter what he thinks or does, and which weighs against his attempts to make certain claims (without doing certain other things), or his adoption of certain criteria. As Cavell puts it:

> [T]he ordinary language critic [is] at the mercy of his opposition – . . . a
> test of his criticism must be whether those to whom it is directed

accept its truth, since they are as authoritative as he in evaluating the data upon which it will be based. . . . But what it means is *not* that the critic and his opposition must come to *agree* about certain propositions which until now they have disagreed about. . . . What this critic wants, or needs, is a possession of data and descriptions so clear and common that apart from them neither agreement nor disagreement would be possible – not as if the problem is for opposed positions to be reconciled, but for the halves of the mind to go back together.[34]

So how is the task of philosophizing to be carried out? As we saw above, in appealing to ordinary language, the philosophical critic introduces a sample. The sample statements and criteria that are based on them "lay out a way of doing or saying something which is to be *followed*."[35] So I take the philosopher's introduction of a sample as *displaying* the ways in which she goes about applying various concepts, displaying these *as* the ways in which *we* do so. This display is an invitation to her audience to follow her ways, to acknowledge those ways as their ways as well.[36] But it follows from the nature of our attunement that nothing insures that this invitation will be taken up:

An initial disagreement may be overcome; it may turn out that we were producing samples of different things . . . or that one of us had not looked carefully at the sample he produced and only imagined that he wished to produce it, and then retracts or exchanges it. But if the disagreement persists, there is no appeal beyond us, or if beyond us two, then not beyond some eventual us. There is such a thing as intellectual tragedy. It is not a matter of saying something false. Nor is it an inability or refusal to say something or to hear something, from which other tragedies may spring (CR, 19).

9 Concluding remarks

In this closing section I begin with some more answers to my opening questions.

The conception of human attunement underlying the philosophy of the ordinary points to a way of answering the final three of my questions. Our common possession of language rests on a convergence in reaction and judgment that may, at any time, fall apart, but that also may, at any time, be in place. Skepticism and traditional epistemology stem from the former possibility, our inheritance and mutual possession of language from the latter; but both arise from the same permanent absence of guarantee. Moreover, that there is never any assurance at all, rational or otherwise, for restoring our mutual attunement is what underlies the conception of philosophizing from the ordinary we have outlined above.

What of the second question? What has now become of the truth of skepticism? On the reading I have been proposing, that truth is not some fact about the skeptic given antecedently to her philosophical engagement with the critic proceeding from the ordinary. This is, of course, a merely negative characterization. But perhaps it must be accepted that what this philosophical conversation with the skeptic can teach us is never any final, positive thesis, something that can take us definitively beyond traditional philosophy. To think that there could be such a teaching is precisely to remain committed to the traditional conception of philosophizing from which the philosopher of the ordinary strives to depart. So, I will venture this: if there is a truth in skepticism, it is that the very idea of a final break with skepticism or with traditional philosophy is itself continuous with the impulse to skepticism.[37]

To conclude, I would like to come back again to the contrast between traditional philosophy and philosophy of the ordinary, to develop some consequences of the fact that the task of philosophizing differs for these two conceptions. For the former, philosophizing is essentially the identification of given facts, in the case of interest, facts about conditions of intelligibility. Thus, the primary duty of the philosophical critic is to represent the facts correctly. The philosophical critic can envision himself as having discharged his responsibility, a responsibility to truth or to reason, once he has gotten the facts right. Once he has done so, he can take himself to be free of the intellectual failings – the vices of ignorance or irrationality or lack of self-knowledge – of those whom he criticizes. That is, traditional philosophy goes with the idea that in philosophizing one may come to possess a truth or occupy a vantage point that is simply missed by those one criticizes. By contrast, for the philosopher of the ordinary, there is no such asymmetry in intellectual position between herself and those whom she opposes. It is not just that, as Mulhall puts it, "there is no crucial piece of knowledge about language that skeptics lack or have forgotten, and that the rest of us possess." It is, additionally, also not the case that while the skeptic is "confused" or "unintelligible" or "abnormal," her philosophical critic is not. In a failure of attunement the loss of intelligibility is mutual. Cavell characterizes the one appealing to the ordinary thus: "I have nothing more to go on than my conviction, my sense that I make sense. It may prove to be the case that I am wrong, that my conviction isolates me, from all others, from myself" (CR, 20). Moreover, since the grounds of mutual intelligibility are not *given*, or not simply given, the philosopher proceeding from the ordinary must see that *she*, in her philosophizing, has a responsibility for achieving that ground. Cavell puts it this way: it is "not just . . . that my understanding *has* limits, but that I must *draw* them, on apparently no more ground than my own" (CR, 115). From this it follows that such a philosophical critic is never in a position to disclaim any implication in philosophical failure, and so never in a position to take herself to be exempt from the difficulties of her audience. What I am suggesting is that, at least from the perspective of the philosophy of the ordinary, the traditional philosopher is what Cavell calls a "moralizer," one who "speak[s] in the name of a position one does not occupy, confronting others in positions of which one will not imagine the acknowledgement" (CR, 326). I

161

end, as is surely only appropriate for this occasion, with some words from *The Claim of Reason*, in which I shall presume to add some emphases and interpolations:

> If philosophy is the criticism a culture produces of itself, and proceeds essentially by criticizing past efforts at this criticism, then Wittgenstein's originality lies in having developed modes of criticism that are not moralistic, that is, that do not leave the critic imagining himself free of the faults he sees around him, and which proceed not by trying to argue a given statement false or wrong [or meaningless or useless], but by showing [to] the person making an assertion [that he] does not really know what *he* means, has not really said what *he* wished (CR, 175).[38]

Notes

1 "Psychoanalysis and cinema: the melodrama of the unknown woman," in Cavell, *Contesting Tears* (Chicago: University of Chicago Press, 1996), pp. 88–9.
2 *The Claim of Reason* (Oxford: Oxford University Press, 1979), p. 241. This book hereafter cited as CR.
3 "Operationalism and ordinary language philosophy," in G. Pitcher (ed.), *Wittgenstein: The Philosophical Investigations* (Notre Dame, IN: University of Notre Dame Press, 1968), pp. 384–419.
4 "Wittgenstein's *Philosophical Investigations*," in Pitcher, op. cit., pp. 84–5.
5 P.M.S. Hacker, *Insight and Illusion*, rev. edn (Oxford: Oxford University Press, 1986), p. 208.
6 Hacker, op. cit., chapter VI, contains a particularly clear account of this view.
7 Michel ter Hark, "The inner and the outer," in H.-J. Glock (ed.), *Wittgenstein: A Critical Reader* (Oxford: Basil Blackwell, 2001), pp. 199–224, at pp. 203 and 205.
8 Some notable exceptions are Steven G. Affeldt, "The ground of mutuality: criteria, judgment, and intelligibility in Stephen Mulhall and Stanley Cavell," *European Journal of Philosophy* 6(1) (1998): 1–31; Richard Eldridge, "'A continuing task': Cavell and the truth of skepticism," in R. Fleming and M. Payne (eds), *The Senses of Stanley Cavell* (Lewisburg, PA: Bucknell University Press, 1989), pp. 73–89; Timothy Gould, "Where the action is: Stanley Cavell and the skeptic's activity," in *The Senses of Stanley Cavell*, pp. 90–115 and *Hearing Things* (Chicago: University of Chicago Press, 1998); and Edward Minar, "Living with the problem of the other," in Denis McManus (ed.), *Wittgenstein and Skepticism*, (London and New York: Routledge, 2004). My overall sense of Cavell on skepticism is, in one way or the other, close, I believe, to those of these essays. But to the extent that I understand the specific arguments and conclusions developed therein, I find that they differ from the ones to be articulated here.
9 Michael Williams, *Unnatural Doubts* (Princeton, NJ: Princeton University Press, 1995), pp. 16, 32, 149.
10 "Hilary Putnam and the relativist menace," in R. Rorty, *Philosophical Papers*, vol. 3 (Cambridge: Cambridge University Press, 1998), pp. 43–62, at p. 47 n. 17.
11 (Oxford: Blackwell, 1989); hereafter cited as SAC.
12 Op. cit., note 9; hereafter cited as UD.
13 (Oxford: Oxford University Press, 1994); hereafter cited as SC.

14 Stephen Mulhall, "The givenness of grammar: a reply to Steven Affeldt," *European Journal of Philosophy* 6 (1998): 32–44, at 43. This paper hereafter cited as GG.

15 Some founding texts of contemporary contextualist epistemology are: Peter Unger, *Philosophical Relativity* (Oxford: Oxford University Press, 2002), Keith DeRose, "Solving the skeptical problem," *The Philosophical Review* 104 (1995): 1–52, and David Lewis, "Elusive knowledge," *The Australasian Journal of Philosophy* 74 (1996): 549–67. For Grice on skepticism see "The causal theory of perception," in Grice, *Studies in the Way of Words* (Cambridge, MA: Harvard University Press, 1989), and also the Introduction of *Studies*.

16 Malcolm Turvey, "Is scepticism a 'natural possibility' of language? Reasons to be sceptical of Cavell's Wittgenstein," in Richard Allen and Malcolm Turvey (eds), *Wittgenstein, Theory and the Arts* (London and New York: Routledge, 2001), pp. 117–36.

17 Bertrand Russell, "On denoting," *Mind* 14 (1905): 479–93; P.F. Strawson, "On referring," *Mind* 59 (1950): 320–44.

18 See Barry Stroud, "Reasonable claims," in *Understanding Human Knowledge: Philosophical Essays* (New York: Oxford University Press, 2000), pp. 51–70, and Edward Witherspoon, "Houses, flowers, and frameworks: Cavell and Mulhall on the moral of skepticism," *European Journal of Philosophy* 10 (2002): 196–208.

19 Charles Parsons's contextualist solution to the Liar Paradox centers on showing that a single liar sentence may be taken to fail to express a proposition in one context, but express a false (or true) one when interpreted from a more encompassing, meta-linguistic perspective. See "The Liar Paradox," in *Mathematics in Philosophy* (Ithaca, NY: Cornell University Press, 1983), pp. 221–51. Clearly this is similar to Mulhall's account of skepticism, but the details of Parsons's views do not seem to me to fit well with Mulhall's account. In particular, there is nothing in the case of skepticism that corresponds to the way in which reflection on how the liar sentence in the original context fails to express a proposition alters the context in such a way that the sentence may then be seen to express a proposition. Reflection on the context of the skeptic's utterance does not alter its context of evaluation; at most it leads one to other contexts of evaluation. I'm grateful to Gary Ebbs for reminding me of the relevance of Parsons's views.

20 Stroud, op. cit., p. 60.

21 Affeldt, op. cit., note 8, at p. 21. This paper will hereafter be cited as GM.

22 As I indicated in note 8 I take Affeldt's essay to be very close in spirit to the present one. Anyone familiar with it will see the extent to which I have learned from it. Indeed, it may well be that at bottom our differences come down to those of formulation. One aim of this essay may then be understood as making explicit that, and how, it is possible for the sort of reading of Cavell that Affeldt might be trying to advance to avoid the kind of assimilation to the standard interpretation sketched in this section.

23 This line of reasoning reflects a deeply entrenched conception of rationality in the analytic tradition. Some closely related versions of it are Rudolf Carnap's adherence to the analytic/synthetic distinction and Michael Dummett's criticism of W.V. Quine's rejection of it. See Carnap, "Intellectual autobiography," in P.A. Schilpp (ed.), *The Philosophy of Rudolf Carnap* (LaSalle: Open Court, 1963), pp. 3–84, esp. pp. 44–5, and Dummett, "The significance of Quine's indeterminacy thesis," *Synthese* 27 (1974): 351–97. For discussion see Thomas Ricketts, "Rationality, translation, and epistemology naturalized," *Journal of Philosophy* 79 (1982): 117–36, and my "Some senses of holism: an anti-realist's guide to Quine," in Richard G. Heck, Jnr (ed.), *Language, Thought, and Logic: Essays in Honour of Michael Dummett* (New York: Oxford University Press, 1997), pp. 71–103.

24 Gottlob Frege, *The Basic Laws of Arithmetic*, ed. and trans. M. Furth (Los Angeles and Berkeley: University of California Press, 1964), Introduction, p. 17.

25 See Frege, op. cit., pp. 14–17.

26 One note in passing: this picture of philosophizing from the ordinary finds an echo in a memorably aphoristic passage with which Kant rewards us for reading all the way to the end of the *Critique of Pure Reason*. I mean a passage from the *Architechtonic of Pure Reason*, which, like most people who quote it, I will quote out of context:

> [W]e cannot learn philosophy; for where is it, who is in possession of it, and how shall we recognize it? We can only learn to philosophize, that is, to exercise the talent of reason . . . on certain actually existing attempts at philosophy (A838/B866).

It need hardly be said, of course, that I am not ascribing Cavell's conception of philosophizing to Kant, or *vice versa*.

27 It should be clear that the conception of philosophical practice just outlined, which appeals to ordinary language, or proceeds from ordinary language, is a different enterprise from "ordinary-language philosophy" as usually understood. Most importantly, unlike much of "ordinary-language philosophy," even some of Austin's work, this conception does not rest on the idea that "ordinary language" is a determinate structure constituted by fixed conventions that are flouted by the "philosophical language" of the skeptic. For such reasons, Cavell does not take himself to be an ordinary-language philosopher, as opposed to a philosopher of the ordinary. I'm grateful to Nancy Bauer for pressing me to be clearer on these differences.

28 Perhaps this is how, in the heyday of Oxford philosophy, the conflict between ordinary-language philosophical criticism and its opposition appeared to both sides. Many early ordinary-language philosophers charge that the skeptic has changed the meaning of the word "know"; in response traditional epistemologists reply that it's the ordinary-language philosophers who refuse to use the word in obviously correct ways.

29 A classic example of a pragmatist with principled tolerance is Carnap. Carnap's project was to display the rationality of the sciences by reconstructing their practices as systems of rules that constitute the framework of various languages. What counts as a claim and what count as reasons for and against claims are fixed by the rules of the linguistic frameworks. Hence no adoption of frameworks can be refuted; this is the principle that underlies Carnap's tolerance. But the choice of frameworks is still governed by rational considerations, ones having to do with the usefulness of the framework for various purposes.

30 In Cavell, *Must We Mean What We Say?* (Cambridge: Cambridge University Press, 1976), p. 52; emphases mine.

31 Just how difficult this vision is may be gauged by the way in which readers of Cavell persistently avoid taking him at his words, just as they persistently avoid taking seriously Cavell's insistence that he is not offering a refutation of skepticism. That nothing guarantees our being able to go on together in language seems barely to register at all; what has gotten taken up are rather the ideas, appearing later in this passage, of "the whirl of organism" or "our form of life" as determinate conditions that enable, i.e. guarantee, after all, our mutual comprehension. Mulhall's idea of criteria as norms or rules agreement to the use of which is a precondition of intelligibility is yet another guise of such an idea of a guarantee of mutuality.

32 Ludwig Wittgenstein, *Philosophical Investigations* (Oxford: Blackwell, 2003), §241.

33 I take this to account for why Cavell often characterizes the skeptic as repudiating ordinary language.

34 "Knowing and acknowledging," in *Must We Mean What We Say?* p. 241; first emphasis mine.

35 "Must we mean what we say?" in *Must We Mean What We Say?* p. 15; emphasis in original.

36 The notion of following here of course leads us back to the ideas of teaching and learning in the passage from "The availability of Wittgenstein's later philosophy." It also suggests why Cavell characterizes philosophy as the education of grownups.

37 I am grateful to Alice Crary for some suggestions that led to this formulation.

38 I would like to thank Bill Bracken, Alice Crary, Gary Ebbs, Mihaela Fistioc, and Arata Hamawaki for comments and criticism of drafts of this paper. I owe a special debt of gratitude to Nancy Bauer, for her insightful criticisms of this essay and unfailing support of my fledgling thoughts on the issues discussed here.

Earlier versions of some materials of this essay were presented at a conference, *Acknowledging Cavell*, at Wesleyan University in 2002, and in a panel discussion, "Cavell and the contested bounds of the pragmatic tradition," at the 2003 Annual Conference of the Society for the Advancement of American Philosophy, in Denver. I am grateful to Henry Abelove and to Harvey Cormer respectively for inviting me to participate in these events.

Stanley Cavell's teaching has been an inspiration to me over some twenty years, although until this essay it has not specifically informed my philosophical work. I am happy at last to remedy this situation, and am grateful to him for comments and suggestions on the two just-mentioned presentations, as well as for encouraging me to make the ideas I voiced in them public.

8

THE DISCOVERY OF THE OTHER
Cavell, Fichte, and skepticism

Paul Franks

Since his earliest publications in defense of the ordinary-language procedures of
Austin and Wittgenstein, Stanley Cavell has repeatedly characterized those
procedures in Kantian terms.[1] In the opening essays collected in *Must We Mean
What We Say?* Cavell compares those procedures to the transcendental logic of
the *Critique of Pure Reason*,[2] then to the categorical imperatives of the *Critique
of Practical Reason*,[3] and then to the judgments made in the universal voice
thematized in the *Critique of Judgment*.[4] But this proliferation of Kantian terms
should already alert us to the fact that Cavell is no orthodox Kantian. By
drawing on all three *Critiques*, Cavell seems to transgress the boundaries that
Kant sought to delineate among the realms of science, morality, and art. And
Cavell's transgressions recall those of the first post-Kantians – Karl Leonhard
Reinhold and Johann Gottlieb Fichte – who undertook to articulate the unity
underlying Kant's three *Critiques* and soon found themselves opposing the letter
of Kant's philosophy in the name of its spirit.

My contention is that the first post-Kantians can be fruitfully reread in the
light of Cavell, in particular that Fichte's seminal struggles with the problem of
the other can be illuminated by Cavell's work on skepticism about other minds.
The fact that past philosophers can be reread in the light of present philosophers is a significant feature of philosophy's relationship with its past, a feature
that brings into question the very notions of philosophical past and philosophical present, even as it calls for constant vigilance against anachronism. And if
Cavell's work can shed particular light on the first post-Kantians, this is not
because, like Heidegger, Cavell has engaged extensively with the first post-
Kantian texts. Rather, it is because, two centuries after Kant, Cavell too is,
among other things and in a particular sense, a post-Kantian – though not in
any specific doctrinal or methodological respect. Like Reinhold, Fichte,
Schelling, or Hegel, Cavell philosophizes in the wake of the Kantian event, an
event whose significance is not yet exhausted. For a post-Kantian, in this sense
of the word, Kant's own assessment of the Kantian event carries no special
authority. And although Cavell has never engaged in a full-length, explicit
assessment of Kant's achievement, he has characterized his own project – at
crucial moments – as an attempt to rescue the Kantian event from Kant's inter-

pretation of it, which is to say that Cavell has himself characterized his own project as post-Kantian.

Cavell regards Kant as having achieved, above all, a fundamentally new insight into human finitude, and he has entirely recast our understanding of thinkers like Emerson, Thoreau, Austin, and Wittgenstein by portraying their work as standing in (complex, often critical) relations to Kant's insight.[5] Furthermore, at crucial moments in his own arguments, Cavell has expressed what amounts to dissatisfaction with Kant's ways of articulating it – as if Cavell thinks that Kant did not fully grasp his own insight. (This is perhaps not an accusation of guilt or negligence when an insight is attained with enormous difficulty, against the grain of long dominant modes of thinking.) In particular, Cavell's complaints center around Kant's notion of the thing in itself. As Cavell has noted, however, dissatisfaction with Kant's notion of the thing in itself is characteristic of post-Kantian sensibilities as different as those of Heidegger and Wittgenstein.[6] Indeed, as Cavell might have noted, almost every post-Kantian since Kant's own day has expressed some such dissatisfaction.[7]

Everything depends, then, on exactly *how* that dissatisfaction is expressed. In the first place, Cavell is dissatisfied with the way Kant interprets his own insight into human finitude when he pictures us as capable of knowing appearances yet incapable of knowing things in themselves. For Kant thereby conceives human finitude as an insurmountable failure of the human, as if there is something we somehow ought to be able to do but that we constitutionally cannot.[8] In contrast, Cavell seeks a positive conception of human finitude that does not understand the human as a privation but rather accepts or acknowledges our finitude.

But how is the acknowledgment of our finitude to be achieved? A full answer to this question would amount to nothing less than a full account of Cavell's work, but it is worth noting here that, at a pregnant moment in the early development of his thought, Cavell offers the remarkable suggestion that Thoreau's *Walden* revises and realizes Kant's insight into human finitude in so far as it "provides a transcendental deduction of the category of the thing-in-itself."[9] Even as he offers this suggestion, Cavell defers its clarification,[10] but he does give

> some explicit justification . . . (for what) seems on the surface at best a play, at worst a contradiction in Kantian terms: the concept of the thing-in-itself is the result, if not exactly the conclusion, of Kant's idea of a transcendental deduction of the categories; it stands for the fact that knowledge has limits, or conditions. The concept, so to speak, just says that it has no transcendental deduction, that its object is not an object of knowledge for us, so to ask for a deduction of it is, on Kant's program, senseless.

Cavell is fully aware, then, of the paradoxical sound of his suggestion, which is bound to sound jarring to anyone familiar with Kant. He proceeds to rehearse one mode of post-Kantian dissatisfaction with the very idea of a thing in itself:

But what is "a thing which is not an object of knowledge for us"? Everyone involved with Kant's thought recognizes a problem here, the implication that there are things just like the things we know (or features of the very things we know) which, not answering to our conditions for knowing anything, are unknowable by us. We oughtn't to be able to attach any meaning at all to such an implication. . . . A thing which we cannot know is not a thing.

It is at this point that many would reject – and it is at this point that many *have* rejected – the concept of a thing in itself as nonsensical. But if Cavell shared this conclusion, then he would hardly be drawn to the project of *deducing* that concept. The distinctive note of Cavell's post-Kantianism is sounded in what follows:

A thing which we cannot know is not a thing. Then why are we led to speak otherwise? What is the sense that something escapes the conditions of knowledge? It is, I think, the sense, or fact, that our primary relation to the world is not one of knowing (understood as achieving certainty of it based on the senses). This is the truth of skepticism. A Kantian "answer" to skepticism would be to accept its truth while denying the apparent implication that this is a failure of knowledge. This is the role the thing-in-itself ought, as it were, to have played.

In these sentences, Cavell replays his seminal criticism of his teacher, Austin. Whereas Austin was, it seems, satisfied by his painstaking demonstrations that everyday words – such as *thing, know, real* – were put to extraordinary use by philosophers, and whereas Austin was, apparently, drawn to the conclusion that we ought to be unable to attach any meaning to philosophers' characteristically extraordinary utterances, Cavell insists that to draw such a conclusion would be false to Austin's own profound insight into the relationship between meaning and the lives of human beings.[11] Instead, Cavell argues that we must account for the sense we have that we are making sense when we are philosophizing, by seeking to imagine a life (our life?) within which our extraordinary utterances are, if not fully intelligible, then not fully unintelligible. Although I cannot hope to explain Cavell's complex realization of this program here, to imagine such a life is, it turns out, to imagine a human life within which the ordinary is always to be achieved against the intimately related threats of isolation from the world and of isolation from others, threats whose possibility is a condition of the possibility of humanity itself and that can therefore never be erased.

Thus, for example, in order to understand the sense Kant has – or the sense any of us has – that he is making sense when he says that we cannot know things in themselves, we must imagine our own lives in such a way as to show how it is possible to be drawn to this skeptical description of our relation to the world, so that we see what *truth* about the human condition (about human conditionedness, human finitude) is expressed by skepticism, and so that we see how that truth can be more satisfyingly expressed, without the implication that we lack something because we are finite. Hence Cavell uses, for the first time, the phrase "the truth of skepticism" – whose articulation is the central theme of *The Claim of Reason* – in the course of a footnote concerned with the claim that Thoreau's *Walden* offers a deduction of the concept of the thing in itself. To deduce the concept of the thing in itself is, then, to demonstrate the possibility – perhaps even, in some sense, the necessity of the possibility – of the skeptical experience of isolation from the world as an unknowable thing in itself; and to deduce the concept of the thing in itself is also to *overcome* skepticism by articulating the underlying truth of human finitude that skepticism expresses in a paralyzing and deformed way: the truth that "our primary relation to the world is not one of knowing it (understood as achieving certainty of it based upon the senses)."

But how is the truth of skepticism to be characterized in positive terms? What is our primary relation to the world if it is not one of knowledge construed as sensation-based certainty? Again, while I cannot hope to do justice to Cavell's thinking here, I can draw attention to a central feature of our primary relation to the world that Cavell himself draws attention to in *The Senses of Walden*: "The externality of the world is articulated by Thoreau as its nextness to me";[12] "What is next to us is what we neighbor."[13] It is essential to Cavell's thought here that the problem of the externality of the world cannot be resolved – the truth underlying the philosopher's sense of isolation of the world as if from an unknowable thing in itself cannot be expressed – independently of some resolution of the problem of whom we neighbor, of who constitutes our community, of whether there are other minds we can know. If we construe knowledge of other minds as certainty based on the senses, then, Cavell argues at length, we are indeed fated – in advance and inescapably – to skepticism.[14] But if, instead, we construe knowledge of other minds as *acknowledgment* of others,[15] then the skeptical problem becomes the practical problem of achieving a meeting of the minds; not a problem that is guaranteed a successful resolution, but not one that is fated to failure either. For Cavell, the neighboring of the world and the acknowledgment of my neighbor are intimately linked, so that skepticism about the external world cannot be satisfyingly discussed in isolation from skepticism about other minds.

Before I return to mark the pertinence of this thought to Fichte, I want to note a further, connected formulation of Cavell's post-Kantian project. Some two decades after his suggestion that a "Kantian 'answer' to skepticism" would amount to a deduction of the concept of the thing in itself, Cavell suggests that Emerson proceeds "as if not just twelve categories (i.e., the categories derived by Kant from the forms of logical judgment in the Metaphysical Deduction) but any and every word in our language stands under the necessity of deduction, or say derivation." The idea of deducing any and every word in our language is further attributed to Wittgenstein, who is said to have "discovered the systematic in the absence of unity." Cavell means to say, first of all, that it is an essential insight of both Emerson and Wittgenstein that there can be no derivation, once and for all, *of* the fundamental categories of human experience, so that there can be no exhaustive list of the concepts that can come into skeptical doubt and so that there can be no final philosophical system that exhaustively overcomes skepticism and expresses its truth. Second, by turning our attention to language – and to words in *our* language – Cavell means to indicate the way in which skepticism involves *both* our relation to the world (to what is worded in language) *and* our relation to each other (as the community of those who share a language). As the heir to Kant's idea of a category,

> Wittgenstein's idea of a criterion . . . is as if a pivot between the necessity of the relation among human beings Wittgenstein calls "agreement inform of life" (§ 241) and the necessity in the relation between grammar and world that Wittgenstein characterizes as telling what kind of object anything is (§ 373), where this telling expresses essence (§ 375) and is accomplished by a process he calls "asking for our criteria."[16]

There is an especially pertinent relationship between Cavell's characterizations of his post-Kantian project – as a deduction of the concept of the thing in itself, as a deduction of any and every word in our language and thus as a response both to skepticism about the external world and to skepticism about other minds – and the post-Kantian project of Fichte. Although Fichte, in some famous passages, seems to dismiss the very notion of the thing in itself, he is actually seeking to overcome the idea of the thing in itself as absolutely independent of the mind in such a way that it is necessarily unknowable: an idea that is made for, or by, skepticism. And he does not object to reformulating the idea of the thing in itself as the idea of a genuinely external yet knowable world, whose independence can be deduced as a necessary condition of the possibility of consciousness and is therefore an independence that is, philosophically speaking, dependent on the self. So it would not be inaccurate – although it would be unusual – to characterize Fichte's project as the deduction of the concept of the thing in itself.[17] Moreover, it is one of Fichte's major insights that there can be no deduction of the concept of the thing in itself without a deduction of the concept of the other.

As I said earlier, my contention in this paper is not only that Cavell's work can be fruitfully considered as post-Kantian, but also that the original post-Kantians can be fruitfully reread in the light of Cavell's work.[18] I want especially to explore Fichte's contribution to what Cavell calls, in *The Claim of Reason*, "the history of the problem of the other."[19] It is important to note that Cavell understands that problem to be under discussion in recent philosophical work – notably by Austin and Wittgenstein – concerning skepticism about other minds, the problem of how I can know that there are minds other than my own.

But, second, Cavell does not take skepticism about other minds to be exhausted by this sort of philosophical debate; for he also finds that problem to be *lived by* us and to be portrayed as such in works of literature – notably, but not exclusively, by Shakespeare.[20] And, third, Cavell takes the problem of the other to be intimately related to skepticism about the external world, so that these two problems are necessarily (if perhaps unconsciously) always discussed together. Now, the fact that Fichte made a significant contribution to the problem of the other has been noted by Fichte scholars, who have argued that he was the first to explicitly thematize the problem of the other within post-Kantian philosophy and, indeed, that he gave the problem of the other the familiar form it takes in Hegel, Husserl, and Heidegger.[21] But this fact is still little appreciated and Fichte's contribution can, I believe, be significantly illuminated by some central themes of Cavell's thought.

In particular, I will discuss (1) as a characteristic of the human the capacity to repudiate humanity, which appears in the first place as the freedom for heteronomy in Fichte's inheritance of Kant, a freedom he takes pains to accommodate; (2) skepticism about the existence of other minds, as a problem that Fichte places at the foundation of his account of human rights – of his system as a whole – and which he undertakes to solve by arguing that the existence of at least one other mind is a necessary condition for the possibility of self-consciousness; and (3) skepticism about other minds, considered as a problem that Fichte lives in virtue of the problematic intelligibility of his philosophical thinking to others. My path through these themes will also trace the course of the following argument: (1) although Fichte takes pains to make philosophical room for the capacity to repudiate the norms expressive of human reason – a task that leads to his first realization of the need to rethink Kant's revolution from the ground up – nevertheless, he does not resolve the difficulties of theorizing that capacity, and those difficulties re-emerge both (2) in his account of the normative significance of the other's role in the genesis of self-consciousness, and (3) in his practical and theoretical struggle with the question of the intelligibility of the *Wissenschaftslehre* to others. It will also emerge in the course of this argument that Fichte's lived skepticism about other minds is also a reappearance – as if by displacement – of a skepticism about the external world that Fichte takes himself to have discarded.

1 The all-too-human freedom for heteronomy

I will begin by considering, not the problem of the other proper, but the problem of heteronomy in Kantian ethics. That the two problems are in some way connected is obvious from the word *heteronomy*, which means receiving the law of one's will from the other. However, no actual other person need be involved in heteronomy, since one may be heteronomous if one acts out of the motive of one's own sensuous desires, which are not, in Kant's view, really oneself. Nevertheless, a controversy about heteronomy provoked Fichte to find his own philosophical voice, and the issues emerging from that dispute are essential to his formulation of the problem of other minds.

To discuss the controversy about heteronomy, I need to recall some familiar features of Kant's moral philosophy. First of all, Kant regards the motivation to action, not the consequences of action, as the locus of moral value. In his view, an action has moral value only if it is *autonomous*, if it is motivated by the law one gives to oneself. Kant also maintains that there is only one law one *can* give to oneself in the relevant way: the moral law. The moral law is a principle of deliberation stating that one ought to adopt only those maxims of action that one could at the same time will as universal law for all rational beings. The moral law is for Kant the only possible *highest* practical principle – the only principle that can serve as the self-justifying justification for all of an agent's maxims. And the moral law is the only practical principle that fully expresses what it is to be a rational agent, to have a rational will, a will that acts for reasons. One can only be autonomous, then, if one acknowledges the moral law as the highest principle of one's practical deliberation, if one gives oneself the law that expresses one's true nature as a rational agent. If, however, one adopts as one's highest principle, say, the maximized satisfaction of one's desires, then one is heteronomous: one is receiving the law from the objects of one's desires, therefore from outside oneself.

If you consider Kantian ethics from the outside, you are likely to ask why *that* is heteronomous. Why regard one's desires as accidental to who one essentially is? If you philosophize from within Kantian ethics, on the other hand, *you are* apt to raise quite a different set of questions: How is heteronomy so much as possible? If the moral law expresses our true nature, then how can we ever fail to give ourselves that law? How can we reject the expression of our own nature? These questions rhyme with a thought Cavell has often expressed, a thought that might be formulated as follows: the wish to reject, or escape from, the human condition is an essential possibility of the human; nothing could be more human.[22] Cavell himself has marked that thought as having Kantian roots.[23] But I do not think it has been realized just how important the thought is for the development of post-Kantian philosophy. The idea of the will to heteronomy is the central focus of a seminal – but now almost forgotten – controversy between Karl Leonhard Reinhold and Carl Christian Erhard Schmid in 1792.[24]

When this controversy began[25] Kant had published several critical works on ethics, but he had not yet clarified his conception of the will. Schmid was the author of a popular dictionary of Kantian terms, in which he defined practical freedom as "dependence of the will on the reason immediately determining it, on the pure moral law; autonomy of the will." Thus Schmid identified freedom with autonomy, with acting out of the motivation of the moral law, from a pure will. At the same time, Schmid understood heteronomy as a function of the impure or empirical will, which he defined as follows: "a will, which is subjected to sensuous nature, where the representations determining it are produced through sensible objects; that refers to the relative good, to happiness and what is bound up with it."[26] This definition is obviously problematic. If freedom is defined as autonomy, then the heteronomous will is not free. But how, then, can I be held responsible for my heteronomous acts? Surely I can always plead that *another is* to blame. I can always say: "sensuous nature" made me do it!

Reinhold attacked Schmid's definitions in one of his famous *Letters Concerning the Kantian Philosophy*, the series of articles most responsible for spreading the Kantian word throughout Germany.[27] Reinhold pointed out that the problem lay, not with Schmid's definition of freedom alone, but with his conception of the will. Or, to be more accurate, the problem lay with Schmid's complete *lack* of such a conception. Schmid thought there were two species of will: the pure will was determined by reason and the empirical will was determined by sensuous nature. But neither of these so-called wills were wills at all, because neither involved the essential feature of a will: *self-determination*. Schmid's error was perhaps excusable on the grounds that Kant had not yet clarified the nature of the will, but the error led to Schmid's denying the very freedom that Kant had set out to defend.

Freedom, Reinhold insisted, is the true spirit of Kant's philosophy, and if we are "to defend freedom then we must distinguish clearly between, autonomy and freedom of the will. Autonomy is reason's spontaneous legislation of the moral law to itself and is entirely independent of us." Freedom of the will is *our* capacity to determine ourselves *either* to autonomy *or* to heteronomy, to acknowledge the moral law as the highest principle of our practical deliberation or not to acknowledge it. So the heteronomous will is no less free – and therefore no less responsible – than the autonomous will. And Reinhold anticipated the distinction Kant would draw, in his 1793 *Religion*, between the autonomous will expressed by the moral law, which he called *Wille*, and the will as the capacity for self-determination or choice, which he called *Willkür*.[28]

It is important to note that Reinhold does not intend to *define* freedom.[29] A real definition must specify the determining grounds of the definiendum, not only its distinguishing marks. But the free will can have no determining grounds except itself. So no informative definition of freedom is possible. Indeed, Reinhold thinks that Schmid has gone astray just because he has converted Kant's true formulations into false definitions: Schmid's fidelity to the *letter* of Kant's philosophy has killed its *spirit*.[30]

This is the first significant use of the concept of spirit in post-Kantian philosophy. It is highly important that, in this first occurrence, spirit is opposed to letter and is identified with the will to autonomy or heteronomy, therefore with our capacity to repudiate the moral law expressing our humanity.

In 1793 Fichte publicly took Reinhold's side against Schmid.[31] But he also accused Reinhold of inadequately grasping the spirit for which he claimed to speak.[32] Fichte argued that Reinhold's understanding of freedom was inconsistent with the deduction of the reality of freedom attributed by Reinhold to Kant. Fichte's criticism of Reinhold marked his first realization that Kantian philosophy was radically incomplete. If the philosophy of freedom had not yet deduced the reality of freedom – of the freedom to autonomous or heteronomous self-determination – then Fichte would have to recast the philosophy of freedom in a more adequate form.

Reinhold thought the reality of freedom could be deduced from what he called "the fact of moral consciousness": "From its effects, through which it comes forth among the facts of consciousness, freedom is fully comprehensible to me; and insofar it is no object of *faith*, but rather of proper *knowledge* for me."[33] Reinhold seems to mean the following. First, the moral law is a fact of consciousness for me, which is to say: I am conscious of the normative force of the moral law; I feel obligated by morality. And second, moral consciousness is an effect of freedom; since the effect is real, the cause must be real; therefore freedom is real.

Fichte thought this line of reasoning deeply flawed because of the distinction Reinhold himself had drawn between autonomy and the freedom to be either autonomous or heteronomous. First, it is important to clarify the nature of what Reinhold calls "the fact of moral consciousness." A fact of consciousness is a determinate state of consciousness that is evident to the subject. Fichte points out that freedom cannot be a fact of consciousness, because the act of self-determination is prior to any particular state of consciousness. The moral law can be a fact of consciousness, in the sense that I can be conscious of moral obligation in my deliberation. But that does not mean that I am conscious of actually being autonomous, because I can never be sure that I actually act on the motivations I consciously represent to myself. The "fact of moral consciousness" is therefore merely my consciousness that I *ought* to be autonomous, and I can never be conscious either of my freedom or of my actual autonomy.[34] Reinhold argues that I can be certain of my freedom as the *cause* of moral consciousness, but Fichte rejects this causal argument. A cause is itself an event determined by a prior cause. If freedom is self-determination, then it cannot be determined and therefore cannot be a cause.[35]

Fichte concluded that the reality of freedom had yet to be proven.[36] And he thought freedom could be deduced only if Kant's philosophy were systematized, if all the necessary features of human life – including freedom – were deduced from an appropriate first principle. But it is important to note how mysterious Fichte's argument leaves our capacity to determine ourselves either to autonomy or to heteronomy. The act of self-determination is not an act of which I can be conscious. The spirit in which I act underlies my actions but cannot be read from my actions. The will to autonomy and the will to heteronomy are not expressed in conscious choices, but are matters of my fundamental self-understanding. If it is possible to understand myself as autonomous, then how can I have failed to do so? And if I have succeeded in understanding myself as autonomous, how can I lapse from that achievement and will heteronomously?

Fichte's work raises these questions but never succeeds in coming to grips with them. His insistence on the freedom for heteronomy haunts his philosophy. For if humans are free to repudiate human nature as expressed in the moral law, then they are also free to repudiate human nature as expressed in the higher principle from which Fichte seeks to derive freedom and morality. How does one philosophize about the human condition in the face of the all-too-human capacity for repudiating the human condition, therefore for repudiating philosophy itself?

2 Skepticism about other minds as a problem for Fichte's system

Fichte first raised the problem of the other proper in the public lectures he gave on his arrival at Jena in 1794:

> Among the questions which philosophy has to answer we find the following two in particular, which have to be answered before, among other things, a well founded theory of natural rights is possible. First of all, by what right does a man call a particular portion of the physical world "his body"? How does he come to consider this to be his body, something which belongs to his I, since it is nevertheless something completely opposed to his I? And then the second question: How does a man come to assume that there are rational beings like himself apart from him? And how does he come to recognize them, since they are certainly not immediately present to his pure self-consciousness?[37]

Here what Cavell calls the problem of the other is explicitly posed as a skeptical problem about our right to some knowledge that we take ourselves to have, and the problem of the so-called assumption of other minds is linked to the question of natural rights and the body, to the fate of the body under the law.

Fichte first saw the shape of a *solution* to the problem of the other in the summer of 1795, and in August he wrote to Reinhold that the incompleteness of Kant's philosophy – of the list of concepts Kant had deduced – was nowhere more evident than in the fact that *Kant had failed* to deduce the *concept* of another mind.[38] And his failure to deduce the concept of another mind was nowhere more evident than in his moral philosophy.[39] For the moral law states, again, that I ought to adopt only those maxims whose adoption by every other rational being I could at the same time will. But how, on Kant's view, are these other rational beings so much as possible? He famously argues that there can be no consciousness without the possibility of self-consciousness – that no representation can be mine unless I could explicitly impute that representation to myself by prefacing it with the phrase "I think." But Kant says nothing about how I might impute representations to *another* self.[40]

Second, the application of the moral law depends upon the distinction between *things* – *which* I am permitted to treat solely as means to my ends – and *persons* whom I am never permitted to treat solely as means. But how do I know which is which? Or: if there are other rational beings besides myself, how would I recognize them as such? As Fichte puts it, I have no qualms riding a horse without asking its permission; so how do I know I need the permission of the man who lends me the horse?

> It will always remain a very delicate question whether, though my act is supported by general opinion, I am not just as unjustified in riding a horse as the Russian nobleman is when he gives away his serfs, or sells them, or beats them for the fun of it for his act too is supported by general opinion.[41]

In order to answer this "very delicate question," whether any particular other is to be ridden like a horse or respected like a fellow human, Fichte thinks we need a principled solution to the problem: how are other minds possible? He sketches his solution in his letter to Reinhold and presents it in detail in his 1796 book, *The Foundations of Natural Right*, where he undertakes to deduce the concept of the other.

As I have already mentioned, Kant argues that the possibility of self-consciousness is a necessary condition of the possibility of consciousness. His strategy in the transcendental deduction is – roughly speaking – to justify concepts by showing them to be necessary conditions of *self*-consciousness, therefore to be necessary conditions of consciousness in general. Fichte's approach to the problem of the other follows Kant's strategy, for he undertakes to show that self-consciousness would be impossible without an a priori relation to another mind. But Fichte alters Kant's strategy in one enormously fateful respect. Kant concerns himself with the necessary conditions of the self-consciousness *with which we presently find ourselves*. He excludes as irrelevant any question about how we *acquired* the consciousness or the particular concepts we now possess. To ask about the history of consciousness is to ask the *quaestio quid facti* – a merely factual or empirical question – but, in Kant's view, the transcendental philosopher is properly concerned only with the *quaestio quid juris* – the question of the a priori legitimacy of our concepts.[42] In contrast, Fichte seeks to show that the concept of the other is an a priori necessary condition of the *genesis* of self-consciousness, of my first coming to think of myself as a self and therefore of my first arrival at consciousness. Fichte thereby introduces the idea of an a priori historical structure. In other words, Fichte's deduction of the other introduces the notion *that reason has its own mode of historicity*, a notion whose importance for the subsequent thinking of post-Kantians like Hegel I hardly need to emphasize.[43]

Fichte's aim, then, is to show that I could not first become aware of myself as a self if I were not at the same time aware of another:

> The rational being cannot posit itself as such, unless a summons to free action [*eine Aufforderung zum freien Handeln*] is addressed to it. But

when such a summons to free action is addressed to it, it must necessarily posit a rational being outside of itself, as the cause thereof; and hence it must posit a rational being outside of itself generally.[44]

The central concept in Fichte's account of the genesis of self-consciousness is the concept of the "*summons*" [*die Aufforderung*].[45] I first find myself as a self when I find myself summoned to free activity by another. Some other wants me to do something. This other has recognized me as a self, capable of free action, and must itself be a self since it is performing a free action in issuing the summons. So I come to myself as an individual with a will of my own, distinct from the will of the other individual, the one who is summoning me to act. And I am necessarily aware of the mind of this other as soon as I am aware of my own mind. I might say that my mind is summoned forth by the mind of another.

It is important to note that Fichte intends this to be a pure or a priori account of the genesis of self-consciousness. It does not matter, from his lofty perspective, *who* is summoning me to act, or *what* that someone wants me to do. The particular instantiation of the a priori concept remains for Fichte an irrelevant *quaestio quid facti* – although we may well imagine it to be fateful for the individual, a matter of the gravest concern for, say, psychoanalysis.

Fichte finds the distinction between what Kant calls *Wille* – the autonomous will expressed in the moral law – and what Kant calls *Willkür* – the will as the capacity for self-determination to either autonomy or heteronomy – to be coeval with the mind itself. The distinction is, in other words, present within the original summons, albeit in a primitive, undeveloped form. Within the summons there is both an element of absolute responsibility and an element of free choice, both human fate and human freedom. My freedom consists in my ability to determine myself *either* to comply with the summons *or* to resist it. My fate consists in the fact that, once I have comprehended the summons as a summons, *anything* I do will count as *a response* to the summons. I may be free to determine myself as I choose, but I am fated to determine myself some way or another. In Fichte's words, "Even my resistance [to the summons] is an expression of my freedom."[46]

When the other summons me, the other assumes problematically that I am a free agent. When I respond to the summons, as I must if I understand it, I recognize the other's recognition of me, recognizing the other as a free agent. I thereby prove *my* existence as a free agent to the other, converting a problematic assumption into a categorical cognition. Since the other may be properly said to know my mind only through my response, it follows that true knowledge of other minds is reciprocal: "No (free being) can recognize the other, unless both recognize each other reciprocally."[47]

Fichte seems to think that every human interaction, not only the original one, has the form of a summons of a reciprocal recognition. And he seeks to derive from this claim the idea of justice (*Recht*) of fundamental human rights. Every interaction between two individuals involves reciprocal recognition,

Fichte argues, and reciprocal recognition involves the recognition of two independent wills, therefore of two mutually exclusive "spheres of free activity"; to recognize the other is thus to ascribe to the other a sphere of activity from which I am excluded; to overstep the sphere of the other's activity is therefore to violate the rights the other possesses merely by virtue of being an individual and to *contradict* an earlier recognition of the other. The notion of contradiction here is intended, Fichte emphasizes, to be the familiar notion *of logical* contradiction, as when one asserts both *p* and not *p*.

In this way, Fichte seeks to deduce the concept of the other as a necessary condition of self-consciousness and then to deduce the rights of each individual from the concept of the other. The fundamental move in the derivation of rights is the transition to the idea of a sphere of activity that it is possible to overstep. And that is equivalent to the idea that it is possible to repudiate the responsibility we bear to the other – an analogue of the idea that it is possible to will heteronomy. Once Fichte has the idea of oversteppable individual spheres of activity, he is able to derive the idea of the body and ultimately the idea of private property. However, I do not think Fichte has earned the idea of oversteppable individual spheres, because he has not adequately theorized the will to transgress the individuality of the other.

I have two reasons for distrusting Fichte's argument. First, the image of a *sphere* suggests too easily a range of already demarcated, yet still merely possible actions that are marked out in advance as mine. The sphere thus anticipates – and makes it easier to derive – the idea of the body and, ultimately, of a realm of property at my disposal. But is it clear that the demarcation and individuation of a range of possible actions follows immediately from the mere possession of a will? We do sometimes talk not only of actual but also of possible actions as being marked out for one individual but, in that sense, it may take me a lifetime to discover which actions are mine to perform.[48]

Second, Fichte fails to explain what *overstepping* the sphere of the other could be and therefore fails to explain in what sense I voluntarily restrict myself when I recognize the other as an individual. If I am the one who is summoned, then I cannot overstep the other's sphere, for I cannot help but recognize the other in so far as I understand the summons. Suppose then that I am the one who has summoned the other and that the other has responded. How might I now overstep the other's sphere? If, to use Fichte's earlier example, I saddle and ride the other like a horse, am I overstepping the other's sphere and contradicting my earlier recognition? Only, it seems, if I genuinely think now that the other is a horse and is not a human being at all. But if I am, *say, humiliating* the other by treating the other *like* a horse, then surely my act presupposes my recognition of the other as a human being and does not contradict that recognition. Suppose, instead, that I *enslave* the other, appropriating the other's body and labor as my own. Might I believe that this other is not human, not capable of free activity? As Cavell has argued in *The Claim of Reason*, Southern slave-owners seem to have believed, not that slaves are not human, but that some humans are slaves – that there are two distinct species of humans.[49] If there is a tension between violating human rights and recognizing the other as a free agent, then that tension is not captured by the idea of logical contradiction.

By insisting on the possibility of overstepping the other's sphere, Fichte is preserving the human freedom to repudiate – not only the moral law – but also the fate of absolute responsiveness to the other. But, just as Fichte lacks an account of the freedom to will heteronomously, he also lacks an account of the freedom to will unjustly. If I can treat the other in ways that do not cohere with my recognition of the other as a rational being, how is this possible? And how can I be brought to a more adequate understanding of the other? In his critical inheritance of Fichte, Hegel thought justice could be derived from the reciprocal recognition necessary for consciousness. But Hegel thought the derivation would require a new dialectical logic and would take nothing less than the whole of human history.

If Fichte underestimates the difficulty of the problem of the other, it is nevertheless largely thanks to him that the problem can be formulated as the problem of human history. And his approach to the problem of the other promises more than the approach known to the English-speaking tradition from the work of J.S. Mill. Mill's idea is that I know other minds in general on the basis of observed *analogies* between my behavior and the behavior of others.[50] But if you start by observing *behavior*, then you have already rendered the other's mind unrecognizable. Fichte's idea is that I know another mind in particular when I find myself responsive to its summons. This raises fruitful questions that Cavell also asks, questions ripe for experimentation: Which responses acknowledge the other? Which avoid responsibility?

Fichte's deduction of the other also plays a crucial role in his deduction of both freedom and the thing in itself, a role I can only indicate here. I have already noted that, by locating *both* an absolute responsibility to respond to the other *and* a choice about how to respond at the very origin of self-consciousness, Fichte is anticipating the practical freedom that he wants ultimately to deduce in his account of morality, for practical freedom is structured in terms of the self-legislation/self-determination (or *Wille/Willkür*) distinction. The idea of the summons also provides Fichte with a promising route to the deduction of the thing in itself, understood as the externality of the world that is necessary for the self to be a self. For, Fichte argues, the summons necessarily involves *two wills* and the individuation of those wills requires that they be situated in distinct loci of agency; that is, that they be separately embodied. Embodiment involves both the existence of matter under the power of the will and the resistance of matter to the will, and, from these features of embodiment, Fichte believes that he can deduce all the necessary features of the external world.[51]

3 Skepticism about other minds as a problem for Fichte's life

It has often been asked whether the skeptic can *live* his skepticism.[52] Cavell's surprising answer is that we do live our skepticism about other minds.[53] Fichte is the first, I have argued, to explicitly thematize the problem of the other in its modern form. But skepticism about other minds is not only a problem addressed *within* Fichte's philosophy; it is also the problem of his *life* in philosophy, the problem he lives. And he lives this problem, as I will suggest, in his shifting attempts to negotiate his difficulties in making himself intelligible to others, difficulties he considers internal to the very nature of philosophy.[54]

One may trace a path from Reinhold's insistence that heteronomy is an essential possibility of the human to the esotericism of Fichte's philosophy. Heteronomy is the repudiation of human nature as expressed in the moral law, the highest principle of practical deliberation. Fichte thinks that Kant has failed to deduce the reality of freedom and failed even to attempt to deduce a priori necessary concepts left out of the table of categories, such as the concept of the other. In order to deduce *all* the concepts necessary to human life, and in order to successfully deduce the reality of our freedom, Fichte undertakes to articulate the highest first principle from which all the necessary concepts, including the concept of the other and the concept of freedom, can be derived. That first principle is supposed to express the most fundamental nature of the self. But if we are capable of repudiating the moral law as an expression of human selfhood, then we are also capable of repudiating the highest first principle as an expression of human selfhood. So Fichte must philosophize about the fundamental nature of the self in the face of the possibility of repudiation, of our capacity to wish to escape from the human condition. Fichte cannot avoid the risk that he will be unintelligible to others, and this risk will lead him into a series of skeptical anxieties that he never succeeds in calming.

Fichte's anxiety about his intelligibility arose as a revised version of what originally seemed to be a skeptical worry about the external world – a genesis worth examining in the light of Cavell's insight that skepticism about the external world and skepticism about other minds are *not merely* different, but intimately connected in their differences. "At each level," Cavell writes, "a feature found to be natural in the one direction will be found to have to undergo inflection or reservation to find itself in the other direction."[55] The two skepticisms, in other words, are not distinct species of a genus, but rather variations of one another. When talking about the one kind – or, as in this case, when ceasing to talk about it – the philosopher finds himself or herself talking about the other kind.

The precise worry about the external world that I have in mind was first raised by Gottlob Ernst Schulze in his skeptical attack on Reinhold and Kant. This polemic, published under the pseudonym Aenesidemus in 1792, was one of the seminal events in the development of post-Kantianism, since it provoked Fichte into a full assessment of Reinhold's achievements and led him to develop his own systematization of Kant's philosophy.[56]

Reinhold was the first to try to systematize Kant's philosophy by deriving it from a single first principle, which identified the faculty of representation as the fundamental essence of the mind. Schulze understood Reinhold to be making the following syllogistic argument:

Major Premise: "Any two things that cannot be *thought* apart from one another can also not *be* apart from one another."[57] *Minor Premise*: "[T]he being and actuality of representations cannot be *thought* apart from the being and actuality of a faculty of representation".[58] . . . [which is] the cause and ground of the actual presence of representations."[59] *Conclusion*: "[H]ence a faculty of representation must also exist objectively, just as certainly as representations are present in us."[60]

Schulze's skeptical response to this argument may be divided into two objections. The first might be called the Reality Problem and is aimed at Reinhold's major premise: with what right does Reinhold assume that the way we cannot help but think corresponds to the way things really are? Even if it were true that we cannot help but think of our representations as grounded in a faculty of representations, with what right would we infer that there really is such a faculty? – especially in light of Kant's own argument that we can never know things as they are in themselves.[61] Schulze's second objection might be called the Uniqueness Problem and is aimed at Reinhold's minor premise: with what right does Reinhold assume that because we – at our present stage of human history – can only think in a certain way, it is *therefore* impossible for anyone to think differently? Even if Reinhold's explanation of representation is the only one available to us, who are we to say that it is the unique possible explanation, to which no future genius will ever provide an alternative?[62]

Fichte thought that post-Kantian philosophy could overcome these objections, but only if Reinhold's version of that philosophy were abandoned for a new systematization. In his 1793 review of Schulze's book, Fichte sounds rather dismissive of Schulze's objections. For example, Fichte thinks Schulze's Reality Problem is misconceived. In the first place, Fichte is suspicious – like Cavell – of the idea that the limits of human knowledge should be conceived as a realm of cognitively inaccessible things.[63] But, second, even if we *could* make sense of things in themselves, it would make no sense to think of the *mind* as a thing in itself. For a thing in itself is a thing as it is independently of the way we think; but the way we think is surely essential to the mind and so the mind cannot *be* as it is independently of the way we think. The mind, Fichte insists, is not a thing at all.[64]

As far as Schulze's Uniqueness Problem is concerned, Fichte concedes that Reinhold has not shown that the grounding of representation in the mind as faculty of representation is the only possible explanation. But that shortcoming simply proves, in Fichte's view, that Reinhold has not succeeded in completing the post-Kantian project – that Reinhold has not succeeded in deriving all the necessary features of human life from a single highest first principle. Fichte has other reasons for rejecting Reinhold's formulation of the first principle of philosophy and proposes himself to establish a first principle based, not on the notion of representation, but on the idea of free and autonomous activity. The necessary conditions of that first principle will indeed constitute the unique explanation of the necessary features of human life. As long as we take pains to ensure that our philosophy proceeds by necessary steps from a necessary first principle, Fichte insists on numerous occasions, we will have no cause to worry about Schulze's skeptical objections.

It is customary to attribute no further role to Schulze's objections than their provoking Fichte to construct his own system, with a first principle differing from Reinhold's – a system that would be immune to Schulze's objections. But I do not think that the Reality and Uniqueness Problems disappear from Fichte's thought. Instead I find that those problems resurface, not as the skeptical problems posed by Schulze about the relationship between philosophy and things in themselves, but rather as skeptical problems about the relationship between Fichte's philosophy and the minds of others.

We can see Schulze's objections resurfacing as issues concerning other minds in a note Fichte wrote, during the winter of 1793–4, while working out his own system for the first time. There, Fichte comments on "the false appearance" of the objection raised against Reinhold by Schulze and by Solomon Maimon, the objection "that [Reinhold] infers that something *must be* from (the premise) that he can think something."[65] This formulation contains both the Reality Problem – Reinhold's illicit inference from thought to being – and the Uniqueness Problem – Reinhold's illicit inference from the possibility of his line of thought to its necessity. But in condemning "the false appearance" of these problems, Fichte seems to imply that they are not *merely* pseudo-problems, that freed from their misleading formulation they are problems he too must face. And indeed Fichte proceeds to reformulate the skeptical objection:

> But how do [Reinhold's] thoughts agree in general with the actions of the spirit; how may such an agreement [*Ubereinstimmung*] be demonstrated? That is really the question: for the object of his philosophy is not the thing in itself, but rather the representing of the thing. The discussion does not concern things outside this representing.

In accordance with this note, the Reality Problem may be reformulated as follows: do the philosopher's thoughts agree with the *real* actions, of the spirit or mind? And the Uniqueness Problem may be reformulated as follows: are the philosopher's thoughts the *only* thoughts whose agreement with the actions of the mind may be demonstrated?

It will be evident that these are now skeptical anxieties about other minds if we reformulate them again. On this reformulation, the Reality Problem becomes: are Fichte's thoughts genuinely expressive of his mind? And the Uniqueness Problem becomes: are Fichte's thoughts expressive of the human mind he shares with others or does he philosophize only for himself?

Reformulated in this way, the Reality Problem divides into two worries: (1) Do Fichte's thoughts in fact proceed necessarily from a necessary first principle? And (2) do Fichte's words express his thoughts? Motivated by the first worry, Fichte obsessively reformulates his system, casting it and recasting it in a dozen quasi-mathematical forms, checking and rechecking the necessity of his every step. But he is fully prepared to attest that his thinking is necessary on the grounds that its necessity is evident to him. To doubt that his evidently necessary thinking is necessary would be to consider the possibility that the steps of his thinking are, instead, taken by free choice, uncompelled by reason. In Fichte's words:

> The confusion of that which is in virtue of free action with that which is in virtue of necessary [action], and vice-versa, is properly speaking frenzy [*Raserei*]. But [if the *Wissenschaftslehre* is a product of frenzy], then who erected such a system?[66]

If anyone has erected an arbitrary system in a fit of frenzy, Fichte is quite sure that it is not he but his uncomprehending critics who have done so, in their interpretation of his system. But while he does not doubt his own sanity, this does not mean that he does not, like Rousseau, run the constant risk of insanity; and it does not mean that he might not, like Nietzsche, go mad. Fichte's repeated, strident declarations of certainty about his constantly changing system struck his contemporaries as maddeningly dogmatic. They strike me differently – as Fichte's own protections against madness.[67]

If Fichte does not doubt that his evidently necessary thoughts express his mind, he can nevertheless doubt that his words express his thoughts to anyone other than himself. And Fichte does worry about the expressiveness of his words – about the ability of the letter to convey the spirit – for example, in an early letter to Reinhold:

> You should not assign to my expressions the same sort of worth which, for example, yours certainly possess. . . . The body in which you clothe the spirit fits it very closely. The body in which I clothe it is looser and is easily cast aside. What I am trying to communicate is something which can be neither said nor grasped conceptually; it can only be intuited. My words are only supposed to guide the reader in such a way that the desired intuition is formed within him. I advise him to go on reading even if he has not completely understood what went before, until at some point a spark of light is finally struck. This spark of light, if it is whole and not half, will suddenly place him in that position in the series of my intuitions from which the whole must be viewed. . . . One enters my philosophy by means of what is absolutely ungraspable. This makes my philosophy difficult . . . yet at the same time this is what guarantees its correctness. Everything that is graspable presupposes some higher sphere in which it is grasped and is therefore not the highest thing, precisely because it is graspable.[68]

Behind Fichte's praise of Reinhold's style, one quickly sees that Fichte thinks Reinhold is a mere philosopher of the letter, while he – Fichte – is a true philosopher of the spirit. And the letter endangers the spirit for reasons that I have already mentioned in my discussion of Fichte's criticism of Reinhold: Fichte understands mind or spirit to be a self-determining act that is prior to any determination of consciousness and therefore cannot be adequately expressed by any determination of consciousness. Language can only convey determinations of consciousness; it cannot ensure that Fichte's audience will experience that internal spark of light that illuminates the ungraspable highest principle of philosophy. What *could* ensure the expression of that principle to others?

Even in his early 1793–4 notes, before he has so much as tried to make his ideas public, Fichte is concerned that some people will be incapable of understanding his ungraspable principle: "(The first, intuitive principle) is to be proven by means of something else, neither by us nor by anyone whomsoever. Whoever has it not, is spoilt [*verdorben*] for philosophy."[69] By the time Fichte publishes his system for the first time in 1794, his concern has grown into a conviction that most others will not understand him:

> The majority of men could sooner be brought to believe themselves a piece of lava in the moon than to take themselves for an I. Hence they have never understood Kant, or read his mind [*und seinen Geist nicht geahnt*]; hence, too, they will not understand this exposition, though the condition for all philosophizing lies at its head. Anyone who is not yet at one with himself on this point has no understanding of any fundamental philosophy, and needs none. Nature, whose machine he is, will lead him, even without his own cooperation, into all the occupations that are his to pursue. Philosophizing calls for independence, and this one can only confer on oneself.[70]

In this last passage, Fichte's skeptical anxiety about his audience is at full pitch. The majority of men, who do not understand him – who do not understand his expression of spirit or mind as such – are not equipped with minds at all; they are mere machines of nature and they should occupy themselves accordingly. But can Fichte really mean that most so-called humans are in fact automata? His official, only slightly less anxious position is that most so-called humans are indeed human, but that their innate capacity for philosophical self-understanding has been corrupted beyond redemption.

I say this is only slightly less anxious because it still worries Fichte that these spiritual wrecks do not wear their corruption on their sleeves, that they are not more easily distinguishable from uncorrupted humans. Some of these impoverished souls even occupy chairs in philosophy! Fichte's wish that these half-humans were more transparent sometimes expresses itself in violent prose that seeks to annihilate their minds – their humanity – entirely. The first target of Fichte's violent prose is his colleague, Professor Schmid, the original champion of Kantian letter over Kantian spirit. In what soon became infamous as the "act of annihilation" [*Tat der Vernichtung*], Fichte proclaimed in 1796 that Schmid was completely incapable of entering the realm of philosophy, and solemnly declared "Professor Schmid . . . to be *nonexistent as a philosopher so* far as I am concerned."[71] A year later, Fichte wrote this remarkable passage about the violent effects he desired for his prose:

> I wish to have nothing to do with those who, as a result of protracted spiritual servitude, have lost their own selves and, along with this loss of themselves, have lost any feeling for their own conviction, as well as any belief in the conviction of others. . . . I would be sorry if I were understood by people of this sort. To date, this wish has been fulfilled so far as they are concerned; and I hope that, in the present case as well, these prefatory remarks will so confuse them that from now on, they will be unable to see anything beyond the mere letters, inasmuch as what passes for spirit in their case will be yanked back and forth by the secret *fury pent up within them.*[72]

Rather than suffer the offense of his readers thinking they understand him when they do not, Fichte wishes his writing to destroy his readers' capacity for reading.

Under the pressures of such violence in his own thinking, Fichte stands in urgent need of an account of the preconditions for philosophy, and of an account of how most humans have been corrupted. He develops a hierarchy of stages of consciousness.

There is the summons that, as we have seen, introduces human rights and makes selfhood and consciousness possible. Then there is moral consciousness – in which one first becomes aware of oneself as autonomous, as capable of giving oneself the moral law expressing one's own true nature[73] – and aesthetic consciousness, in which one understands the human capacity to create an entire world embodied in a work of art.[74]

Fourth and finally, after all these stages, there is philosophical consciousness, in which one becomes aware of oneself as the autonomous source of all the necessary features of the world one already inhabits. Without moral consciousness and aesthetic consciousness, philosophical consciousness is impossible. Not everyone attains moral consciousness, and Fichte is sometimes led to suggest that those who misunderstand his philosophy must be immoral scoundrels. But his more temperate position is that men like Professor Schmid lack aesthetic taste:

> If it is a painting which is supposed to be evaluated, one listens to the opinion of people that can see. However bad a painting may be, I do not think that it should be criticized by people who are blind from birth.[75]

Fichte also develops an account of how the Schmids of the world have become corrupted, incapable of aesthetic taste, and therefore incapable of philosophy.

Aesthetic taste requires the integration and harmonization of the various faculties of the individual. But the development of civil society requires the division of labor and therefore educates individuals to particular tasks, allowing certain faculties to flourish and others to atrophy. So the very development of social and economic civilization tends to destroy the possibility of aesthetic and philosophical cultivation. This is Fichte's version of the paradox of progress first formulated by Rousseau[76] and then reformulated by Schiller.[77] Fichte's solution to the paradox is distinctive and significant. He suggests in his *Philosophy of Masonry* that civilization has always been accompanied by an esoteric counterculture that counteracts the division of labor required by the exoteric culture.[78] Whether this historical speculation is correct or not, Fichte proposes just such a counterculture as an antidote to the fragmentation of humanity that stands in the way of the attainment of philosophical consciousness, and he believed that this counterculture could be constructed through the reformation and refinement of the existing Masonic lodges, within which class and occupation were irrelevant and an integrated humanity could be cultivated. Fichte's involvement in Freemasonry began as early as 1792–3[79] but it was only after the atheism controversy – the disastrous encounter with the inability to comprehend philosophy that forced Fichte to leave Jena[80] – that he participated energetically in Fessler's reorganization of Masonry in Berlin from 1800 to 1801.[81] Thus, the high point of Fichte's Masonic activity coincided with his realization that philosophy required an initiation that he could not trust his own writing – or perhaps writing as such – to provide.

Turning now from the Reality Problem to the reformulated Uniqueness Problem: suppose Fichte's philosophy *is* genuinely expressive of the mind. Does it follow that Fichte speaks for *all* other minds? Or might *some* other minds differ from his so radically as to be expressed by another philosophy? Supposing that Fichte's system proceeds necessarily from a first principle expressive of selfhood, might there be an alternative, equally necessary philosophy? Fichte sometimes says that the provision of such an alternative would be the only serious challenge to his philosophy.[82] And he is well aware that attempts to provide such alternatives are inevitable because, as he had already said in criticism of Reinhold's deduction of freedom, it will always be possible to give naturalistic accounts of human life, accounts that explain freedom away as an illusion.

Instead of starting from a first principle expressive of autonomous, free selfhood, naturalistic accounts start from a first principle expressive of *thinghood*. *Fichte* insists that no such account can ever give a satisfying explanation of human life, but he recognizes that there can be no theoretical argument against naturalism or in favor of freedom, because there is no common ground here, no shared higher principle to which the disputants might appeal. Furthermore, there is a sense in which these alternative naturalistic explanations of human life are genuinely expressive of the minds of their proponents, whom Fichte calls dogmatists. As he explains in 1797:

there are two different levels of human development, and, so long as everyone has not yet reached the highest level in the course of the progress of our species [*unseres Geschlechts*], there are two main sorts [*Hauptgattungen*] of human beings. Some people – namely, those who have not yet attained a full feeling of their own freedom and absolute self-sufficiency – discover themselves only in the act of representing things. Their self-consciousness is dispersed and attached to objects and must be gleaned from the manifold of the latter. They glimpse their own image only insofar as it is reflected through things, as in a mirror. If they were to be deprived of these things, then they would lose themselves at the same time. Thus, for the sake of their own selves, they cannot renounce their belief in the self-sufficiency of things. It is really through the external world that they have become everything that they are, and a person who is in fact nothing but a product of things will never be able to view himself in any other way. He will, furthermore, be correct – so long as he speaks only of himself and of those who are like him in this respect.[83]

Do we yet know the risks one runs when one divides humanity into *Hauptgattungen?* Fichte runs a risk, among others, that he will come to believe that he philosophizes only for himself, that he is the last human being. What prevents him from concluding that these uncomprehending ones who surround him are, if not machines, then rational beings of a different species, a species to which he does not belong and for which he cannot speak? Nothing prevents him except his conviction that the two *Gattungen* are in fact two stages in the *development* of humanity.[84] Since it is hard to see how any evidence for Fichte's developmental theory could compete with the constantly mounting evidence that his contemporaries are incompetent to understand the *Wissenschaftslehre*, Fichte's conviction that he lives among fellow humans must hang by a terrifyingly narrow thread.

It is in this sense, then, that I claim Fichte not only thematizes the problem of other minds within post-Kantian philosophy but also lives that problem. For the Reality Problem and the Uniqueness Problem raised by Schulze against the post-Kantian philosophy of Reinhold – raised as skeptical worries about the agreement between thought and the external world – resurface for Fichte as skeptical anxieties about the agreement between his thought (or its linguistic expression) and the thought of others. Those anxieties express themselves as the fear that others are mere machines, or that they are members of an alien species of rational beings. Much of Fichte's frenetic intellectual activity can be seen as an attempt to hold those fears at bay without sacrificing his conviction in the truth of his own insights, and without sacrificing his sanity.

What Fichte needs above all – and what Fichte does not possess in any adequate form – is an account not only of the development toward full humanity, but also of what *resists* that development. From the beginning of his career as an independent philosopher, Fichte insists on preserving the possibility of heteronomy as essential to human freedom. But the freedom to repudiate the moral law as expression of autonomous human nature is also the freedom to repudiate Fichte's philosophy as expression of fully self-conscious human nature. And Fichte never finds the right level at which to characterize this darkness of the spirit, which cannot (as I have already argued) be represented as a conscious choice of a course of action. Fichte's achievement remains incomplete, since it remains without an account of the ways in which human beings can become obscure to themselves, and without any sense of how we might be helped out of our darkness.

This incompleteness is evident in Fichte's attitude toward writing. We have already seen that Fichte is inclined early in his career to be suspicious of the letter's capacity to express the spirit. The suspicion mounts – in the course of events, leading to Fichte's forced departure from his teaching position – until, in 1804, Fichte renounces written publication as an appropriate vehicle for philosophy. He writes to the royal cabinet of ministers to the King of Prussia, insisting that they hear him out. For he has discovered the philosophical system that will finally enable "a rebirth of mankind and of all human relationships." But he cannot make his discovery known in writing because he

> has become sufficiently confident that the conditions necessary for understanding a system of this sort have, for the most part, been destroyed by the academic method that has prevailed until now, and he is also convinced that more errors are in general circulation at the present time than perhaps ever before. Consequently, he has no intention of publishing his discovery in its present form and exposing it to general misunderstanding and distortion. He wishes to confine himself to oral communication so that misunderstanding can thereby be detected and eliminated on the spot.[85]

Cavell has often written of the importance of a certain pedagogical passivity or patience, a presentation of the teacher's self for the pupil's acknowledgment.[86] And Cavell has found this patience exemplified in the writing of Emerson, Thoreau, and Wittgenstein. I might say, then, that – in this sense – Fichte is *impatient*, unwilling to present himself for reading. Wishing to eliminate misunderstanding on the spot, Fichte denies his audience the freedom to work their own passage to insight. He never entirely abandons the desire to exercise a causal influence on his audience or, to use his own desperate words, "to force the reader to understand."

This is a new version of an old criticism. The old criticism – heard already in Fichte's day – is that his philosophy leaves no room for the passivity involved in knowing the world. My new version is that Fichte's way of living his philosophy leaves no room for the passivity involved in being acknowledged by another.

However, I emphatically do not wish to underestimate how difficult a reconception of the task of writing Fichte would have had to undertake – and how much suffering he would have had to undergo – in order to achieve the patience of which Cavell speaks. So I emphatically do not mean to accuse Fichte of simply not doing something he might simply have done. Precisely because Fichte puts at stake, in his relation to his audience, nothing less than the resolution of skepticism about other minds, the assurance that he is not alone; precisely because the stake is so enormous that it cannot be supported by writing as he conceives it, perhaps by writing as philosophy in his day conceives it; and because this crisis might be thought to call for philosophy to reconceive writing or for writing to reconceive philosophy, Fichte can be fruitfully juxtaposed to the Emersonian perfectionists whose philosophical practice of writing Cavell has done so much to illuminate and to inherit.

A full assessment of Fichte's contribution to the history of the problem of the other would have to reckon with, not only his highly suggestive account of the origin of consciousness in the summons of the other, but also with what I might call his *life with other minds*: his troubled authorship, his problematic pedagogy, and his humanity, which he was not afraid to put at risk. Furthermore, both the theoretical and practical issues of the existence of other minds arise *within* Fichte's general project of completing Kant's revolution and responding to the threat of skepticism by systematically deducing the concept of freedom and the concept of the thing in itself from the original activity of the self. So the problem of Fichte's life with other minds, which some philosophers might dismiss as merely biographical or psychological, cannot be separated from what are generally recognized as central *philosophical* issues for post-Kantian philosophy. I reach this conclusion in acknowledgment of the significance of Cavell's work, because to read Cavell is, among other things, to make the discovery – at once terrifying and exhilarating – that the problems of philosophy and the problems of human life are all inescapably linked.[87]

Notes

1   The idea that Wittgenstein's project is post-Kantian is almost commonplace now, but this was not the case when Cavell first made the claim. See *This New Yet Unapproachable America: Lectures after Emerson after Wittgenstein* (Albuquerque: Living Batch Press, 1989), p. 80:
    As for the underwriting of ordinary language philosophy [by Emersonian transcendentalism], that had been in preparation in my work since the first things I published that I still use – the title essay and its companion second essay *of Must We Mean What We Say?* – which identify Wittgenstein's *Investigations* (together with Austin's practice) as inheritors of the task of Kant's transcendental logic, namely to demonstrate, or articulate, the *a priori* fit of the categories of human understanding with the objects of human understanding, that is, with objects. Within a couple of years, I was attacked so violently for this Kantian suggestion – on the grounds that it made the study of language unempirical – that a well-placed friend of mine informed me that my philosophical reputation was destroyed in the crib. And now a quarter of a century later, when just about anyone and everyone agrees that the *Investigations* is a

Kantian work, I will not even get the solace of being credited with having first pointed it out. (Ah well. If you live by the pen you perish by the pen.)

2 Title essay, *Must We Mean What We Say?* (Cambridge: Cambridge University Press, 1976), hereafter cited as *MWM*, 13.

3 *MWM*, 24–5.

4 "Aesthetic problems of modern philosophy," *MWM*, 96.

5 I do not mean to suggest that Cavell began by developing an interpretation of Kant and then extended his thinking to others. (Although the dissertation he was originally planning, prior to Austin's visit to America, was concerned, in part, with Kant's conception of human action. See *A Pitch of Philosophy: Autobiographical Exercises* (Cambridge: Harvard University Press, 1995), p. 55.) Rather, it was while working on lines of thought suggested by Austin and Wittgenstein that Cavell came to see a profound relationship between that work and Kant, a relationship that had not been made explicit and that was bound to seem surprising in light of the explicitly anti-Kantian tone of much work inspired by aspects of Wittgenstein's thinking at that time. Cavell has remarked in conversation that he was particularly struck, when working on Wittgenstein, by the way in which *Philosophical Investigations* (trans. G.E.M. Anscombe, New York: Macmillan, 1953), §90 – "Our investigation . . . is directed not towards phenomena, but, as one might say, towards the 'possibilities' of phenomena" – suggested that Wittgenstein's grammatical investigations could be regarded as *transcendental* in Kant's sense. See "The availability of Wittgenstein's later philosophy," *MWM*, 64–6. See also *In Quest of the Ordinary: Lines of Skepticism and Romanticism* (Chicago: University of Chicago Press, 1988), p. 38, and *Pursuits of Happiness: The Hollywood Comedy of Remarriage* (Cambridge: Harvard University Press, 1981), p. 77.

6 See *This New Yet Unapproachable America*, p. 49:

> It is as if such a perplexed sensibility shared Kant's sense of the *a priori* as the possibility of language but then could not tolerate two of Kant's intellectual costs: (1) the thing in itself as a remainder or excess beyond the categories of the understanding; and (2) the Aristotelian table of judgments as the key to the completeness of those categories.

In this passage, Cavell is describing dissatisfaction with these two Kantian costs as motivations both for Wittgenstein's "idea of a criterion, hence of grammar" and for "Heidegger's reconception of the idea of the *thing* that is fundamental to his later philosophy."

7 The list begins with Jacobi, Maimon, Fichte, Hegel, and Schopenhauer, continues with figures such as Cohen, Green, and McTaggart, and includes many contemporary philosophers. See, for example, Hilary Putnam, *The Many Faces of Realism* (LaSalle: Open Court, 1987). For the first, seminal criticism of Kant's notion of the thing in itself, see F.H. Jacobi, "On transcendental idealism" (supplement to *David Theme on Faith*) in *The Main Philosophical Writings and the Novel Allwill*, trans. and ed. George di Giovanni (Montreal: McGill University Press, 1994), pp. 331–8, where Jacobi famously remarks: "*Without* that presupposition [that is, the presupposition of the thing in itself affecting the subject and thereby giving rise to sensible impressions] I could not enter into the system, but *with* it, I could not stay within it."

8 See Cavell, *In Quest of the Ordinary*, p. 31.

9 *The Senses of Walden: An Expanded Edition* (San Francisco: North Point Press, 1981), pp. 106–7 n.

10 It is unclear whether the time for Cavell's clarification of this idea has yet arrived. However, the theme recurs in *The Claim of Reason* (Oxford: Clarendon Press, 1979), pp. 53–4, in a passage closely related to the footnote under discussion here, a passage

in which Cavell remarks: "The problem with the thing in itself is that it should itself have received a transcendental deduction." It is highly significant that this passage occurs just at the moment when Cavell, criticizing Austin's criticism of traditional epistemology for not focusing on what Cavell calls "specific objects," introduces the highly important idea of "generic objects" as essential to the project of traditional epistemology. In Cavell's view, Austin has performed an enormously significant task by showing that epistemologists are *not* concerned with knowing "specific objects" about which some specific question of knowledge has arisen, such as birds whose identity must be established by marking their specific characteristics. But Austin is mistaken in thinking that this amounts to *a criticism* of epistemology; on the contrary, it points to the *essence of* epistemology. For the epistemologist is concerned with "generic objects" such as pieces of wax and tomatoes precisely *because* no specific question of knowledge has arisen about them, because *in so far as there is a question of knowing them,* it must be quite generally the question of knowing *the world as such.*

11 See "Austin at criticism," MWM, 111:

> Austin's criticisms, where they stand, are perhaps as external and snap as any others, but he has done more than any philosopher (excepting Wittgenstein) in the AngloAmerican tradition to make clear that there is a coherent tradition to be dealt with. If he has held it at arm's length, and falsely assessed it, that is just a fault which must bear its own assessment; it remains true that he has given us hands for assessing it in subtler ways than we had known. The first step would be to grant to philosophers the ordinary rights of language and vision Austin grants to all men: to ask of them, in his spirit, why they should say what they say where and when they say it, and to give the *full story* before claiming satisfaction.

This criticism of Austin at criticism amounts to a call for a new relation to the history of philosophy, a relation made possible by Austin but quite contrary to the relation taken up by Austin himself. Hence, for example, Cavell's capacity for the relation to Kant I am discussing, a relation significantly different from that of Austin, who remarked, in a characteristic witticism, and in allusion to Kant's famous statement that Hume awoke him from his dogmatic slumber, "On these matters (i.e., matters concerning the spurious phrase, 'the meaning of a word') dogmatists require prodding: although history indeed suggests that it may sometimes be better to let sleeping dogmatists lie" ("The meaning of a word," in J.L. Austin, *Philosophical Papers*, 3rd edn (Oxford: Oxford University Press, 1979), p. 75).

12 *Senses of Walden*, p. 107 n.

13 Ibid., p. 105.

14 See "Knowing and acknowledging" and "The avoidance of love: a reading of *King Lear*," both in MWM; and Part Four of *The Claim of Reason*.

15 It is important here to recall Cavell's remark:

> But I do not propose the idea of acknowledging as an alternative to knowing but rather as an interpretation of it, as I take the word 'acknowledge', containing the 'knowledge' itself to suggest (or perhaps it suggests that knowing is an interpretation of acknowledging) (*In Quest of the Ordinary*, p. 9).

Cavell is therefore not to be understood as recommending that, since knowledge cannot withstand the threat of skepticism, we ought to adopt some alternative attitude. Santayana is mentioned by Cavell as making this sort of recommendation; among Kant's contemporaries, one might recall Jacobi, whose initiation of the criticism of Kant's notion of the thing in itself I have already noted.

16 *This New Yet Unapproachable America*, pp. 49–50.

17 See, for example, *Foundation of the Entire Science of the Knowledge, Foundation of Knowledge of the Practical* in *Fichte: Science of Knowledge*, trans. P. Heath and J. Lachs (Cambridge: Cambridge University Press, 1982), p. 249, J.G. *Fichte-Gesamtausgabe der Bayerischen Akademie der Wissenschaften* (henceforth GA), eds Reinhard Lauth, Hans Jacob, *et al.* (Stuttgart-Bad Cannstatr: Friedrich Frommann Verlag, 1964–), I, 2: 414:

> The thing-in-itself is something for the self, and consequently in the self, though it ought *not* to be *in the self* it is thus a contradiction, though as the object of a necessary idea it must be set at the foundation of all our philoso-phizing, and has always lain at the root of all philosophy and all acts of the finite mind, save only that no one has been clearly aware of it, or of the contra-diction contained therein. This relation of the thing-in-itself to the self forms the basis for the entire mechanism of the human and all other finite minds. Any attempt to change this would entail the elimination of all consciousness, and with it of all existence.

18 I can only note here–what goes almost without saying – that there are significant differences between Cavell and early post-Kantians like Fichte and Reinhold. In particular, Reinhold and Fichte see Kant's problematic use of the concept of the thing in itself as symptomatic of his failure – at some moments, apparently self-confessed – to *systematize* his philosophy. A system must derive its concepts from a single first principle, as Kant himself sometimes says, and Reinhold and Fichte think that all of Kant's difficulties could be resolved, and all of his insights preserved, if only *they* could formulate the right first principle. Then space, time, the categories, the idea of freedom, the idea of the thing in itself, etc., could all be derived within a single system, and the thing in itself would not remain left over as a source of embar-rassment. For Cavell, in contrast, it is one of Wittgenstein's major insights that human reason is systematic without, at the same time, being capable of organization into a system. Human reason is systematic, in so far as any concept could, under presently unforeseeable circumstances, bear the pressure of a skepticism that puts *every* concept – the world as a whole – at risk. But human reason cannot be system-atized, because skepticism may strike *at any* concept in this fashion and its occasions cannot be known in advance of their occurrence, so that we cannot know in advance which concepts will stand in need of deduction at the moment of skeptical crisis, and no first principle can afford philosophy a vantage point from which to survey human reason as a single, timeless whole. This difference between Cavell and his post-Kantian predecessors – for that matter, between Kant's idea of a category and Wittgenstein's idea of a criterion – seems too massive not to mention and too immeasurable to discuss in the present context.

19 *The Claim of Reason*, pp. 468–78. Note especially p. 468: "The idea is that the problem of the other is discovered through telling its history."

20 See the papers collected in *Disowning Knowledge in Six Plays of Shakespeare* (Cambridge: Cambridge University Press, 1987).

21 There has been much discussion of the problem of other minds in Fichte, particu-larly since the publication of Reinhard Lauth's seminal article, "Le Problème de l'interpersonnalité chez J.G. Fichte," *Archives de Philosophie* 35 (1962): 325–44, and Alexis Philonenko's thesis, *La Liberté humaine dans la philosophie de Fichte* (Paris: Vrin, 1966). A useful recent discussion, relevant to the period in Fichte's develop-ment discussed here, can be found in Ives Radrizzani, *Vers la fondation de l'intersubjectivité chez Fichte* (Paris: Vrin, 1993). However, none of the literature with which I am familiar regards the problem of the other as internally related to the

problem of skepticism about the external world in the way that I am suggesting. Conversely, none of the discussions of Schulze's effect on Fichte with which I am familiar regard the problem of the intelligibility of the *Wissenschaftlehre* as a displacement of that effect in the way that I am suggesting. See, for example, Peter Baumanns, *Fichtes Wissenschaftslehre: Probleme ihres Anfangs* (Bonn: Bouvier Verlag Hermann Grundmann, 1974), pp. 47–50, 69–80; Daniel Breazeale, "Fichte's *Aenesidemus* review and the transformation of German Idealism," *Review of Metaphysics* 34 (1981): 545–68; Frederick Neuhouser, *Fichte's Theory of Subjectivity* (Cambridge: Cambridge University Press, 1990), pp. 69–75, 103–7. In the development of the reading of Fichte of which this essay is a part, I have repeatedly found that, sensitized as my reading is by the work of Cavell, I am not so much disagreeing with existing Fichte interpretations as noting lines of thought that seem not to have been noted before. I should note here that I do not pretend to carry out in this essay an exhaustive investigation of Fichte's various accounts, offered at different stages of his philosophical development, of relations among minds and their role in the constitution of the world. I restrict myself here to the origins of Fichte's thought about other minds in his influential writings of the 1790s, and to some ramifications of these origins for the problem of the intelligibility of Fichte's philosophy. Thus I will not consider here the significant developments in Fichte's thought at Berlin, except in so far as they relate directly to the issue of philosophical intelligibility already raised at Jena.

22 See, for example, MWM, 96; *The Claim of Reason*, p. 207.

23 See, for example, *Pursuits of Happiness*, p. 80, where Cavell characterizes "moral evil," on a Kantian view, "as the will to exempt oneself, to isolate oneself, from the human community. It is a choice of inhumanity, of monstrousness." In this passage Cavell is contrasting Kant's practical philosophy, where such a will to inhumanity is conceived as possible, with Kant's theoretical philosophy, where it is not. On the interpretation I am offering here, however, Fichte's attempt to unify the theoretical and the practical in a single principle can be regarded as showing how the will to inhumanity can express itself as a resistance to philosophy, both theoretical and practical.

24 To provide some brief background information: Schmid was the first to teach Kantian philosophy at the University of Jena and his popular *Worterbuch* (see note 26) was republished many times. Reinhold was at first an anti-Kantian who changed his mind and massively increased Kant's fame with his *Briefe über die Kantische Philosophie* and was then appointed to the first chair established expressly for Kantian philosophy, also at Jena, in 1787. Fichte, who experienced a conversion to Kant's philosophy in 1790 when he was an obscure private tutor, became suddenly famous in 1792 when his *Kritik aller Offenbarung*, published anonymously, was mistaken for Kant's own work. When Reinhold left Jena for Kiel in 1793, Fichte, who had never before occupied a university position, was appointed his successor. For more on Schmid, see the biographical sketch in *Aufklärung* 7(1) (1992): 73–4; on Reinhold, see Frederick Beiser, *The Fate of Reason: German Philosophy from Kant to Fichte* (Cambridge: Harvard University Press, 1987), pp. 266–84, and D. Breazeale, "Between Kant and Fichte: Karl Leonhard Reinhold's 'elementary philosophy,'" *Review of Metaphysics* 35 (1982): 785–822; on Fichte, see "Editor's introduction: Fichte in Jena" in *Fichte: Early Philosophical Writings*, trans. and ed. D. Breazeale (Ithaca: Cornell University Press, 1988), pp. 1–49.

25 Some light was shed on Kant's conception of the will in *Religion within the Limits of Reason Alone*, Book One of which appeared in the *Berlinische Monatsschrift* in 1792, although the whole book was not published (due to government censorship) until 1793. But even Book One does not seem to have been available to Reinhold when he criticized Schmid, and Kant did not explicitly clarify his conception of the will until he published the *Metaphysics of Morals* in 1797.

26 Carl C.E. Schmid, *Worterbuch Zum leichtern Gebrauch der Kantischen Schriften nebst einer Abbandlung*, 2nd edn (Jena: Croker, 1788), pp. 356–7. In later editions, Schmid replied to Reinhold's attack, invoking Kant's authority (see note 29 below). See, for example, the fourth edition of 1798, ed. Norbert Hinske (Darmstadt: Wissenschaftliche Buchgesellschaft, 1976), pp. 3–4, 251.

27 For what follows, see Reinhold, *Briefe uber die Kantische Philosophie, vol. 2* (Leipzig: Georg Joachim Göschen, 1792), Achter Brief, pp. 262–308.

28 There is no adequate English translation of this distinction, so I will use the German words. On the problem of translation, see Ralf Meerbote, "*Wille* and *Willkür* in Kant's theory of action," in Molcke Gram (ed.), *Interpreting Kant* (Iowa City: University of Iowa Press, 1982). Although Kant does not officially formulate this distinction until the 1797 *Metaphysics of Morals*, it is generally recognized that Kant already makes use of the distinction in the 1793 *Religion within the Limits of Reason Alone*.

29 Hence the injustice of Kant's 1797 attack, apparently aimed at Reinhold, on those who seek to define freedom as the capacity to make a choice for or against the law. See *Metaphysics of Morals*, p. 52 (Ak. 6, 226). Reinhold replied to the attack in "Einige Bermerkungen über die in der Einleitung zu den metaphysischen Anfangsgrunden der Rechtslehre von I. Kant aufgestellten Begriffe von der Freiheit des Willens" in *Auswahl vermischter Schriften*, vol. 2 (Jena: J.M. Mauke, 1797). Some recent discussion of this dispute has recognized Kant's injustice to Reinhold. See Gerold Prauss, *Kant über Freiheit als Autonomie* (Frankfurt am Main: Vittorio Klostermann, 1983), pp. 85–9, and Henry Allison, *Kant's Theory of Freedom* (Cambridge: Cambridge University Press, 1990), pp. 133–6.

30

> An essential component part of this discussion would be missing if, in it, I passed over in silence the relation of the concept of free will established by me to the *results of the Kantian philosophy*. That concept has been *prepared* through this [Kantian] philosophy, and is so completely in accordance with the *spirit* of the same, that it contradicts the *letter* of certain utterances of the *Critique of Practical Reason* only if one takes them for what they are in no way supposed to be according to the purpose of the author: for *logical explanations* [i.e., definitions of the sort given by Schmid] of the free will.

Reinhold is, of course, invoking Paul's polemic against the role of the law in Judaism (2 Corinthians 3: 6: "for the letter killeth, but the spirit giveth life"), and thus Reinhold is the first post-Kantian to interpret his relation to his competitors in terms of the Christian claim to supersede Judaism, an interpretation that Fichte will turn against Reinhold and that Hegel will turn against Fichte.

31 See Fichte's reviews of Creuzer's *Skeptische Betrachtungen über die Freiheit des Willens*, GA, I, 2: 7–14, and Gebhard's *Uber die sittliche Gute aus uninteressiertem Wohlwollen*, GA, I, 2: 21–9, both published in 1793. These two reviews, which appeared on consecutive days, 30 and 31 October 1793, in the Jena *Allgemeine LiteraturZeitung*, provide a fascinating glimpse of developments in Fichte's thinking. Already in the Creuzer review Fichte affirms the importance of Reinhold's distinction between freedom and autonomy, but argues that Reinhold has not fully grasped the implication of his distinction, that the reality of freedom cannot be regarded as knowable. Only in the Gebhard review, however, does Fichte see that this creates a crisis for Kantianism.

32 See Creuzer review, GA, I, 2: 10, where Fichte calls, in criticism of Reinhold, for a

> return to that which seems to the reviewer the true spirit of the critical philosophy.... Namely – the principle of sufficient reason can absolutely not be applied to the *determining* of absolute self-activity by itself (to *willing*); for it is

> One and a Simple, and a completely isolated action; the determining itself is at the same time the being-determined, and the determinant is that which becomes determined.

In this characterization of the immediate self-relation of the free will one can see a preliminary formulation of what Fichte would later call intellectual intuition.

33 Reinhold, *Briefe*, vol. 2, p. 284. I do not think Reinhold's interpretation of Kant's deduction of freedom by means of the *Faktum* of reason is correct, but some contemporary commentators read *the Critique of Practical Reason* in a strikingly similar way although, unlike Reinhold, they take this interpretation to be a reason for sharp criticism of Kant.

34 In the Creuzer review, GA, I, 2: 9, Fichte argues that

> one must distinguish between the *determining*, as free action of the intelligible I; and the *being-determined*, as phenomenal state of the empirical I. The first expression of the absolute self-activity of the human spirit mentioned above appears in a fact: in the being determined *of the higher faculty of desire*, which certainly must not be confused with the will, but must equally not be passed over in a theory of the will; the self-activity gives this faculty its *determinate form, which is only determinable in one manner*, which appears as the moral law. The expression of absolute self-activity in the *determining* of the *will* – which is to be distinguished from the former – does not appear and cannot appear, because the will is originally *formless*; it is assumed merely as postulate of the moral law given to consciousness by means of that form of the original faculty of desire, and is therefore no object of knowledge, but rather of belief.

Similarly, in the Gebhard review, GA, I, 2: 26, Fichte argues that Kantians cannot appeal to facts of moral consciousness against their determinist opponents, "for (the opponent) concedes what is actually a fact [i.e. moral feeling], and it is not a fact that [pure] reason is practical and produces that (moral) feeling through its [practical] capacity."

35 See Creuzer review, GA, I, 2: 10: if one makes Reinhold's causal argument, "then one drags an intelligible into the series of *natural causes*; and one thereby brings about the placement [of freedom] in the series of *natural effects*; the assumption of an intelligible which is no intelligible."

36 See Gebhard review, GA, I, 2: 27–8: "[Pure] practical reason . . . cannot be passed off as a fact, nor postulated as the consequence of a fact, rather it must be proven. It must be proven *that* [pure] reason is practical." Immediately following this declaration, Fichte sketches – in an extremely cursory form – "such a proof, which could at the same time very easily be the foundation *of all* philosophical knowledge (in accordance with its matter)." For a discussion of this first published hint at the project of Fichte's *Wissenschaftslehre*, see F. Neuhouser, *Fichte's Theory of Subjectivity*, pp. 35–41.

37 *Some Lectures Concerning the Scholar's Vocation*, 1794, Fichte. *Early Philosophical Writings*, p. 153; GA, I, 3: 34.

38 Kant does not seem ever to address the problem of other minds explicitly and almost all his commentators have followed him in this. An exception is Carol A. Van Kirk, "Kant and the problem of other minds," *KantStudien* 77 (1986): 41–58, who argues that Kant did not *need* to address the problem, which only arises for those who privilege self-knowledge over cognition of objects. But even if Kant is not committed to incorrigible self-knowledge, he is surely committed to a significant asymmetry between the first-person point of view and the views others can have of me, which is sufficient to motivate a Kantian problem of other minds.

39 Cavell also sees a connection between Kant's moral philosophy and the problem of the other. See *Pursuits of Happiness*, pp. 73–80, especially p. 79, where Cavell argues that the idea of human finitude is significantly different in Kant's *practical* philosophy:

> One inflection of the moral law is that its necessity and universality are to be viewed as holding in "the realm of ends," which may be thought of as the perfected human community. This realm is also a world "beyond" the world we inhabit, a noumenal realm, open to reason, standing to reason; but I am not fated to be debarred from it as I am from the realm of things-in-themselves, by my sensuous nature; for the perfected human community *can* be achieved, it may at last be experienced, it is in principle presentable. Yet, there is between me and this realm of reason also something that may present itself as a barrier – the fact that I cannot reach this realm *alone*.

Might we say that Fichte reconceives Kant's theoretical philosophy in just the terms in which Cavell here understands Kant's practical philosophy, so that the other is to provide me with access to the intelligible world of things in themselves?

40 Fichte might have argued that Kant's theoretical philosophy also presupposes the possibility of other minds. For in *Prolegomena* 18–19, Kant identifies the objective validity I claim when I make an empirical judgment with "necessary universal validity (for everyone)":

> For instance, when I say the air is elastic, this judgment is as yet a judgment of perception only. I do nothing but refer two sensations in my senses to one another. But if I would have it called a judgment of experience, I require this connection to stand under a condition which makes it universally valid. I desire therefore that I and everybody else should always necessarily connect the same perceptions under the same circumstances" (*Prolegomena to Any Future Metaphysics That Will Be Able to Come Forward at a Science*, trans. Paul Carus, revised by James W. Ellington (Indianapolis: Hackett, 1977), p. 43; Ak. 4, 299).

For a helpful discussion of the difficulties attending Kant's distinction here between judgments of perception and judgments of experience, and for an illuminating indication of the connections between universal validity and the notion of the universal voice in the *Critique of Judgment*, see Lewis White Beck, "Did the sage of Konigsberg have no dreams?" in *Essays on Kant and Hume* (New Haven: Yale University Press, 1978).

41 Letter to Reinhold, 29 August 1795, *Fichte. Early Philosophical Writings*, pp. 407–8; GA, III, 1, no. 305.

42 See *Critique of Pure Reason*, trans. N. Kemp Smith (New York: St Martin's Press, 1965), A84/B117.

43 Note that, while in Fichte's thought the historicity of reason emerges in the context of the problem of the other, Cavell writes in *The Claim of Reason*, p. 468, that "the problem of other minds is a problem of history (the problem of modern human history; the modern problem of human history)."

44 *Foundations of Natural Right* (1796) in *The Science of Rights*, trans. A.E. Kroeger (New York: Harper & Row, 1970), p. 60; GA. I, 3: 347.

45 This aspect of Fichte's thought has so far received very little attention in the burgeoning English-language literature on him. See, however, Allen Wood, *Hegel's Ethical Thought* (Cambridge: Cambridge University Press, 1990), pp. 77–83, and Robert Williams, *Recognition: Fichte and Hegel on the Other* (Albany: State University of New York Press, 1992), pp. 49–70.

46 *Fichte. Foundations of Transcendental Philosophy (Wissenschaftslehre) Nova Methodo* (1796/9), trans. and ed. D. Breazeale (Ithaca: Cornell University Press, 1992), p. 357; GA, IV, 2: 180.
47 *Foundations of Natural Right* (1796) in *The Science of Rights*, p. 67; GA, I, 3: 351.
48 Fichte may be entitled, not to the spatial image of a *sphere*, but rather to the temporal image of a *trajectory*, for it is central to his thinking that the finite rational being is essentially directed toward the future, a thought easily derived from the idea of the summons. See *The Science of Rights*, p. 77; GA, I, 3: 357.
49 See *The Claim of Reason*, pp. 372–8, especially p. 375: "What he really believes is not that slaves are not human beings, but that some human beings are slaves."
50 See J.S. Mill, *An Examination of Sir William Hamilton's Philosophy and of the Principal Philosophical Questions Discussed in His Writings*, chap. 12 ("The psychological theory of the belief in matter, how far applicable to mind") in *Collected Works of John Stuart Mill*, ed. J.M. Robson *et al.* (Toronto: University of Toronto Press, 1979), pp. 188–95. For an illuminating discussion of the difficulties attending the argument from analogy – in particular of the difficulties attending its claim about the *likeness* of my body and the other's – see *Claim of Reason*, pp. 393–416, especially pp. 393–95.
51 The intricate and problematic details of this ambitious program – the *Wissenschaftslehre Nova Methods* of 1796–9 – are not my concern here.
52 The question, usually hostile, is associated with Hume. For an important recent discussion that takes seriously the ancient skeptic's claim that skepticism is a way of life, see Myles Burnyeat, "Can the skeptic live his skepticism?" in *The Skeptical Tradition*, ed. Myles Burnyeat (Berkeley: University of California Press, 1983), pp. 117–48.
53 In this way, Cavell argues, skepticism about other minds differs from skepticism about the external world, which cannot be lived. Arriving at and exploring this difference is one of the main tasks of Part Four of *The Claim of Reason*. See especially pp. 432–40, 453.
54 In my view, it has not been sufficiently appreciated that each of the major German Idealists – Kant, Fichte, Schelling, and Hegel – was not only aware of the obscurity of his philosophy but also sought to account for that obscurity as arising from the very nature of philosophy. Here I can only hope to show how one might establish this thesis with respect to Fichte. Just as Fichte's account of the obscurities of the *Wissenschaftslehre* is rooted in his struggles with central philosophical problems such as freedom of the will, the prospects of transcendental argumentation, and skepticism about other minds, so the obscurities of the other Idealists arise (in their views, at least) from their treatments of central philosophical issues. Those obscurities should therefore not be treated (without explicit justification) either as peripheral issues of style or as symptoms of easily avoidable confusion.
55 *The Claim of Reason*, p. 451.
56 See Beiser, *The Fate of Reason*, pp. 266–84.
57 Schulze, "Aenesidemus;' in *Between Kant and Hegel*, trans. George Di Giovanni and Henry S. Harris (Albany: State University of New York Press, 1985), p. 108; *Aenesidemus oder uber die Fundamente der von dem Herrn Professor Reinhold in Jena gelieferten Elementar-Philosophie*, ed. Arthur Liebert (Berlin: Reuther & Reichard, 1911), p. 99.
58 Ibid., p. 108; *Aenesidemus*, p. 99.
59 Ibid., p. 107; *Aenesidemus*, 97.
60 Ibid., p. 108; *Aenesidemus*, 99.
61 Although Schulze has not been mentioned, to my knowledge, in the renewed discussions of transcendental method that have occurred since the 1960s, the most important objections raised against the Kant-inspired strategies of "transcendental arguments" associated with P.F. Strawson were in fact rediscoveries formulated in a

contemporary idiom – of Schulze's original objections to Kant and Reinhold. The parallel to Schulze's Reality Problem is Barry Stroud's famous charge that transcendental arguments that eschew Kant's transcendental Idealism are implicitly relying upon an unargued-for verificationism to bridge the gap between the necessities of thought and the nature of reality. See Stroud, "Transcendental Arguments," in *Journal of Philosophy* 65 (1968), reprinted in *Kant on Pure Reason*, ed. Ralph C.S. Walker (Oxford: Oxford University Press, 1982), p. 129:

> Kant thought that he could argue from the necessary conditions of thought and experience to the falsity of "problematic" idealism and so to the actual existence of the external world of material objects, and not merely to the fact that we believe that there is a world, or that as far as we can tell there is. An examination of some recent attempts to argue in analogous fashion suggests that, without invoking a verification principle which automatically renders superfluous any indirect argument, the most that could be probed by a consideration of the necessary conditions of language is that, for example, we must *believe* that there are material objects and other minds in order for us to speak meaningfully at all.

62 The contemporary parallel to the Uniqueness Problem is the argument made by Stephan Koerner in "The impossibility of transcendental deductions" (*The Monist* 51 (1967) 3: 321) that "the impossibility of demonstrating a schema's uniqueness . . . renders transcendental deductions impossible."

63 "Review of *Aenesidemus*," *Fichte: Early Philosophical Writings*, pp. 72–3; GA, 1, 2: 60–1:

> Aenesidemus says: "It is simply ingrained in the entire structure of our nature that we can be satisfied with our knowledge only when we have completely seen the connection and agreement between our representations and the features contained within them and something *which exists entirely independently of them*: Thus, here at the foundations of this new skepticism, we clearly and distinctly have that old mischief which, until Kant, was perpetrated with the thing in itself. It seems to the reviewer anyway that neither Kant nor Reinhold has by any means declared himself loudly and strongly enough against this mischief, which has been the common source of all the objections – skeptical as well as dogmatic – which have been raised against the Critical Philosophy. However, it is by no means ingrained in human nature to think of a thing independent of *any* faculty of representation *at all*; on the contrary, it is downright impossible to do so."

64 Ibid., pp. 66–7; GA, I, 2: 50–1.
Aenesidemus raises the question of how the Elementary Philosophy (of Reinhold) is supposed to be able to arrive at this effusive knowledge of the *objective existence* of a thing of the sort which the faculty of representation is said to be. Aenesidemus cannot express sufficient amazement that Reinhold, as a Critical [i.e. Kantian] Philosopher, should make the following inference: "Anyone who admits a representation at the same time admits a faculty of representation. The reviewer, or perhaps anyone very inclined toward amazement, *may* express no less amazement over the skeptic, for whom only a short time ago nothing was certain except that there are various representations in us, and who now, as soon as he hears the words 'faculty of representation,' can think only of some sort of thing (round or square?) which exists as a thing in itself, *independently of its being represented*, and indeed, exists as a thing which *represents*. The reader will soon see that this interpretation involves no injustice to our skeptic. The faculty of representation exists *for* the faculty of

representation and *through* the faculty of representation: this is the circle within which every finite understanding, that is, every understanding that we can conceive, is necessarily conceived. Anyone who wants to escape from this circle does not understand himself and does not know what he wants."

In Fichte's view, it is one of Kant's major insights – albeit one that Fichte is the first to fully grasp – that the mind is not a thing but a self-determining activity.

65 *Eigne Meditationen*, GA, II, 3: 23–4.

66 *Science of Rights*, p. 11; GA, I, 3: 314.

67 The suggestion is that Fichte's struggle with the skeptical problem of the other not only makes him look insane to others but also implies that he needs to protect himself against insanity. It is essential to Cavell's understanding of skepticism that, in its commitment to the rational examination of reason, which seems the opposite of madness, skepticism nevertheless shows the possibility – or even runs the risk – of madness. At the very beginning of his *Meditations*, when he proposes to doubt all knowledge based upon the senses, Descartes accuses himself of being like a madman fantasizing wildly about his body. The accusation seems overcome when Descartes realizes that he "regularly has all the same experiences when asleep as madmen do when awake – indeed sometimes even more improbable ones." Since his dreams are sometimes indistinguishable from waking experiences, Descartes finds a reason for doubting that he is "here, in his dressing-gown, sitting by the fire," as he would appear to know on the basis of his senses. The existence of "some reason for doubt" marks a difference between Descartes and the madmen, marks his commitment to reason itself. See *The Philosophical Writings of Descartes*, vol. 2, trans. John Cottingham, R. Stoothoff, and D. Murdoch (Cambridge, UK: Cambridge University Press, 1984), pp. 12–13, and *The Claim of Reason*, pp. 130–1. However, anxiety about one's own sanity, once raised, is not so easily banished. Although Descartes has reason for his fantasies; these are nevertheless fantasies that madmen might well share, like the fantasy of a "supremely powerful . . . malicious deceiver," so that reason itself puts Descartes (at least temporarily) in the company of madmen. And if Descartes cannot at last leave the company of madmen by defending reason against skepticism, then there is no reason to distinguish reason from unreason and madness is the only *honest* expression of the human condition. Thus Cavell remarks, in his interpretation of Shakespeare's *The Winter's Tale* as a study of skepticism, that "Descartes' discovery of skepticism shows, you might say, what makes Leontes' madness possible, or what makes his madness representative of the human need for acknowledgment." See *In Quest of the Ordinary*, p. 85. I am grateful to Cavell for illuminating conversation on this topic.

68 Letter from Fichte to Reinhold, 2 July 1795, *Fichte: Early Philosophical Writings*, pp. 398–9; GA, III, no. 294.

69 *Eigne Meditationen*, GA, II, 3:144.

70 *Foundation of Theoretical Knowledge* (1794), *Fichte: Science of Knowledge*, pp. 175 n., GA, 1, 2: 326 n.

71 *A Comparison between Professor Schmid's System and the Wissenschaftslehre* (1796), *Fichte. Early Philosophical Writings*, pp. 334–5; GA, I, 3: 266.

72 Preface, *An Attempt at a New Presentation of the Wissenschaftslehre* (1797), *J.G. Fichte: Introductions to the Wissenschaftslehre and Other Writings* (1797–1800), trans. and ed. D. Breazeale (Indianapolis: Hackett, 1994), pp. 5-6; GA, I, 4: 185.

73 For Fichte's most famous statement of the need for moral consciousness prior to philosophical consciousness, see *Second Introduction* in *Introductions to the Wissenschaftslehre*, p. 49; GA, I, 2: 219:

> [T]o confirm, on the basis of something even higher, the *belief* in the reality of this intellectual intuition, with which, according to our explicit admission,

transcendental idealism must commence, and to show the presence within reason itself of the very interest upon which this belief is based. The only way in which this can be accomplished is by exhibiting the ethical law within us, within the context of which the I is represented as something sublime and elevated above all of the original modifications accomplished through this law and is challenged to act in an absolute manner, the sole foundation of which should lie in the I itself and nowhere else. It is in this way that the I becomes characterized as something absolutely active.

74 For the statement that aesthetic sense is a prerequisite for philosophy because the aesthetic standpoint mediates between the ordinary standpoint and the transcendental (philosophical) standpoint, see, for example, GA, IV, 2: 266:

> From the aesthetic point of view, the world appears to be something given; from the transcendental point of view, it appears to be something produced (entirely within me). From the aesthetic point of view, the world appears to be given to us just as if we had produced it and to be just the sort of world we would have produced. The philosopher has to possess an aesthetic sense.

See *Science of Ethics*, p. 368; GA, 1, 7: 307–8. I do not mean to suggest that Fichte is committed to the claim that moral consciousness must always develop before aesthetic consciousness. Although moral consciousness is certainly prior to aesthetic consciousness in Fichte's plan of the *Wissenschaftlehre Nova Methodo*, he also describes aesthetic sense as "a preparation for virtue" in *Science of Ethics*, p. 369; GA, I, 7: 308. Aesthetics is the least developed area of the *Wissenschaftslehre* and has been little discussed by Fichte scholars. See, however, C. Piche, "L'Esthetique a-t-elle une place dans la philosophie de Fichte?" in *Les Cahiers de philosophie*, "Le bicentenaire de la Doctrine de la Science de Fichte (1794–1994)," numéro hors série, Printemps 1995, pp. 181–202. I suggest, however, that the place originally left for aesthetics is actually filled by Fichte's philosophy of Freemasonry. See notes 79 and 81 below. Both aesthetic sense and initiation into a secret society without distinctions of class and rank are supposed to help establish that integral harmony of the whole human that tends to be destroyed by the development of consciousness within society and that is required for philosophical recognition of the world as a totality possible only through freedom.

75 *A Comparison between Professor Schmid's System and The Wissenschaftlehre*, 1796, *Fichte: Early Philosophical Writings*, p. 335; GA, I, 3: 265.

76 In the *Discourse on the Sciences and the Arts* that made him famous when it won the competition of the Academy of Dijon in 1750.

77 See, for example, *On the Aesthetic Education of Man in a Series of Letters*, trans. R. Snell (New York: Ungar, 1965), pp. 39-40:

> Why was the individual Greek qualified to be the representative of his time, and why may the individual modern not dare to be so? Because it was all-uniting Nature that bestowed upon the former, and all-dividing intellect that bestowed upon the latter, their respective forms. It was culture itself that inflicted this wound upon modern humanity. As soon as enlarged experience and more precise speculation made necessary a sharper division of the sciences on the one hand, and on the other, the more intricate machinery of States made necessary a more rigorous dissociation of ranks and occupations, the essential bond of human nature was torn apart, and a ruinous conflict set its harmonious powers at variance. . . . Eternally chained to only one single little fragment of the whole, Man himself grew to be only a fragment; with the

monotonous noise of the wheel he drives everlastingly in his ears, he never develops the harmony of his being, and instead of imprinting humanity upon his nature he becomes merely the imprint of his occupation, of his science.

Here Schiller is combining (1) Rousseau's idea that scientific progress is accompanied by increasing disharmony between humanity and nature with (2) the post-Kantian idea of the understanding or intellect as dividing nature in order to know it in order to solve (3) the problem posed by Winckelmann's valorization of the Greek relation to nature as the condition for great art. The *Letters* were written during a time when Schiller and Fichte were both teaching at Jena and, although Schiller referred favorably to Fichte in the *Letters* (31 n.), the similarities between their views combined with the significant differences between them led to a schism in 1795 when Schiller rejected Fichte's second contribution to *Die Horen* ("A series of letters concerning the spirit and the letter within philosophy") because (among other reasons) it overlapped too much with Schiller's own *Letters*. See *Fichte: Early Philosophical Writings*, pp. 392–6 and Breazeale's helpful note.

78 See *Philosophy of Masonry: Letters to Constant*, trans. Roscoe Pound (Seattle: Research Lodge, No. 281, F. & A. M., 1945), p. 59; GA, I, 8: 454, where Fichte suggests that it is

> in the highest degree likely that from the beginning in addition to the public training in society there was a secret training which went on beside it, rose and fell with it, had an unobserved influence upon the former and, on the other hand, was gained or tolerated through the influence of the former. For example, there was Pythagoras and his famous band in the states of Magna Grecia. Hence we put as the first proposition which deserves our attention the following: It may well be, so far as history reaches, there were always secret institutions of training separate and necessarily separate from the public institutions.

These institutions are secret, not only in so far as they are separate from the public culture, but also in so far as the "secret teaching can only be transmitted through oral and in no wise through written tradition. Written communication must be strictly forbidden." See ibid., p. 62; GA, I, 8: 458–9.

79 The exact date of Fichte's initiation remains unknown, but it was certainly between 30 September 1792 and 20 September 1793, as shown by his correspondence with von Schon. See GA, II, 3: 372–3 and III, 1: 434; K. Hammacher, "Fichte and die Freimauerei," *Fichte Studien* 2 (1990): 138–59; I. Radrizzani, "La Doctrine de la science et la maconnerie," *Le Bicentenaire de la doctrine de la science*, pp. 237–52. In Berlin Fichte was allied with the reform movement of Ignatz Aurelius Fessler, with whom he soon fell out. See Peter F. Barton, *Ignatius Aurelius Fessler: Vom Barockkatholizismus zur Erweckungsbewegung* (Wien: Bohlau, 1969), and *Maurer, Mysten, Moralisten: ein Beitrag zur Kultar- and Geistesgeschichte Berlins and Deutschlands 1796–1804: Fessler in Berlin* (Wien: Bohlau, 1982). The involvement of a major philosopher in Freemasonry may seem eccentric to us now, but should be seen against the background of the Masonic activities of a very high proportion of important German intellectuals in this period – including Goethe, Schiller, Wieland, Reinhold, and Hegel – and in light of the philosophical interpretation of Masonry given by Lessing in his *Ernst and Falk: Dialogues for Freemasons*.

80 For details of the controversy, which erupted in 1798, see Breazeale's introduction to *Introductions to the Wissenschaftslehre*. There can be no doubt both that the controversy was based on a misunderstanding of – or perhaps a failure to read – Fichte's writings and that, in responding to the accusations, Fichte committed a series of political blunders that made it easier for the Duke of Weimar to accept his resignation

than to defend him. In any event, Fichte regarded the controversy as a symptom of the deeply rooted tendency to grasp the letter of his writings at the expense of the spirit. His 1800 *From a Private Letter* thematizes this issue and argues that the misunderstandings arise from the fact that in what he calls philosophy, "all is act, movement and life," whereas what is often called philosophy by others is merely "trafficking in dead concepts"; those who interpreted Fichte's thesis that "God is the moral world order," subsuming God under the "dead concept" of a "determinate being-alongside-one-another and being-one-after-another of a manifold," were correct in taking the thesis to be atheistic *on their understanding*, but they had completely failed to understand Fichte's meaning, which essentially involved the concept of "an *active ordering (ordo ordinans)*," a meaning for which these readers lacked the requisite "organ.' See *Introductions to the Wissenschaftslehre*, pp. 160–1; GA, I, 6: 373. Clearly, Fichte was prepared for this interpretation of the atheism controversy by the developments in his thinking since 1793 that I am tracing.

81 According to Fichte, the goal of Masonry is "[t]o do away with the disadvantages in the mode of education in the greater society and to merge the one-sided education for the special vocation in the all-sided training of men as men" (*Philosophy of Masonry*, p. 34; GA, I, 8: 426).

82 See, for example, Fichte's *A Crystal Clear Report to the General Public Concerning the Actual Essence of the Newest Philosophy: An Attempt to Force the Reader to Understand* (1801), trans. J. Botterman and W. Rasch, in *Fichte, Jacobi and Schelling: Philosophy of German Idealism*, ed. Ernst Behler (New York: Continuum, 1987), p. 89; GA, 1, 7: 239:

> Is it therefore so, that absolutely no one could have a judgment concerning any proposition of this science, and, in case it should be the only possible philosophy, which it certainly maintains, concerning any philosophical proposition; – no one who has either not proven in fact that he himself has invented the *Wissenschaftslehre*, or, if this is not the case, who is not conscious of having studied it long enough to make it his own invention, *or – because this is the only possible alternative – who can ascertain another system of intellectual intuition opposed to that of the Wissenschaftslehre?* Reader [with whom Fichte's authorial stand-in is conversing]: Try as I might, I cannot deny that it is so.

83 *First Introduction* in *Introductions to the Wissenschaftslehre and Other Writings*, p. 18; GA, I, 4: 194. I have altered the translation in one respect: where Breazeale translates *Hauptgattungen* as "main sub-species," I have given the translation "main sorts" in order to avoid the suggestion that Fichte is making a biological distinction among human beings, a suggestion that Fichte explicitly denies. (See next note.) The term *Gattung* was not yet inseparably associated with the biological notion of species at this time. I am grateful to David Polly for bringing this point to my attention.

84 Unlike Schelling, Fichte always denied that anybody is *innately* incapable of philosophy. See *Second Introduction* in *Introductions to the Wissenschaftslehre and Other Writings*, p. 91; GA, I, 4: 258:
We have not maintained that there exists any sort of original and innate difference between human beings which makes some people capable of thinking of or of learning something that others, because of their very nature, are simply unable to think. Reason is the common possession of everyone and is entirely the same in every rational being.

85 Fichte to royal cabinet of ministers to Prussian government, 3 January 1804, trans. Breazeale in *Fichte. Foundations of Transcendental Philosophy (Wissenschaftslehre) Nova Methodo* (1796/9), pp. 31-32, from GA, III, 5: 222–4. Although the cabinet did not grant Fichte's request, it is only fair to note that Fichte did not fade into obscurity in

Berlin. On the contrary, he began both to give private classes on the *Wissenschaftslehre* for those who were philosophically prepared, and also to give public Sunday lectures that gave him a position of some importance within intellectual and political circles in Berlin. Some of his lectures were published in written form, such as the *Anweisung zum seeligen Leben* and *Reden an die Deutsche Nation*. Fichte was also involved in the foundation of the University of Berlin, which he served as Chancellor and where he continued his private lectures on the *Wissenschaftslehre*. The economy of oral and written discourse during Fichte's Berlin period requires discussion elsewhere. On Fichte's establishment of a new pedagogical situation at Berlin, see R. Lauth, "Uber Fichtes Lehrtatigkeit in Berlin von Mitte 1799 bis Anfang 1805 and seine Zuhbrerschaft" and "Fichte in den Jahren 1802 and 1803" in *Vernünftige Durchdringung der Wirklichkeit: Fichte und sein Umkreis* (Neuried: Ars Una, 1994), pp. 191–250.

86 See, for example, *The Senses of Walden*, especially pp. 98–119; *The Claim of Reason*, pp. 123–5, 442–51, 459–63; "Finding as founding," in *This New Yet Unapproachable America*; and *Conditions Handsome and Unhandsome*, especially chap. 2, "The argument of the ordinary: scenes of instruction in Wittgenstein and in Kripke."

87 The author wishes to express his gratitude for helpful conversations with Stanley Cavell, James Conant, Eli Friedlander, Arata Hamawaki, David Hills, Andrew Janiak, Hindy Najman, Frederick Neuhouser, Barry Stroud, the Boston Fichte reading group, and the Michigan Society of Fellows.

9

ON EXAMPLES,
REPRESENTATIVES, MEASURES,
STANDARDS, AND THE IDEAL

Eli Friedlander

Stanley Cavell manifestly turns to Kant at central junctures of his writing. He inherits and transforms such Kantian matters as the notion of conditions, the idea of human finitude, the vision of the human as divided – living in two worlds, the figure of limits, as well as the nature of the metaphysical transgressive drive. In the present essay I take up the notion of exemplification, central to Cavell's Moral Perfectionism, and traceable not only to Emerson and Nietzsche, but also to Kant's *Critique of Judgement*. I begin by doing little more than listing and distinguishing several features of exemplification – which I draw from moments in Cavell's writings where their Kantian resonance is clearest, thus providing an intuitive sketch of the dimensions of that idea. The main part of my paper consists then in deriving those features, showing their internal articulation, by providing a partial reading of Kant's "Analytic of the Beautiful". I do not wish to prejudge whether I make succinct the Kantian inspiration of Cavell's writing or give a Cavellian reading of Kant, in part since the issue is best addressed by understanding the inner logic of exemplification.

1 Practices of exemplification

Early on, in *Must We Mean What We Say?*, Cavell relates the ordinary-language practices of Austin and Wittgenstein back to Kant' s account of the aesthetic judgement, writing that "Kant's 'universal voice' is, with perhaps a slight shift of accent, what we hear recorded in the philosopher's claim about 'what we say'" (MWM, 94).[1] Lacking any empirical grounds, the conviction in the philosopher's claim depends in part on his or her ability to make what is thus exemplified appear surprisingly natural to us, testifying to our form of life, as if a "natural ground of our conventions" (CR, 125), hidden by our more conventional wisdom. Justifying the claim to "what we say" would further demand realizing the *necessity* of an arrogation of the right to speak without external authorization or objective grounds, that is accounting for the peculiar inner connection between self-reliance and universality (as in Emerson's "Speak your latent conviction and it shall be the universal sense" ("Self-reliance")). The investigation of the ordinary opens onto the perfectionist representativeness, showing the higher self to speak for common sense.

In thematizing this investigation of the grammar of language, Cavell appeals once more to a Kantian term pertaining to judgement, to the schematism of judgement. The grammar of ordinary language reveals the lines of projection of the imagination that provides, if not quite an illustration, then the presentation or intuitive design of the space of possibilities of our concepts. Cavell takes Emerson (and Wittgenstein) to be broadening the Kantian idea "so that it speaks not alone of deducing twelve categories of the understanding but of deriving – say schematizing – every word in which we speak together" (CHU, 39). The idea of a perspicuous presentation, as well as the extension of the schematism to judgement as such (beyond its transcendental use in cognition), in effect points to the Critique of Judgement as that philosophical place in and from which this future of the Kantian philosophy is opened.

A further articulation of the concept of exemplification is made possible in linking it not only to the schematism of concepts but also to the capacity that underlies the use of rules (the capacity for following apart from a rule). This potential is best brought to light by an investigation of teaching and learning, where it is not the necessity of speaking for the other that is emphasized, but rather the problem of bringing the other to speak with me. In particular taking teaching and learning into the account of what language is, problematizes just as much its mature use as the entry into it. As though the fact that there is a state of infancy in language makes the education to meaning something of a constant task. It is in the context of the teaching of philosophy that one can become most sensitive to the way that in exemplification the showing, even the enacting, of what counts must replace telling that always risks preaching "for no one is in a position to know more about this than any other, hence in no position to tell anyone of it, to offer information concerning it" (CHU, 44).

The exemplification that allows mutuality can also become mutual exemplification as in the idea of conversation that demands a certain improvisatory interplay in which following and being followed, changing places, taking the lead and being led are essential to the way each reflects for the other further possibilities of the self. Cavell's investigation of (re)marriage as "a meet and happy conversation" is probably the central context in which that structure is elaborated. Here too a Kantian inflection exists as when Cavell describes the way in which "what [the pair in the remarriage comedies] do together is less important than the fact that they do whatever it is together" and calls this quality of their relationship "the achievement of purposiveness without purpose" (PH, 113). Kant's account of the aesthetic judgement is further echoed when perfectionist friendship is conceived as "the finding of mutual happiness without a concept" (CHU, 32).

Mutual exemplification in remarriage itself exemplifies a possibility of mutuality for society at large (see in particular Cavell's reading of The Philadelphia Story). It is essential to the vision of the democratic need for perfection, taking the path "from the idea of there being one (call him Socrates) who represents for each of us the height of the journey, to the idea of each of us being representative for each of us"(*CHU*, 9). In community it is not only I who speak for others, but others who must also be allowed to speak for me. A society in which that possibility is not experienced as conspiratorial is not just one in which I can tolerate a degree of injustice without compromising my integrity, but also one in which my consent in the face of compromise can be affirmative. Rather than being essentially a justification to myself upon reflection, consent takes the form of cheering expression of the higher possibilities of this society, so to speak creating the city of words next to it. (Thus raising the question of how expression must be constitutive of consent, and how a certain pleasure or cheerfulness can be internal to expression itself – issues no doubt essential to the nature of the aesthetic judgement as well.) The expression of consent can thus be seen to involve a task of providing a standard for intuition to measure the distance of the departure of society from its ideal (something just left by Rawls's theory of justice to intuition). This feature of consent is not captured by the notion of bringing higher- and lower-order beliefs and principles to reflective equilibrium but rather by the Kantian reflective judgement in which "the idea is of the expression of a conviction whose grounding remains subjective – say myself – but which expects or claims justification from the (universal) concurrence of other subjectivities, on reflection; call this the acknowledgement of matching" (*CHU*, xxvi).

Issues of standards and measures point to a further dimension of the idea of exemplification; when what is at issue is "the acceptance of an exemplar, as access to another realm", Cavell interprets Emerson's "I will stand here for humanity" as addressing "the Kantian idea that man lives in two worlds, that is, is capable of viewing himself from two 'standpoints' (in Kant's term)". As Emerson "assigns his pages as standards (flags and measures)" he takes our relation to his writing, in reading, to stand for our relation to the intelligible world (*CHU*, 50–1). The idea of the constraining standard places particular emphasis on a certain stance, on standing rather than following or advancing, even without purpose. It is, so to speak, standing apart and setting a standard, manifesting not only the nextness and attraction of the idea, but also its unapproachability. The structure of the standard is not modelled upon the judgement of beauty, with its inherent ever-evolving reflectiveness, but rather on a transferential return that has something of the sublime to it, for through it "we recognize our own rejected thoughts. They come back to us with a certain alienated majesty" (Emerson, "Self-reliance").

Finally, it is possible to find in Cavell's writing what I would call an ideal of a content (following, conversation and transference are all formal characterizations of representativeness). By this I mean an absolute measure formed from the contingent material of experience (an absolute pitch). I would identify it with the understanding of the higher self in terms of the proper name.[2] It is in autobiography that the contingent can put on the figure of philosophical necessity.

2 Beauty and representative expression

The aesthetic judgement is pronounced with a universal voice as the judge of taste "judges not merely for himself, but for all men, and then speaks of beauty as if it were a property of things" (5:212). A peculiar form of universality is characteristic of the aesthetic, one that initially cannot be referred to an objective law, whether in the constitution of the object (as in cognition) or in what ought to determine subjects (as in morality). To account for that peculiarity, it is not sufficient to point to Kant's distinction between universality in the subject matter of judgement and the general validity which judgements can have, that is the agreement all subjects are expected to give to correct judgements about that subject matter. For the question is precisely how such generality is to be possible without an objective subject matter to agree upon. Moreover, beauty is estimated by relying on oneself with no expectations from others. I do not judge for myself and then infer from the sense of the correctness of the judgement that it must be valid for all, thus expecting others to agree. Rather, universality is internalized into the very making of the judgement. In passing judgement I *already* speak for others, in giving words to what is singular I am representative.

Taking the political domain as an initial context for that possibility of speaking for others, we can say that it is essential for the representative to give expression, internal to his or her task to voice the needs of those he or she represents. In doing so, the representative is not an emissary, who gets directives from his or her constituency, but takes it upon himself or herself to make explicit what remains implicit, unsaid. Put differently, even if there is an agreement in principle, the representative addresses the shifting circumstances and events by showing what it would be for such principles to *apply* in new conditions (rather than remain mere slogans). In so doing, the representative provides an example, exemplifies a possibility by putting things in words, shows a way to address the matters at hand.

The aesthetic judgement is essentially representative because what one testifies to has not yet been worded. Both because what is judged is singular and because to pronounce a judgement on that singularity which is called beautiful is to speak for an *idea* of universal agreement. "[The] universal voice is . . . only an idea" (5:216). Whereas there are only instances, examples, of *general* laws, the universality pertaining to the idea demands the representativeness of subjects. The subject must be manifest in his judgement, meaning that the way of judging, not the content, must show the judgement to be speaking for an idea. The singular beauty in itself does not simply embody the idea and merely to claim that one is judging with the idea in mind carries no authority. The fact that others might not agree with my judgement is further insufficient, for this would be true of countless occasions of disagreement in which we would not call the insistence on one's position a case of speaking for an *idea*. It is only by making the judgement itself manifest the endlessness characteristic of the idea, the way it can never be fully and determinately realized in experience, that one can claim to be judging for it. Such endlessness is expressed in the notion of "purposiveness without purpose". It is also to be found in speaking of beauty as an "aesthetic idea for which a rational concept can never be found" (5:210), which Kant elucidates as follows:

> Just as the *imagination*, in the case of a rational idea, fails with its intuitions to attain to the given concepts, so *understanding*, in the case of an aesthetic idea, fails with its concepts to attain to the completeness of the internal intuition which imagination conjoins with a given representation.
>
> (5:212)

In order to fail to attain to the completeness of the intuition, one has to *try*, thus the aesthetic judgement is not merely a silent appreciation of beauty. Moreover, there is no difficulty finding some concept or other to apply to beauty ("It is a Picasso"). The point is that certain concepts will stifle judging by eventuating in a judgement, imposing a preconception, as though judging beauty is determining properties of an object. Thus what is demanded are words that evolve by being attuned to the singularity of beauty, showing it to be pregnant with meaning (in the reflective judgement concepts not only evolve from the singular, but also strive to remain true to it, to ultimately name it, to do justice to its beauty). It is necessary for the judgement to insist on this inexhaustibility, to make it manifest by having one word lead to another, finding ever-new ways to avoid bringing words to an end. It is in going beyond common agreement and in thereby showing that there is always more to express in relation to the singular beauty that the judgement of taste speaks for an idea of agreement. Thus what might be called the *total* singularity of beauty, precisely allows the idea of agreement, allows to bypass the rule of the concept.[3]

What is exemplified by the judgement is thus nothing more than the possibility of being intelligible in relation to that singularity which is beautiful:

> nothing is postulated in the judgement of taste but such a *universal voice* in respect of delight that is not mediated by concepts; consequently, only the *possibility* of an aesthetic judgement capable of being at the same time deemed valid for every one.
>
> (5:216)

To speak of "the possibility of an aesthetic judgement" is not to say that the judgement is only possibly correct, but rather that it is inherently showing something to be possible. To show something to be possible does not preclude other ways of bringing words to beauty, but rather calls for them. Indeed it is the very gap between the idea and any attempt to give it body (which, of necessity, will be partial) that requires further exemplifications. Far from damaging the universality of the aesthetic judgement the multiplicity of takes on, say, a work of art, is precisely adequate to its nature. It is not incompatible with the idea of the universal voice but precisely expresses it. Even if genius is authoritarian a community of taste will be essentially democratic. In such a community agreement need not be thought of in terms of identical reactions to beauty. Rather there is agreement in being equally attuned to beauty, that is attuned to one another through the beautiful thing. Just as in the realm of ends I view myself equally as legislator and subject, in the community of taste I am a party to a conversation that gives expression to beauty.

The idea of the universal voice is thus not reducible to common reactions to an object of delight in an ideal case. For voice implies, first and foremost, giving expression. Voicing something is expressing it, making it *available* to others. Internal to the aesthetic judgement there are others from which agreement is *demanded*. This demand for agreement differentiates the aesthetic judgement from cognition in which agreement is *expected*. It is also fundamentally different from the moral judgement in which a demand for agreement would amount to moralism. To argue that a demand is *internal* to making a judgement precisely does not mean that after making the judgement one has to convince, request or require agreement from others (just as in speaking for others one need not ask for their permission). One can appeal to others precisely by judging for oneself, by being self-absorbed. A demand can arise by expressing oneself in a language that is *demanding*, higher. The language of the judgement is higher when it shows it to be possible for more meaning to be found. In so speaking one is attracting or shaming, but either way constraining, producing a demand upon others. In passing an aesthetic judgement "we are suitors for the agreement of every one else" (5:237). The language of the suitor is tempting but he or she also must be ready "often enough to put up with rude dismissal" (5:214).

Actual communication is not assumed to be internal to the aesthetic judgement but rather communicability. That something is communicable is evidenced by its *being put into words*. Expression allows beauty to be in common. It is the very expression, the very putting into words, that is pleasurable. This is not pleasure in *communicating* to others. Indeed *that* pleasure is threatened by an interest in society and cannot be the ground of the aesthetic judgement. The pleasure must be in the opening of meaning itself thus in *communicability* rather than interest in actual communication. Communicability is evidenced by expression. In being expressed something shows itself to be communicable. The judgement is thus not an essentially pleasurable reaction to the object, which upon reflection is expected to arise in anyone with the same faculties under the same conditions. This would make the pleasure antecedent to communicability, thus essentially an agreeable pleasure of the senses. Rather as Kant puts it in section 9, which he calls "the key to the critique of taste", "it is the universal capacity for being communicated incident to the mental state in the given representation which, as the subjective condition of the judgement of taste, must be fundamental, with the pleasure in the object as its consequent"(5:217).

Expression is, by definition, pleasurable when it furthers itself, when it opens to more meaning. For pleasure is not understood sentimentally as the conscious-ness of a specific *quality*, but rather "the consciousness of the causality of a representation in respect of the state of the Subject as one tending to *preserve a continuance* of that state, may here be said to denote in a general way what is called pleasure"(5:220). The enhanced activity of the mind, the furthering that shows the mind's potential, in giving expression to beauty, *is* the pleasure of the aesthetic judgement.

3 Exemplification and common sense

It should not be surprising that exemplification plays a central role in the *Critique of Judgement*. Indeed the notion of the example appeared already, without being given a systematic function, in the transcendental doctrine of judgement in the *Critique of Pure Reason*. There Kant famously claims that it is impossible to provide rules for judgement, to give rules to the faculty that is in charge of applying them. Lacking rules, judgement in general (to be contrasted with the transcendental use of judgement that rests on schemata for the appli-cations of the categories to the manifold of intuition) depends on natural talent, "so called mother-wit [whose] lack no school can make good", as well as on its, albeit poor substitutes, examples that are "the go-cart of judgement" (A 133/B172).

In Kant's discussion of genius in the "Third Critique" examples and natural talent are already aligned. For the gift of genius is precisely "bestowed directly from the hand of nature upon each individual", who "needs no more than an example to set the talent of which he is conscious at work on similar lines"(5:309). But the most sustained thematization of the inner relation of natural ground and exemplification occurs in the Fourth Moment of the Analytic of the Beautiful: "such a necessity as is thought in an aesthetic judge-ment . . . can only be termed *exemplary*. In other words it is a necessity of the assent of *all* to a judgement regarded as exemplifying a universal rule incapable of formulation" (5:237). It is in the aesthetic judgement that exemplification is more than a mere pedagogical aid for the awakening of nature. It becomes *necessary*. Common sense is that quasi-natural faculty, the common ground that exemplification expresses.

Exemplification demands not only the forward projection of an ideal agree-ment, the universal agreement of judging subjects, or the idea of the universal voice, but also the assumption of a common ground given to all subjects implic-itly. Common sense is a *presupposition* whereas the possibility of the universal voice is *imputed*. One can impute agreement to others only on the presuppposi-tion of the common ground. "We are suitors for agreement from every one else, *because we are fortified with a ground common to all*" (5:237, my emphasis) The idea of universal agreement discussed in the second moment and the idea of a common sense discussed in the fourth are linked together by the logic of exemplification. It is the formation of universal agreement (the artificial) by expressing the given ground in common (the natural).[4] We speak for all by resting on, sensing, that unexpressed ground in common. Or in other words the common sense is the sense of meaningfulness given to be expressed. Voice assumes sense and sense demands voice.

In order to initially elaborate why Kant thinks of taste as presupposing something like a sense, we might point out that it is not enough to claim the communality of feeling. Indeed it must be feeling that arises by way of how one is aware of beauty. And it is that awareness that must be construed on the model of a sense ("we want to get a look at the Object with our own eyes, just *as if* our delight depended on sensation" (5:216, my emphasis)). But common sense cannot depend on the external causality of perception, on the real existence of the object. It is not, as Kant puts it, "to be taken to mean some external sense, but the effect arising from the play of our powers of cognition". This is not to say that the play of the powers of cognition is empty of content. It occurs as they *bring into play* various meaningful matters. Those matters, independent of the actual sensuous material, are brought to bear, by our faculties, in judging, thus opening a space of significance by way of the beautiful thing. Indeed only thus can our judgement be more than a judgement of perception depending on the real existence of an object, that is take place in a space of meaning. Or as Kant puts it "everything turns on the meaning which I can give to this representation, and not on any factor which makes me dependent on the real existence of the object"(5:205).

Sense, thus, is not just feeling, but a certain contentful awareness. Similarly, the common would not only be referring to the plurality of subjects that feel in the same way, but also to the communality of what is brought to bear on the given, of what is related, tied together, by way of beauty.[5] To sense that relatedness (which is neither causal, conceptual, nor analogical) is to sense significance, even before being able to say what its meaning is.

Above all, it is important not to think of the actual sensuous manifold as that which is to be systematically related (as though we are speaking of structural matters such as harmony or composition). Rather, the identity of the beautiful, *what* it is that is beautiful, is revealed by what is brought to bear on it. What is at stake is the gathering power of beauty. Beauty gathers within itself irreducible dimensions of meaning, making the beautiful thing into their meeting point. To allow beauty to be such a meeting point requires not reducing it to one register of significance (i.e. not determining it under a concept), that even opposed dimensions of meaning can touch each other, can be concentrated and brought to bear on each other in what is beautiful. Beauty draws us by drawing things together.

Interpreting common sense in this way, it becomes clear why Kant views "common sense as the necessary condition of the universal communicability of our knowledge, which is presupposed in every logic and every principle of knowledge that is not one of scepticism" (5:239). Indeed, common sense would precisely address the sceptical threat that Kant raises in the introduction to the *Critique of Judgement*:

> For it is quite conceivable that, despite all the uniformity of the things of nature according to universal laws, without which we would not have the form of general empirical knowledge at all, the specific variety of the empirical laws of nature, with their effects, might still be so great as to make it impossible for our understanding to discover in nature an intelligible order.
>
> (5:185)

Assuming that we cannot achieve a reduction of the variety of fields of experience to one set of fundamental laws (for instance the laws of mechanics), a different form of ordering must be given by judgement, where all the field of experience, all its dimensions, come together, bear on each other while retaining their irreducible independence. Common sense is the presupposition of such an ordering; call it a sense of the world as a whole.

This non-reductive idea of the totality of experience points to the possibility of relating the notion of common sense to its more common use, to mean what is ordinary. Kant seems, at first, intent on separating common sense from what he calls "common understanding", for the judgement of the latter is not one by feeling, but always one by concepts, though usually only in the shape of "obscurely represented principles" (5:238, 82). Such "mere sound understanding" is an average, minimal or even vulgar characterization of "what is everywhere to be met with – a quality which by no means confers credit or distinction upon its possessor" (5:293, 51). And yet, Kant's elaboration of taste as a common sense might precisely give a better understanding of the measured nature of the ordinary, a higher sense of that idea which is not reducible to average conformity.

This turns on properly interpreting Kant's use of the figures of ratio and proportion in characterizing common sense:

> But if cognitions are to admit of communication, then our mental state, i.e. the way the cognitive powers are attuned for cognition generally, and, in fact the relative proportion, suitable for a representation (by which an object is given to us) from which cognition is to result, must also admit of being universally communicated . . . But this disposition of the cognitive powers has a relative proportion differing with the diversity of the Objects that are given. However there must be one in which this internal ratio suitable for quickening (one faculty by the other) is best adapted for both mental powers in respect of cognition (of given objects) generally; and this disposition can only be determined through feeling (and not by concepts).
>
> (5:238)

Kant expresses the issue by speaking of the proportion between the two faculties, the imagination and the understanding. But I take it that the proportion of the faculties is itself dependent on what is brought to bear by the imagination to make the given manifold into a meaningful object. To put it crudely, the proportion is dependent on how much imagination is needed to grasp the possibilities that make a thing what it is.

Common sense is that sense of proportion. In common sense nothing is excessive, everything gets its right weight, in balance.[6] That balance is provided by occupying a certain standpoint, by a stance toward things. It is not standing against, as a ruler might be placed next to the object. But rather it is placing oneself *in the midst of things*, forming so to speak a *milieu* by attempting to take everything into account. It is a way of balancing the plurality that encircles and thereby keeps open a place, not allowing any side to disproportionately take over. This balance of common sense is not an average, but as a sense of the world that takes beauty as the meeting point of its dimensions, the centre of its co-ordinates. To have a sense of all dimensions is, one might say, to feel at home in the world. In beauty one feels oriented in the world.[7] Whether that sense of orientation can be expressed as a true measure is a question that must be raised by the account of the ideal of beauty.

4 The measure and the ideal

Beauty might be ruleless but it is not measureless.[8] It admits of an ideal. In the *Critique of Pure Reason* Kant writes that the ideal is "the idea, not merely *in concreto*, but *in individuo*, that is, as an individual thing, determinable or even determined by the idea alone"(A568/B596). Such ideals exist, but have, according to Kant, only "*practical* power (as regulative principles) and form the basis of the possible perfection of certain *actions*"(A569/B597). He warns that the attempts to view the ideal, which exists only in thought, as realized in the field of appearance (to think that a particular human being, for instance, embodies the stoic ideal of wisdom), "are constantly doing violence to the completeness of the idea". Even when blatantly illusory, such attempts can "cast suspicion on the good itself – the good that has its source in the idea – by giving it the air of being a mere fiction" (A570/B598).

Ideals are not "figments of the brain" but rather serve as archetypes of judgement. They are indispensable standards to measure the degree to which a particular is adequate to an idea. "As the idea gives the *rule*, so the ideal in such cases serves as the *archetype* for the complete determination of the copy." Although it is the creative imagination that provides standards of judgement, Kant is keen to distinguish the archetype from a

> representation such as painters and physiognomists profess to carry in their heads, and which they treat as being an incommunicable shadowy image of their creations or even of their critical judgements.

Such representations may be entitled, though improperly, ideals of sensibility, inasmuch as they are viewed as being models (not indeed realizable) of empirical intuitions, and yet furnish no rules that allow of being explained and examined.

(A570/B598)

In reading this last passage one becomes acutely aware of the shift that takes place in Kant's position in the *Critique of Judgement*, providing as he does for a legitimate notion of an ideal of beauty, while at the same time trying to distinguish it from a problematic realization of the idea in the field of appearances. But at the same time it raises the question of how beauty can admit of an ideal at all. On the one hand, it is essential not to characterize the ideal of beauty in terms of perfection, as the highest specimen of a given genus. For a judgement of perfection would no more be an aesthetic reflective judgement, but rather a determinant one. On the other hand, to truly be a standard, the ideal must be a "determinate image", not merely "a blurred sketch drawn from diverse experiences" (A570/B598).

It is through the figure of concentration, of an intensity of expression in an individual that it is possible to understand the ideal of beauty. The total determination of content provides a notion of determinateness that does not depend on the perfection of a pre-given concept. It is the idea of the particular turned singular: singular not through its immediate intuitive presence, but rather by being fully determined in meaning. From the idea of fully determinate content it follows that the ideal is uncriticizable.[9] Uncriticizability does not mean that a work is so good that there is nothing to say against it, for there is also nothing to say *for* it. It allows no further expression, for it is *totally* determined. In the ideal of beauty, the potential of meaning sensed (common sense) is fully actualized. It is one might say an unapproachable ideal of *content*. (Note that in the Kantian aesthetics form is always also a mode of approach; it is always correlative with the purposive advance of judgement without a purpose.)

The uncriticizable, that is the unjudgeable, can nevertheless be a *standard* of judgement. The standard is in a different logical space from the instances of judgement, in essence different, though it might be perceptually indistinguishable from particularly successful or perfect examples. To take Wittgenstein's example, the standard metre in Paris is to be distinguished from examples of things one metre long. That standard provides for the possibility of the measurement of length at all. The model, or standard, is necessary for the very recognition of facts that involve determinate length. We produce facts of measurement by having the model or standard in view.

Whereas temporal schemata are such standards for the application of the categories and the lawfulness of nature serves as an analogical archetype for the application of the moral law, it is seldom asked whether there is a schema of judgement as such, an archetype of taste. It is the ideal of beauty that is such a standard of taste, an archetype for "everything that is an object of taste, or that is an example of critical taste, and even of universal taste itself" (5:232).

For reasons that now become clear, the human figure alone can be an ideal of beauty. The ideal is not the highest instance of a specific kind of beauty, of human beauty, but is the ideal of beauty *as such*, showing beauty to be cut to human measure. To understand this anthropomorphism correctly it is necessary to think of the possibilities of things depicted, the space of meaning opened around something beautiful, as fit for the higher possibilities of man.[10] This does not imply a sovereignty of man over nature, as he uses it for his purposes. Rather, nature brought by man to expression will show its attunement with the highest moral ends, with his moral being.[11] It will provide signs of hope for the possibility of a world fit for human dwelling. The ideal of beauty in the human figure is the standard for this poetic task of man, making it possible to imagine second nature, just next to this one here and now.

Here we come upon a last complication in Kant's account. The ideal of taste cannot simply be given by models of the past, so called classical works. "[T]aste must be an original faculty. . . . Hence it follows that the highest model, the archetype of taste, is a mere idea, which each person must beget in his own consciousness"(5:232). But with what material available to each, can such an ideal be fashioned? Kant does not provide an answer, but I would suggest that the ideal is for each, their own life determined in meaning. This can further explain why only the human figure allows of an ideal of beauty. For it alone provides the possibility of the coexistence of infinitude and determinacy, both required for a true ideal. It is infinite in that it is always in a world, determinable in so far as that world can be gathered and refracted through it. A human life is that wherein a world can be meaningfully concentrated. It can bear enough meaning to express the world. Aesthetically speaking, it is a monad.[12] The ideal each must beget in themselves is that of one's own life as an origin of the world. Call it after Wittgenstein, the world as I found it, the ideal of a philosophical autobiography.

Notes

1   References to Cavell's writings will be by page number immediately after the quotations according to the following abbreviations: *Must We Mean What We Say? –* MWM, *Conditions Handsome and Unhandsome – CHU, The Claim of Reason – CR, A Pitch of Philosophy – PP, Pursuits of Happiness – PH.* References to Kant's writings will similarly be given in the body of the text, to the *Critique of Pure Reason* according to the A/B notation and to the *Critique of Judgement* according to the pagination of the *Akademie* edition.

2   A particularly interesting genealogy for this idea appears in the introduction to *A Pitch of Philosophy*, where Cavell moves from Europe to America, and back to Europe to find himself in Israel. Epigraphs from Gershom Scholem's reading of Walter Benjamin's text "Agesilaus Santander" provide hints for the inflection of the perfectionist higher self in term of the name, and for "the idea of the true name, that of the secret self, being hidden" (*PP*, xiii).

3   The notion of total singularity will be further elaborated in the discussion of Kant's understanding of the ideal of beauty.

4   We are tempted to say either that the projected ideal determines our sense of what is given, or that the given determines the formation of the ideal agreement. But Kant

makes clear that the temporality that links nature and the artificial is much more complex:

> But does such a common sense in fact exist as a constitutive principle of the possibility of experience, or is it formed for us as a regulative principle by a still higher principle of reason, that for higher ends first seeks to beget in us a common sense? Is taste, in other words, a natural and original faculty, or is it only the idea of one that is artificial and to be acquired by us, so that a judgement of taste, with its demand for universal assent, is but a requirement of reason for generating such a *consensus*, and does the "ought", i.e. the objective necessity of the coincidence of the feeling of all with the particular feeling of each, only betoken the possibility of arriving at some sort of unanimity in these matters, and the judgement of taste only adduce an example of the application of this principle? These are questions which as yet we are neither willing nor in a position to investigate (5:85).

The indeterminacy of the question is constitutive of the aesthetic as a bridge between nature and freedom

5   In thinking of this sixth sense, it might be useful to recall the Aristotelian notion of a common sense, not as a further sense that has it own mode of access to the world, but rather as the gathering of the other senses.

6   For instance, to apply the concept of "table" to a certain perceptual manifold, I do not merely recognize a certain arrangement in space, but must, for example, imagine what it is to sit at such table, imagine it having the solidity required to write on it (thus have at least a sense of human stature and human manners as well as of the resistance of matter and the pliancy of the human body). See in that context Cavell's discussion of the appeal to projective imagination in ch. 7 of *The Claim of Reason*, as well as his discussion of Kripke's interpretation of Wittgenstein in ch. 2 of *Conditions Handsome and Unhandsome*.

7   This relation between totality or world and orientation is raised in Kant's essay entitled "What is orientation in thinking" where precisely the idea of taking into account and balancing all the needs of reason is raised as the ultimate task of philosophy. The assessment of the proper balance is aesthetic, by way of feeling:

> orientation will be the business of pure reason in directing its use when, starting from known objects of experience, it tries to extend itself beyond all boundaries of experience, finding no object of intuition but merely space for it. For it is then no longer capable of bringing its judgements, in the determination of its own faculty of judgement, under a definite maxim according to objective grounds of knowledge; it can do so only by a subjective ground of distinction. This subjective means which remains is nothing else than the feeling of a need belonging to reason ("What is orientation in thinking," in *Kant's Political Writings* (Cambridge: Cambridge University Press, 1991), p.296).

8   In elaborating this distinction between the rule and the measure I am indebted to Walter Benjamin's essay "The concept of criticism in German Romanticism", in *Walter Benjamin, Selected Writings* vol. 1 (Cambridge, MA: Harvard University Press, 1996). See in particular the esoteric epilogue entitled "The early Romantic theory of art and Goethe", in which the distinction between the idea and the ideal is fleshed out.

9   Kant stresses the uncriticizability of models by writing:

> Models of taste with respect to the arts of speech must be composed in a dead and learned language; the first to prevent their having to suffer the changes that

inevitably overtake living ones, making dignified expressions become degraded, common ones antiquated, and ones newly coined after a short currency obsolete; the second to ensure its having a grammar that is not subject to the caprices of fashion, but has fixed rules of its own (5:232, footnote 1).

But this feature of models, which pertains to the contingent agreement on classical works of antiquity, is still to be distinguished from the necessary unchangeability of the ideal.

10 In the First moment Kant writes that "beauty has purport and significance only for human beings, i.e. for beings at once animal and rational (but not merely for them as rational – intelligent beings – but only for them as at once animal and rational)"(5:210). In the ideal of beauty we get a much stronger case for the relation of beauty to the human.

11 The extreme case of free beauty is significant, in so far as it answers to man's higher interest that the existence of beauty in nature has nothing to do with his purposes. Only thus can beauty be a sign of hope for the ideal inner attunement of nature and morality, for the possibility of the highest good.

12 Compare with our previous example of the table. While the concept of table might have a complex grammar to it, the imagination cannot gather a world around it. Even animals that have an environment cannot be said to express their world.

10

HABITUAL REMARRIAGE

The ends of happiness in *The Palm Beach Story*

Stuart Klawans

I begin with an observation that any number of readers must have made, that a thought is left dangling in Stanley Cavell's magisterial *Pursuits of Happiness: The Hollywood Comedy of Remarriage*. After Cavell drops an aside about Preston Sturges's *The Palm Beach Story* (1942), he at once passes on, never again to mention that remarkable film. I can't know what Cavell might have written about *The Palm Beach Story* had he not dismissed it so quickly – so suspiciously, one might say. But I now propose to tug on the loose end he left, to discover whether it will unravel part of his argument or instead lead through a labyrinth.

If I say that the all-too-casual mention of *The Palm Beach Story* is suspect, it's because no other film would seem more appropriate to a study of "the comedy of remarriage." Just on the level of plot, the film meets Cavell's elaborate and elastic criteria for the genre he has invented.

Very early in the picture, the airily self-confident Gerry (Claudette Colbert) announces that she no longer wants to be married to angry, failure-haunted Tom (Joel McCrea). Or perhaps she doesn't need to be married to him, or feels she shouldn't be. Her stated reasons for leaving are open to interpretation – but while Tom and the audience are busy interpreting, she takes off. What moral and social obstacles must Tom overcome to win her again? What experiences will convince her to give herself back to him? The plot's chief work is to answer these questions, once Tom gets past his helpless indecision and resolves to run after Gerry.

Already we're dealing with themes and situations that Cavell identifies as characteristic of the genre, primary among which is the explicit posing of the question: What constitutes a marriage? Is the glue merely the habit that two people form for one another? If so, and if the habits are bad (as Gerry says), then it's plausible to define marriage as something to be broken. But perhaps a true marriage is something more. Maybe it's something that Gerry and Tom will discover in one another through the course of the movie.

We know this something more must have to do with happiness, since Sturges refers to that condition explicitly, at the beginning of the picture. During the opening credits, he shows us a chaotic, as yet inexplicable affair, which turns out to be Gerry and Tom's wedding. Upon reaching the altar, the breathless pair are framed by a title, written in the script of a Valentine's Day card: "And they lived happily ever after." The camera then pulls back to reveal a second title: "Or did they?" The soundtrack music imparts an aural sneer to this afterthought; but the question still demands an answer. We need to learn whether Gerry and Tom lived happily ever after: an "ever" that covers not just the period beyond their marriage, but also the one after their break-up.

Now, the happiness that's at stake for Gerry and Tom has dimensions beyond the personal. Their circumstances suggest that it's a kind of Jeffersonian happiness, which America encourages them to pursue. So important is this theme to Cavell when it emerges in other comedies of remarriage that he writes it into the title of his book – another reason to be surprised that he neglects *The Palm Beach Story*.

Gerry's formal name is Mrs Thomas Jeffers; and her husband, like the sage of Monticello, is a great improver. He knows that "something is bound to come through" with his schemes, because he's got "too many good ideas." Nevertheless (as Gerry is not too delicate to mention), Thomas Jeffers has yet to achieve even one success – that is, a success in business – and for this shortcoming she blames herself, or at least claims to do so. She will therefore pursue happiness on her own, which to her means having it bestowed on her by men who have amassed wealth, or had it amassed for them by their grandfathers.

The first of her gift-givers, the Wienie King (Robert Dudley), is an elderly, brusquely candid little man, scarcely taller than his own black hat, who sets off the plot by handing Gerry 700 dollars and the impetus to abandon her husband. Having left, she will soon attract the attention of John D. Hackensacker 3rd (Rudy Vallee), who offers her far more costly presents, along with the prospect of remarriage as soon as her Palm Beach divorce is final. So Gerry's pursuit of happiness takes place within an America where people can enrich themselves, if they're canny enough. ("It's a good business," says the Wienie King of his sausage-making, "if you know where to buy the meat cheap.") This is also a society where the wealthy can spend freely – although they should do so within principled limits, as John D. Hackensacker firmly believes. He draws the line at tipping and the hiring of private railroad staterooms, both of which are "un-American."

As someone who knows herself to need money, and a lot of it, Gerry intends to make the most of the opportunities America provides. But, beyond that, she also needs to prove that she can create business opportunities for Tom. Her happiness depends upon his recognizing that her good looks and ready wit are worth as much, in dollars, as his ideas. To be more precise: he must overcome his sexual jealousy and recognize that it's all right for her good looks and ready wit to have economic value.

Cavell's readers may now mark off another of his principal themes: the need for the man to acknowledge the woman's autonomy, and for her to see that he acknowledges it. Only by doing so will he make himself worthy of her, so that she may at last give herself to him. In the films discussed in *Pursuits of Happiness*, this mutual recognition requires a process of transformation, either in the woman or in the way the man views her, a process that Cavell sometimes calls "the creation of a woman." As in Genesis, this creation is accomplished through the word: the women in Cavell's comedies of remarriage are subjected to endless lectures. But in *The Palm Beach Story*, Gerry recognizes her own value from the start – and so does Tom, evidently, since he chafes at it. What's more, Gerry is the one to do the lecturing, giving Tom several minutes of practical advice about the duties of helpmates and the role of sex in the business world.

Here, *The Palm Beach Story* diverges from the other films Cavell discusses. I intend to track that divergence – but before I do, I want to point out one more way in which this movie conforms to his model.

Cavell believes that movies are inherently self-referential; that they often toy with their own movieness by alluding to earlier films; that their stars are more vivid to us than the characters they portray. (We watch an adventure of Claudette Colbert, more than of Gerry Jeffers.) In its relationship to the Frank Capra–Robert Riskin movie *It Happened One Night* (1935), *The Palm Beach Story* confirms Cavell's ideas so strikingly that I wonder, why didn't he say so and take credit?

You will recall that in *It Happened One Night*, Claudette Colbert escaped from her father's yacht, then made her way overland from Florida to New York, traveling most of the way without money or luggage. I doubt it's mere coincidence that, in *The Palm Beach Story*, Colbert escapes from a Park Avenue duplex, then makes her way overland from New York to Florida, traveling most of the way without money or luggage. In *It Happened One Night*, Colbert needed considerable help from Clark Gable to make her trip; but in the mirror image of *The Palm Beach Story*, she announces in advance her plan to make her own way, then proves beyond doubt her ability to do so.

It would be hard to exaggerate the popularity of *It Happened One Night* or the degree to which it defined Colbert, who would from then on be known as the woman who hitch-hiked by baring her legs. Clearly, then, Sturges builds some of the pleasures of *The Palm Beach Story* upon his audience's familiarity with Colbert and her past adventures. In thinking about the film, I find that I want to think about *her*. The moment of this realization marks the moment of my enforced departure from Cavell.

As often as he insists upon the importance of the star, never once in *Pursuits of Happiness* does Cavell inquire into an actor's performance or looks. Faces, bodies, tones of voice, gestures, postures, tempos, inflections, attitudes – all suggestions of these are missing from *Pursuits of Happiness*, except for the meager evidence of photographs and the repeated assertion that the story involves *this particular* actor. But what makes the actor particular? Cavell never tells us; and the omission is as troubling to me as the neglect of *The Palm Beach Story*.

So I begin my inquiry again, this time with Colbert.

She wore her hair short in *It Happened One Night*, sucked in her cheeks to produce a kewpie-doll pucker, and often kept her face to the camera while peeking sideways at Clark Gable, so her big eyes looked bigger on their upward roll. All this made her seem juvenile – a "brat," as Gable called her – an impression strongly reinforced by the sight of her flopping around in his pajamas.

Of course, her body contradicted the childish image. The celebrated legs were not so much long or sleek as propulsive, powering forward her rounded hips and automobile-figurehead bosom. Capra established this womanly presence first, before turning Colbert into a kid. For her introductory scene, on the yacht, he posed her in a clinging white robe with hands on hips, thereby demonstrating her defiance of her father's authority while giving the audience a good look at her figure. Capra then had her snarl, chase the crew from her stateroom and finally fling herself overboard.

Nothing about her lush, apparently luxury-bred person suggested athleticism; she was more likely to soak in a bath of asses' milk than to swim long distances in the open sea. But in *It Happened One Night*, it seemed plausible that she could swim fast enough to outpace a pursuing boat. If she was not an athlete, then Colbert at least had the vitality, and ferocity, of a healthy and mature animal.

How did she bring together these two aspects of the character she was playing, the marriageable young woman and the wayward brat? One obvious link was her quickness of gesture; Colbert moved more abruptly than anyone else in the picture. When she lifted an arm, crossed a yard, hitched a hem, you might have imagined you were seeing not only the action but also, at its onset, the decision to act. Impatience and impulsiveness merged in her performance with alertness, when the character was at her best.

If this description is accurate, then the circumstances where languor overtook her demand special attention. I can think of two such moments.

The first happened when she and Gable were preparing to sleep in the open, on beds of hay. Gable had slipped off without her realizing it, to scrounge for food. When she saw that he was gone, she became frightened – so frightened that, upon his return, she threw herself into his arms. In the aftermath of this first embrace, in the stillness as the two settled down on the hay, there was a pause when it seemed as if Gable would kiss her. She looked like she wanted to be kissed. Then, with the camera hovering over her in close-up, she asked what he was thinking. Her voice was suddenly pitched much lower than at any previous moment. All trace of childishness was gone; the sound was that of a woman's invitation. And yet Colbert still was alert. Newly sensual but without any of the somnambulism of desire, she asked what Gable was thinking in a tone that made it clear: she knew.

The second and last time Colbert used her chest tones, she was playing the scene where she began to reconcile with her father. By this point, she had abandoned Gable; she had resolved, unwisely, to make official her marriage to a high-society aeronaut. (By around this point in the picture, she also had resumed her hands-on-hips stance – no more a child, but a woman again.) When her father, at long last grown sympathetic toward her, asked why she would marry a man she didn't love, Colbert slowed down and made her voice husky: "I'm tired, Dad. Tired of running around in circles. . . . I've got to settle down. It really doesn't matter how – or where – or with whom."

Perhaps it seems paradoxical that the voice Colbert had used to convey sexual arousal, and an attunement to Gable's thoughts, should also serve for fatigue and resignation. But this was only the start of the contradiction, which soon broke into the dialogue as well. When her groom came in, and Colbert forced herself to be lively, she told him she wanted their marriage to be "full of excitement. . . . We'll get on a merry-go-round and never get off. . . . We don't want to stop to think, do we? Just want to keep going."

So this was what it meant to settle down, once you had accepted the proposition that any mate was acceptable: it meant living on a merry-go-round. A funny way to stop "running around in circles."

Of course, Colbert wasn't entirely wrong. You may become dizzy on a merry-go-round, but you can't go anywhere. The film even illustrated this peculiar form of stasis, using two images – one seen, and one merely described. The unseen image was that of the groom's intended entrance to the wedding: He was said to be planning to land in a helicopter. (The spin of the rotor; the idiot whirl of self-regard.) The visible image was that of Colbert in a fancy gown, drink held high, standing on a platform amid a circle of bachelors – as if they were the carousel's horses, and she the center pole.

This latter image was part of the scene of sterile, brainless revelry upon which Gable stumbled, to his disgust and Colbert's shame, when he visited her home just before the wedding. In judging his harsh reaction, the viewer does well to remember that Gable was playing not merely a newspaper reporter but a *writer*, someone who had been fired for submitting his copy in the form of blank verse. He, too, liked to take a drink – he was drunk in his introductory scene – but he didn't drink thoughtlessly. So it would be too simple to say that, at this point, he was contemptuous of Colbert for being a spendthrift rich woman, lapping up cocktails while millions starved in the Depression. Nor was he angry with her solely because she was about to throw herself away on a worthless clubman. What she was squandering most grievously was her mind. As she herself had just said of life on a merry-go-round, "We don't want to stop to think, do we? Just want to keep going."

No wonder, then, that for the climax of the movie, Capra and Riskin showed us Colbert thinking about things. The wedding scene consisted almost entirely of the sight of her struggling in silence to come to a decision. Her womanliness had returned; so now did her mindfulness (a mindfulness first achieved on the road, during her childlike period). And her vigor returned: having thought, she ran, much as she'd swum away at the beginning of the picture. Perhaps feminists will object that Colbert thought only about which man to marry. True enough. But considering the range of new experiences she'd had with Gable, I would suggest there was more than a little substance to her decision.

We never got to see her marry Gable; we didn't even see her give him a kiss.

Our last sight of Colbert, in this definitive role, was of a woman in a wedding dress, dashing flat-out for a future in which she wouldn't go around in circles.

You will understand why I have narrated all this in the past tense when I turn to *The Palm Beach Story* and the first glimpses it offers of Claudette Colbert. She is in a wedding dress, dashing flat-out for a future in which she and Joel McCrea will live happily ever after – or will they?

This brief but eventful opening-credits sequence plays like a complete screwball comedy in itself, run at forty times the normal speed. It's all fainting housemaids, disrupted phone calls, careening vehicles, disarrayed costumes, and mysteriously trussed-up women, as if Sturges were beginning *The Palm Beach Story* by giving us the high points (and only the high points) of some story about Colbert's progress toward marriage with a large, handsome man.

The movie that follows this prelude will show us, in effect, how Colbert and her husband were getting on, several years after *It Happened One Night*.[1] It's impossible, of course, to imagine Gable himself performing in this update; he never would have made himself glower through an entire film, as Joel McCrea does here. But then, it's the unrelieved grumpiness of McCrea's performance that underscores the basic conceit. Once upon a time, Colbert married for love. As she herself says in *The Palm Beach Story*, she chose a man who looked like a movie star. (And no wonder – he *was* a movie star.) But what was likely to have followed her wedding to that dashing lug? Endless nights in motor courts, innumerable benders, perpetual unemployment, an inexhaustible store of indignation: That's what Colbert had coming as Mrs Gable. Now, at the start of this new picture, she's stuck with the stone-faced Mr McCrea. Her movie-star husband still looks good, but he seems to be no fun at all.

And yet, as *The Palm Beach Story* starts in earnest, we discover that fun is what Colbert still wants. She proves it by playing hide-and-seek with the little Wienie King.

On the surface, she has no reason to make sport of their meeting. The plot has her facing eviction from her apartment, into which potential renters have been invited to pry; and her physical presence now is unsuited to children's games. No longer an actress who might be addressed as "brat," Colbert wears her hair and eyelashes long, and comes onto the screen in a form-defining wrapper, looking very like the beautiful and mature woman you think you might encounter in a Park Avenue boudoir. She also sounds like Park Avenue. She keeps her pitch to a rich middle register, and her smooth-flowing vowels declare their origins in her stage training.

A lovely clear voice, like a bell – so says the Wienie King, after he discovers Colbert behind the shower curtain. She pretends, momentarily, to be offended. But why did this mature, sophisticated woman hide in the first place? What made her hop from room to room, sneaking looks at the Wienie King and trying to stay out of his sight? As Gerry, she's still a woman in her own home – and as Colbert, she towers over the intruder, both physically and as a leading player. Neither the character nor the star has anything to fear; so I conclude that they must both be amusing themselves, indulging an aptitude for games and a willingness to plunge ahead experimentally.

To sum up: at the beginning of *The Palm Beach Story*, Colbert is trying to hold onto a girlishness that may already have slipped away. Once she enjoyed life on the road with a raffish adventurer. Now she's stranded on Park Avenue, unwilling to leave but too broke to stay. Evidently she wants to go on playing, but her opportunities to do so would seem to be vanishing. For these reasons, I take to heart the worldview articulated in this scene by the Wienie King. Given the setting, I'd have to call it a philosophy of the bathroom, more than of the boudoir; but it's a philosophy all the same: "Cold are the hands of time that creep along relentlessly destroying slowly but without pity that which yesterday was young. Alone our memories resist this disintegration and grow more lovely with the passing years."

Do I laugh at this pronouncement? Yes, every time. And I especially love the kicker: "That's hard to say with false teeth." But then, the funniest thing about the punch line is its justice. Once the cold hands of time have pitilessly wrenched out your teeth, you bet it's hard to talk. It seems the Wienie King is not only a philosopher, but also an elegant one. He knows how to deflate his own solemnity while pointedly confirming its message.

If you've responded to the way Sturges uses Colbert – if you've allowed the Wienie King's words to register – then you'll feel what a terrible mistake McCrea makes in the scene that follows. Colbert phones him in high spirits, meaning to share the news that the rent is paid and they're going out on the town; and McCrea cuts her off. He's too busy at the office, trying to sell an airport scheme to a potential investor. It seems a grim business, the way he goes about it; and yet it needn't be. What's he doing, if not playing with model airplanes? He, too, might make a game out of his encounter with a rich older man. (The investor, in his own words, is retired and has plenty of time.) But to McCrea, the occasion is a burden, which prevents him from responding to his wife, or even listening to her.

No wonder she demands a divorce, as soon as he gets home.

She says she's holding him back in his career; she implies he can't make enough money for her. Though slightly incompatible, these twin reasons for wanting a divorce seem equally valid – but the viewer may guess that neither is as important to this "long-legged gal" as the possibility of becoming "an adventuress," and neither speaks to her unhappiness in marriage so much as her husband's display of sexual jealousy. To put the matter crudely, she wants some fun – now, before time claims her teeth (and her legs); and she's hurt that he reduces fun to sex. If her body is truly hers to enjoy, then his body needn't be the limit of enjoyment. Why shouldn't she also get physical pleasure from, say, a 300-foot yacht?

By proposing this line of argument, *The Palm Beach Story* again makes itself the mirror image of *It Happened One Night*. Once, Colbert had abandoned her yacht for the simple life with Clark Gable; now Colbert abandons Joel McCrea, and a life that threatens to become simple, for the prospect of a yacht. Or, to phrase the issue in terms of communication: In the earlier film, Colbert felt she made contact with the world through her man. In this film, she feels her man blocks out the world.

But the problem that Sturges poses for Colbert is more complex than that. Very soon after we learn of her dissatisfaction, we find that she wriggles uncontrollably when McCrea sits her in his lap. "Hold still," McCrea orders; but even in movies made after Hollywood abandoned the Production Code, no one has acted out more vividly than Colbert the excitement of buttocks rubbing groin. Momentarily, McCrea's stolidity seems attractive. He enjoys giving her this order that he knows she can't obey. She wouldn't squirm so helplessly, if he weren't so proudly and completely a stiff.

At last we get to Topic A, as McCrea will later call it with disdain. He provides her with only one kind of fun, but one that's so powerful that she might give up the world for it. Sex keeps Colbert in her marriage, or threatens to. It's more than a habit, bad or otherwise. It's an irrational bond, whose absurd power she later acknowledges when she gives McCrea the pseudonym of "Captain McGlue." When Colbert flees her marriage, running so precipitously that she asks a taxi driver where to get a divorce, she is in effect struggling to change her relationship to her own sexual desires. Until now, she has been their agent. From this time on, she hopes, they will be her instrument.

This isn't a bad problem for an American movie to address, in its capacity either as American or as a movie. One of the ways in which Americans have not only pursued happiness but also changed the meaning of that pursuit is to have turned against such considerations as economics and clan solidarity as overt reasons for marriage. To a degree that is uncommon in history, Americans believe themselves to marry for love – which translates, in the movies, into marriage for sex. Outside of the movies, most people know that they must strike a balance between their sexual dreams and other needs: companionship, empathy, clan solidarity, economics. This balance is "love." But for cases in which a person has given up too much of the sexual ideal, Americans have coined an unlovely term: "settling."

Movie stars generally do not settle. They attain their sexual ideals, on big screens set up in public places, so that the rest of us may find it easier to believe in our compromised version of marriage for love. But in *The Palm Beach Story*, Colbert gives up her sexual ideal, precisely with the aim of settling. She does so in the expectation of embodying the dream of some wealthy man. (To amend my earlier formulation: she hopes to make *someone else's* sexual desire into her instrument.) And the first thing she learns is that it's not easy to lower her sexual expectations.

When she boards the train to Palm Beach with the "rich millionaires" of the Ale and Quail Club, she proves that her charm is as potent as she imagines; but she also learns that wealthy suitors, as a class, are a trial. By the time they break into her sleeping compartment to serenade her, Colbert is smiling in a way that recalls her forced gaiety toward the end of It Happened One Night, with the difference that she and Sturges allow her misery to show through for a moment. She can't imagine providing sex to any of these men; she can't bear the thought of keeping one of them aroused while fending him off. And for what it's worth, she's not even in her own sleeping compartment. The members of the Ale and Quail Club may feel free to enter because the place belongs to them.

The humor of this sequence becomes hectic, until it's no longer humor but something almost frightening. How should I take the "comic" mistreatment by the all-white Ale and Quail Club of their black bartender? Maybe audiences in 1942 – white audiences, at any rate – thought it unambiguously hilarious that these men should terrorize Fred "Snowflake" Toones. Or maybe some viewers, starting with Sturges himself, felt uneasy to see the rambunctiousness take this turn. It's impossible for an American of my generation to know with any certainty the full complexity of the first audience's response. But I do know that Sturges was capable of creating a black character as dignified as the preacher at the end of Sullivan's Travels. I also know that he had Colbert hide in fear from the pursuing mob, with their shotguns and baying dogs. Is it too far-fetched to think that the Ale and Quail Club turns into a lynch mob, once its collective sexual hopes have been frustrated? Is there no lesson in this for Colbert, as she starts her career as an adventuress?

From frustrated desire to little or no sexual urge: the next marital prospect Colbert meets is John D. Hackensacker 3rd, played by Rudy Vallee as if he had a zipper under his zipper. Vallee seems a perfect choice on whom to settle, especially when he's compared to the men Colbert has just escaped. He's younger and better looking than anyone in the Ale and Quail Club, and he has more money than the lot of them. It may also be a mark in his favor that he's so polite in his sexual interest, expressing it entirely in the subjunctive. If Colbert were to choose him, we understand, she could satisfy him with very little, and without having her sensibilities offended. After all, he's kind of cute. A woman could learn to call him Snoodles.

But then, "Captain McGlue" shows up, and Colbert feels what it would mean to settle. To paraphrase Snoodles: it is one of the tragedies of this life that the men of whom Colbert is most in need are always enormous.

By now, through emulation, I hope to have demonstrated how highly I value Cavell's dual process of translation and exegesis. By carrying meanings across from one vocabulary to another – from the language of Hollywood comedy to that of American philosophy – and by leading the reader through his texts as if by a thread, Cavell has done more than endorse these films as works of art. His real achievement is to have shown how these movies may be understood as sustained arguments, carried out about subjects that continue to matter to people. I might compare his method of translation and exegesis in *Pursuits of Happiness* to the way Emanuel Levinas read excerpts from the Talmud. Though Cavell's source material is nothing sacred, I believe both writers shared the goal of making their texts speak to real human problems.

In *Pursuits of Happiness*, Cavell favors those films that speak convivially, optimistically, about these problems. But in carrying out my own reading of *The Palm Beach Story*, I have now reached the place in the film's argument where conviviality fails and optimism falters.

It might seem perverse to say such a thing about *The Palm Beach Story*, when *Pursuits of Happiness* so brilliantly discusses another Sturges film, *The Lady Eve*, in which the characters are richer and the surface far more troubled. (Where in *The Palm Beach Story* are Barbara Stanwyck's bitter tears?) But just as the uproariousness of the Ale and Quail Club turns ugly, so is there something desperate in the screwball lightness of the film as a whole.

To resume the reading: Captain McGlue returns, and Colbert understands at last that she must have him. In conventional translation, "They were made for each other." This formula may be applied to the couples in all the films discussed in *Pursuits of Happiness*, and in a great many lesser films, just as it is applied in life to the lead actors in the average wedding. Perhaps we acknowledge that marriage-for-love aspires through the movies to become marriage-for-sex; perhaps we admit that sexual energy is no respecter of persons. Even so, we are supposed to keep in place the fig leaf of individualism and imagine that only *this particular man* can provide satisfaction to *this particular woman*. If *this particular woman* goes by the name of Gerry Jeffers, we're to forget that she has tested as alternative mates only a small, symbolic sampling of men. If the particular woman is Colbert, we must ignore the satisfaction previously given her by Gable (and by others, too, in a rather larger sampling).

Yet in *The Palm Beach Story*, Sturges won't let us maintain our genteel fiction. It turns out, at the end, that there are *two* Colberts and *two* McCreas: enough to go around. And so, in the final shot, Snoodles attains his sexual ideal (though he might not know what to do with her); his too-much-married sister gets her ideal, too, in the extra McCrea (and will probably tire of him within the month); and the original, sexually compatible pair remain together.

That closing shot, of the three couples at the altar, resembles the conclusion of a fairy tale, in which life offers three neat possibilities: too cold, too hot, and just right. But if the Colberts and McCreas are multiple and interchangeable, there can be no fairy-tale ending. This time, when we read "And they lived happily ever after – or did they?" we know how to answer. They did not, because the story has turned out to be circular, and dissatisfaction must come around again; because sexual desire is a merry-go-round, which you may enjoy so long as you don't stop to think; because Colbert, doubled, gets to have both of her choices, which means that neither choice is uniquely right for her.

I know – I'm making a lot out of something that viewers may take simply as a surprise ending. The sudden production of twin Colberts and McCreas seems teasingly gratuitous, as if the author were showing us his hand at work. What's more, the device isn't even novel. In some of Cavell's other comedies of remarriage, the woman was also doubled or split, the most pertinent example being Stanwyck in *The Lady Eve*. First Stanwyck appeared to Henry Fonda as "Jean"; then she came to him as Jean's fictional creation, "Eve." By showing up twice – thereby inciting Fonda to go twice through the same limp courtship speech – Stanwyck exposed the language of romance as being so much cardboard from Hallmark (a revelation that, for most viewers, is less than shocking). At the end of *The Lady Eve*, though, the fiction held. It still turned out that Stanwyck and Fonda were made for each other and no one else.

The finale of *The Palm Beach Story* makes nonsense of this notion of sexual exclusivity. It shows us that Colbert can make love to Joel McCrea and also to Rudy Vallee, that McCrea can make love to Colbert and to Mary Astor, too. We know it's in the nature of movies for stars to enjoy more than one partner; but it's not in the nature of movies to remind us of the fact. We observe a compact with the movies, a tacit agreement that allows us to enjoy a star's present adventure on condition that we pretend ignorance of the previous exploits. We pretend while knowing that we're pretending; that's a large part of the willing suspension of disbelief we practice at the movies. At the end of *The Palm Beach Story*, Sturges playfully violates this compact.

In so doing, he also violates his particular compact with the audience. His work appeals to moviegoers who like to think of themselves as wised-up. These are people who might identify with Gerry Jeffers as she appears in the early scenes of *The Palm Beach Story*, full of practical experience, fluent cynicism, and practiced sophistication. At the end, though, the worldly wisdom she mouthed is proved to have been so much hot air. She couldn't live by her principles; she succeeded in being an adventuress but wound up with her "bad habit" anyway. Bright chatter is futile – a revelation that Sturges's core audience really *may* find shocking.

Finally, and most outrageously, Sturges violates the notion that our choices make a difference. The conclusion of *The Palm Beach Story* reminds me of that moment in *It Happened One Night* when Colbert claimed that "It really doesn't matter how – or where – or with whom" she settled down; only here there's neither huskiness nor fatigue in her voice. There's no voice at all (words being nothing more than idle self-justification). Colbert, doubled, exercises both her choices simultaneously, and neither is likely to prove satisfactory.

As a philosopher other than the Wienie King might have said, "Either you marry Rudy Vallee or you don't marry Rudy Vallee. Marry Rudy Vallee or don't marry Rudy Vallee, and you will be unhappy."

There are also convivial, optimistic ways to phrase the same notion. As Molly Bloom put it at the end of *Ulysses*, "I thought well as well him as another." But for all the laughter it provides, the conclusion of *The Palm Beach Story* doesn't convey to me any of Molly's affirmation. The finale is jeering, discordant – a trick played on the characters and audience alike.

With that understood, I feel I know why Cavell omitted *The Palm Beach Story* from *Pursuits of Happiness*. Despite all its outward conformity to the genre, this picture is not a comedy of remarriage. It's a comedy of disillusionment. I also feel I know why, in *Pursuits of Happiness*, he dwelled so little on the actors' bodies and their ways of using them. Contingency, frailty, the creeping of the cold hands of time: these facts, which are so unavoidably bound up with our sense of someone's physical presence, have no role to play in his American commonwealth.

Now, Cavell does admit disillusionment into his philosophy and his film-going. Here, for example, is his reading of the final shot of another movie:

> the woman puts her hand on the man's shoulder not because she forgives his betrayal, or even his inability to offer tears and beg forgiveness, but because she accepts that there is nothing to forgive, to forgo, no new place to be won on the other side of this moment. There is no man different from any other, or she will seek none. Her faithfulness is to accept their juxtaposition in a world of uneventful adventure (one event is as adventurous or routine as another, one absence or presence as significant or unimportant as another, change as unthinkable as permanence, the many as the one) and to move into that world with him (*The World Viewed*, p. 96).

This, of course, is the ending of *L'Avventura*. Would Cavell admit that an American woman, too, might feel that "there is no man different from any other, or she will seek none"? Would he further admit that, given enough money, she might greet futility with laughter? Perhaps he would – but such a possibility lies outside the scheme of *Pursuits of Happiness*.

So I lay down my thread, having concluded that Cavell's argument holds up well against unravelling. It seems that the dropped thread of *The Palm Beach Story* does lead through a labyrinth. It's just a different maze from the one we've been exploring.

Note

1   The reader may reasonably wonder whether I'm imposing my way of thinking upon Sturges. For an answer, see his 1947 film *The Sin of Harold Diddlebock*, which opens with the final reel of Harold Lloyd's *The Freshman* and then shows us the same actor and character twenty years on.

11

THE RECOVERY OF GREECE AND THE DISCOVERY OF AMERICA

James Conant

"Greek Hellenism" . . . has not yet been created.

(George Seferis)[1]

America exists only in its discovery.

(Stanley Cavell)[2]

The first of these two epigraphs is from a *Greek poet* – where that combination of words will need to mean something more here than just "a poet who happens to be Greek"; the second is from an *American philosopher* – where that combination of words will need to mean something more here than just "a philosopher who happens to be American". The topic of each of the quotations is what more each of these combinations of words can mean.

Each of these remarks flirts with a paradox. More familiar – hence less overtly paradoxical – labels for the respective clusters of problems at issue in each of these remarks would be: "modern Greek culture" and "American culture". Do either of these latter two locutions involve a contradiction in terms? There is a temptation, in each case, to think so. To what extent do the two clusters of problems thus named – problems about what it means to be a modern Greek poet or writer or philosopher or intellectual and what it means to be an American poet or writer or philosopher or intellectual – resemble one another and to what extent do they differ? In order to answer this question, we will need to explore the concept of Greece that underlies the founding myth of the modern Greek state and the concept of America that underlies the founding myth of the United States of America.[3]

Let's begin with Seferis's remark: "'Greek Hellenism' has not yet been created." The most superficial layer of looming paradox here comes from the temptation to hear the expression "Greek Hellenism" as a tautology – as if what it says could be reformulated without loss of meaning as "Hellenic Hellenism" or "Greek Greekness" – and thus to hear the remark as a whole as making no sense; for if "Greek Hellenism" has not yet been created, then neither has Hellenism. Or, conversely, if such a thing as Hellenism has already been achieved, as it famously has – as the founding and guiding paradigm of Western cultural achievement – then whatever else it is, surely it is Greek. So what can

Seferis's remark mean? I have lifted the remark from a sentence in an essay devoted to the question of the *hellenicity* of works of art – a topic that, Seferis says, "has never ceased to attract attention and inquiry, and one which is still very much alive, since it involves two or three basic problems in our Greek intellectual life".[4] Seferis, of course, has no wish to deny the trivial historical truth that Hellenism was originally a Greek creation. But he avoids speaking of the origin of Hellenism as itself constituting a Greek variety of Hellenism, reserving the expression "Greek Hellenism" to designate a moment of subsequent return to that moment of origin.

Seferis's remark affirms four things: first, the relatively uncontroversial historical claim that the cultural, literary and philosophical achievement of classical Greece represents a founding moment of Western civilization; second, the trivial historical claim that subsequent epochs have sought to inherit and appropriate that cultural, literary and philosophical legacy; third, the equally trivial claim that over the course of history there has been a wide variety of such efforts of inheritance and appropriation – such Hellenisms – increasingly less ancient and less Greek than their forerunners;[5] fourth, the not at all trivial thought, that what still remains a problem (especially for those who today wish to take pride in thinking of themselves as Greek[6]) – what has not yet been created – is a constellation of cultural achievement worthy of the appellation "modern Greek Hellenism".

Now Cavell's remark: "America exists only in its discovery." The most superficial layer of looming paradox here comes from the temptation to think that what the locution "the discovery of America" must name is some documented matter of historical fact concerning a first moment of human contact with a certain portion of the earth's landmass – as if what the remark says could be reformulated without much loss of meaning as "A certain portion of the earth's landmass would not exist but for its discovery." It will be urged by some – let's call them moderate social constructionists – that a second, more fruitful paradox looms here as well. They will urge the importance of a thought they, too, will want to formulate by saying something like the following: "America could not exist until it was discovered." But, in so far as they have a point, it can be expressed in less paradoxical fashion.[7] Now there are yet others – let's call them raving social constructionists – who will feel this still misses something yet deeper. They will tell us that because geographical concepts are socially constructed so must be the entities to which they refer. But we have now lost all control of our paradox: it no longer has anything in particular to do with America.[8] Cavell's remark aims to illuminate something not about practically all our concepts, but rather about one concept in particular: the concept of America.[9]

The discovery of America that concerns Cavell is an event that must occur subsequent – not prior – to the settling of the New World. The first ship whose arrival in America Cavell cares about is the *Mayflower*. I take his remark to affirm at least the following four things: first, the relatively trivial historical truth that the passengers of the *Mayflower*, and those that followed them, sought a new life in a new world that they sought to settle, under the protection of a new social order that they sought to found; second, the slightly less trivial truth that what they therefore sought, in seeking "America", were possibilities of life, liberty and the pursuit of happiness that remained not only to be realized, but also still to be discovered; third, the far less trivial claim that a faithfulness to that project of foundation and discovery are constitutive of what, on a certain use of the word, the "America" in "the United States of America" stands for; and fourth, the far from trivial thought, that it still remains an open question (especially for those who wish to take pride in thinking of themselves as American) to what extent such a discovery has taken place, hence to what extent America, thus understood, can be said to exist.

To better understand our two remarks – from Seferis and Cavell – it will help to have some further context. Here, first, in preparation for the context of Seferis's remark, is some information from the *Michelin Green Guide to Greece* about three famous buildings in (what is today) downtown Athens:

> The University, Academy, and National Library – three 19th-century buildings in white Pentelic Marble – compose an architectural group in the elegant but slightly arid neo-Classical style. The university in the center is the oldest of the three buildings; it was designed by Christian von Hansen, the Danish architect, and built between 1837 and 1864; the pure design of the façade is outstanding. . . . The Academy (to the right) was paid for by Baron Sina, a Greek banker in Vienna, and designed by Theophilos von Hansen, Christian's brother, in the style of an Ionic temple; it is flanked by two tall columns surmounted by statues of Apollo and Athena.[10]

The Blue Guide to Athens adds that the university's outstanding façade features an Ionic portico whose inner walls "have frescoes depicting a variety of characters from ancient art, learning, and mythology".[11] Now let us ask: Are these buildings *Hellenic* in style? Well, as these guidebooks attest, the buildings in question certainly bear the earmarks of a classical revival in their manner of architectural design as well as in their manner of decoration – one of them, after all, displays paintings of the sages and deities of ancient learning and lore, while the other is dominated by statues of Apollo and Athena. So, in one sense, each of these buildings is as Hellenic as a building could hope to be. But their Hellenism is not of a sort that Seferis will categorize as Greek. Why not?

It would be a misunderstanding to think that it could count as a mitigating circumstance here that one of these buildings was paid for by a Greek banker; and it would be positively desperate to take comfort in the fact that one of the architects is named Theophilos. But it would be no less desperate a misunderstanding to think that for Seferis the disqualification of their Hellenism as Greek is to be traced solely to facts about these buildings such as their architects hailing from Denmark. Let us suppose that new historical research were to bring to light that the putatively Danish brothers had all along really been Greeks pretending to be Danes – or suppose, even mere fancifully, that these buildings were designed, constructed and adorned by prodigiously talented Athenian veterans of the Greek War of Independence who, without ever stepping off of Greek soil, managed to teach themselves architecture between skirmishes with the Turks – all this would make no difference. As long as these buildings retain any semblance of their present appearance, in architectural conception or style, then their Hellenism would be, by Seferis's lights, no more Greek than it presently is. If buildings like these were products of entirely Greek labor, they would merely be Greek contributions to a relatively modern and not at all Greek variety of Hellenism.

These buildings provide the point of departure for Seferis's remark. Here is the full context:

> We all know the buildings of the modern academy in Athens, an example of pseudo-classical architecture. But we do not realize that very often when we are speaking of the "Hellenism" of some work of art, we are really speaking about [something like] the buildings of the Academy. "And what shall be done?", I shall be asked. I said that Hellenism is something difficult. And this comes about because if, in the realm of the intellect, European Hellenism was created (and who knows, perhaps in our days is dying), our own "Greek Hellenism", if I may be permitted so to call it, has not yet been created and not yet recovered its tradition.[12]

Hellenism long ago went into cultural diaspora and became a European affair. That self-avowed "good European", Friedrich Nietzsche, speaks for many other Europeans of the nineteenth century when he confesses a longing for the "only place one would want to be at home: the *Greek* world". Nietzsche here declares not a desire to visit contemporary Greece, but a nostalgia for an earlier Hellenic civilization whose achievements haunt our own.[13] (Though for many others in the nineteenth century, such as Lord Byron, a longing for the Greece of the past was tied to an interest in visiting contemporary Greece and to hopes for a renewed Greece of today and tomorrow.)[14] If today's Greeks are to find a way to their own "Greek Hellenism", they must first, Seferis thinks, find a way to recover that lost world – where such a recovery is not a matter simply of reversing the direction of history (to be accomplished, say, by ridding oneself of subsequent "foreign" impurities), it is also a matter of forging something new. It must be both a re-creation and a new creation.[15] It requires finding a way neither simply to incorporate nor simply to repudiate European Hellenism.[16] It requires finding a way to re-inherit what was once Greek so that it may once again be Greek.[17]

Now let us turn to the context of Cavell's remark. I have lifted the remark from the middle of a sentence from his book about *Walden*. But, before we look at its context, it might help to have before us a sample of the way in which the topic of America haunts Thoreau's prose. Here is a representative passage from *Walden*:

> Let us settle ourselves, and work and wedge our feet downward through the mud and slush of opinion, and prejudice, and tradition, and delusion, and appearance, that alluvion which covers the globe, through Paris and London, through New York and Boston and Concord, through church and state, through poetry and philosophy and religion, till we come to a hard bottom and rocks in place . . . a place where you might found a wall or a state.[18]

This passage is about, among other things, what it is to settle a land and to found a state. Its author wishes his fellow citizens to re-open questions that he imagines they wish to regard as settled – questions about whether America, the land, has been discovered and successfully settled and whether the United States of America, the state, has been founded and stands fully constituted. The author, as the rest of the book makes clear, wishes to suggest that the task of settling still remains ahead of his readers – indeed, that the task of settling America stands hardly more accomplished in New York and Boston and Concord than in Paris or London – and that, for it to be accomplished, America's present, essentially European, understanding of what a church is and what a state is (and hence what the relations between church and state can be) must undergo radical transformation, as must America's present, equally European, understanding of what poetry and philosophy and religion are (and hence what the relations between poetry and philosophy and religion can be), and that, only once such transformations are underway, will a foundation have been dug secure enough to sustain the founding of a state able to fulfill the promise of America.

Here is the full context of Cavell's remark – it is a commentary on the (inseparability of the) literary and religious and philosophical and political ambitions of a work such as *Walden*:[19]

> We know the specific day in the specific year on which all the ancestors of New England took their abode in the woods. The moment of origin is a national event reenacted in the events of *Walden*, in order this time to do it right, or to prove that it is impossible; to discover and settle this land, or the question of this land, once and for all. . . . Any American writer, any American, is apt to respond to that event in one way or another; to the knowledge that America exists only in its discovery and its discovery was always an accident; and to the obsession with freedom, and with building new structures and forming new human beings with new minds to inhabit them; and to the presentiment that this unparalleled opportunity has been lost forever.[20]

The discovery of America is here represented as something that has yet to take place. Cavell takes Thoreau to take "America" to name something that those who wish to think of themselves as American must work to make happen: America exists only to the extent that the work of making America happen – the work of building new structures and forming new human beings with new minds to inhabit them – is actively undertaken, in anticipation of there being something thereby to discover. The implication is that, in so far as the fruits of such labor are (as Thoreau thinks they everywhere are) taken for granted, as having already been brought to completion, America is fading out of existence. Its discovery remains yet to be accomplished.

If, for Seferis, the task of those who wish to take pride in Greece is to forge a re-inheritance of what was once Greek so that it may once again be Greek, for Cavell, following Thoreau, the task of those who wish to take pride in America is to discover what is alleged already to have been discovered so that America can one day be what it now too often pretends already to be. The arresting initial parallel here – in the cases of Greece and America – is the possibility of a pseudo-cultural variant of the pseudo-religious phenomenon that Kierkegaard called the monstrous illusion. For Kierkegaard, the monstrous illusion was Christendom – a state of affairs in which everyone imagines he or she already is a Christian, simply in virtue of his living in a Christian country, having been baptized in a Christian ceremony, going every Sunday to hear a Christian sermon, etc., so that the struggle for faith and against sin once constitutive of the task of living a Christian life come to seem inessential to a person's claim to be a Christian. A Christian is taken to be something one already is, rather than someone one must become. Since everyone already knows himself or herself to be a Christian, no one undertakes the arduous task of becoming a Christian. It is a state of affairs in which there are no longer any Christians just because everyone thinks he or she already is one. The illusion is sustained by the apparent presence of evidence everywhere – in the form of well-maintained churches, Sunday services, baptismal ceremonies, theological publications, etc. – that Christianity continues to thrive in nineteenth-century Denmark.

For Seferis, the monstrous illusion that threatens the culture of modern Greece is the illusion of an already accomplished Greek Hellenism – a state of affairs in which a Greek writer or artist imagines himself or herself able to participate in a living Hellenic tradition, simply in virtue of his or her speaking Greek, living in Greece, remaining committed to the heritage of Greece, and purifying his or her style or thought of elements deemed not to be Greek, so that the struggle to create a new tradition (one that can lay rightful claim to having reclaimed some part of the glory that was Greece) which ought to be the task of a properly Greek Hellenism comes to seem inessential to a writer's or artist's claim to represent a living continuation of Hellenic tradition. The resources for a Greek Hellenism are taken already to lie ready to hand, within an easy arm's reach, rather than to be ones first needing to be fashioned through a laborious piecemeal process of literary and intellectual experimentation.[21] The illusion here consists in a state of affairs in which there are no genuine examples of Greek Hellenism, yet everyone thinks they are to be found in any contemporary Greek bookstore or art gallery.[22] The illusion is sustained by the apparent presence of evidence everywhere – in the form of modern demotic verse laced with classical illusions, municipal architecture incorporating Ionic temple elements, interior spaces adorned with allusions to Minoan wall-painting, mantelpieces decorated with reproductions of Cycladic sculpture, etc. – that Greece has recovered its classical traditions.[23]

For Cavell, following Thoreau, the monstrous illusion that threatens America is the illusion of an already discovered America – a state of affairs in which every American citizen imagines that the sole obstacles to reaping the benefits of the American dream are of a local and logistical variety. Each citizen takes the existence of America to be confirmed by facts such as that he or she lives on a continent called America, in a nation known as the United States of America, in a place where the words used to formulate the promise of America (words about freedom and democracy, about each citizen's counting equally, about a new beginning and a new hope, about being open to all people, regardless of creed, race or nation of origin, about life, liberty and the pursuit of happiness, equally guaranteed for all) are words repeated by every politician and pundit – and as fervently by the shameless as the sincere – so that the task of ensuring that these words retain a meaning (so that America can rightfully lay claim to having lived up to its promise), which ought to be the abiding concern of every American citizen, comes to seem inessential to one's claim to be a citizen. The discovery and constitution of America are taken to be accomplished facts, rather than ongoing projects whose vitality measures the pulse of America's heartbeat. The illusion consists in a state of affairs in which America no longer exists, just because every American takes the existence of America to be self-evident. The illusion is sustained by the apparent presence of evidence everywhere – in the form of up-to-date passports, shiny public buildings, closely contested elections, boisterous Fourth of July celebrations, etc. – that America exists.

Seferis not only says that Hellenism is something difficult for the contemporary Greek intellectual, but also that it is something dangerous:

> "Hellenism" as applied to a work of art is a big word to use. A big word and a fine word. But if we want to pin down exactly what is meant by it, we shall find it a difficult and a dangerous word to use. . . . Those who agitated for the artificially "purist" language aimed just at this; they sought for just this kind of "Hellenism". With touching obstinacy, with sweat and toil they tried to purify the national language from the stains of "barbarism" and hoped that slowly but surely we should attain once more the language and the art of Sophocles and Plato. And their reward was what might have been expected – a destruction and a drying up of Hellenism's fairest and truest streams. . . . This is why I used the word "dangerous", because we run the risk, as was the case of

the purists, of destroying in the name of "Hellenism" those values which are most purely Hellenic.[24]

On this analysis of the problem, nothing is more potentially destructive of a fruitful Greek Hellenism than the misguided attempt to secure it at too cheap a cost.[25] The misguided solution that Seferis particularly singles out is a quest to purify Greek writing and art of all supposedly "foreign" influences, in the hope of restoring a lost past. Such a project of reinstating the language and the art of a Sophocles or a Plato by purging today's language and art of the traces of twenty-five centuries of history – thereby supposedly placing Greece in a position where it will be ready simply to repeat the accomplishments of Sophocles and Plato – can strike one as almost comically chimerical.[26] Plato was as revolutionary a thinker as has ever lived. One cannot recapture either the style or the spirit of his philosophy or his art without also inheriting Plato's utopian ambition to transform the souls and the lives of his fellow citizens. (And what sort of conception of language is it that imagines that it can appropriate Plato's language while utterly divorcing it from the substance of his thought?) A project of turning the clock of Greek language and culture back two and a half millennia has no chance of bearing the imprint of Plato's style or spirit – for nothing could be further from these than such a project of cultural nostalgia. Such a project will only contribute, Seferis says, to a destruction and a drying up of Hellenism's streams – to a destruction in the name of "Hellenism" of those values that are most properly termed Hellenic. The first step to recovering the language of the dialogues of a Plato or a Sophocles must be to breathe life into their respective conceptions of what kinds of goods philosophy and tragedy were supposed to be. And the task of finding fruitful ways to bring such goods to bear on the souls and lives of the citizens of a modern (or postmodern) Greece constitutes a formidable challenge. The possibilities of thinking and living able to lend substance to such forms must be tested against contemporary needs and hopes to see what in them can withstand the pressures and demands of the present.[27] The unfruitful conception of a recovery of Greek culture, for Seferis, lies in a merely retrospective attachment to the bare forms of past ways of speaking, emptied of their substance – thus in a misplaced understanding of the ground of the present deficit of genuinely Hellenic forms and in an incoherent conception of how such a deficit is to be remedied.

An obstacle to the discovery of America, for Emerson and Thoreau, is also to be traced to an attachment to mere forms of speech emptied of their substance. Emerson writes: "[S]ometimes the life seems to be dying out of all literature and this enormous paper currency of Words is accepted instead."[28] Cavell elaborates why for Emerson's student, the author of *Walden*, the reader and the word can only be awakened together:

Everyone is saying, and anyone can hear, that this is the new world; that we are the new men; that the earth is to be born again; that the

237

past is to be cast off like a skin; that we must learn from children to see again; that everyday is the first day of the world, that America is Eden. So how can a word get through whose burden is that we do not understand a word of all this? Or rather, that the way we understand it is insane, and we are trying again to buy and bully our way into heaven, that we have failed, that the present is a task and a discovery, not a period of America's privileged history; that we are not free, not whole, and not new, and we know this and are on a downward path of despair because of it.[29]

The form of self-deception at issue here attaches not to a conception of how one might go about recovering the former grandeur of past forms of discourse, but to a conception of these forms as requiring no recovery. These forms of speech seem not to require recovery because they have always been with us and are everywhere still with us. We still hear people, in America, echoing the currently fashionable – often secularized – equivalents of thoughts such as these: "This is the new world"; "We are the new men"; "The earth is to be born again"; "The past is to be cast off like a skin"; "America is Eden". The rhetoric has been modernized but the sentiment remains much the same and threatens to degenerate into a form of chauvinistic sentimentality. Sentiments such as these, after several centuries of repetition, are asked not to lose any of their original expressive capacity. Yet those who make confident use of them persist in living in ways that must deprive them of meaning: as the call for us to be new men gives way to a fantasy of freezing time – to a call to disregard any needs or hopes deemed not to accord with the supposed "intentions of the founders"; as America, having proclaimed the earth's rebirth and itself a new Eden, now appears to its neighbors to be bent on perfecting the means to forever spoil the garden; and as the new world, having pledged to cast off its past like an old skin, seems now, much like the old world, weighed down by layers of history. In the face of such failures on America's part to be able to mean its descriptions of itself, the task of a properly American philosophical and literary and political discourse became, already over a century and a half ago, for authors such as Emerson and Thoreau, that of finding a way, first, to tell us, such that we are able to hear it, that we no longer understand the forms of words we call upon to articulate the promise of America, and, second, to demonstrate that these very words, their present apparent expressive impotence notwithstanding, can still be called upon, in speaking of America, to say something we are still able to understand and believe.

The essential parallel between Seferis and Cavell lies in their wanting the linguistic compounds *Greek poet* and *American philosopher* respectively to signify something more than an individual who happens to fall under two independently intelligible predicates – *Greek* and *poet*, *American* and *philosopher*. They want these complexes to denote a unity, such that the meaning of each of the terms occurring in the complex is decisively altered through its participation with the other in such a unity. Seferis's conception of the calling of the Greek poet is one according to which what it is for a poet to be a *Greek* poet is to be gauged not merely by the passport he or she holds or where he or she lives or which language he or she speaks, but by the manner in which he or she crafts and inhabits the linguistic and other expressive resources through which he or she seeks to establish a relation to a broader Hellenic artistic, literary and intellectual tradition;[30] and according to which what it is for a Greek to be a Greek *poet* is to be measured not merely by his or her producing work that is recognizably poetry, but by his or her poetry itself serving as a vehicle for the expression and further articulation of what it now means to be Greek. Cavell's conception of the calling of the American philosopher is one according to which what it is for a philosopher to be an *American* philosopher is to be gauged not merely by the passport he or she holds or where he or she lives or which flag he or she salutes, but by the manner in which he or she seeks to further (what Cavell calls) the discovery of America; and according to which what it is for an American to be an American *philosopher* is to be measured not merely by his or her producing work that is recognizably philosophy, but by his or her philosophy itself serving as vehicle for the expression and critical articulation of what it now means to be an American.

It might appear to one, at first blush, as if Seferis's conception of the sort of unity that is available to be denoted by the complex expression "Greek poetry" is far more coherent than Cavell's conception of the sort of unity that is available to be denoted by the complex expression "American philosophy" – especially if one is attracted to an argument along the following lines:

> Poetry by its very nature partakes of the particularity of a language, a culture, a people and a place; indeed, only to the extent that it partakes of these can it succeed as poetry; and thus any poetry that is not deeply marked by such particularities is bound to be shallow and bloodless. Philosophy, on the other hand, is an entirely different matter. It must rise above such particularities. In its quest for reason and universality, a philosophical effort partakes of such particularities only to the extent that it fails as philosophy.[31]

The soundness of such an argument depends upon the soundness of the respective conceptions of poetry and philosophy (and the corresponding conceptions of "language", "culture", "reason", etc.) upon which it relies.

It is just such conceptions that Seferis and Cavell, each in his own way, seek to challenge.

First, there is the question of what *poetry* and *philosophy* each are – of the supposedly ineluctably provincial nature of poetry (so that it pertains to its essence that a poetic production have a recognizably modern French or ancient Greek or early American provenance) and the supposedly equally ineluctably cosmopolitan nature of philosophy (so that it pertains merely to its accidents

239

that a philosophical production have a recognizably modern French or ancient Greek or early American provenance). Seferis and Cavell seek to contest such pictures of poetry and philosophy and the correlative picture of the separability of their essences from their accidents. Their respective conceptions of poetry and philosophy each assume an intertwining of moments of particularity and universality. Poetry for Seferis (rooted in particularities though it must be) always seeks to give voice to something universally human.[32] And philosophy for Cavell (its claim to be philosophy depending on its capacity to speak in the universal voice notwithstanding) must not shrink from the recognition that whoever seeks to speak for everyone must first speak as the particular person he or she is – rooted in the particularities of his or her time and place.

Second, Seferis's and Cavell's respective conceptions of the *Greek* and *American* moments in Greek poetry and American philosophy can also be seen, upon closer examination, themselves each to involve a further intertwining of particularity and universality – an internal complexity that makes a difference to the sort of thing Greek poetry and American philosophy can each aspire to be. Seferis's conception of Hellenism rests on the possibility of the universal appeal of the Hellenic ideal, while seeing such an appeal as constitutively tied to the emergence of a very particular sort of tradition – one that sought to artic-ulate universal demands of reason – a synthesis of tradition and criticism in which the possibility of an aspiration to universality depended upon the devel-opment of very particular sorts of practices and institutions. A set of practices and institutions – not merely a new way of thinking, but a new way of *living*, of relating to tradition and language and other people – came into being and enabled the cultivation of a heightened sensitivity to the requirements of an ongoing enterprise of rational self-criticism and self-correction. "Hellenism" therefore is the name both of a very particular tradition with a very particular history and an aspiration to a perspective on the world and one's place in it that transcends the parochialism of the merely traditional. Cavell's conception of America is not of an ideal of community that can be of concern only to a certain group of people who happen already to live in a certain place. It is constitutive of America as originally conceived that it be open to everyone and that it can claim to exist only to the extent that a nation exists in which each American's claim to be American does not depend upon his or her rootedness in the particularities that constitute most other national communities – particu-larities of language, or creed, or race, or place of birth or ethnic heritage. "America" therefore is both the name of a very particular people with a very particular history and the name of a certain ideal of national community – one that is to be an example to the rest of the world – that not only is able to tran-scend the parochial ties that previously bound together other peoples, but that, through the degree and manner in which such transcendence is achieved, is able to transform the world's understanding of what a nation should be.[33]

The depth of the parallel notwithstanding, the unities that Seferis and Cavell respectively seek to designate with the terms "Greek poetry" and

"American philosophy" are of very different sorts. After remarking upon the risks of "destroying in the name of 'Hellenism' those values which are most purely Hellenic", Seferis goes on to warn of a second danger:

> But the opposite may happen, too; and this is why I used the adjective "difficult". We may also, in the confidence that we are "hellenizing", come under the sway of values which are not Hellenic at all or only remotely so.[34]

He explains:

> Since the time of Alexander the Great we have scattered our Hellenism far and wide. We have sown it throughout the world. . . . And this vast diaspora was to have a significant result. Hellenism was worked upon, reformed and revivified, right down to the time of the Renaissance, by personalities who were sometimes Greek and sometimes not. And after that time, which marks the enslavement of the Greek race, it was shaped by personalities who were not Greek at all and who worked outside the Greek area. And we should remember that it was in this period that were created those great works which crystalized the form of the civilization which we know today as European. . . . No Greek had any decisive or immediate influence at that time on the trends which were taking shape in the West as a result of the contact with Greek values. . . . This was how things stood until the time of the awakening of the race. Then, just as is done today, the best among us studied in or went to the West and tried to bring back to liberated Greece the heritage that had left our country in order to be preserved. But this heritage was not a matter of lifeless gold; it was a living thing that had fertilized its surroundings and taken root and borne fruit. And through these functions it gradually came to be a general and abstract framework inside which many powerful intelligences came to find their places, each completely different from the others and more consonant with their own selves than with anything else. Dante's Ulysses, Shakespeare's Venus and Adonis, Racine's Phèdre and Hölderlin's Hyperion, apart from their worldwide significance and value, belong basically to the times and the races of their creators; their Hellenic subject matter is, as motivation, something external and superficial. We, however, with most legitimate and commendable motives, burning, as we were, with the desire to bring back to Greece everything that was Hellenic and seeing signs of Hellenism everywhere, brought back, without looking more deeply into the matter, countless foreign values which in fact had nothing to do with our own land at all.[35]

Thus it comes to pass that there are such things as the buildings of the modern academy in Athens – examples of an architecture that is as unquestionably

241

Hellenic as it is questionably Greek. The call to hellenize Greek arts and letters faces, in Seferis's view, a dilemma. The first horn of the dilemma is a suffocating nostalgia and the accompanying appetite for lifeless anachronisms (which Seferis thinks is the inevitable consequence of a fixation on the ideals of "cultural purity" and a merely backward retreat to "traditional" Hellenic values). The second horn of the dilemma is a pseudo-classical hodgepodge that is neither Greek nor Hellenic (which Seferis thinks is the inevitable consequence of an undirected cultivation of neo-classical forms as mere ends in themselves).

What is the way out of this dilemma? Why has a genuinely Greek Hellenism yet to emerge? And, when it does, what will it look like? Seferis, wisely, has only this to say in answer:

> Sometimes there is a foreknowledge of this "Greek Hellenism" among some of the best of us, "for wise men perceive what is approaching". But before we can say that we can see its face clearly, many great works will have to be created and many men, great and small alike, will have to work and to struggle. For this particular Hellenism will only show its face when the Greece of today has acquired its own real intellectual character and features.[36]

Whereas the American is haunted by the fear that what was once possible can no longer become actual, the modern Greek is haunted by the fear that what was once actual will never again be possible. Whereas, according to Cavell, the American intellectual disguises the cultural accomplishments of America from himself and remains haunted by a "presentiment that the unparalleled opportunity [named America] has been lost forever". According to Seferis, what the Greek intellectual is tempted to hide from himself or herself is that there are no accomplished instances of a currently Greek Hellenism and hence that knowledge of such a possibility can exist *only* in the form of a presentiment. A more definite knowledge of its possibility is not to be had in advance of its actuality – that is, until its face can clearly be seen. This can happen only once modern Greece has expressed itself philosophically, poetically and artistically – when sufficiently many distinctively modern Greek works have been created of sufficient intellectual and aesthetic scope and consistency to establish and inspire a new tradition of Hellenic values. One reason this day is slow in coming is the illusion that Greece can only create something of permanent value by specifically creating again what can no longer be recreated. If Greece adheres to such a backward-looking formula for progress, Seferis suggests, it will be doomed to underpraise its innovators and overvalue its imitators.

This comes close to being the reverse of an American malady Cavell seeks to diagnose:

> Study of *Walden* would perhaps not have become such an obsession with me had it not presented itself as a response to the questions with

242

which I was already obsessed: Why has America never expressed itself philosophically? . . . In re-reading *Walden*, twenty years after first reading it, I seemed to find a book of sufficient intellectual scope and consistency to have established or inspired a tradition of thinking. One reason it did not is that American culture has never really believed in its capacity to produce anything of permanent value – except itself. So it forever overpraises and undervalues its achievements.[37]

Cavell's opening question here ("Why has America never expressed itself philosophically?") can sound a bit like a worry Seferis has about modern Greece. But Cavell rejects the underlying premise of his opening question. The problem, according to him, is not why a distinctively modern American cultural voice has yet to emerge, but why, each time it emerges, America fails to acknowledge it as such. In *Walden*, Cavell claims to be able to identify the American counterpart of that to which Seferis claims he can only look forward: a book of sufficient intellectual scope and consistency to establish or inspire a tradition of thinking. So, in each case, an indigenous intellectual tradition has yet to catch fire and clear a new space, but for almost opposite reasons: in the case of Greece, according to Seferis, it is because there is at present no flame and little point in lighting one as long as the cultural landscape remains too dry and barren to sustain a blaze; in the case of America, according to Cavell, it is because, though a flame intermittently burns bright in the densely wooded landscape, no one believes sufficiently in its capacity to sustain itself to want to contribute a handful of kindling. If the curse of modern Greek culture lies in its conviction that Greece has already proved its capacity to produce something of permanent value, the curse of American culture, according to Cavell, lies in its inability to believe in its capacity to produce anything of permanent value. On this analysis, Cavell's diagnosis would appear to be the opposite of Seferis's: the problem is not how to reduce the paralyzing glare of an unavoidably visible cultural achievement, but rather how to render finally visible cultural events that remain almost inexplicably invisible. Cavell finds this only almost – and not utterly – inexplicable, because he sees America's obliviousness to such achievements as itself characteristic of a chronic American tendency to be able to praise in American culture only as much as a European sensibility will ratify.

Seferis and Cavell are each concerned with something that remains to be discovered. But Seferis's name for what remains to be discovered – "Greek Hellenism" – requires realigning two nearly synonymous terms: together they come to signify something neither term previously was able to stand for by itself, their combination simultaneously marking a relation (through the second term) to a glorious but dangerous past and (through its qualification by the first term) to a difficult but possible future, with the ensuing complex failing to refer to anything in the present. Cavell's name for what remains to be discovered – "America" – requires only one term: it either refers simultaneously to a past of

243

promise and a future faithful to that promise or it fails to refer to anything at all, depending upon whether it stands for something happening in the present.

We can disguise the depth of the difference here by saying that for Seferis the modern Greek must discover for himself or herself what is Hellenic and for Cavell the American must discover for himself or herself what is American. But Seferis's and Cavell's own formulations are more nuanced, exploding this surface appearance of a parallelism. Seferis writes: "If I am right, the whole question is this: how profoundly and how truly can a Greek confront his own self and that nature of his which must inevitably be part of the greater nature which is Hellenic?"[38] To say that the confrontation of the Greek with himself must also involve a confrontation with "that nature of his which must inevitably be part of the greater nature which is Hellenic" is to say that the confrontation in question here is of necessity also a confrontation with a no longer living Greek past as well as with an only partially living (and thus partially dying) European inheritance of that same past.

The confrontation of the American soul with itself, for Cavell, also involves a question about how to inherit a European past; but it takes a rather different form. The following remarks are from a lecture Cavell delivered to an assembly of Austrian philosophers:

> The interests among philosophers here in the richness of specifically Austrian thought has helped my own preoccupation with the richness, and the poverty, of specifically American thought, above all with the extraordinary fact that those I regard as the founders of American thinking – Ralph Waldo Emerson and Henry David Thoreau – are philosophically repressed in the culture they founded. My efforts to realize this repression are not interested, perhaps I should say explicitly, any more than I understand the attention to Austrian thought here to be interested, in ridding itself of foreign influence and participation. On the contrary, my wish to inherit Emerson and Thoreau as philosophers, my claim for them as founding American thinking, is a claim both that America contains an unacknowledged current of thinking, *and* that this thinking accomplishes itself by teaching the inheritance of European philosophy – an inheritance that should make me not the master of this European philosophy, but also not its slave.[39]

Thus for Cavell, as for Seferis, an effort to purify oneself of foreign influences represents a misunderstanding of what the desired process of discovery requires. And for Cavell, as for Seferis, this process can accomplish itself only by acknowledging and reanimating a European legacy. And, for Cavell, as for Seferis, this inheritance of a European legacy should make me neither its master nor its slave. But for Cavell's America, now unlike Seferis's Greece, the confrontation of the American soul with itself does not of necessity also involve a confrontation with a subsequent European transmogrification of American values. This is the great difference between the heir of the ancient world's and the heir of the new world's respective relations to the old world. Whereas the recovery of a distinctively Greek Hellenism remains beholden to Europe's intervening discovery of Greece, America's discovery of itself ought not to remain beholden to Europe's intervening discoveries of America.

This might seem wrong. One might object along the following lines: "Even though America has perhaps never exactly enjoyed anything quite as triumphant as an Alexander the Great of its own, has it not enjoyed its own version of cultural imperialism, scattering vestiges of Americanism far and wide? Elaborations on American music, film, television, clothes, advertising, etc., are now to be found the world over. So doesn't an American's confrontation with the nature of America today necessarily involve a confrontation with the presently global phenomenon of American culture?" This rejoinder fails to register the critical difference between Seferis's and Cavell's respective problematics (and this is not just because American culture has never yet gone into cultural diaspora, but rather continues to absorb the diasporas of the world). The claim of Cavell's here missed is that America's continuing discovery of itself does not have to wait upon a reabsorption of the old world's crystallizations of her achievements. If her culture is to be a living thing able to fertilize its own native surroundings, take root and bear fruit, it must be something that can be homegrown. The point is not that European Americanism is unable to rival the achievement of European Hellenism – that Sergio Leone's Westerns, Jean-Luc Godard's film noir and Lars Gulin's jazz saxophone are not the equal of Dante's Ulysses, Racine's Phèdre or Hölderlin's Hyperion. It is that – however much pride or joy or affection these tasteful European adaptations of American culture may excite in an American soul – their distinctively European accents preclude them from furnishing decisive articulation for an American of what America is. However much such pockets of Italian or French or Swedish Americanism may enrich world culture, such European discoveries of America are not contributions to what Cavell means when he speaks of "the discovery of America".

Here Seferis's and Cavell's concerns appear to run in opposite directions. Seferis wishes to teach the Greek intellectual to be suspicious of any call for a Greek culture that abjures the achievement of subsequent European Hellenism on the ground that "the only possible genuine [Greek] life" must spring exclusively "from the selfsame source of Hellenic life".[40] Whereas Cavell wishes to teach the American culture-vulture to be suspicious of his or her tendency to single out as significant products of American life only what a European sensibility will immediately be inclined to single out as such – hence to be suspicious of his or her own chronically American tendency to underestimate the powers of renewal inherent in the self-same source of American life.

Seferis, as we have seen, charges those most eager to champion Greek cultural forms with forgetting what lent those forms substance. This makes for the possibility of a kind of Greek intellectual who (like Seferis) deplores the

245

stultifying effects of a backward-looking cultural chauvinism but who (unlike Seferis) does not think that all modern Greek philosophy derives (as Nietzsche thought all German philosophy derived) "its real dignity from being a gradual reclamation of the soil of antiquity".[41] This kind of modern Greek intellectual recoils from a shallow enthusiasm for ancient philosophy – one that makes much of its being Greek and little of its being philosophy – by refusing the classics altogether. Just as there are American intellectuals who (to Cavell's disappointment) refuse to interest themselves in the possibility of a distinctively American philosophy, so there are also Greek intellectuals who (to Seferis's disappointment) refuse to interest themselves in ancient Greek philosophy.

There is both a symmetry and an asymmetry here. The superficial symmetry lies in the fact that the typical modern Greek philosopher (who has no time for Seferis's enthusiasm for ancient Greek philosophy) and the typical American philosopher (who has no time for Cavell's preoccupation with America expressing herself philosophically) each aspires, in the first instance, to be a *philosopher* and each, in his or her own way, fears that a preoccupation with what it is to be a Greek or an American will constitute at best a distraction from (and at worst a corruption of) that aspiration. The asymmetry lies in the fact that, quite unlike his or her American counterpart, the Greek intellectual, who refuses the classics of Greek thought, is refusing something he or she had forced upon him or her from an early age in a fashion that deprived it of its possible significance. Many a modern Greek intellectual has been taught to believe, from an early age, that for something to be a genuine cultural achievement it must speak in a discernibly Greek accent; thus he or she often comes to distrust the cultivation of such an accent as much as he or she has come to disdain the varieties of sterile nationalism that he or she associates with it.[42] Many an American intellectual has been led to believe that for something to be a genuine cultural achievement it must bear the earmarks of a European provenance; and, if he or she has never come to distrust this equation of culture with Europe, then the cultivation of a distinctively American variety of high culture is bound to seem to him or her an inherently paradoxical undertaking: a chauvinistic affirmation of provincialism in the name of cosmopolitanism.

The deeper symmetry here lies in the ensuing possibility of someone who is compelled, in the name of a higher patriotism, to stand alone and to speak in ways that are bound to appear (at least to many of his or her countrymen) decidedly unpatriotic. Cavell says of America: "Those who voice politically radical wishes for this country may forget the radical hopes it holds for itself, and not know that the hatred of America by its intellectuals is only their own version of patriotism."[43] And something similar sometimes holds of modern Greek intellectuals. For, often despite a professed impatience with the excessive celebration of the ancient Greeks, they remain moved by the radical hopes that philosophy in its beginnings, among the Greeks, held for itself – moved by the memory of Socrates, allowing his fellow citizens to put him to death, out of a loyalty to Athens. So even those contemporary Greek philosophers who now refuse to study the classics of Greek philosophy (on the grounds that they are interested in *doing* philosophy, not merely studying what it once was), they, too, in their own way, are maintaining a faithfulness to Greek thought – helping to keep alive the possibility of its inheritance as philosophy. For philosophy in Greece to become worthy of the title "Greek philosophy" again it must first become philosophy, which means overcoming the apparently dead weight of a distinctively Hellenic philosophical legacy. For philosophy in America ever to become worthy of the title "American philosophy" it must first discover America, which means overcoming the apparent weightlessness of a distinctively American philosophical legacy.

Seferis and Cavell are each attuned to the way in which the predicates "Greek" and "American" respectively denote, at one and the same time, a belonging to a people and a place as well as to an ideal that holds that people together and binds them to their place. For Seferis, as for Cavell, *Greece*, like *America*, is neither merely an objective concept nor merely a subjective one. The difficulty in each case lies in achieving a proper alignment between the objective and subjective dimensions of the concepts in question. The quest to attain such alignment invites opposition from opposite quarters. Those who pride themselves on being "patriots" tend to collapse the concept of "Greece" or "America" into a merely objective one, draining it of its moral force, while imagining they thereby increase its moral weight, representing their causes as if they were the inexorable obligations of all who fall under the (merely objective) concept in question. Those who pride themselves on being "intellectuals" conclude that the only obligations that could accrue from a person's happening to fall under such a (merely objective) concept are bogus ones. But in rejecting such obligations, they take themselves to have uncovered the bankruptcy in the very idea that the word that named that (merely objective) concept could ever denote a legitimate source of obligation. Both sides thereby overlook the concepts *Greece* and *America* that concern the likes of Seferis (and the Greek poets he admires – Sikelianos, Antoniou, Cavafy) and Cavell (and the American authors he admires – Emerson, Thoreau, Whitman). Thus the hopes these authors entertain for Greece and for America are overlooked by those on both ends of the political spectrum. The "patriots" are repelled by the radicalism in their form of patriotism. They are unable to see it for what it is: a form of patriotism. The "intellectuals" notice just that – that it is a form of patriotism – and are repelled by just that, thereby missing just what the "patriots" notice: its radicalism. Unable to hold together the subjective and objective poles of the concepts in question, the "intellectuals" threaten to turn intellectual criticism into an ineffectual oppositionalism without any critical bite, while the "patriots" threaten to turn patriotism into an all too effectual jingoism, ready to take a bite out of just about anything. This leaves their countrymen with a forced choice between a politics of bloodless abstraction and critical detachment or one of bloody reaction and unreflective entrenchment. Given such a forced choice, there is reason to prefer the former over the latter. But must the choice be forced?

The asymmetry between Seferis's and Cavell's respective concerns comes sharply into focus in Seferis's essay comparing the poetry of Constantine Cavafy with that of T.S. Eliot. The comparison provides him with an occasion to reflect on the difference in the mode of relation to tradition that an American and a modern Greek intellectual must each inhabit:

> Eliot is very different from Cavafy. . . . Sprung from a line of puritans, Eliot sets out from America. . . . For him tradition is not a matter of inheritance; if you want it, you must work hard to acquire it. An Englishman would not feel like this. But Eliot comes from a rootless place, a place without a past. He feels strongly how paper-thin, how groundless, how unreal and anarchic is, in fact, the order offered by the mechanical civilization of today, his inheritance of material good. He is aware of the drying up of the sources of inspiration. . . .
>
> Cavafy is something different. He comes from one of the intellectual capitals of the world which, though almost submerged, is still great and can boast of being "Greek from ages past" . . . from the capital of an intellectual fatherland which is marked by innumerable graves, but is still immense . . . of this immensity he is the last inhabitant. . . . The "common language of the Greeks" which he inherited and came to develop "like an eavesdropper" is the language of the great masters of Hellenism. He is their last heir.
>
> Cavafy is not burdened by the absence of a tradition. On the contrary, what he feels is the dead weight of a tradition which is thousands of years old and which he has done nothing to acquire, since he "carries in him" this "glorious" literate tradition of the Greeks. He is the solitary of an extreme period of Hellenism, the period of the twentieth century. . . . And the whole question is whether the graves will suck him down or whether he will be able to bring to life with his own blood even so much as a single dry twig in this dead garden – a thing that, for a thousand years before him, no one has yet done in this tradition.[44]

Seferis begins here by touching on an aspect of the problem of America that preoccupies Cavell: "Sprung from a line of puritans, Eliot sets out from America. . . . For him tradition is not a matter of inheritance; if you want it, you must work hard to acquire it." But, by Cavell's lights, Seferis retains here a very European picture of what sort of hard work it is the American must do in order to acquire a culturally resonant poetic voice. Cavell is bound to be suspicious of the choice of Eliot as the prototype of the accomplished American poet. This choice leaves unquestioned the assumption that in order for an American poet to attain accomplishment he must emigrate at least spiritually, if not literally, to Europe.

Seferis's discussion is structured around the following opposition: the American poet is burdened by the absence of a tradition while the Greek poet is not thus burdened. Now there is certainly something right about this formula.

But it stands in need of further qualification if it is to avoid being doubly off the mark. As it stands, it is off the mark about poets such as Walt Whitman or William Carlos Williams or Robert Frost (that is, poets who strove to be *American* poets) for the very reason that it is on target about Eliot (whose ambition was to become not an American, but rather a European, poet). Those who sought to write an American poetry *were* burdened by the presence of a tradition: they labored not in the absence of a tradition, but in the absence of a tradition they were prepared to claim as *theirs*. And, as it stands, the formula is not quite right about the modern Greek poet for reasons Seferis understands only too well: the Greek poet's burden would not be what it is, if the tradition in question were already alive and kicking, rather than in need of resurrection. Seferis is certainly right about the problem of the Greek poet not being that of the American – burdened by the absence of a body of tradition that he or she can claim as his or her own. The modern Greek's problem is that the body that remains his or hers to claim is a corpse. The Greek poet is burdened by the absence of a *living* tradition. Indeed, what Seferis here says about Cavafy's relation to tradition illuminates why the task of forging a contemporary Greek Hellenism is bound to be fraught with difficulty. One the one hand, a poet such as Cavafy carries within him a glorious literary tradition that he has done (and needed to do) nothing to acquire; on the other hand, he fights almost alone to revivify this tradition, to convert it into something more than a dead weight – a thing that no one has done for a thousand years. The question that haunts his entire poetic enterprise is whether he can succeed or whether the graves of his literary forebears will suck him down into the soil of a no longer living tradition.

This resonates with a moment in Emerson's work that Cavell repeatedly underscores: the American scholar will come into existence only when America herself comes into existence by learning to think for herself, where this requires first throwing off all that is no longer living in the ossified edifice of European scholarship. This partial symmetry notwithstanding, it is important to notice how significantly Seferis's account of the loneliness of the modern Greek intellectual differs from Cavell's account of his American counterpart:

> [C]ontemporary Greece, attempting, as she is, to find the right attitude towards her ancient tradition, which is known to her exclusively through foreign sources; beginning only now to become conscious even of her recent history, and forced to import the greater part of her intellectual requirements, presents a kind of intellectual landscape in which there are scarcely any discernible landmarks and all around lie tracts of barren and largely unknown country. As for the artist who wishes to live in this land, he is sometimes, if I may say so, very cruelly isolated among these barren tracts, parched up, and withered away. And this is why we see so many at the starting point and so few reaching the end of the course.[45]

249

Cavell would also be willing to say of America that it presents the appearance of "a kind of intellectual landscape in which there are scarcely any discernible landmarks and all around lie tracts of barren and largely unknown country". But he would want to qualify this in various ways. First, such a remark would be, for Cavell, a remark about how the intellectual landscape of America is apt to *appear* to an American intellectual – that is, someone who is apt to undervalue America's achievements. (Seferis's remark is not about how the intellectual landscape of Greece is *apt* to appear to a Greek intellectual, but about how it *ought* to appear, if seen in proper perspective.) Second, the solution to this problem of apparent barrenness, for Cavell, lies (not in deciding, as most American intellectuals are apt to, that America is "forced to import the greater part of her intellectual requirements", but rather) in dissipating the appearance of barrenness by bringing the actual contours of the landscape properly into view. Third, for Cavell, some of the most significant resources available for accomplishing this task (of dissipating the appearance of cultural barrenness) are to be located in just those products of the culture most passionately consumed, while least valued as expressions of America, not only by its self-professed intelligentsia, but also by its average citizens – for example, American movies.

But why should the American case differ from that of other cultures in this way? Why does the once seemingly serviceable distinction between high and low culture come to the particular sort of grief that it does when one attempts to apply it to the American scene? Is it because, for the most part (that is, with the occasional exception), the highest America has to offer in the way of a distinctively American culture is something that is not all that high? Or is because America was from the beginning founded on an ambition to realign the relation between high and low – between the aristocratic and the popular – so that her high culture cannot remain utterly divorced from (what a certain aristocratic model of culture dictates must be) the "low" and still remain a part of a genuinely American culture?[46]

Notes

1 George Seferis, "Dialogue on poetry: what is meant by Hellenism?", in *On the Greek Style: Selected Essays on Poetry and Hellenism* [Henceforth OGS], trans. Rex Warner and Th.D. Frangopoulos (Denise Harvey Publisher: Limni, Evia, Greece, 1982), p. 94.
2 *The Senses of Walden*, expanded edn (San Francisco, CA: North Point Press, 1981) [henceforth SW], pp. 8–9.
3 The attempt to single out such concepts and elucidate their logic apart from any broader empirical inquiry is apt to strike many a serious practicing historian as a peculiar activity – one that is apt to arouse a certain discomfort. Such concepts and the founding myths that presuppose them can breed mythical histories and dangerously distorted forms of national self-understandings (e.g. "Prior to its liberation the Greek race suffered five centuries of uninterrupted enslavement at the hands of the Turk", or "The Vietnam War was a struggle between the guardians of the free world and the forces of totalitarianism"). But a proper acknowledgement of the manifold ways in which myth is repeatedly mistaken for history does not itself constitute a showing either that such concepts are merely pernicious or even that an under-

standing of them is irrelevant to an understanding of history. To understand what one is *qua* modern Greek or American requires, among other things, coming to terms with how one's identity is profoundly shaped by certain national myths.

4   Seferis, OGS, p. 86. In his translator's introduction, Rex Warner notes:

> The problem of style, of finding the precise expression appropriate to the writer's own insight, to his tradition and to the air which he breathes, is, of course, a problem which must be faced by every writer in every country; but in Greece, which is not only very old but also very new, the problem has been and has been seen to be one of very special urgency and complexity (OGS, p. vi).

5   The adjective "Hellenistic" in English is used in scholarly circles to refer exclusively to the first – the most ancient and Greek – of these subsequent Hellenisms. According to this scholarly usage, the so-called "Hellenistic Period" marks the first flowering of that broader cultural phenomenon which Seferis seeks to designate through his more inclusive use of the term 'Hellenism'. Seferis uses (the term here translated as) 'Hellenism' to refer not only to this first extended dissemination of classical Greek culture in the so-called "Hellenistic period", but to subsequent inheritances as well – in, e.g., the Italian Renaissance, the French Academy, the German Enlightenment, etc. To avoid confusion with the (aforementioned scholarly use of the) term "Hellenistic", I will employ "Hellenic" as the adjectival form of Seferis's "Hellenism". Seferis's employment of this latter term – due to the grandiosity of his conception of Hellenism – is hardly uncontroversial. But it has a distinguished pedigree. Jakob Burkhardt writes:

> The meaning of Hellenism is that the whole world made use of and laid claim to the [ancient] Greek world; it was to be the medium of spiritual continuity between antiquity, the Roman world and the Middle Ages. . . . Hellenistic Rome was the indispensable basis for the spread of Christianity, and Christianity, apart from its role as a religion, was to be the single bridge destined to unite the old world with its Germanic conquerors. In this whole chain of cause and effect, Hellenism is the most important link (*The Greeks and Greek Civilization*, trans. Sheila Stern (London: Fontana Press, 1998), pp. 282–3).

6   "In English the expression 'ancient Greece' includes the meaning 'finished', whereas for us Greece goes on living for better or for worse; it is *in* life, has not expired yet" ("Conversation with Seferis", in Edmund Keeley, *Modern Greek Poetry: Voice and Myth* (Princeton, NJ: Princeton University Press, 1983), p. 183).

7   An insistence on this sort of (social constructionist) paradoxical formulation mostly just leads to confusion. It threatens to leave no room for sense to be made of what is asserted by those who wish to claim that "Erik the Red discovered America". Iceland is full of such people – we do not deny what they claim on behalf of their Viking ancestor, if we hold to the paradoxical formulation (and insist that Erik could not have got there first because America came into existence only with the arrival of Columbus's vessel). More importantly, for my purposes, as we shall see, it obscures what Cavell is after in his own rather different and (in my view, more fruitful, but) equally paradoxical formulations.

8   If what the latter sort of social constructionist wants to claim about America were something of which sense could be made, it would apply equally to France or Greece (or, for that matter, to the North Pole and the rings of Saturn).

9   I mean to leave it open whether there are other concepts like it (and, if so, how many). Concepts such as *German* or *Japanese* – i.e. concepts that have historically, in the first instance, denoted a *Volk* individuated by lines of racial and ethnic descent –

cannot work the way the concept *American* does. But it is an open question to what extent concepts such as *Australia* – the inception of which also marks the settling of a new world – obey something resembling the logic of America. And, of course, there will be all sorts of intermediate cases of concepts that intertwine in different ways objective geographical or national references with subjective ethical, political or religious dimensions of significance – concepts such as *Iceland* (the name of an ancient land and the world's oldest continuously existing democracy), *Greece* (the name of a young nation and the cradle of Western civilization), *Israel* (the name of an even younger nation and a covenant between God and His people), and so forth.

10 *Michelin Green Guide to Greece*, 4th edn (New York: Michelin Travel Publications, 2001), p. 97.
11 *The Blue Guide to Athens*, 4th edn (New York: W.W. Norton & Company, 1999), p. 128.
12 Seferis, OGS, p. 95.
13 The full context of the quotation from Nietzsche runs as follows: "One is no longer at home anywhere; at last one longs for that only place in which one can be at home, because it is the only place one would want to be at home: the Greek world" (Friedrich Nietzsche, *Werke: Kritische Gesamtausgabe*, Vol. 3, eds G. Colli and M. Montinari, *Nachgelassene Fragmente Herbst 1884 bis Herbst 1885* (Berlin: Gruyter), p. 412).

Though Nietzsche himself may not have had the least interest in modern Greece – that is, in a geographically and culturally Greek community that sought to constitute itself as a modern state and take its place as one among the other European nations – it would be a mistake to conclude that the sort of nostalgia he evinces for a lost "Greek world" is irrelevant to an understanding of the dilemma of the modern Greek intellectual that Seferis seeks to explore. The broader classicist enthusiasm in which Nietzsche participated contributed substantially to the formation and subsequent self-understanding of modern Greece – thanks, in particular, to the English incarnation of that enthusiasm, typified in the work of figures such as Byron and Shelley who laid a far greater emphasis than their German counterparts (with the notable exception of Hölderlin) on the notion that (as Terence Spencer nicely puts it): "there existed an urgent moral obligation for Europe to restore liberty to Greece as a kind of payment for the civilization which Hellas had once given to the world" (*Fair Greece Sad Relic* (London: Weidenfeld & Nicolson, 1954), p. vii). Aristides Baltas writes:

> The Romantic and more general philhellenic movements played a very important role in gathering support worldwide for the cause of Greek independence and the idea that modern Greeks are direct descendents of Plato and Aristotle was thereby enhanced, forming a very important part of modern Greek identity. By considering himself the direct descendent of such glorious ancestors, a modern Greek could find some kind of ideological support with respect to many problems, both internal and external, that the small and undeveloped Greek society and Greek state were facing (unpublished manuscript).

This philhellenic legacy forms an important background to Seferis's quest for a genuinely "Greek Hellenism". Without it, Seferis's quest would be unable quite as easily to achieve its particular blend of nationality and universality. This moment of universality is nicely highlighted in E.M. Forster's remark "Greece is a spirit which can appear, not only at any time, but also in any land" (*Abinger Harvest* (New York: Harcourt Brace Jovanovich, 1964), p. 187).

14 In nineteenth-century Europe, Byron's case – partly due to the extraordinary influence of Byron himself – was at least as typical as Nietzsche's. For Byron, admiration for ancient Hellenic civilization went hand in hand with a felt imperative to visit contem-

porary Greece and experience the site of Hellenism first-hand. And Byron went on to claim that such experience not only enhanced but also transformed one's appreciation of the classical texts themselves: "It is one thing to read *Iliad* at Sigaeum and on the tumuli . . . and another to trim your taper over it in a library – *this* I know" (*Childe Harold's Pilgrimage*, canto iii, note 19). Those who accepted this claim (i.e. that a full appreciation of the classics depends upon a first-hand experience of Greece) were easily brought around to the view that support for the cause of Greek independence remained an outstanding obligation of the entire civilized world. Shelley expressed the sentiment succinctly in his preface to *Hellas*: "We are all Greeks. . . . [T]he final triumph of the Greek cause is . . . a portion of the cause of civilization and social improvement" (*Shelley's Poetry and Prose* (New York: Norton, 1977), pp. 408–9). Here we discern a crucial element of the philhellenic background of modern Greek identity – one that finds a counterpart in the Puritan background of modern American identity and allows for the possibility of the parallelism between Seferis's call for a Greek Hellenism and Cavell's call for a discovery of America. In each of these cases, the universal and the national become intertwined to a degree that allows Shelley and Emerson, with equally unabashed metaphysical emphases, respectively to assert "We are all Greeks" and "Anyone can become an American". And here we can also already discern the crucial moment at which the parallelism breaks down: For Shelley, we all *already* are Greeks, whereas, for Emerson, an American is something we must first *become* in order for there to be anything which is America.

15 The shape of this difficulty was already anticipated by Byron:

> Fair Greece! Sad relic of departed worth!
> Immortal, though no more; though fallen, great!
> Who now shall lead thy scatter'd children forth,
> And long accustom'd bondage uncreate? . . .
> Oh,! Who that gallant spirit shall resume,
> . . . and call thee from the tomb?
> (*Childe Harold's Pilgrimage*, II, lxxiii)

In this stanza, we can discern the outlines of Seferis's problematic: Greece is to be re-created by having her present condition uncreated through a new creation. The immortality of Greece is to be recovered only through a prior acknowledgement of her mortality. As things stand, Greece is the name of a sad relic of merely departed worth and of an ideal to which we are obliged to contribute our assistance so that Greece may attain worth once again. Hellas can be resumed and called from the tomb only by our thus enabling Greece to embark upon such a second infancy.

16 Seferis's conception of the task of fashioning a genuinely Greek Hellenism thus requires a delicate balancing of the claims of the past against those of the future. The modern Greek artist and intellectual must learn to live with one eye on the future and one on the past – to retain a fidelity to the past without ceasing to make the future his task. Henry Miller speaks in this connection of Seferis's peculiar "way of looking forwards and backwards" at once (in *The Colossus of Maroussi* (New York: New Directions, 1941), p. 47). In Seferis's own work, this struggle to negotiate between past and future often arises in a manner that recalls the second of Nietzsche's *Untimely Meditations, On the Uses and Disadvantages of History for Life* – as a problem of memory and forgetting: of how best and how much to remember. Thus, for example, in Seferis's poem "Mr Stratis Thalassinos Describes a Man", we find this:

> We found ashes. What remains is to discover our life, now that we've nothing left. . . . What can a flame remember? If it remembers a little less than is neces-sary, it goes out; if it remembers a little more than is necessary, it goes out. If

only it could teach us, while it burns, to remember correctly (*Collected Poems*, trans. Edmund Keeley and Philip Sherrard (London: Anvil Press, 1995), pp. 74–5).

17 One might argue that this is equally true of all of the Balkan states and merely shows that Greece is part of the Balkans. Mark Mazower writes:

> [The] states in the Balkans look back to the medieval or classical past for their national roots, and encourage their historians to pass over the period of Ottoman rule as quickly as possible, as though nothing good could have come out of those years" (*The Balkans*, London: Weidenfeld & Nicolson, 2000).

The extent of the Serbian national obsession with the battle of Kosovo in 1389 has recently helped to bring this phenomenon (and the attendant desire to wipe the slate of history clean) to the attention of the rest of the world. It is certainly true that modern Greece suffers from a characteristically Balkan form of amnesia in its relation to her Ottoman legacy. Does this mean that the problematic that Seferis views as peculiar to modern Greece is characteristic of the Balkans as such? Todor Zhivkov, Bulgaria's communist leader, echoed an oft-repeated view (still echoed by Bulgaria's leaders today) when he proclaimed in 1981: "When at the end of the fourteenth century Bulgaria fell under Ottoman domination, the natural course of her historical development was stopped and reversed" (quoted by Mazower, p. 14). The call here is for a return to and preservation of a moment of continuity with a European past. The accent falls on what Bulgaria has *in common* with Europe. The guiding myth here is voiced (and endorsed) by Sir John Marriott at the outset of his history of the Eastern Question: "[T]he primary and most essential factor in the problem is the presence, embedded in the living flesh of Europe, of an alien substance. That substance is the Ottoman Turk" (*The Eastern Question* (Oxford: Oxford University Press, 1917), p. 3). Operative though this particular (Balkan) myth no doubt continues to be in contemporary Greek consciousness, the founding myth of modern Greece is a different one and has quite a different logic – one that seeks to turn the tables on the condescension of a Sir John Marriott – and, in the process, threatens to designate all cultural contents imported from without (thus not merely from the Orient but also from the Occident) as alien substance. This myth rests on a proclamation far more hubristic than Zhivkov's. For it requires the recovery of a moment of past cultural fertility that radically differentiates Greece from the rest of Europe – one that is the supposed prior condition of the subsequent possibility of Europe. Hence the occurrence of the following sort of phrases in modern Greece's descriptions of itself: "the fountainhead of European culture", "the birthplace of enlightenment", "the cradle of Western civilization", etc. The differences between the two cases notwithstanding, the hubris of such rhetoric matches the hubris of America's rhetoric regarding its unparalleled uniqueness. Without these parallel claims to unparalleledness on the part of modern Greece and America, Seferis's and Cavell's respective problematics would not parallel one another in the various ways that they do.

18 *Walden*, Chapter II, paragraph 22; *Walden and Other Writings*, p. 88.

19 Cavell says about Thoreau: "His problem – at once philosophical, religious, literary, and I will argue, political – is to get us to ask the questions, and then to show us that we do not know what we are asking, and then to show us that we have the answer" (*SW*, p. 47).

20 *SW*, pp. 8–9.

21 Seferis speaks of the remaining vestiges of a once genuine form of Hellenism in ways that are reminiscent of some of Kierkegaard's characterizations of how someone in Christendom might experience the remaining vestiges of a Christian way of life – for

example of their being "fragments of a life which was once complete, disturbing fragments, close to us, ours for one moment, and then mysterious and unapproachable"
(*Delphi*, trans. Philip Sherrard (Hanover: Munich & Ahrbeck, 1963), p. 8).

22 Seferis's poem "In the Manner of G.S." begins: "Wherever I travel Greece wounds
me" (*Collected Poems*, p. 52).

23 Seferis's poem, "The Return of the Exile", contains the following rebuke: "Your
nostalgia has created a non-existent country, with laws alien to earth and man"
(*Collected Poems*, p. 52).

24 OGS, pp. 91–2. The mention here of "those who agitated for the artificially 'purist'
language" is a reference to one side in a fractious ongoing debate in modern Greek
history – simultaneously conducted in the political, religious and literary arenas –
concerning which form of the Greek language is to be used by whom and on what
occasions. After the liberation of Greece in 1832, the debate began as to which
language to adopt as the official language of the new nation. It was clear that Attic
Greek – in its "pure" classical form – was no longer viable but many advocated the
use of a form of the language "cleansed" of all foreign elements that was close to
Attic and that had been employed in the Greek Orthodox Church; and from this
sprang a movement that continues until this day. A supporter of this movement, a
katharevusianos or "purist" (often a politically right-wing or a religiously conservative
Greek – these are not always the same), favors a return to formality in the language
and the use of (what has become known as) *katharevousa* – the purifying language.
The opposing side in the debate support as the official language of the state (what
has become known as) *Dhimotiki* – Demotic Greek, the people's language – the
language most people use most of the time. *Dhimotiki* is often held by the purists to
be not only replete with "impure words" (i.e. words of foreign origin – most notably
from Latin, Italian and especially Turkish, and more recently from English and
French) but also to be intellectually and/or spiritually lacking in clarity. (The verb
katherizo means to cleanse, clear, peal, pare or purify, but also to explain, clarify,
settle or clear up.) Since Seferis's time, the populists have won out over the purists in
this debate (though *katharevousa* was briefly re-introduced as the official language of
the state under the military dictatorship in 1967, until the fall of the dictatorship, in
1974, when *Dhimotiki* was re-established as the official language.) Though essentially
a foreign language to vast portions of the Greek population, *katharevousa* remained
until very recently (basically until the rise to power of the political party PASOK in
the early 1980s) the official language of the law and most spheres of education and
the Church. It is still employed today by many doctors, lawyers, professors and even
a handful of journalists. In Seferis's time, the debate was a charged one and one in
which a poet had no choice but – in every line he or she penned – to take part.
Seferis's own position was one of seeking to explode the terms of the debate by
insisting on the importance of a modern Greek poetic practice that both sought to
cultivate the poetic potentiality of the vernacular and sought to establish forms of
continuity with ancient Greek literary traditions.

25

> [I]f we consider how much bad art – I mean to say how much academic art – has
> been produced in the name of the classics, we should be all the more severe in
> our judgment on those very mediocre people who try to cling tight to the
> "eternal values" and who deform them like parasites that settle like a blight on
> the perennial trees (OGS, p. 83).

26 But is it less comic than some of the complementary forms of American cultural
chauvinism? It is surely less tragic. I will probably never lose a boyhood memory I
have, from the time of the Vietnam War, of traveling on an international flight filled

with the sound of a voice with an unmistakably American accent, loudly explaining, to a Cambodian passenger sitting nearby, just why it was that America had to drop bombs on his country in order to make that corner of the world safe for democracy.

27 Edmund Keeley and Philip Sherrard write in the introduction to their edition of Seferis's *Collected Poems*:

> [E]ven as one does catch the sound of a richly traditional voice, a voice learned in the best poetry of previous ages, one is also aware that the voice is very much of the present age and that the poet's sensibility couldn't be farther from that of an antiquarian delving nostalgically back into the past in order to escape the bewilderments and afflictions of modern life: the past is always there to shape and illuminate an image of the present (p. xv).

It should be (and Seferis would have been the first to have) acknowledged that not all anti-antiquarian, forward-looking forms of attachment to a Hellenic ideal – ones for which "the past is always there to shape and illuminate an image of the present" – are equally attractive. The point can be made succinctly by citing the following sentence from a letter of 6 August 1942 (shortly after the occupation of Greece by the Axis Powers) in which, after saying how much he envies him his recent visit to the Acropolis, Hitler tells Mussolini: "I perhaps better than anyone else can share your feelings with regard to a place where all we today call human culture found its beginning" (quoted by Mark Mazower in *Inside Hitler's Greece* (New Haven: Yale University Press, 1995), p. 67).

28 Emerson, *Journals* (in *Emerson in His Journals*, ed. Joel Porte (Cambridge, MA: Harvard University Press, 1982), p. 125. The full context of this remark runs as follows:

> We all lean on England, scarce a verse, a page, a newspaper but is writ in imitation of English forms, our very manners and conversation are traditional and sometimes the life seems to be dying out of all literature and this enormous paper currency of Words is accepted instead (ibid., p. 125).

Emerson immediately goes on to indicate a possible source of remedy:

> I suppose the evil may be cured by this rank rabble party, the Jacksonism of the country, heedless of English and of all literature – a stone cut out of the ground without hands – they may root out the hollow dilettantism of our cultivation in the coarsest way and the new-born may begin again to frame their own world with greater advantage (ibid., p. 125).

To gauge just how desperate a remedy Emerson thought this – and thus as how great an evil he viewed the hollow dilettantism of America and how eager he was to see the new-born nation begin again to frame its own world – one needs to appreciate just how rank he considered Jackson and his rabble party:

> It is said public opinion will not bear it. Really? Public opinion, I am sorry to say, will bear a great deal of nonsense. There is scarce any absurdity so gross whether in religion, politics, science, or manners, which it will not bear. . . . It will bear Andrew Jackson for President (ibid., p. 65).

I know how he feels.

29 *SW*, pp. 59–60.

30 Thus, though someone can be a Greek citizen and a poet, and yet not be (someone Seferis is prepared to call) a Greek poet, so also someone (e.g. Constantine Cavafy)

can be neither a citizen nor a resident of Greece and yet be (one of the few whom Seferis is prepared to regard as) an exemplary Greek poet.

31 Someone attracted to this argument might imagine he or she can find passages in Seferis that support his or her case. Seferis, for example, quotes with admiration the following words from T.S. Eliot's *Tradition and the Individual Talent*:

> [T]he historical sense involves a perception, not only of the pastness of the past, but of its presence. . . . [It] compels a man to write not merely with his own generation in his bones, but with the feeling that the whole of the literature of Europe from Homer and within it the whole of the literature of his own country has a simultaneous existence and composes a simultaneous order. . . . [It is] what makes a writer most acutely conscious of his place in time, of his own contemporaneity (quoted by Seferis in "Cavafy and Eliot – a comparison", OGS, p. 150).

A first question here is whether Seferis (or Eliot, for that matter) imagines the writer of philosophy to constitute an exceptional case – the case of someone who, unlike the poet, ought to attempt to exempt himself or herself from the requirement to cultivate such an acute consciousness of his or her own contemporaneity. A second question is whether the cultivation of such a consciousness is in tension with philosophy's aspiration to reason.

32 Henry Miller says of Seferis that he was able "to ripen into a universal poet – by passionately rooting himself into the soil of his people" (*The Colossus of Maroussi*, p. 47). Seferis would have been pleased by this compliment. Nonetheless, Miller himself, though no doubt meaning what he says here, and wishing thereby to pay homage to Seferis's achievement, is also evidently unable to overcome his own sense that there is something inherently paradoxical in Seferis's poetic ideal. Miller's various remarks about Seferis in *The Colossus of Maroussi* bear testimony to his inability to comprehend how the aspiration to be a universal poet can be made to harmonize with the aspiration to cultivate a distinctively Greek poetic voice.

33 Here we encounter some of the moments of hubris in the founding myth of America that are able to match those in the founding myth of modern Greece ("the fountainhead of European culture", "the birthplace of enlightenment", "the cradle of Western civilization", etc.).

34 OGS, pp. 91–2.

35 OGS, pp. 92–4.

36 OGS, p. 95.

37 SW, pp. 32–3.

38 OGS, pp. 95–6.

39 In *Quest of the Ordinary* (Chicago: University of Chicago Press, 1988), pp. 181–2.

40 Such a recommendation purports to offer a criterion of value – a criterion for condemning or approving intellectual or artistic work. But, Seferis notes, its method of application altogether bypasses the task of serious criticism – of attending to the detail of a work, and thus to its actual intellectual or aesthetic merits or defects (cf. OGS, p. 91).

41

> Maybe a few centuries from now one will judge that all German philosophy derives its real dignity from being a gradual reclamation of the soil of antiquity, and that all claims to "originality" must sound petty and absurd in relation to that higher claim of the Germans to have renewed the bond with the Greeks – the hitherto highest type of man. . . . [W]e are growing more Greek by the day. . . . Herein lies (and has always lain) my hope for the German character! (Nietzsche, *Werke*, op. cit.).

42 Aristides Baltas sums up the situation of philosophy in modern Greece from the formation of an independent state (1821) up through the rule of the Junta (1973) as follows:

> [A]fter the national revolution of 1821 . . . in the institutions of higher learning created within the tiny Greek state of the time, lip service was . . . paid to philosophy. However . . . there was no native philosophical or theoretical tradition to speak of – that is, a tradition comparable to what had in the meantime been achieved in the West. This gap was filled by an appeal to the glory of Ancient Greece, an appeal blown beyond all proportions, and which, in a sense, continues even today. . . . [A]ll of the humanities were stiflingly dominated by the uncritical glorification which formed the core element of official ideology. . . . Philosophy thus acquired a bad name among students. . . . [S]ick of the uncritical discourse that was taken to be philosophy, students whose interests and talents might have naturally directed them towards philosophy in a more balanced academic environment, chose science and engineering instead (unpublished manuscript).

43 *Must We Mean What We Say?: A Book of Essays* (Cambridge, MA: Harvard University Press, 1969), p. 345.
44 OGS, pp. 154–6. This passage is from Seferis's essay "Cavafy and Eliot – a comparison". The remarks in the passage that occur in quotation marks are quotations drawn from Cavafy's work.
45 OGS, pp. 96–7.
46 The text is drawn from a larger manuscript titled "The concept of America." Explanations of some of the distinctions and terminology employed here (e.g., the distinction between subjective and objective concepts) can be found in my "Cavell and the Concept of America" – a further excerpt from the same manuscript – collected in *Contending with Stanley Cavell*, edited by Russell Goodman, Oxford: Oxford University Press, 2005, pp. 55–81.

INDEX

259